THE POLITICS AND POETICS
OF CICERO'S *BRUTUS*

Cicero's *Brutus* (46 BCE), a tour-de-force of intellectual and political history, was written amidst political crisis: Caesar's defeat of the republican resistance at the battle of Thapsus. This magisterial example of the dialogue genre capaciously documents the intellectual vibrancy of the Roman republic and its Greco-Roman traditions. This book is the first study of the work from several distinct yet interrelated perspectives: Cicero's account of oratorical history, the confrontation with Caesar, and the exploration of what it means to write a history of an artistic practice. Close readings of this dialogue – including its apparent contradictions and tendentious fabrications – reveal a crucial and crucially productive moment in Greco-Roman thought. Cicero, this book argues, created the first nuanced, sophisticated, and ultimately "modern" literary history, both crafting a compelling justification of Rome's oratorical traditions and also laying a foundation for literary historiography that abides to this day. This title is also available as Open Access on Cambridge Core.

CHRISTOPHER S. VAN DEN BERG is Aliki Perroti and Seth Frank '55 Professor in Classical Studies and Professor of Classics at Amherst College. He is the author of *The World of Tacitus' Dialogus de Oratoribus* (Cambridge University Press, 2014) and has published and researched broadly in ancient and modern political rhetoric.

T0371520

THE POLITICS AND POETICS OF CICERO'S *BRUTUS*

The Invention of Literary History

CHRISTOPHER S. VAN DEN BERG

Amherst College, Massachusetts

CAMBRIDGE
UNIVERSITY PRESS

University Printing House, Cambridge CB2 8BS, United Kingdom

One Liberty Plaza, 20th Floor, New York, NY 10006, USA

477 Williamstown Road, Port Melbourne, VIC 3207, Australia

314–321, 3rd Floor, Plot 3, Splendor Forum, Jasola District Centre, New Delhi – 110025, India

103 Penang Road, #05–06/07, Visioncrest Commercial, Singapore 238467

Cambridge University Press is part of the Cambridge University Press & Assessment.

It furthers the University's mission by disseminating knowledge in the pursuit of education, learning, and research at the highest international levels of excellence.

www.cambridge.org
Information on this title: www.cambridge.org/9781009281355

DOI: 10.1017/9781009281386

First published 2023
Reissued as Open Access, 2023

A catalogue record for this publication is available from the British Library.

Library of Congress Cataloging-in-Publication Data
NAMES: Van den Berg, Christopher Sean, author.
TITLE: The politics and poetics of Cicero's Brutus : the invention of literary history / Christopher S. van den Berg.
DESCRIPTION: New York : Cambridge University Press, 2021. | Includes bibliographical references and index.
IDENTIFIERS: LCCN 2021024758 (print) | LCCN 2021024759 (ebook) | ISBN 9781108495950 (hardback) | ISBN 9781108811354 (paperback) | ISBN 9781108856447 (epub)
SUBJECTS: LCSH: Cicero, Marcus Tullius. Brutus. | BISAC: LITERARY CRITICISM / Ancient & Classical
CLASSIFICATION: LCC PA6296.B7 V36 2021 (print) | LCC PA6296.B7 (ebook) | DDC 875/.01–DC23
LC record available at https://lccn.loc.gov/2021024758
LC ebook record available at https://lccn.loc.gov/2021024759

ISBN 978-1-009-28135-5 Paperback

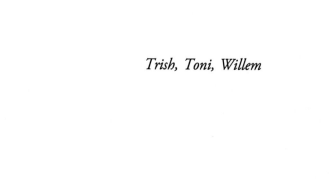

Trish, Toni, Willem

Contents

Preface and Acknowledgments

This book began as one chapter of a project on the Greco-Roman literature of literary criticism, history, and theory. Early on it became clear, largely at the prompting of others, that more space was needed to give the *Brutus* its due. David Quint, and then Pramit Chaudhuri and Ayelet Haimson Lushkov, dispelled my initial reluctance to devote so much time to Cicero.

Several other scholars and institutions assisted immeasurably along the way. Sander Goldberg, Chris Kraus, Irene Peirano, and James Uden read early drafts of an article that appeared in *Classical Philology*, "The Invention of Literary History in Cicero's *Brutus*" (© 2019 by The University of Chicago). That article, with several revisions and corrections, forms the basis for Chapters 5 and 6. I thank *Classical Philology* for permission to reuse the material.

Audiences at the 2015 meeting of the International Society for the History of Rhetoric, and at the annual meetings of the Society for Classical Studies in 2016, 2018, and 2019 provided stimulating feedback. Some of the earliest work was presented at the 2014 "Cargo Culture" conference at Stanford, some of the latest at "Historiography Jam III," 2019, also at Stanford. In addition, audiences at the American Academy in Rome, Boston University, Bucknell, Smith, Tulane, University of California at Los Angeles, University of Illinois at Urbana-Champaign, University of Kansas, and Yale offered stimulating responses to several aspects of the project.

At various stages the manuscript, in part or whole, was improved immensely by the astute comments of Mont Allen, Yelena Baraz, Bettina Bergmann, Tom Frazel, Sander Goldberg, Charles Guérin, Joanna Kenty, Larry Kim, Bryant Kirkland, Christopher Krebs, Stephanie Pearson, Bethany Schneider, Kate Thomas, Chris Trinacty, and Chris Whitton. I have also benefited from discussions with Andrea Balbo, Susanna Braund, Corey Brennan, Tom Carpenter, Tony Corbeill, Nicola

Courtright, Scott DiGiulio, Jackie Elliott, Joe Farrell, Andrew Feldherr, Kirk Freudenburg, Karissa Haugeberg, Maria Heim, Elizabeth Heintges, Steve Johnstone, Lynne Lancaster, Courtney Luckhardt, Evan MacCarthy, Duncan MacRae, Melissa Mueller, Ingrid Nelson, Nigel Nicholson, Matthew Roller, Jeremy Simmons, Friedrich Spoth, Michael Squire, Henriette van der Blom, Ann Vasaly, Chris Waldo, and Jarrett Welsh.

I am grateful to Katarzyna (Kasia) Jazdzewska for sharing chapters of her forthcoming book on Greek dialogue, and to Peter White and Jim Zetzel for sharing unpublished work on the *tirocinium fori* and on *de Legibus*, respectively. Adam Gitner at the Thesaurus Linguae Latinae assisted with queries concerning the material on *rectus/recte*. Julia Scarborough was an insightful Latin reading partner for Cicero's *Letters to Atticus*. Chris Hallett generously responded to queries about the Roman heroic (nude) costume. Katharina Volk valuably commented on a draft and shared with me her forthcoming study of Roman intellectuals in the late republic. A manuscript exchange with Bob Kaster allowed me to profit from his excellent new translation with notes. His comments improved this book immeasurably and made me thoroughly rethink Caesar's role in the *Brutus*. Jim Zetzel read the final draft, offering several crucial suggestions and saving me from several errors.

Michael Sharp supported the project early on and secured two readers who suggested several improvements. I wholeheartedly thank them and the editorial and production staff at Cambridge University Press. Amelia Wrigley, a Gregory S. Call Academic Intern at Amherst College, assisted with the first full rewrite. Pam Scholefield deserves thanks for judicious indexing. Mary Bellino provided editorial guidance, improvements, and corrections that were well beyond anything I could have ever expected.

The suggestions and improvements of scholars and friends are evident, to me at least, on nearly every page. If there are still passages in which the detail is tedious, the error unfixed, the argument muddled, or the speculation wild, the blame cannot be theirs.

Librarians seldom get the credit they deserve, and this book could not have been written without the assistance and resources of the libraries at Amherst College and Tulane University. Steve Heim (Amherst) and Hayden Battle (Tulane) were essential at several points. I'm also grateful to Sebastian Hierl and Paolo Imperatori (American Academy in Rome). The ongoing COVID-19 pandemic made it painfully clear how valuable such resources and their gatekeepers are. Even with widespread electronic resources, double-checking references and tracking down bibliography without physical access to a library has been challenging, to say the least.

I completed final revisions to the manuscript as Italy began to face COVID-19 and the United States began to turn its back on the pandemic's reality. My cohort of fellows at the American Academy in Rome were suddenly uprooted while struggling to finish projects to which we had devoted months if not years. I am thankful to each of them for intellectual encouragement and, above all, for friendship and compassion, virtues that may, one sometimes forgets, not only exist but even flourish in academic and artistic institutions. This book, or at least the completion of it, is in so many ways theirs.

This is not to overlook nearer examples. Katie Edwards provided patience, support, and encouragement well beyond what should be expected of anyone. Several pages of this book, including this one, have been written while holed up in an apartment across the street from the house of my sister's family in Galveston, Texas. Here I typically write in the mornings and help out in the afternoons with household tasks and childcare while my sister, Patricia, faces a harrowing and protracted battle with cancer. The subject of this book is, from a certain perspective, how an individual might respond not to unexpected disaster, but to the slow and hopeful expectation that it will never fully arrive. I am impressed daily by my sister's courage, by the love of her wife, Toni Ricigliano, and by the boundless and sometimes devilish joy of their son, my nephew, Willem. This book is dedicated to them.

A Note on the Text

All translations are mine unless otherwise noted. In rendering Cicero's *Brutus* into readable English, I have benefited immensely from Robert A. Kaster's translation and hope that the reader will have had a chance to consult it (if not the Latin) before reading this book. I have sought to be fairly literal in translating, while also seeking to avoid clumsy or outdated English. I follow the Teubner text (E. Malcovati, 2nd rev. ed., 1970) with changes as noted, several of which are adopted from Kaster (2020). Latin passages quoted are accompanied by translations, except when occasionally the immediate discussion paraphrases the Latin. Citations of the *Brutus* are not preceded by its title, so section numbers appearing without further attribution refer to it. To avoid footnote fatigue, citations and quotations of the *Brutus* typically occur in the body of the text. All dates are BCE unless otherwise noted.

Journal titles are abbreviated in the References according to the conventions of *L'Année philologique*. The abbreviations for Greek and Latin works are from the *Oxford Latin Dictionary*, when available, and otherwise from the *Oxford Classical Dictionary*. Other abbreviations are listed below.

Lastly, in a study of the intellectual framework and rhetorical crafting of the *Brutus*' literary history, succumbing to the explanatory allure of Cicero's vision is almost inevitable. One motivation for writing this book was precisely to expose the sway Cicero has held over modern conceptions of literatures and their histories. Nonetheless, to appreciate and explain Cicero's choices and characterizations is not to accept his prejudices and flaws. Still, it seemed a graver error to repeatedly pepper the text with interjections such as "so Cicero claims" or "as Cicero would have us believe." I hope the reader understands that economy of exposition is meant to convey the enticing power of Cicero's narrative even when, as often happens, I tacitly disagree with his ideas or the unquestioned assumptions that sustain them.

Abbreviations

CAH^2	*The Cambridge Ancient History*, 2nd ed. (Cambridge, 1961–)
CHLC	G. A. Kennedy (ed.), *The Cambridge History of Literary Criticism*, vol. 1: *Classical Criticism* (Cambridge, 1989)
CIL	*Corpus Inscriptionum Latinarum* (Berlin, 1863–)
FRHist	T. J. Cornell (ed.), *The Fragments of the Roman Historians*, 3 vols. (Oxford, 2013)
GRF	H. Funaioli (ed.), *Grammaticae Romanae fragmenti*, vol. 1 (Leipzig, 1907)
HWRh	G. Ueding et al. (eds.), *Historisches Wörterbuch der Rhetorik*, 11 vols. (Tübingen, 1992–2014)
LIMC	*Lexicon iconographicum Mythologiae Classicae*, 8 vols. (Zurich, 1981–2009)
LTUR	E. M. Steinby (ed.), *Lexicon topographicum urbis Romae*, 6 vols. (Oxford, 1993–2000)
MRR	T. R. S. Broughton (ed.), *The Magistrates of the Roman Republic* (American Philological Association, 1951–86)
OCD^4	S. Hornblower, A. Spawforth, and E. Eidinow (eds.), *The Oxford Classical Dictionary*, 4th ed. (Oxford, 2012)
OLD	P. G. W. Glare (ed.), *Oxford Latin Dictionary*, 2nd ed. (Oxford, 2012)
ORF^4	E. Malcovati (ed.), *Oratorum Romanorum fragmenta liberae rei publicae*, 4th ed., 2 vols. (Turin, 1976–79)
RLM	K. Halm (ed.), *Rhetores Latini Minores* (Leipzig, 1863)
RRC	M. H. Crawford (ed.), *Roman Republican Coinage* (Cambridge, 1974)
TLL	*Thesaurus Linguae Latinae* (Leipzig/Munich/Berlin, 1900–)[1]
TLRR	M. C. Alexander, *Trials in the Late Roman Republic: 149 BC to 50 BC* (Toronto, 1990)

---

[1] Citations of the *TLL* include the notation [author, year] to indicate the lemma's author and the publication date of the fascicle in which the lemma appears.

This title is part of the Cambridge University Press *Flip it Open* Open Access Books program and has been "flipped" from a traditional book to an Open Access book through the program.

Flip it Open sells books through regular channels, treating them at the outset in the same way as any other book; they are part of our library collections for Cambridge Core, and sell as hardbacks and ebooks. The one crucial difference is that we make an upfront commitment that when each of these books meets a set revenue threshold we make them available to everyone Open Access via Cambridge Core.

This paperback edition has been released as part of our Open Access commitment and we would like to use this as an opportunity to thank the libraries and other buyers who have helped us flip this and the other titles in the program to Open Access.

To see the full list of libraries that we know have contributed to *Flip it Open*, as well as the other titles in the program please visit http://www.cambridge.org/fio-acknowledgements

Introduction

At last Cicero broke his long silence. After years away from Rome and its politics – first as proconsular governor of Cilicia in Asia Minor, then as a reluctant participant and witness to the horrors of civil war that enveloped Italy and were still spreading across the Mediterranean – at last it was time to resume his customary labors on behalf of the Roman state. Though Rome's preeminent orator and one of its oldest living consulars, he would speak again, but not via public oratory. There was no venue in which to do so. The forum and its *rostra* were vacant, the courts closed. His efforts instead took on a different shape, in the form of a literary dialogue. Sometime during the spring of 46 he completed the *Brutus*, a fictional conversation about the history of oratory with his lifelong friend Titus Pomponius Atticus and his protégé (he hoped) Marcus Junius Brutus, the soon-to-be Caesaricide.

To write a history of Roman orators in the midst of civil war was hardly the most obvious response to what ailed Rome. Yet however bleak the state of politics, the cultural conditions for that endeavor were remarkably felicitous. The dialogue appeared at a moment when curiosity about the natural and historical worlds, influenced by a tradition of Greek philosophy and scholarship, had enthralled Rome. Several thinkers, following Greek precedent, helped to craft an intellectual culture of individuation and rationalization of knowledge and the systems that produce it.[1] Yet the immediate crisis has overshadowed just how innovative, even revolutionary, Cicero's project was. Ultimately, it amounted to far more than just a consolatory catalogue of Rome's oratorical luminaries.

---

[1] Moatti (1997) connects these changes to the development of *ratio*/reason; cf. Rüpke (2012) 204 for an overview of Weberian *Rationalisierung* as a framework to understand the developments, and the objection to both in MacRae (2016) 53–75. See further Rawson (1985), Lehoux (2012), Volk (2021), chap. 1.

This book's purpose is to examine the intellectual and political frameworks of the *Brutus*, and my abiding concern is the extent to which Cicero
invented what we now think of as literary history. In writing a historical
account of Roman orators, Cicero offers a sustained critique of how to
document an artistic tradition across time. His conclusions about literary
historiography – themselves integrated into an oratorical history – were
necessarily imperfect and did not emanate from his mind alone.[2] Drawing
on several discourses about literatures and their pasts, Cicero theorized
about literary change even as the world he inherited was itself rapidly
changing. Close study of the *Brutus* is warranted not only for the precious
details of Roman history it preserves, but for its lasting contribution to
ongoing conversations about the public role of literary creation. Cicero
absorbed and gave shape to intellectual debates and developments that
continue to define our own thinking about how to categorize and chronicle the passage of time, systems of power and empire, and the interrelated
forces of artistic and political history.

When Cicero – along with his intellectual and political peers such as
Varro, Atticus, Nepos, and Caesar – undertook to investigate, chronicle, or
systematize cultural production, their efforts shaped not only Rome's sense
of its past but also its contemporary imperial and civic identities. The
Brutus illuminates several issues that his contemporaries found increasingly
urgent in the protracted crisis: the close relationship between knowledge
and power; the impossibility of presenting factual evidence without impos-
ing an interpretive narrative onto that evidence; the competing Roman
mindsets for how to document the past in the service of the present; the
conflict between traditional and new forms of knowledge; and the resulting desire to craft and control new systems with which to organize and
interpret history.

Perhaps the most memorable new system was the controversial calendar
that Julius Caesar was putting into place. Calendrical reform was inherently connected to the vibrant intellectual clashes among the Roman elite
in the late republic. The calendar was more than a neutral mechanism to
organize days, months, or years. Its workings and the information it
contained had for centuries been in the hands of political and religious

---

[2] C. Steel (2005) 146: "His achievements as a writer gain much of their meaning from the interaction
with other writings that they spring from." See Rawson (1985), esp. 143–55, 215–49. In many
respects the simultaneously evaluative and productive role of what we can call the "scholar orator"
goes back at least as far as the Hellenistic conception of the "scholar poet" (if not to Isocrates or
perhaps Antiphon in the rhetorical tradition); cf. Montana (2015) 69.

authorities who crafted a sense of state identity and civic purpose.[3] Similarly, Cicero's putatively neutral account of oratory's past involved much more than a disinterested catalogue of noteworthy speakers. His system of oratorical history is inextricable from a civic vision of the Roman state and of what it means to be Roman. Furthermore, Romans, like Greeks, conceptualized time and its passage as part of a network of interrelated individuals and events. The mechanisms to mark time, such as the naming of years after the consuls, are simultaneously historical data and historical frameworks for understanding that data: "not placing events within a pre-existing time frame," observes Denis Feeney, but "constructing a time frame within which the events have meaning."[4] Cicero in the *Brutus* does not merely provide a chronological account of orators; he crafts a literary history in which Roman orators are players in part of a larger civic drama.

It had long been the case that the organization of time and the past was inextricable from the tenure of power, perhaps most notably in the control of the calendar days (*fasti*) by the Roman aristocracy. Only at the end of the fourth century (304 BCE) did the curule aedile Gnaeus Flavius, under the influence of Appius Claudius Caecus, publish the *fasti* and so make available the days for public business and legal procedures. This was pivotal in freeing access to the legal system from the stranglehold of the aristocracy.[5] The *Brutus* likewise constantly reminds us that the forms we impose on the past through memory and history are inherently connected to power: Roman magistracies and martial achievements anchor the chronological framework of its individual and cultural biographies.

The year 46 was marked not only by the defeat of the republican army at Thapsus and the suicide of Cato the Younger, but also by a calendrical monstrosity. It was the infamous "(last) year of disorder,"[6] which lasted 445 days in order to realign the inherited Roman calendar with the seasons to prepare for the introduction of the Julian calendar on the Kalends of January 45. Julius Caesar took a long-standing Roman mechanism for managing days and months and redesigned it in accordance with Greek astronomical knowledge. Under the guidance of Sosigenes of Alexandria, he introduced to Rome a new way of reckoning the year and thereby secured a powerful hold over this fundamental civic and religious institution.[7] The

<hr/>

[3] Laurence and Smith (1995). Feeney (2007) on Caesar's reforms.
[4] Feeney (2010) 887, with Wilcox (1987).
[5] Cic. *Mur.* 25. Moatti (2003) 311 nicely dubs the power inherent in such knowledge "savoirs de puissance."
[6] Macrobius' *annus confusionis ultimus* (*Sat.* 1.14.3).
[7] The account of Plin. *Nat.* 18.211–12, at least; cf. (differently) Plut. *Caes.* 59.2, Macr. *Sat.* 1.14.2.

new calendar took effect fully in the year 709 *ab Vrbe condita* ("since the city's foundation" – itself a calculation involving contemporary scholarly controversy). In the year before, when Caesar began to reform Roman administrative time, Cicero wrote the *Brutus*, a chronological and descriptive account of literary time. Other scholars eagerly crafted chronologies as well: Atticus' recently produced "Yearly Book" (*Liber Annalis*) greatly influenced Cicero. Marcus Terentius Varro labored diligently to establish himself as Rome's great antiquarian scholar. Cornelius Nepos had published his *Chronica* in three books, which Catullus memorializes in his prefatory poem. Time – its organization, political and aesthetic effects, and explanatory allure – was on the minds of Romans.

Such reforms and reconceptualizations were hardly infallible, and there is much that we will never know about them. Even those that have had a lasting effect can be eclipsed by later innovations: Caesar's calendar gave way to our Gregorian calendar, after all (more on that below). Similarly, modern literary historians do not always know the Ciceronian theoretical foundations on which their accounts are built. The labors of Atticus, Nepos, and Varro, however valuable to contemporaries, have largely been lost (Varro has fared best of the trio, though we know Nepos as a biographer and Atticus as a blank screen onto which Cicero's letters project so much of himself). Still, it is worth considering some of the vicissitudes, challenges, and flaws in such efforts to organize knowledge so that we may understand what is at stake in reconceptualizing a given field of scholarly inquiry or technical advancement, whether in ancient or modern times.

Because political will often trumps common or scientific sense, certain paradoxes are inevitable in aligning national identity with technical or scholarly systems. The development and control of systems that potently organize the past and the future rarely depend on disinterested observers making neutral choices; they more often reveal political identity or chauvinism. The Gregorian calendar was adopted in Russia only in 1918 and in China in 1949, as communism meant not just a new political dispensation but also a new way of organizing bureaucratic and administrative relationships to the past, and the future, all with the aim of legitimizing the new regimes.[8] And it is exceptionalist chauvinism, as much as cost or convenience, that explains why the United States, formed in revolt against its British lords, persists in using the English rather than

---

[8] Russia may still have been smarting from the calendrical disgrace of a decade earlier: Czar Nicholas II's national delegation to the 1908 Olympic Games in London arrived twelve days after the contests; Richards (1998) 247. The French Revolutionary Calendar (implemented with the contentious yet longer-lived metric system) is another prime example of calendar as civic ideology.

the metric system. In a similarly patriotic spirit, but in a Roman context, Cicero depicts oratorical history not merely as a cultural acquisition from the Greeks, but as a centuries-long process that culminates in his own aesthetic and political values. Most importantly, he portrays the greatness of Rome's oratorical past as indistinguishable from the greatness of Rome itself, each a prerequisite for the success of the other.

Without a professionalized bureaucracy, technical-administrative systems may encounter serious obstacles to proper management. The most noteworthy Roman example, to turn again to the calendar, remains the bungling of the leap year by the *pontifex maximus* Marcus Aemilius Lepidus, the triumvir whom Shakespeare memorably dismissed as a "slight, unmeritable man."[9] Macrobius tells us in the *Saturnalia* that Lepidus added a leap day every three years rather than every four years. The error would persist until Augustus became *pontifex maximus* upon Lepidus' death in 13 or 12.[10] One cause of such confusion was the complexity, even for Romans, of traditional systems; another was the paucity or inaccuracy of precedent or physical records providing instruction and guidance.[11] The management of time did not typically fall to professionals invested in neutrality or even accuracy. Technical knowledge might come from experts, but its interpretation and implementation were typically in the administrative purview of the Roman elite, who occupied the magistracies and priesthoods. Such men usually had axes to grind. In a similar fashion, Cicero's understanding of the pasts of poetry and oratory is derived not only from his fellow scholars, who were pursuing their own intellectual agendas, but also from ancient records, *commentarii* (possibly also used by those same scholars). The information found there could be unreliable or subject to misinterpretation, sometimes willfully. Several errors and omissions in the *Brutus*, alongside Cicero's willingness to meaningfully misinterpret the record of the past or its documenters, are nevertheless valuable because they can reveal his civic and intellectual commitments.[12]

Even with improved scientific knowledge or access to it and to experts, apparent questions of fact may still yet be contested. If we or some scholar

[9] Coin issues of 43/2, financed by proceeds from the brutal proscriptions announced in 43, advertise his two roles: "Lepidus, triumvir for restoration of the republic and pontifex maximus" (*triumvir rei publicae constituendae Lepidus pontifex maximus, RRC* 495). The obverse (with minimal variation) reads: LEPIDUS PONT MAX III V R P C. The reverse depicts Octavian.

[10] The error and the reasons for it are still debated. See Plin. *Nat.* 18.211, Suet. *Aug.* 31.2, Solinus 1.46–47, Macr. *Sat.* 1.14.13–15. Wardle (2014) 249–50 (on Suet. *Aug.* 31.2) judiciously summarizes. Cf. Bennett (2003), Feeney (2007) 196–97, Rüpke (2011) 111–21, Stern (2012) 204–27, esp. 214–16, Stern (2017). The vagaries and manipulations of the calendrical system are well studied and continue to captivate modern observers, not least because they reveal a great deal about the vibrant intellectual clashes among the Roman elite in the late republic.

[11] Culham (1989) discusses the lack of reliable centralized archives.

[12] Several examples are listed and discussed below.

from antiquity were to ask in what year the Julian calendar began, one can easily imagine the sort of heated tongue-lashings likely to arise during the initially cool assessment of the facts. The year 45 seems like the best candidate, and yet one could just as easily say that the corrections to the calendar in 46 were already an indication of the new calendrical system. By this logic 46 is the beginning of the calendar even if a single year would not run according to the new system until 45. That is, the calendar was "all there" in 46, but the old system was just being brought up to date in accordance with the new. An institutional purist might propose a later date, arguing that the Julian calendar took effect only when correctly instituted by the *pontifex maximus*. In this reckoning the Julian calendar began at Rome only after Augustus' realignment decades later. Such investigations may seem provincially academic in certain contexts. Yet the comparable questions in the *Brutus* – for example, when and with whom did oratory or poetry begin at Rome? – are central to understanding Cicero's aesthetic and political motivations. The beginnings of artistic traditions in the *Brutus* involved both decisions about which events merit historical notice and also justifications of those decisions. As will become apparent, Cicero's carefully crafted beginnings anchor the ideology and aesthetics of his entire literary-historical enterprise.

The calendrical mishaps of the Julian leap year also serve as a powerful reminder that Romans had their own relationship to time, the past, and its accounting. How strange is it that the pontiffs not only got the leap year wrong, but also persisted in the error, one that probably resulted from a misunderstanding of inclusive counting? Even this basic chronometric element reveals a mindset, formed on relative chronology, with which to organize and interpret historical data.[13] The mental habits of Romans primed them to calculate chronologies relative to their own achievements, understanding events in relation to other major events and not to the absolute dating system we so take for granted.[14]

In reading the *Brutus* it is crucial to recognize the underlying mental structures on which narratives of the past were built. Cicero does not simply have at his disposal knowledge that was different or more primitive than our knowledge; rather, his and his contemporaries' assumptions and habits of mind opened explanatory avenues that may not be readily

---

[13] Feeney (2007) 7–67 is especially good at explaining the mindset.

[14] Our system, however, does pose similar problems, such as the momentary delay that arises when we recall, for example, that the twentieth century comprises the years 1900 through 1999 – and purists will scoff at that claim and note that the century is actually 1901 through 2000, since the year 0 was never counted.

available to the modern scholar. He relies on the customary consular dating to indicate years, but also had several other criteria for structuring literary history, and these undoubtedly had conceptual advantages: generational overlap, birth and death dates of authors and orators, significant literary events, the synchrony or parallel development of events or individual lives (again, a feature of hellenizing scholarship).[15]

When, for example, Cicero highlights the spatial aesthetics of Atticus' *Liber Annalis* he is also telling us something about the *Brutus*. Atticus' *Liber* allowed him to see the order of all history unrolled in a single sweeping view (*ut explicatis ordinibus temporum uno in conspectu omnia viderem*, 15). Cicero similarly conceives of his own literary history as a unified account of the past, useful for what it contains and pleasing as a learned object of aesthetic consumption. Cicero adapts preexisting categories of explanation and forges new ones in order to construct an innovative account of oratorical history. Little has been said about the chronological markers and unusual categories that shape Cicero's literary history, and much less about the attendant conceptual framework or its effects: what choices were made, what people and concepts emphasized or excluded, what possibilities and innovations exploited or abandoned?

Cicero relied on distinct, even potentially conflicting, temporal or conceptual categories to construct a narrative of oratory's past, which might initially strike us as odd. Yet common sense and experience again tell us that there is nothing peculiar about switching between systems of assessment or criteria of categorization, even when one system is unquestionably better. Most of us today do just that, despite living in an age that is far more scientific and – despite the whimsical (or malicious) rise of "alternative facts" since 2016 – far more invested in accuracy. We have longitude and latitude, for example, perfectly serviceable criteria for pinpointing physical location. Yet we rarely use them in everyday contexts. You'd find it odd if, when asked for directions to my hometown of Amherst, I told you to head to 42°20′25.3752″N and 72°29′48.5484″W – one possible set of geospatial coordinates. It is also not the case that an advance in the knowledge furnished by technology actually ensures knowledge of a topic – the advent of global positioning and navigational systems, which calculate the distance, trajectory, and length of a trip with astonishing accuracy, has contributed in

---

[15] As Sumner (1973) has shown, Cicero relies most of all on birth years to form groups of orators, which is perhaps the most striking feature of his chronology and a clear indication that biology and biography hold an important place in the work's conceptual framework.

no small measure to many a traveler's ignorance about where they are and how they got there.

Modern humans are keenly pragmatic and key their consumption and distribution of information to their aims in using it. Romans were no different, and neither was Cicero when writing the *Brutus*. He certainly claims access to better knowledge derived from the research of Atticus and Varro and occasional forays into old records, *commentarii veteres* or *antiqui*. Yet to claim as he does that such advances are a natural part of a broader intellectual trajectory is to assume that all artistic forms, including research into the past, evolve over time, and that change is necessarily improvement. Cicero was above all skilled in rhetorical presentation, and the superior information of his contemporaries may well have served his desire to illuminate the grand landscape of Rome's oratorical past; but it served no less his craftiness in selecting and presenting the shades and hues of truth as he envisioned them. His academic enterprise and its presentation reflect his belief in artistic progress, especially for oratory, up to his day. Many scholars today, imagining him to be a forerunner of positivism's advancement of knowledge, have stumbled into Cicero's intellectual trap. Even in the *Brutus*, Cicero's most historical work – more so than even *de Republica* or *de Legibus* – he is not a disinterested historian, but, true to character, a self-interested rhetorician, desperately seeking salvation for a state in crisis and, just as desperately, vying to be its savior.

The vicissitudes of the Roman calendar also shed light on contemporary cultural tensions that are crucial to the writing of the *Brutus*. The conflict and convergence of traditional forms of power with innovations in knowledge are yet another version of an inveterate challenge: maintaining inherited customs while realigning them with new ideas. The new calendar's 365 and ¼ days were keyed to a solar cycle rather than the customary, if temperamental, (soli)lunar year, which had served Rome's ancestors well enough across the several centuries during which the tiny city-state nestled on the Tiber river had grown into the largest sustained empire known to the Mediterranean, stretching out dominion toward the Rhine and Thames in the north and west, as well as the Nile and Euphrates in the south and east.[16] From the newly captured lands Rome brought back books, coins, slaves, statues, and scientific knowledge. Like most of Rome's empire the calendar wasn't even truly Roman, but rather intellectual booty taken from Greek Egyptian astronomers. They had calculated, with an

---

[16] Or, as Cicero says, "Rhine, Ocean, Nile" (*Marc.* 28), perhaps minimizing Caesar's September 46 quadruple triumph over Africa, Egypt, Gaul, and Pontus.

impressive mix of accuracy and prejudice, the sun's 365¼-day trajectory around the earth.

Hellenization lies at the heart of Rome's imperial redefinitions and at the heart of Cicero's definition of great oratory. One of the oldest tales Romans tell about themselves is that of foreign influence: they adopted, often with reluctance or suspicion, Greek artistic and intellectual forms in order to explain and order the world. Inherited ideas and values were put to serious proof once Romans left their sovereign stamp on the world order. Changing these inheritances could seriously challenge, and for some thoroughly destroy, a shared sense of Roman identity. The *Brutus* recognizes this instability while trying to synchronize Roman history and aesthetic ideals with Greek events and literary models.

The *Brutus* also crucially intervenes in contemporary intellectual debates, staging a conflict, for example, over Caesar's recently published *de Analogia*. This treatise on language formation and reformation provides yet another perspective, in addition to the calendar, on how Caesar sought to assert control over the minds and mouths of Romans.[17] Cicero countered Caesar's analogical system by indirect rhetorical means, pointing up its shortcomings and implicitly relating them to a tangential debate: the conflict of rhetorical styles, "Atticism" versus "Asianism."

Cicero paints the Atticists as unrepentant philhellenes, hopeless lovers of all things Greek, whose penchant for the foreign undermined Roman traditions and, implicitly, the state and social orders. No stranger himself to Greek influence, he strove instead to guide and control the reception of Greek intellectual goods through an alternative model of appropriation that still accorded pride of place to Romans over Greeks and to his view of Roman identity over the views of his similarly enterprising competitors. Cicero's imperial ambition, however, was not the same as Caesar's, who through warfare monopolized power and glory. Yet it was like Caesar's, if we remember L. P. Hartley's adage that "the past is a foreign country." Cicero set his imperial sights on Roman history, impressing his sovereign mark onto the intellectual history of artistic practices at Rome and their forerunners in the Greek world.

As noted above, a fundamental aim of this book is to highlight the contribution of Cicero's *Brutus* to literary historiography, to how we think about the organization of an artistic practice across time. Such a legacy can often be obscured by subsequent developments, and this is the case for Cicero's *Brutus*. Once again, the history of Caesar's contemporary calendar

---

[17] Cf. Feeney (2007) 197.

sheds light on an abiding problem in intellectual traditions and their reception: how much change is required to claim ownership of a system or tradition? This is the implication of our belief that we use the Gregorian rather than the Julian calendar, when in fact the difference is almost microscopic: in 1582 about 0.002 percent was subtracted from the year's length, and we'll have to wait some eight decades before any person alive when this book is published will experience the result – the skipping of leap year in centuries not divisible by four.[18] By right of this momentous change, Pope Gregory XIII also erased the calendar's ascription to Julius Caesar and thereby "invented" our Gregorian calendar.[19] This is not to dismiss Gregory's changes, which are if anything another object lesson in the dynamics of intellectual appropriation as a response to political crisis.[20] The writing and theorization of literary history has likewise continued apace since Cicero wrote the *Brutus*. Yet subsequent efforts have either misunderstood or overshadowed Cicero's initial work, and this despite the fact that he anticipated and proposed workarounds or solutions for several problems that still bedevil the writing of literary history.[21]

Similar jockeying over the meaning of a tradition or innovation can be seen in the history of the related field of astronomy. Still well over the horizon from the reforms of Caesar and Gregory lay Copernicus' *Revolutions*, which would have the earth go around the sun (although Aristarchus of Samos had already proposed heliocentrism).[22] Our planet, however, was still round – nineteenth-century thinkers had yet (falsely) to ascribe to medieval scientists a belief in the earth's flatness, an allegation used to argue for the incompatibility of science and religion or to denigrate Catholics in sectarian disagreement. The attempts of nineteenth-century intellectuals to discredit medieval science (the so-called "Flat Earth Theory" of the Middle Ages) show the extent to which later authorities

---

[18] We have leap years in 2000 and 2400 (centuries 20, 24) but not in 2100, 2200, or 2300 (centuries 21, 22, 23).

[19] The annual change was approximately 10 minutes and 48 seconds. In 1582 ten days, 5 October through 14 October, were deleted, i.e. 15 October immediately followed 4 October; Richards (1998) 365–66.

[20] As Pope – the Catholic office formerly known as *pontifex maximus* – Gregory was responsible for determining and announcing the day of Easter to millions of the faithful. To calculate accurately the anniversary of the resurrection of the Lord and Savior of Man for a religion predicated on the salvation and resurrection of humanity was no trivial matter. Richards (1998) 3–123; 239–56 (Gregorian reforms); 345–78 (Easter). D. Steel (2000) 93–136 (Easter and AD/BC dates); 157–82 (Gregorian reforms). Stern (2012) 380–424 (earliest disputes over Easter).

[21] Perkins (1992) remains the most accessible study of literary historiography and its limitations.

[22] A fact that Copernicus knew for his initial investigations but seems to have unlearned by the time he published the pioneering *Revolutions*.

both appropriate earlier authors and, by relying on the thinnest pieces of evidence and consulting the prejudices of their contemporaries rather than plausible facts, may also make false assertions about their earlier counterparts as part of that appropriation.[23] Distorting the past and then belittling it for being distorted is an old trick – just ask any scholar of the Middle Ages laboring in the wake of Renaissance prejudices.

Cicero was a forerunner to such appropriations and distortions: several stories in the *Brutus* about literary authorities and their motivations are wrong. This is probably the case for Accius, for example.[24] Cicero tendentiously discredits Accius' work and offers a self-serving appeal to factual accuracy: Accius bungled the beginning of Latin literature by placing it in 207, while Cicero and his prudent contemporaries know that 240 is correct. Cicero similarly distorts the scholarly past when he places upon Ennius the mantle of the literary historian: Ennius is the first documenter of the first Roman orator, Marcus Cornelius Cethegus. Yet, it is unimaginable that Ennius, when he used the term *orator* in connection with Cethegus, thought that he was making a claim about the history of an artistic tradition, much less about its origin. It is equally unimaginable that Ennius called Cethegus the *Suadai medulla* ("marrow of Persuasion") because he was referring to Eupolis' characterization of Pericles as possessing *Peitho* ("Persuasion") on his lips. Both moves – highly tendentious and shrouded in brilliant rhetorical misdirection – allow Cicero to appropriate a tradition of literary history, the details of which are largely his own invention. With Accius and his alternative chronology safely out of the way, Cicero can arrogate to himself the authority he has created and attributed to Ennius, and he can further portray Ennius as being involved in a philhellenic habit of intellectual appropriation. In this inventive scheme, the documentation of oratorical history has not only a valid Roman precedent to justify it but also a justification that is itself born of cultural translation of the Greek world. What enters Cicero's rhetorical filter as tendentious and revolutionary emerges as circumspect and traditional.

Approaches to the *Brutus*

I have spent so much time considering a range of intellectual discourses in order to defamiliarize the terms of Cicero's *Brutus* and to situate it within

---

[23] J. B. Russell (1991).

[24] On Accius see Welsh (2011), who shows the extent to which Cicero distorts Accius' *Didascalica* and the Porcian chronology on which it was (probably) based. See below on Ennius.

scholarly traditions upon which it built or with which it competed. Cicero, this book argues, deftly interwove various strands of inquiry into a crucial and innovative document of contemporary political and intellectual discourse. He invented literary history not simply as a scholarly endeavor but as a sophisticated response to contemporary aesthetic debates and to civic crisis. The most prominent features of the *Brutus* – a self-serving trajectory toward the Ciceronian present, a detailed account of Roman orators, and gestures toward scientific accuracy – have garnered it a mixed reputation as a historical survey of orators that promotes its author's inevitable triumph. The tendentious reframing of history and unabashed self-promotion figure in most of Cicero's writings, but modern observers' often squeamish attention to his alleged vanity has failed fully to capture the unique merits of the *Brutus*: what it accomplishes intellectually, how it lures readers into its ideological and critical programs, and why it is a serious intervention in Rome's political crisis.

Scholars have long shown a grudging respect for Cicero's investigations (Douglas thought them "remarkable"), admiration for all that he gathered and appreciation for the details about orators and politicians who otherwise would have passed forever into silence.[25] Praise is often paired with regrets about Cicero's careless omissions or unscrupulous emphases.[26] Inconsistent, temperamental, and rhetorically inclined, Cicero just wasn't a very good modern historian. Yet the scholarly pose he strikes over and again should not lull us into complacency about his motives and techniques: Cicero is not a modern scholar, or an ancient one either. Above all he is a political orator skilled in rhetorical presentation. What Cicero discovers is the past as he wishes to see it, not as he finds it – or perhaps it's more accurate to say that Cicero discovers the past as he wishes to see the present and future.[27]

The greatest scholarly emphasis has been on the work's most salient feature, the evolutionary catalogue of orators culminating in Cicero's and Brutus' accomplishments. The oratorical collection and the teleology underlying it were a significant achievement and a methodological advance

---

[25] Douglas (1966a) xxiii, assessing the "literary merits" of the *Brutus*, even as he elsewhere recognizes the distortions and omissions. Rawson (1972) 41: "Cicero's most sustained, sensitive and successful historical achievement."

[26] The split attitude is perhaps best exemplified by Suerbaum (1996/1997), largely positive, and Suerbaum (1997), which focuses on the shortcomings in Cicero's catalogue.

[27] Cicero's rhetorical use of evidence is similarly in full effect in *de Republica*, in which he selectively details early Roman history based on the facts that he claims to discover, all while criticizing Plato's fictional account in the *Republic*. Criticism of Plato strategically justifies and conceals his own omissions and emphases.

over previous Hellenistic and Roman scholars.[28] Yet attention to the self-serving and somewhat predictable teleological design can shed only so much light on the work's innovations in the field of literary historiography or on the civic vision underlying the oratorical history.[29]

Several discrete topics in addition to the work's teleology have tended to capture scholarly attention: prosopography, the history of early poetry, the textual economy of Cicero's work and afterlife, its possible function as a commemoration and swan song of republican oratory, the technical oratorical polemic with the so-called Atticists, the debate over Analogy and Anomaly, or the oblique relationship to Caesar's political monopoly under the shadow of the republican losses in Africa.[30] Numerous exemplary readings of the *Brutus* exist, but, this book argues, understanding the breadth and depth of Cicero's intellectual insights requires us to examine closely the terms of his explanations and to treat his dialogue as a complex piece of literature worthy of complex analysis. This claim is not made to cast aspersions on the many valuable contributions thus far: I don't wish to be a Gregory to past Caesars.[31] This book is an attempt to read the *Brutus* as we might an extended poem or a work of drama, with attention both to the specifics of language and formal presentation, and to the recurrence of key ideas and motifs, which are all essential to a coherent account of its political message and intellectual innovations.[32]

---

[28] Douglas (1966a) xxii, Bringmann (1971) 22, Narducci (1997) 103–4, Schwindt (2000) 96–122.

[29] Fox (2007) 177–208 is reluctant to accept Cicero's scheme of progress, noting the (at times contradictory) interplay of "chronological progression" and "conceptual progression." Dugan (2005) 172–250 takes the account at face value, as do Goldberg (1995) 3–12 and Hinds (1998) 52–98, even as they challenge its assumptions.

[30] These topics undoubtedly merit scholarly attention, and will be examined throughout. The main contributions in the immense bibliography are listed here. Prosopography: in addition to Broughton's *MRR*, Douglas (1966b), Sumner (1973), with bibliography, David (1992), Fogel (2007); history of poetry: Barchiesi (1962), Goldberg (1995) 3–12, Hinds (1998) 52–98, Suerbaum (2002) 80–83, Welsh (2011); afterlife and swan song: *CHLC* I: 236, Heldmann (1982) 17–21, Gowing (2000), C. Steel (2002), Charrier (2003), Dugan (2005) 172–250, Fox (2007) 177–208, Stroup (2010) 237–68; Atticism: Wilamowitz (1900), Dihle (1957), Leeman (1963) 91–111, 136–67, Lebek (1970) 83–114, 176–93, T. Gelzer (1979), May (1990), Wisse (1995), Guérin (2011) 342–49; Caesar: Haenni (1905), M. Gelzer (1938), Rathofer (1986), Strasburger (1990), 29–38, Narducci (1997) 98–101, Dugan (2005) 244–46, Lowrie (2008), Bishop (2019) 173–218; Analogy: Garcea (2012), with bibliography. Bringmann (1971) 13–40, Narducci (2002), and the essays in Aubert-Baillot and Guérin (2014) are good starting points for several issues.

[31] As Badian (1967) 229 noted, though surely with different aims in mind, "more can be written about the *Brutus* than about any other of Cicero's works."

[32] This aspect of the analysis is essentially text-immanent (a technique reaching back at least as far as Aristarchus' "to elucidate Homer from Homer"). Schwindt (2000) on the methodological implications of text-immanent criticism.

My readings build on the widespread acknowledgment that Roman dialogues are sophisticated pieces of literature, even if no consensus exists about how to translate that methodological insight into the practical business of literary analysis. This approach is also in sympathy with developing understandings of related prose genres – historiography and epistolography in particular – in which the selection, presentation, and emphasis or omission of material are all crucial to isolating the message and experience of the text. Beyond the dialogue, in the subsequent reception of the *Brutus* by literary critics, Cicero's innovative model of literary evolution came under close scrutiny, and so this study occasionally gazes forward to the imperial reception to understand the first stages in the legacy of Cicero's innovations.[33]

In addition to offering a global close reading of the *Brutus*, this book also lays great stress on several apparent omissions, errors, or inconsistencies in the dialogue, seeking to understand them not as flaws but as a productive feature of its literary design. Several problems confront any reader of the *Brutus* and might suggest that Cicero, in the course of slapdash composition, either committed numerous errors or could not be bothered with consistency of presentation. While one organizational principle, chronology, emerges clearly, digressions are numerous, scattered throughout the account, and seemingly unconnected to one another or to the advancing timeline. Cicero repeats emphases and phrasing, as when he twice notes Caesar's running of the senate in 59 (*senatum Caesar consul habuisset*, 218). "Many such superfluous repetitions are found in our treatise," says G. L. Hendrickson, who later criticizes the "obtrusive habit of repetition, when he wishes to urge a point important for his argument." Other passages, including the tortuous explanation of Ennius' *Suadai medulla* (59), "may be an index of rapid composition (or dictation)."[34]

The *Brutus* is replete with exaggerations and errors: the assessment of Calvus contradicts most other evidence;[35] for his protégé Caelius Cicero counts three speeches but at least five are attested;[36] several orators, such as Marius, Sulla, Catiline, and Clodius, are omitted without notice or apology; Cicero refuses to discuss living orators but circumvents his own

---

[33] See especially Hardie (1993) as a model for reception as interpretation, who in this respect builds on H. R. Jauss, especially the fifth principle laid out in Jauss (1982).

[34] Hendrickson (1962) 186 n.a; 220–21 n.a. Bringmann (1971) 35–39 sensibly criticizes overzealous attempts to excise repetitions.

[35] Leeman (1963) 138–42, Gruen (1967), Lebek (1970) 84–97, Fairweather (1981) 96–98, Aubert (2010) 92–93 n.26, Guérin (2011) 342–49. See Chapter 7 for full evidence.

[36] Kaster (2020) 146 n.425.

injunction by having Brutus and Atticus discuss Marcellus and Caesar; the assessment of Brutus' speech for King Deiotarus is fulsome beyond Cicero's assessment elsewhere of Brutus' essentially philosophical style;[37] Cicero claims oral sources for material he probably read;[38] the interpretations of Ennius are grossly distorted; parts of Accius' claims are probably misreported; the insistence on Naevius' death in 204 engages in special pleading; Cicero discusses Torquatus (he is thus presumably dead), but not the oratory of Cato and Scipio (suggesting they were still alive, although they died with Torquatus).[39]

The list could go on. Context or convention explain some of its items: for example, praise of Brutus' oratory makes sense in light of his central role in the dialogue and Cicero's desire to court him as a political ally.[40] Hastiness of composition may well explain certain errors or repetitions – I am not suggesting that every minor blemish necessarily betrays some grand distortion of Ciceronian propaganda. When Cicero nods and remarks on writing (*scribi*, 181) about past orators in his spoken dialogue, indulgence is warranted, however much the slip may meaningfully remind us that the drama is a fictional screen for a written account. Even the most cautious authors and scholars, ancient or modern, succumb to occasional slips and hope to enjoy readerly charity.

Picking apart Cicero's distortions, errors, or tendentiousness can always get caught up in a kind of latter-day "gotcha-ism." I seek rather to explain why he meaningfully shapes, distorts, and even falsifies material as part of his intellectual project. These apparent errors or problems open up new avenues for approaching the work because, paradoxically, they reveal his purpose most plainly. In this way we can discover novel meaning in the thorniest moments of the text. For example, the strident admonitions

---

[37] On his oratory see Filbey (1911) 333, Balbo (2013), Tempest (2017) 26–28, 50–52, 66–67, 128–29, and 234. On his philosophy see Tempest (2017) 94–97; Sedley (1997), highlighting Antiochean leanings, challenges the long-held belief in his Stoicism; Rawson (1986) offers detailed source analysis of Brutus' intellectual and political views.

[38] Cicero's claim to have heard Accius praise Decimus Brutus may be an invention (107); *Arch.* 27 makes no such connection, even though it could have supported Cicero's arguments.

[39] Other problems are worth noting (this list is not exhaustive): Brutus states that he couldn't have heard Julius Caesar speak because Caesar had been away from Rome (248); Brutus also claims ignorance of Scaevola Pontifex's oratory (147) before praising the *elegantia* of his speeches (163); allegations of the untrammeled ambition of Publius Crassus, son of the triumvir, are otherwise unsubstantiated (281–82); the depiction of Cicero's speech defending Titinia against Curio is highly suspect (and represented differently and perhaps accurately in *Orator*, cf. W. J. Tatum 1991).

[40] Similarly, the praise for Cicero's former son-in-law C. Calpurnius Piso (272) is probably excessive: Cicero practically admits as much. Yet there seems to be no ulterior motive other than (expected) praise for a family member.

against discussing the living do not square with the equally strident choice
to discuss Caesar and Marcellus at length (and we cannot explain away the
irregularity just because Cicero creatively outsources the task to his interlocutors). The inconsistency and the sustained attention on these two
figures prompt us to consider all the more closely why and how they are
discussed. Such a passage is ideal for close reading because it reveals the
motivations underlying the surface rhetoric. This in turn helps to explain
why, despite several apparent problems or flaws, the *Brutus* is a captivating
and pathbreaking document of intellectual history. Whatever one's
approach, A. E. Douglas' assertion about "its freedom from discernible
historical error" requires revision: the basic chronology of Roman orators is
mostly full and mostly accurate (Douglas' true concern), but that is only
one topic; and Cicero's professions of accuracy often obscure how he
fashions the material to suit his larger designs.[41]

In many ways the remarks on *inventio* (the discovery of the most
serviceable evidence and arguments) from the *Orator* (also 46 BCE) tellingly reveal the *Brutus'* techniques:

> Unless considerable selection is employed by the orator's judgment, how
> will he linger over and dwell on his good points or soften harsh ones, or
> hide and thoroughly suppress, if possible, what can't be explained away, or
> distract the minds of the audience or offer another point, which, when put
> forward, is more convincing than the one that stands in the way?

> nisi ab oratoris iudicio dilectus magnus adhibebitur, quonam modo ille in
> bonis haerebit et habitabit suis aut molliet dura aut occultabit quae dilui
> non poterunt atque omnino opprimet, si licebit, aut abducet animos aut
> aliud adferet, quod oppositum probabilius sit quam illud quod obstabit?
> (*Orat.* 49)

Cicero's distortions, errors, or inconsistencies – no less than his stated
choices – often serve a greater purpose: to offer a sustained critique of
literary history, to construct a view of the past that is plausible and
coherent even as it tends toward Cicero's own development, to challenge
Caesar, to promote Cicero's understanding of philhellenism, and to attack
the Atticists. Seemingly chance distortions and details often indicate some
political or intellectual motive or reinforce a key idea or theme. When
Cicero tries to force the evidence into a particular mold, his efforts often
reveal the larger designs of the *Brutus*.

---

[41] Douglas (1966a) liii.

Chapter Outline

Each of the book's eight chapters examines a major topic or significant digression in the *Brutus*. Chapter 1 begins with the "Ciceropaideia" (301–29), the account of Cicero's education and training. I begin with the end of the *Brutus* in order to get a sense of what the dialogue has been building up to. Cicero's concluding discussion of himself reveals and brings together several assumptions, problems, and techniques of presentation that are crucial to the earlier parts of the dialogue. In the Ciceropaideia he carefully shapes biographical and historical details into a tandem narrative, intertwining his ascent with the decline of Hortensius. The account suggestively documents Cicero's development of a moderate "Rhodian" style and implicitly undermines his Atticist detractors.

Chapter 2 focuses on the dialogue's intellectual filiations. It begins by examining the preface's (1–25) insistence on remaining silent about the civic crisis even as the interlocutors' exchange of written texts incessantly circles back to the woes besetting the Roman state. Atticus' *Liber Annalis* and Brutus' *de Virtute* inspired the *Brutus*, but to what extent and to what purpose remain initially unclear. In aligning their texts with *de Republica* and the *Brutus* Cicero creates a complex web of learned exchange in the service of the republic. The chapter then considers other potential intellectual predecessors: Varro's writings on literature, the history of the dialogue genre, and Cicero's own works. The *Brutus* draws together several intellectual currents and promises significant innovations in how to document and conceptualize the literary past.

Chapter 3 examines the *Brutus* as an intervention in contemporary politics. It begins by revisiting the preface but focuses on the contemporary civic crisis (1–25). In both the preface and the digression on Julius Caesar (254–57) Cicero presents an alternative civic vision as a response to the crisis. The chapter concludes by considering the portrayal of the younger generation of orators: Curio (*filius*), Caelius, Publius Crassus, and Marcellus. The last figure merits special attention because Cicero's oratorical canon includes only two living figures: Marcellus and Caesar. Marcellus is accorded a prominent role as part of Cicero's attempt to offer a coherent vision of the republic, one based on the restoration of the senatorial elite and the reinstatement of the traditional institutions of government.

Chapter 4 turns to the pedagogical workings of the *Brutus*, which instill in the reader a new sense of how to organize and assess the literary past. Syncrisis is central to conceptualizing the past and to portraying

individuals and groups across cultures and generations. The dialogue also
spends a considerable amount of time reflecting on historical accuracy, for
example in the discussions of Coriolanus and Themistocles (41–44), the
laudatio funebris (62), the beginning of Latin literature with Livius
Andronicus (72–73), and Curio's dialogue about Caesar's consulship
(218–19). Taken together these reflections on rhetorical presentation of
the past explain Cicero's license in handling the data of literary history.
Several claims, exaggerations, and fabrications can be explained by Cicero's
desire to craft meaningful parallels in his history of Latin oratory and
literature, including his insistence on Naevius' death in 204 BCE (60).
Such parallels reveal in turn the close interconnection of his intellectual
and ideological commitments.

Chapter 5 takes up the work's beginnings: why did Cicero choose
Marcus Cornelius Cethegus as the first Roman orator? Appius Claudius
Caecus made more sense, and Cicero's reasons for excluding Caecus from
his canon tellingly reveal his literary-historical principles. The literary
history presented ultimately justifies his own role as a literary historian
and confirms his prejudices about the past, present, and future of oratory.
His manicuring of the past emerges prominently in the perplexing "double
history" of Greek oratory (26–51), which is a methodological template for
Roman oratorical history, and in Ennius' special place as a literary historian
(57–59).

Chapter 6 shows how Cicero establishes a normative framework for the
writing of literary history. Across the dialogue and through the various
speakers he offers a sustained critique of literary historiography. Several
fundamental tensions and conflicts emerge: absolute versus relative criteria
in assessing literature and building canons; presentism and antiquarianism;
formalism and historicism; and the recognition that all literary histories are
subject to their crafters' emphases and agendas.

Chapter 7 considers stylistic imitation and appropriation in the debate
over Atticism and Asianism, with a special focus on how Cicero distorts
the aims and positions of his detractors in the diatribe against the Atticists
(285–91). He trades on various meanings of *Atticus/Attici* in order to make
a rhetorical – rather than strictly logical – case. He downplays Atticism as
outdated and relegates its stylistic virtues to the plain style (*genus tenue*).
Rejecting Atticism does not entail rejecting the plain style. Instead he
acknowledges it as one of many oratorical virtues to be subsumed under
the capable orator's broad stylistic repertoire. Cicero promotes a model of
stylistic diversity, examples of which are found in the long histories of
Greek and, especially, Roman oratory.

Chapter 8 turns to the famous judgment of Julius Caesar's *commentarii* (*nudi, recti, venusti,* 262). Not only textual aesthetics but also visual analogies and the plastic arts underlie Cicero's judgments. An analysis of statuary analogies and of the fuller contexts for Cicero's statements suggests a deft ploy on his part. He portrays himself as Phidias crafting a statue of Minerva (the Parthenon Athena) and Caesar as Praxiteles crafting a statue of Venus (the Aphrodite of Knidos). The fundamentally different symbolic resonances of the goddesses simultaneously challenge Caesar's military accomplishments and underscore Cicero's civic achievements. Cicero thereby promotes his vision of the need to restore the Roman republic once the civil war has concluded. The Conclusion brings the disparate pieces together in order to underscore Cicero's lasting influence on the writing of literary history.

CHAPTER I

Ciceropaideia

A Brief Biography

Cicero's life is well attested and well known, in part because the *Brutus* chronicles his education, training, and advocacy. It does not provide, however, a full biography by modern (or ancient) standards, and so a biographical sketch can help us assess what it does offer. Born in 106 BCE to an equestrian family in Arpinum, a hillside town some 65 miles southeast of Rome, Cicero would go on to have one of the most remarkable careers of any "new man" (*novus homo*).[1] His early education soon brought him to Rome and to the guidance of Quintus Mucius Scaevola "the augur" (cos. 117), after whose death Cicero attached himself to Quintus Mucius Scaevola "the pontifex" (cos. 95). Both were eminent legal authorities; the latter published some eighteen books on civil law, and his edict while governor of Asia guided Cicero's proconsulship in Cilicia in 51–50.[2] Cicero's *tirocinium fori* ("orator's apprenticeship in the forum"), the informal institution that Andrew Riggsby has memorably called "political boot

---

[1] On Cicero as *novus homo* and how he worked around this limitation, Earl (1967) 44–59, Wiseman (1971) 107–13, Dugan (2005), Kurczyk (2006) 121–211, van der Blom (2010), Hölkeskamp (2011a). Modern biographies of Cicero are legion. The following list is partial (and egregiously Anglophone-centric). M. Gelzer (2014, third edition in German) is the best for comprehensiveness, Rawson (1983) as an extensive study in English, Tempest (2011) as an introduction, and Everitt (2001) for entertainment. Stockton (1971) and Mitchell (1979) and (1991) emphasize political aspects. Shackleton Bailey (1971) is engaging or idiosyncratic, depending on one's expectations; he focuses on the letters and on Cicero's later life and tends to dismiss his politics and rhetoric. Andrew Dyck's 2015 *BMCR* review of M. Gelzer (2014) remarks that "a new biography . . . is overdue." Mary Beard's *LRB* review of Everitt (2001), reprinted as Beard (2013), desiderates an account of reception "to explore the way his life-story has been constructed and reconstructed over the last two thousand years" (87). The *Cronologia Ciceroniana*, Marinone (2004), is indispensable on details and slowly coming to receive its due. The latest version is on the website of the International Society of Cicero's Friends, www.tulliana.eu.

[2] Van der Blom (2010) 238–41 for a succinct account; also see below.

camp," introduced him to the forum's inner workings under the guidance of an experienced member of the Roman aristocracy (Scaevola Augur).[3]

Cicero undertook legal advocacy rather late in comparison to his ambitious peers, many of whose family backgrounds facilitated their public entrée. Only in 81 did he take up his first civil case (*pro Quinctio*) and in 80 his first criminal case (*pro S. Roscio Amerino*). A sojourn through Greece in 79–77 interrupted his forensic activity and saw him studying under Greek masters of philosophy and rhetoric. He returned to Rome to restart his legal and political career with a refined oratorical style. His rise was exceptional given his background and limited connections. The quaestorship in 75 had him assigned to western Sicily. The Sicilians soon presented him the opportunity of prosecuting Gaius Verres in 70, the peccant propraetorian governor from 73 to 71. Success against Verres on charges of extortion (*repetundae*) marked a breaking point in his career. The defeat of Verres' advocate, Quintus Hortensius Hortalus, the premier orator of his day, heralded Cicero's triumphant arrival in the cutthroat arena of the Roman forum. He was elected aedile for 69 (before the trial's conclusion), urban praetor for 66, and finally consul for 63, the first year he was eligible (*anno suo*).[4]

Cicero's pursuit of Catiline and his followers while consul garnered him considerable and lasting renown: he received a *supplicatio* ("thanksgiving") and was hailed as *pater patriae* ("father of the fatherland"). Execution of the conspirators also made him several enemies and left him exposed to legal reprisals. While continuing to be active in defense cases and politics, he would soon make one of the many political miscalculations that plagued his later career. He testified in 61 against Publius Clodius, who had snuck into Caesar's house dressed as a woman at the festival of the *Bona Dea*, which prohibited men from attending. Clodius' pursuit of revenge would lead to Cicero's exile for eighteen months in 58–57. He was recalled by the people, with considerable help from Pompey, Atticus, and other allies, resuming forensic advocacy but with little scope for independent political action. During the so-called First Triumvirate he turned to the writing of dialogues in the tradition of Plato, which was one response to being sidelined from political affairs while Caesar, Crassus, and Pompey dominated domestic and overseas politics. He wrote three major treatises on

---

[3] Riggsby (2010) 59. Peter White has kindly shared an unpublished paper questioning the institutional status of the *tirocinium fori*; cf. Richlin (2011).

[4] For a succinct overview of the *cursus honorum*, see Lintott (1999) 144–46, Brennan (2014) 50–53; Beck (2005) examines its early development.

political philosophy: *de Oratore*, *de Republica*, and *de Legibus* (On the Orator, On the Republic, On the Laws).[5] *De Republica* indirectly inspired the *Brutus*, and the magisterial *de Oratore* looms constantly in the background.[6] Pompey's new laws in response to the urban chaos at Rome governed the courts in 52 and meant a busy year for Cicero. A proconsular assignment in 51–50 sent him to Cilicia (southeastern coast of modern Turkey), where he governed the province on the model of his former mentor Scaevola Pontifex, curbing corruption, ensuring the administration of justice, and limiting personal expenditures. He also defeated local mountain tribes in skirmishes.

This military success (and backroom political maneuvering in Rome) brought a second *supplicatio*, although Cicero's true goal was a triumph, with the justification that he had ensured stability in Cilicia.[7] The achievement was not trivial given the threat posed by the Parthians after Crassus' disastrous defeat in 53 in the neighboring province of Syria. Cicero's hopes, however, were dashed by great events and even greater men: civil war between Caesar and Pompey broke out in January of 49 as Cicero waited patiently outside the walls of Rome with his proconsular lictors, expectantly retaining *imperium* for a triumph that never materialized. He followed the Pompeian forces to defeat at Pharsalus in Greece in 48 and returned sheepishly to Italy, landing at Brundisium with the lictors still in tow. He would not relinquish *imperium* until pardoned by Caesar late in 47. The *Brutus* is written in the progressing aftermath of the civil war, which though still ongoing in the spring of 46 was essentially over after the defeat of the republican resistance in north Africa and the deaths of its leaders, Cato and Scipio.[8]

The "Ciceropaideia" (301–29)

The outline presented above is the barest sketch of Cicero's biography, with details cherry-picked for their relevance to the *Brutus*. That cherry-picking in

---

[5] On the triad in Cicero's writings and career, see C. Steel (2005) 70–75 (*de Orat.*), 75–78 (*Rep.*), 78–80 (*Leg.*).

[6] The record of *de Legibus* is murky. Cicero probably never completed or published it while alive, although its mood seems to reflect the (late) 50s. See Dyck (2003) 5–7. Zetzel (2017) xxii–xxvi emphasizes connections to the 40s. Jim Zetzel has kindly shared an (unpublished) essay that challenges dating the work to the 50s and reading it in tandem with *de Republica*. Cavarzere (1998) on how Hortensius bridges the end/beginning of *de Oratore*/the *Brutus*.

[7] On this *supplicatio*, see Wistrand (1979), Rollinger (2017), and Morrell (2017) 197; Chapter 8.

[8] The resistance was "only mostly dead" (to borrow from *The Princess Bride*). Caesar subdued the holdouts in Spain on 17 March 45.

some sense copies Cicero's own self-presentation (301–29), which is not an autobiography in any full sense, but what could be called a "Ciceropaideia," on account of Cicero's widespread interest in Xenophon's *Cyropaideia* ("Education of Cyrus").[9] Like the *Brutus*, this riveting account of Cyrus' rise to command the Persian empire has far greater moral and political aims than just documenting its stated subject. Biography plays a crucial role in the *Brutus*, which adapts the tradition of Hellenistic biographical scholarship, repeatedly cites Roman (auto)biographers, and culminates in Cicero's intellectual training and his political oratory.[10] It heavily emphasizes intellectual (and physical) connections with the Greek world: reading, declamation, philosophy, and rhetorical instruction, both at Rome and in the Greek East. It also closely intertwines the biographies of Cicero and his chief forensic rival, Quintus Hortensius Hortalus, honored at the dialogue's beginning and end.

Alert to biography's potential for self-promotion, Cicero also promotes his intellectual and political achievements while reflecting on the appropriate use of Greek culture. The *Brutus* contains the oldest remains of extended autobiography from Greco-Roman antiquity, building on (now mostly lost) Greek and Roman forerunners. We learn too of Latin autobiographies of Catulus (132) and Scaurus (112). These are contrasted with Xenophon's *Cyropaideia*, a laudable yet overvalued Greek model (112), despite Cicero's praise elsewhere.[11] Cicero fashions the Ciceropaideia with these models in mind.[12] Its details are unlikely to satisfy the expectations of either ancient or modern readers: anecdotes and the assessment of moral character, so scintillating to ancient biographers, are largely absent. Absent too are the basic details relished by modern readers: nothing about his early years, family, or friends. Instead the focus is on his oratorical development, which mirrors the evolutionary account of Greco-Roman oratory.

In addition to recounting his rhetorical training and trajectory, Cicero interconnects his life with that of his slightly older rival Hortensius.[13]

---

[9] E.g. *Leg.* 2.56, *Fin.* 2.92, *Tusc.* 5.99, *Sen.* 30, 79–81, with J. G. F. Powell (1988) 256–58; *Att.* 2.3.2 (SB 23), *Fam.* 9.25.1 (SB 114), *Q. fr.* 1.1.23 (SB 1). The last letter emphasizes that Xenophon focused more on depicting the just ruler than chronicling the truth.

[10] On the *Cyropaideia* see Due (1989), J. Tatum (1989), and Gera (1993).

[11] E.g. *Fam.* 9.25.1 (SB 114).

[12] No mention is made, however, of Catulus' Greek biography or Sulla's memoirs; the latter colored much of the post-Sullan accounts of Roman history. Cicero may also occasionally draw on Rutilius Rufus' memoirs. See Chassignet (2003), Smith (2009), W. J. Tatum (2011), Scholz, Walter, and Winkle (2013), and Flower (2014) on memoirs and autobiography.

[13] Dyck (2008) examines Hortensius' career and Ciceronian evidence for it. Kurczyk (2006) 312–26 discusses Cicero's autobiography and Hortensius' role in it, but what follows differs fundamentally

Hortensius may seem like an obvious choice in light of his oratorical prominence, but other motivations undoubtedly play a role. By inserting Hortensius into the narrative Cicero emphasizes the importance of syncrisis for aesthetic evaluation; he also reinforces the general impression that the art of oratory progresses from generation to generation as a kind of shared intellectual project fostered and transmitted by the Roman elite.

Cicero might have considered other candidates for comparison, such as his coeval Servius Sulpicius Rufus (106/5–43 BCE, cos. 51). Sulpicius accompanied Cicero to Rhodes in 78 and was an eminent jurist and stylist, as evidenced by two famous letters (*Fam.* 4.5, 4.12 [SB 248, 253]), the first consoling Cicero after Tullia's death and the second detailing the death of Sulpicius' consular colleague M. Claudius Marcellus (cos. 51), who was murdered at Piraeus in 45 while on his way back to Rome from exile. Sulpicius had also prosecuted Murena in 63 after losing the consular elections to him, and won fame for three speeches that survived to Quintilian's day.[14] Like the earlier Mucii Scaevolae he excelled in Roman jurisprudence but took pride of place because he was the first to make it an art (151–54). Still, Sulpicius was hardly the orator that Hortensius was, and the prohibition on discussing living orators precluded evaluation of him.[15]

Hortensius' life becomes a foil for Cicero's, shedding light on Cicero's oratorical development throughout his lifetime.[16] Both in its comparison to Hortensius and in its overall presentation, the Ciceropaideia is highly manicured, selective, and tendentious. It not only paints Cicero in the best possible light but also interweaves into Cicero's oratorical development several themes and disputes central to the *Brutus*: the geography of Rome and Greece (especially Rhodes), including the stylistic debate over Atticism and Asianism; the philosophical and practical virtue of moderation; the idea of development and decline in individuals and in cultures; the manipulation of chronology to present a coherent narrative; the use of syncrisis as the key means to evaluate individuals; and the fundamental connection between oratory and politics.

from her account. Frazel (2009) 38–45 invaluably illuminates Cicero's devotion to rhetorical training and its importance to the portrayals of the prosecution of Verres and Hortensius' oratory.

[14] See *ORF*⁴ no. 118; Quint. *Inst.* 4.2.106, 6.1.20, 10.1.22, 10.1.116, 10.7.30.

[15] Van der Blom (2016) 236 on how oratory helped Sulpicius secure the consulship in 51.

[16] Leo (1901) 150 on the exemplary use of biographical syncrisis: "Die vollkommensten Beispiele bietet uns Cicero im Brutus." The contest between Aeschylus and Euripides in the second half of Aristophanes' *Frogs* is the *locus classicus* of syncrisis in literary criticism.

The Ciceropaideia closely resembles yet meaningfully diverges from the work's comprehensive oratorical history. The nearly year-by-year reckoning shows far greater granularity than does the account of the *aetates* of Rome's orators, for which no identifiable chronological principle exactly determines the narrative's progress.[17] Cicero skips the earliest years before his arrival in the forum in 91 (*nos in forum venimus*, 303) but the details then come thick and fast up through his consulship. Cicero condenses his post-consular travails and quickly brings us to the year 50, when Hortensius and the practice of eloquence are said to find simultaneous ends.[18]

As is clear from annalistic history and the *fasti*, the names of consuls were the primary means to designate a year and thus place it within a continuous timeline. The *Brutus* draws on consular dating but frequently attaches additional significance to the tenure of office by implicitly aligning it with an event of oratorical or artistic merit. Thus the consulships mentioned, for example, do not successively connect in annalistic fashion the unbroken passage of time but instead often punctuate the progress of oratorical history by highlighting meaningful change.

The accounts of oratorical history and of Cicero's life stress key markers such as the tenure of office or the reliance on births and deaths to mark out different generations (the birth of Cicero, death of Crassus, and death of Hortensius). Magistracies likewise provide boundaries to signal significant advancements (Crassus in 95 and Hortensius' debut; Cicero and Hortensius as aedile-elect and consul-elect, respectively, in 70). As a result, greater emphasis falls on events in the lifetime of the artists: births, deaths, the offices that they hold, and significant civic or intellectual achievements connected to literary activity. These details are present in the Ciceropaideia no less than in the main narrative, and Cicero's emphasis on them in his

---

[17] See Sumner (1973) 151–54 for a general overview of the main *aetates*, which are taken from 333: Cato; Galba; Lepidus; Carbo (and the Gracchi); Antonius and Crassus; Cotta and Sulpicius; Hortensius. The fuller account across the dialogue would warrant adding (at least) the *aetates* of Q. Catulus; Caesar Strabo; Cicero; Brutus. Sumner (1973) 154 rightly speaks of the "variability of the concept *aetas*."

[18] The "end" of oratory is also the beginning of the narrative in the *Brutus*, since Cicero starts with the year 50 (*cum e Cilicia decedens Rhodum venissem*, 1). He learns of the death of Hortensius while returning from his governorship of Cilicia and landing at the island of Rhodes, and thus the chronological narrative offers a ring-composition with the work's beginning that is bolstered by thematic parallels such as the emphasis on *dolor* (1–8, 21/23, and 330–31) and the visual focus on Brutus as representative of the next generation (*in te intuens*, 22 and 331). On the (misleading?) account of Cicero's forensic advent in 91/90, see below.

own biography reinforces the importance of such markers to structure oratorical history throughout the work.[19]

The Ciceropaideia is a well-balanced diptych, two narrative panels of roughly equal length (301–16 and 317–29) that intertwine the lives of Cicero and Hortensius. Each half of the diptych illuminates the other by drawing attention to the parallels and differences in their lives. Nearly every significant topic of the *Brutus* is discussed or alluded to in some way, and the biographical microcosm of the Ciceropaideia encapsulates the macrocosm of oratorical history. Along the way Cicero grants himself considerable latitude in aligning his own life with the life of oratory, identifying his biological existence with the historical essence of oratory. Perhaps no single term better demonstrates this than *maturitas*, used only three times in the dialogue but to great effect (8, 161, 318). It twice describes Cicero himself and once describes oratory's first maturity at Rome in 106 BCE. *Maturitas* also connects a key moment in his professional life (his return from Sicily and subsequent prosecution of Verres, 318) to a key moment in oratory's life, the first maturity (*prima maturitas*) of oratory in the generation of Crassus (161). Cicero asserts that oratory had reached its "first flourishing" (*prima maturitas*) in the age of Crassus, highlighting in particular Crassus' speech in defense of the *lex Servilia* of 106 BCE: "so it can be known in which age Latin oratory had first reached maturity" (*ut dicendi Latine prima maturitas in qua aetate exstitisset posset notari*, 161).

Two distinct yet interrelated aspects of Crassus' speech motivate the special attention it receives. The speech must have been in reality a powerful model for Cicero. Crassus defended the interests of the senate by arguing for the inclusion of senators in the panels of court judges, which for two decades had been controlled by the equestrians. The distinctive value of Crassus' speech lay in the use of *popularis* rhetoric to assert the authority of the senate. He aroused indignation against the equestrians and prosecutors and then – with a highly emotional appeal – asked that the senate's authority, which ultimately derives from the people, be saved from the tyranny of the equestrian panels. Cicero would memorialize the speech in *de Oratore*, citing passages filled with emotional appeals and the complex yet powerful claim that the senate's autonomy could only be saved by making it subject to the will of the people.[20] Cicero had learned his lesson

---

[19] The significance of such dates and the attempt to emphasize or even manufacture coincidences are explored fully in Chapter 4. The framework helps to "cluster" data as much as to "space out" that data, creating an almost visual map of history in which meaningful events stand out.

[20] *De Orat.* 1.225. *ORF*[4] no. 66 fr. 22–26, with Morstein-Marx (2004) 28, 235–36. In *de Oratore* Antonius roundly criticizes the speech for failing to meet Crassus' philosophical positions. This

well – to appropriate *popularis* rhetoric in the service of the senate's wishes. It is precisely the strategy he would use four decades after Crassus' speech in the debate over yet another *lex Servilia*, the agrarian law proposed in 63 by the tribune of the plebs, Publius Servilius Rullus.[21] Cicero marvelously adapted *popularis* rhetoric to defend senatorial interests and authority and to defeat the agrarian law.[22] Crassus' speech had taught him well the political and rhetorical maneuvering of contional speech.

The speech's exemplary status was but one half of the equation, since its chronology was equally crucial to Cicero's construction of an oratorical history. 106 BCE is, of course, the year of Cicero's birth, and he will suggest, but not dictate, the obvious conclusion: oratory reaches full maturity with Cicero. Oratory could only advance in the hands of someone better instructed in philosophy, law, and history (*a philosophia a iure civili ab historia fuisse instructior*, 161), someone such as Cicero himself. The contemporary setting of the dialogue is the endpoint of Cicero's *maturitas* (signaled by the pairing with *senectus*, 8). Life, history, and text are thus intricately interwoven throughout the *Brutus*.

Another essential parallel between the life of the art and the life of its principle artist exists in the theme of artistic evolution. The major change comes during Cicero's sojourn to the East while in his late twenties for

---

earlier ambivalence is wholly absent from the *Brutus*. It is also perplexing that the *Brutus* highlights a contional speech but largely ignores the *contio* (see the following notes). A partial answer may be found in the observation at C. Steel (2002) 203: "Cicero seeks to eliminate content from his discussion, or at least the content of deliberative speeches, and to explain success in terms of technical skill."

[21] Morstein-Marx (2004) 190–202. His discussion of the contional rhetoric of *de Lege Agraria* is exemplary. The idea that oratory reached its *prima maturitas* may be more than a biological conceit (though it is also that). Cicero may have seen Crassus' speech as a crucial turning point in the senatorial elite's appropriation of the relatively new *popularis* rhetoric – so fixed to the figures and memory of the Gracchi – to defend the interests of the senate.

[22] Cicero's limited interest in the *contio*, described in *de Oratore* as virtually the greatest stage for the orator (*maxima quasi oratoris scaena, de Orat.* 2.338, cf. 2.334). The *Brutus* mentions the *contio* only ten times (54, 56, 165, 176, 178, 192, 223, 273, 305–6 [×4], 333); Mouritsen (2013) 65 n.17. The *contio* and the extent of "the sovereign power of the people" (Millar 1998 12) have become hotly debated topics in the study of the late republic. No note can do justice to the burgeoning bibliography, but van der Blom (2016) 3–4, 33 n.35 and Pina Polo (2012) offer judicious overviews. Morstein-Marx (2004) remains to my mind the most astute study of elite management of *popularis* discourse. The debate was sparked by several influential essays that culminated in the book by Millar (1998); cf. Yakobson (1992); North (1990) calls for reconceptualizing Roman democracy. Millar champions a democratizing thesis. It has in turn been challenged. Mouritsen (2001) emphasizes the non-representative nature of the contional crowd, while Hölkeskamp (1995), (2010), and (2017) stresses the lack of genuine democratic debate. Flaig (2003) details the various venues and mechanisms for elite communication. On the history and mechanics of the *contio*, see also Taylor (1966) 15–33, Pina Polo (1996), Tan (2008), Hiebel (2009), van der Blom (2016) 33–38.

what Susan Treggiari has called his "graduate study."[23] Cicero's style when younger endangered his physical well-being, and during his time in the East he changed his style considerably through training with experts, especially by studying with Apollonius Molon in Rhodes (313–16). Cicero's account of his development concludes the first of the two panels in the biographical diptych. Set against it is the analysis of Hortensius at the end of the second panel (325–28). Yet unlike Cicero and his artistic progress, Hortensius failed to evolve and gradually declined after being consul. The careers of the two orators have opposite trajectories that are represented in geographical terms. Hortensius remains an unrepentant Asianist. Cicero forges a middle path between Asianism and Atticism that he identifies with the island of Rhodes.[24] The geographical details crucially connect his educational development with the stylistic debate over Atticism and Asianism. In the syncrisis with Hortensius, Cicero both champions the middle path and also intertwines geography and evolution to demonstrate the superiority of the Rhodian alternative. Just as the life of oratory evolves toward a Rhodian compromise between two extremes, so too does Cicero evolve on his way to measured stylistic maturity.

Cicero's evaluation of Hortensius is richer than that of any other speaker yet still simpler than Cicero's account of himself. While Hortensius is the main feature of the second panel, his presence there offers a useful entrée into the larger issues and aims of the Ciceropaideia. He is immediately identified as an Asianist, which explains his shortcomings in his later years, because "the Asian style of speech was permitted more to youth than to old age" (*genus erat orationis Asiaticum adulescentiae magis concessum quam senectuti*, 325). This genre of speech contains two main styles, which correspond roughly to the traditional division of content and form (*res* and *verba*) that Cicero emphasizes elsewhere.[25] One style relies on "thoughts that are not as weighty and stern as they are sonorous and charming" (*sententiis non tam gravibus et severis quam concinnis et venustis*, 325). The other uses swift and impetuous language (*verbis volucre atque incitatum*, 325) along with words that are elaborate and elegant (*exornato et faceto genere verborum*, 325), although it lacks the careful symmetry of thought of the first style (*ornata sententiarum concinnitas non erat*, 325).

---

[23] Treggiari (2015) 240, with Barwick (1963) 13–17. On (Greco-)Roman education, see Marrou (1971), Bonner (1977), Corbeill (2001), Sciarrino (2015), with *de Orat.* 1.147–59, Quint. *Inst.* 2.1–7 on rhetorical education and training.

[24] Dugan (2005) 225–26 on Rhodes' importance.

[25] The division is prominent in *de Oratore*, although Cicero is adamant there that the two are inseparable.

Hortensius won acclaim for having mastered both, although they ultimately lacked weighty distinction (*gravitas*, 326; cf. *auctoritas*, 327). He
partly followed the striking polish of the Asian orator Menecles of
Alabanda, preferring charming expression over the practical demands of
speaking (*magis venustae dulcesque sententiae quam aut necessariae aut
interdum utiles*, 326). Attention to effect over effectiveness essentially
repeats earlier criticism of the Atticists, who subordinate persuasiveness
to aesthetics.[26]

Through Hortensius Cicero also underscores, indeed makes paramount,
the role of individual development and the accommodation of style to
audience expectations. Yet there are two distinct aspects to this accommodation. First, style must be appropriate to the *ethos* of the speaker by
matching his station or age. Second, different historical periods have
different stylistic expectations, a main premise of the *Brutus*. For this
reason Cicero notes that the masses and young men approved of
Hortensius' style, whereas older men such as Philippus (cos. 91) angrily
ridiculed his youthful exuberance (*saepe videbam cum irridentem tum etiam
irascentem et stomachantem Philippum*, 326).[27] Although Hortensius' style
lacked authority, he still excelled while young because "it nonetheless
seemed appropriate to his age" (*tamen aptum esse aetati videbatur*, 327).
Cicero seems to refer primarily to Hortensius' status as a young man, but
the ambiguity in the term *aetas* likewise suggests that his style was
appropriate to the expectations of the younger generation in contrast to
the older generation of Philippus, who is grouped with other *senes* in 326.

The analysis of Hortensius soon grows critical: he failed to curb his
immature exuberance. When he was older, his style no longer matched his
status or (perhaps) evolving tastes. Mock imitation of his style drives home
the point: "although at that point official honors and the prominent
authority of old age demanded greater gravity, he stayed the same and
was ineptly the same" (*cum iam honores et illa senior auctoritas gravius
quiddam requireret, remanebat idem nec decebat idem*, 327). The last clause
concludes with a sing-song *sententia* of the sort that ensured the checkered
reputation of the declaimers of the early imperial period catalogued by the
elder Seneca. Its form perfectly captures its criticisms: the claim that style
must acquire gravitas as individuals age is ostentatiously made in a style

---

[26] See Chapter 7 on Atticism. At *Orat.* 65 the *sophistae* have the same shortcoming. The centrality of
pragmatic realism (*utilitas* and *veritas*) would become a refrain of Quintilian's prescriptions for
imperial orators. See Brink (1989).

[27] It is often argued that Hortensius prosecuted Philippus in 95; see *TLRR* no. 90, Fantham (2004)
299–300, Dyck (2008) 144. No clear evidence indicates a prosecution; cf. Kaster (2020) 127 n.348.

that lacks all grandeur. The repetition of verbs in -*ebat* and the pronoun *idem* produce a cloying parallelism that is reinforced by isocolon: two clauses of six syllables each (*remanebat idem / nec decebat idem*). Rhythm diminishes its grandeur by concluding with three trochees, the rhythmic sequence so prominent, for example, at the conclusion of Catullus' hendecasyllabic love poems.[28] Division of the clause makes all the more apparent its rhythmic monotony: ditrochee precedes the concluding triple trochee.[29]

The subsequent criticism of Hortensius' development focuses on his continued penchant for balanced phrasing and thought even as his command of adornment slackened: *manebat* (327) may slyly allude to the immediately preceding *remanebat* and its parodied ending -*ebat*. A contrast of style in Cicero's concluding flourish drives the point home and suggests how Hortensius should have written: "perhaps he pleased you less than he would have if you could have heard him burning with zeal and possessing his full talents" (*minus fortasse placuit quam placuisset, si illum flagrantem studio et florentem facultate audire potuisses*, 327). Cicero's conclusion varies the language of the thought (*placuit/placuisset*), relies on the balanced fullness of two participles with accompanying ablatives, alliterates *f*, *p*, and *s*, and employs the rhythm for which he would become known: resolved cretic plus trochee.[30] The superfluity of *audire potuisses*, where *audivisses* would suffice for the meaning but spoil the *clausula*, suggests that Cicero strove after the rhythmic effect, masterfully and damningly concluding the assessment of Hortensius.[31]

Cicero credits his own move away from extravagance – which he never calls Asianism – to an education received in the Greek East. His studies are directly tied to his portrayal of hellenizing influences and the Atticism debate. They are not merely biographical facts but rather part of a larger strategy, as the geography presented is calculated to elucidate his adherence to the golden mean. The arguments of the *Brutus*, Cicero's fulsome style,

---

[28] The triple trochee: ¯ ˘ ¯ ˘ ¯ ×. On ditrochee as an ending popular in Asia, see *Orat.* 212, and 212–15 on the need for variation; cf. Dion. Hal. *Comp.* 18, Quint. *Inst.* 9.4.103. Cicero says ditrochee is popular in Asia (*est secuta Asia maxime*, 212), Quintilian that it is popular among Asianists (*quo Asiani sunt usi plurimum*), said with Cicero's passage in mind.

[29] The two six-syllable clauses are *remanebat idem / nec decebat idem*: ˘ ˘ ¯ ˘ ¯ × / ¯ ˘ ¯ ˘ ¯ ×.

[30] Often dubbed the "esse videatur" ending: ¯ ˘ ˘ ˘ ¯ ×.

[31] Cicero rarely uses *audivisses*, however (only *Div.* 1.59). Brutus (probably) could have heard Hortensius at his height, even if we give credence to Cicero's claim about Hortensius' decline after the consulship of 69, in which year Brutus would have been about sixteen years old. This assumes, however, a birth year of 85, and not later (78/77). Badian (1967) 229 insists on the earlier date. Tempest (2017) 11 and 102 urges caution.

and his disagreement with the Atticists have often been taken to mean that he was essentially an adherent of the Asianist school of oratory in a debate against the Atticists – yet he nowhere confirms that and in fact goes to great lengths to offer a different perspective.[32] The geographical symbolism portrays him as being between two poles, one represented by various Atticists (unnamed at this point in the text but discussed at length earlier) and the other by the Asianist, Hortensius. Cicero himself appeals to the laudable "middle" between these extremes, represented geographically by the island of Rhodes. This explains the island's importance, including in its first sentence and in Cicero's repeated emphasis on training with Apollonius Molon of Rhodes. Cicero develops his oratorical skills in order to evolve toward a superior middle ground, whereas the Atticists and Hortensius persist in their one-sided inclinations.[33]

Cicero begins by noting the harm his oratorical delivery caused him before outlining the changes he underwent on Rhodes. His strained style endangered his health, almost mortally (*non procul abesse putatur a vitae periculo*, 313). Vigorous tension (*contentio*) is the prevalent term to describe his early style, which he successfully curbed on Rhodes under the guidance of Apollonius . Whereas Hortensius continued to pursue the charms of Asianism, Cicero had to adapt, and the account makes a virtue of necessity by highlighting the stylistic merits of a required change.

Prized above all else is moderation, signaled by *moderatio* and *temperatius dicere* at the beginning of his biography (314) and *mediocris* at its conclusion (317). Cicero acquired variety and a restrained blending of stylistic effects, but the terms also suggest the "golden mean," the happy middle ground between stylistic extremes. Cicero had already reminded Brutus of the philosophical principle when discussing Crassus and Scaevola: "since the whole of excellence rests in the mean, as your Old Academy tells us, Brutus, each of these men strove after a kind of middle ground" (*cum omnis virtus sit, ut vestra, Brute, vetus Academia dixit, mediocritas, uterque horum medium quiddam volebat sequi*, 149).[34] This is yet another example of how an earlier and seemingly unrelated

---

[32] See Chapter 7 on Atticism/Asianism.

[33] Plutarch (*Cic.* 3) claims that Cicero left Rome because in his defense of Roscius of Ameria he exposed the machinations of Sulla's freedman, Chrysogonus.

[34] Cicero's claim is perplexing. Douglas (1966a) 97–98 adduces Antiochus' reliance on Peripatetic ethics. Cf. Ar. *Eth. Nic.* 2.5–7, esp. 2.6.13. The mean is prominent in the notion of emotional limitation (*metriopatheia* versus Stoic *apatheia*). See *Ac.* 2.135 (cf. *Ac.* 1.39) and *Tusc.* 4.38–47 (cf. *Tusc.* 3.12 on Crantor, a figure of the Old Academy) on *mediocritates* and the Peripatetic view of the mean as the best (*mediocritatem esse optumam existiment*, *Tusc.* 4.46), with Graver (2002).

principle anticipates a later topic, in this case the arguments for
stylistic moderation.

Cicero's move toward moderation relies on two conceits: the geography
of the Greek East and a commonplace image, the constraining of a violent
river. Although the Ciceropaideia nowhere mentions Asianism or Cicero's
disagreements with the Atticists, that debate remains central to his and
Hortensius' biographies. The syncrisis of Cicero and Hortensius gives their
stylistic developments far greater meaning by making clear which alternatives each could or should have embraced, and in light of earlier orators
who sought out moderation, like Crassus and Scaevola, it suggests how
much Hortensius, unlike Cicero, failed to learn from the past. Although
youthful exuberance and Asianist tendencies are not in themselves liabil-
ities, they become so when Hortensius cannot adapt as he matures.
Allusion to the Atticism/Asianism debate may prompt Cicero to single
out Asia when describing his educational sojourn (*ea causa mihi in Asiam
proficiscendi fuit*, 314). More directly he mentions Menippus of
Stratonicea, "in my opinion the most fluent speaker of all Asia at the
time" (*meo iudicio tota Asia illis temporibus disertissimus*, 315). A pointed
barb notes that this Asian orator could be classified as an Atticist: "if having
nothing bothersome or useless characterizes Atticists, this orator can rightly
be counted among their number" (*si nihil habere molestiarum nec ineptiarum Atticorum est, hic orator in illis numerari recte potest*, 315). While
faultless style is a minimum requirement for all oratory, it is neither the
preserve of Atticism nor sufficient for great oratory (284). The discussion
of the Asian orator Menippus again stresses that geography alone cannot
guarantee stylistic affiliation or greatness, and singling him out both drives
home this point and underscores the weakness of the label "Atticist."[35]

Further details of geography are central to this intervention in the
Atticism/Asianism debate. Cicero arrived first in Athens to study
philosophy for six months with Antiochus of Ascalon, who claimed to
have returned to the original doctrines (the "Old Academy") in distinction
to the "New Academy" of Arcesilaus, Carneades, and Philo.[36] Cicero
proceeded from Athens to Asia to be in the company of the most
prominent *rhetores*. They proved insufficient for his needs, and only at
Rhodes did he flourish under Apollonius Molon (*quibus non contentus*

---

[35] Chapter 7 discusses this rhetorical strategy.
[36] See Brittain (2001) on Philo, Sedley (2012) on Antiochus, Woolf (2015) on Cicero's Scepticism.

Rhodum veni meque ad eundem quem Romae audiveram Molonem adplicavi, 316).[37]

The subsequent account of Cicero's stylistic development is guided by one central metaphor, that of a raging river whose waters are contained: "when I was overswollen and flowing high on account of my style's youthful rashness and license, he strove to constrain me and to keep me from overflowing the riverbanks, so to speak" (*is dedit operam … ut nimis redundantis nos et supra fluentis iuvenili quadam dicendi impunitate et licentia reprimeret et quasi extra ripas diffluentis coerceret*, 316). The metaphor is continued in Apollonius' successful interventions: Cicero's "style had simmered down, so to speak" (*quasi deferverat oratio*, 316), with *defervescere* commonly used of boiling water that stops bubbling or rivers that settle after a flood crest.[38] The sustained river metaphor reemerges in connection with Hortensius and Asianism's unchecked stylistic flow (*flumen … orationis*, 325) and swift course (*orationis cursus*, 325). Cicero sums up his own improvements by focusing again on his body (*corpus*) and his moderation (*mediocris habitus*, 317).[39]

Cicero transposes this emphasis on moderation from a Greek educational context to the Roman forum. Upon his return Hortensius and Cotta were the preeminent orators (317), each of whom embodied a stylistic extreme that Cicero longed to imitate: Cotta restrained and Hortensius vigorous. Cicero is more like Hortensius, who becomes a role model, but only partially. The middle path is crucial and is anticipated by the earlier, connected syncrisis of Cotta and Sulpicius (202–4). Here again, each exemplified a stylistic extreme, uncoincidentally portrayed with the same vocabulary and imagery of the Ciceropaideia: Cotta abandoned any straining (*contentionem omnem remiserat*, 202) while Sulpicius' ebullient swiftness avoided overflowing exuberance (*incitata et volubilis nec ea redundans tamen nec circumfluens oratio*, 203).[40] Even the selection of whom to emulate is guided by restraint and moderation between extremes.

---

[37] *Contentus* may allude to Cicero's claim that his early style was dominated by *contentio*, which he overcame (*contentio nimia vocis resederat*, 316). Cicero would then be playing on different roots of *contentus*: *contendere* "to strain" (producing *contentio*) and *continere* "to restrain."

[38] See *TLL* v.1.321.81–322.4 [Gudeman, 1910] for literal uses; 322.9–10 for the metaphorical usage in the *Brutus*. Bringmann (1971) 27–28 (with bibliography) notes the Callimachean background to the river metaphors. Cf. Keith (1999), Gutzwiller (2014) 21, Goh (2018).

[39] There is a curious inverse relationship between the physical and the stylistic developments: Cicero's style has thinned out as he has physically bulked up. Bishop (2019) 204 astutely suggests that the narrative of overcoming physical limitations ties Cicero to similar accounts about Demosthenes. Leeman (1963) 111 concludes that Cicero exaggerates these stylistic changes, which were part of a much longer development.

[40] The interlinking of Cotta/Sulpicius with Cotta/Hortensius is also an excellent example of Cicero's nested syncrises, in which one pair or group partially overlaps with another, creating a network of

Equally instructive in historical terms is the earlier stylistic account of oratory's demise in the post-classical Greek era, when Cicero discusses the journey of *eloquentia* through Greece and Asia.[41] Here key language from the river metaphor first appears and the geographical symbolism meaningfully expresses stylistic development:

> And in fact outside of Greece there was great devotion to speaking, and achieving the greatest honors for this accomplishment gave prominence to orators' renown. You see, as soon as Eloquence sailed out from Piraeus it wandered through all the islands and made its way through all Asia, so that it smeared itself with foreign habits, lost so to speak all that wholesomeness and health of Attic style, and nearly unlearned how to speak. From here came the Asian orators who shouldn't be despised at all either for their swiftness or for their fullness, but because they lack concision and are overly verbose. The Rhodians are healthier and are more like the Attic stylists.

> At vero extra Graeciam magna dicendi studia fuerunt maximique huic laudi habiti honores inlustre oratorum nomen reddiderunt. nam ut semel e Piraeo eloquentia evecta est, omnis peragravit insulas atque ita peregrinata tota Asia est, ut se externis oblineret moribus omnemque illam salubritatem Atticae dictionis et quasi sanitatem perderet ac loqui paene dedisceret. hinc Asiatici oratores non contemnendi quidem nec celeritate nec copia, sed parum pressi et nimis redundantes; Rhodii saniores et Atticorum similiores. (51)

Linguistic parallels again drive the conceptual narrative by equating the lives of artist and art. The Asians are *nimis redundantes*, a fault of which Apollonius cured Cicero (*nimis redundantis*, 316). *Eloquentia* toured Greece and Asia as Cicero did (*a me Asia tota peragrata est*, 315).[42] Unlike Cicero, it followed a trajectory of decline, leaving Athens for the islands (presumably including Rhodes) and finally reaching Asia, a gradual decline from restraint (Athens) to exuberance (Asia). Cicero by contrast first visited the extremes of Athens and Asia before finding the happy medium at Rhodes.

The decline of Greek oratory, symbolized geographically by its movement to Asia, only highlights Cicero's successful pursuit of moderation. He left Rome to study in Asia (*in Asiam*, 314) but returned to Rome having studied in Rhodes, suggesting that he may have initially pursued

---

mutually illuminating syncrises. The description of Sulpicius here either conflicts with *de Oratore* or perhaps makes Sulpicius a model for the development away from his earlier style: cf. *de Orat.* 2.88 (where Sulpicius resembles a young Hortensius/Cicero).

[41] For later versions of the allegory in Dionysius and Longinus, see de Jonge (2014).

[42] Cf. also the adjacent citation of Menippus as the leading orator in all Asia (*tota Asia*, 315).

Asianism but ultimately found Rhodianism. Allegiance to the latter style (whatever it might entail) rather than Asianism results from experience and learning. He does not defend Asianism against Atticism but instead rejects the limitations of both: Atticism and Asianism are two sides of the same coin, beholden to an extreme and inferior to Rhodian moderation.[43]

The Rhodians' importance can explain their initial inclusion almost as an afterthought in the allegory of *eloquentia* (*Rhodii saniores et Atticorum similiores*, 51). It anticipates their ultimate triumph as the locus of moderation and creates a ring-composition in the text: Rhodes appears in the first and last sentences of the long preface (1–51). The island also suggests a connection between Roman imperialism and oratory, as Cicero's journey back from Cilicia via Rhodes in 50 creates a parallel between his provincial command and his oratorical education.

Truthiness in the Ciceropaideia[44]

Halfway through the Ciceropaideia Cicero gestures toward self-effacement: "I think too much is being said about me, especially since I'm the one talking" (*nimis multa videor de me, ipse praesertim*, 318). The statement could serve as a lightly ironic motto for the work, since Cicero and his values are ultimately the subject of the dialogue even when he isn't the subject of the discussion, as the comparisons with Hortensius demonstrate. Like so many other orators Hortensius is a foil for Cicero, and the choices and judgments made concerning the history of oratory are remarkably self-serving. The larger conceptual framework in which Cicero compares himself to Hortensius only reinforces several ideas Cicero assumes to be valid, for example, that successive generations imitate their predecessors

---

[43] Quintilian confirms the *Brutus'* portrayal, contrasting moderate Rhodianism with Atticism and Asianism: "Then those who made this division added the Rhodian style as a third, which they understood as a kind of middle ground and mixture of each" (*tertium mox qui haec dividebant adiecerunt genus Rhodium, quod velut medium esse atque ex utroque mixtum volunt, Inst.* 12.10.18). The topos was malleable: Isoc. *Antid.* 296 claims moderation (μετριότης) for Attic (presumably between Doric and Ionic). Cf. Gutzwiller (2014) 26 and 31 on the middle style: "The middle was a useful concept in part because it was not a clearly distinct style but flexible in its in-betweenness, mixing elements of other styles in various ways, sometimes ameliorating the grandeur of the high and sometimes adorning the plainness of the low." The middle style and Rhodianism share this slippery quality, though Rhodianism should not be confused with the middle style. Cicero uses Rhodianism to implicitly distinguish himself from the extremes of two stylistic currents.

[44] The term "truthiness" was implanted in the American political lexicon in 2005 by television comedian Stephen Colbert and roughly means the intuitive sense that a statement is or should be true based on its general appeal or plausibility rather than accuracy or fact. For the Latin-abled, Colbert also offered the term "veritasiness," a composite not so unlike Sisenna's infamous "spittlicious" (*sputatilica*, 260), on which see Chapter 6.

and that orators transmit their abilities across each *aetas*. The comparison with Hortensius also assumes that individual style should evolve during one's lifetime, which explains Hortensius' decline and Cicero's rise.

The evolutionary account of the Ciceropaideia and the larger historical narrative of oratory are mutually reinforcing. Cicero's trajectory is a miniature version of oratory's evolution at Rome since its origins, once again giving the impression that his accomplishments are the inevitable result of oratory's history and the encapsulation of its artistic principles. Cicero manipulates and guides the material at hand while making larger points and arguments through indirection and implication. The massive network of parallels and coincidences gives the impression of connection and continuity, imperceptibly endowing history with a sense of purpose and meaning: the vicissitudes of oratorical history seem to be guided by a visible yet authorless intelligent design.

Cicero's autobiography also illuminates several claims made elsewhere about oratory. Some are more obvious, such as his enumeration of philosophy (*philosophia*), civil law (*ius civile*), and history (*memoria rerum Romanarum*) as essential departments of knowledge for great oratory (322). It is nearly impossible not to glance back from there to the first maturity of oratory in the age of his role models, Crassus and Antonius, who would be surpassed "only by someone who was more learned in philosophy, civil law, and history" (*nisi qui a philosophia a iure civili ab historia fuisset instructior*, 161).

Less obvious perhaps is the significance or even logic of certain seemingly stray details, such as his repeated mention of Apollonius Molon of Rhodes at Rome (307, 312, 316). He supposedly first came to Rome along with other Greeks in 87 (307), a detail whose accuracy has been questioned.[45] Later mention of Apollonius in Rome in 81 as an envoy during Sulla's dictatorship reprises the earlier passage's language (*Moloni dedimus operam*, 312) without noting the earlier visit.[46] And lastly Cicero crucially changed his speaking style under Apollonius while on sojourn in Rhodes in the early 70s. On that occasion it was Apollonius who took pains (*is dedit operam*, 316) to reshape Cicero's oratory.

[45] Douglas (1966a) 221 summarizes the arguments against it and defends the possibility that Apollonius was at Rome, since Posidonius was at Rome as an envoy at the time (citing Plut. *Mar.* 45). Caesar also studied with him (Suet. *Jul.* 4.1, Plut. *Caes.* 3.1). On the three mentions of Apollonius and Cicero's selective reporting of the years 90–89 (see below), including the *lex Varia* and the suspension of the courts, Badian (1969) 452–58 is essential, though we differ on certain aspects of Cicero's motivations.
[46] Hendrickson (1962) 270 n.a: "an awkward intercalation, suggesting later insertion." On the language, cf. *Att.* 2.1.9 (SB 21), with a joke at the expense of Favonius.

The three separate periods of tutelage create an overall image of Cicero's training, and in order to produce that image he inevitably shaped or even fabricated certain details. As a young man he observed legal cases and *contiones* (forensic and deliberative oratory), studied law under Scaevola Pontifex, and philosophy under Philo (304–6). The curriculum thus far is impressive, but as Ernst Badian explains: "there was an obvious gap in the structure of his studies: he had not yet studied rhetoric under a master. It was essential for the completion of the picture that, no later than 87, he should do so."[47]

This is the first instance of three in which Cicero connects crucial stages of his career to formal training with Apollonius, and it essentially caps the studies of his youth, which took not only the shape of formal pedagogy but also observation of real speeches in the Roman forum. The second stage has again a close connection to Apollonius, when Cicero studies with him in 81 and notes that his initial forensic activity depended on adequate learning (*ut . . . docti in forum veniremus*, 311). It is after this argument that he inserts mention of his simultaneous training with Apollonius (*eodem tempore Moloni dedimus operam*, 312) and nearly credits him with the success of his oratorical debut: "and therefore my first public trial, spoken on behalf of Sextus Roscius, won so much approval that no other case seemed not to deserve my services" (*itaque prima causa publica pro Sex. Roscio dicta tantum commendationis habuit, ut non ulla esset quae non digna nostro patrocinio videretur*, 312).[48]

In the final phase of influence Apollonius guided Cicero toward a mature Rhodian style (discussed above). No figure is as important to his early years: he dedicated himself to Apollonius during the hiatus of the courts in the early 80s, his forensic debut in the late 80s, and his crowning transformation in Greece (79–77 BCE). The three passages closely mirror one another, as Cicero first devotes himself to Apollonius, who later responds in kind (*operam dedimus ~ dedit operam*), a parallel reinforced by the changed location: Cicero requites his teacher's visits to Rome by traveling to Rhodes. And Cicero stresses that Apollonius was not merely a teacher but also a speaker (307, 316) and writer (316): *actor, magister, scriptor*, all activities that describe Cicero, if one considers his pedagogical role in the *Brutus*. Most crucial is Apollonius' connection to Rhodes, which, as we have seen, is so central to Cicero's self-portrayal as a moderate Rhodian orator against the extremes of the Atticists and Asianists.

---

[47] Badian (1969) 456.
[48] Badian (1969) 456 n.24 says that the insertion and temporal indication wholly undermine Cicero's arguments. They do, however, emphasize how important Apollonius was to Cicero's early success.

The repeated notice of Apollonius, the details of language, and the geographical relevance of Rhodes all conspire to elevate Apollonius to an importance no other figure attains, likening the two individuals to one another.[49]

Omissions in the Ciceropaideia are as important as its emphases. The most glaring instance skips over his post-consular career, abbreviating the years between 62 and 51 with the notice that he and Hortensius harmoniously managed several notable cases together. The protracted dispute with Clodius, exile, and the so-called First Triumvirate all vanish from the record. We fast-forward to the new courts under Pompey's laws in 52. When the narrative is more detailed, in Cicero's rise to prominence, the picture is remarkably flattering. Cicero's suggestion of how much diligence and hard work were necessary to become a capable speaker may appeal to modern scholars, with their own protracted journey toward professional competence, but most of all he makes a virtue of necessity. He spent his early years largely in the shadows, of other rhetorical luminaries and of the greatness to which he aspired. It may be true that Cicero seemed ready to take on any case after defending Roscius, but seemed so to whom?

The available evidence suggests that Cicero handled cases of limited importance until the prosecution of Verres in 70 – and even then he fought for the right to prosecute, a struggle memorialized in the *Divinatio in Q. Caecilium*.[50] Until 70 Cicero's cases were largely "small beer,"[51] mostly for provincial Italians. It was not until the aedileship of 69, at age thirty-seven, that he broke into the ranks of premier patrons; he first defended a senator, Marcus Fonteius, on charges of provincial extortion in Transalpine Gaul.[52] That year brought three cases, including two for

[49] Contrast the quite different source of influence emphasized in *de Oratore*: esteemed Romans gathered around the figures of Crassus and Antonius. I am of course not suggesting that Cicero portrays himself as a Greek rhetorician or that he considered Apollonius a social equal. Cic. *N.D.* 1.6 indiscriminately cites Diodotus, Philo, Antiochus, and Posidonius as Cicero's teachers.

[50] See now C. Steel (2016) for a survey of early-career prosecution, esp. 219–20 on the considerable social and political capital required to mount such a case; 222–23 on how unusual and risky his prosecution of Verres was.

[51] Borrowing the phrase for certain imperial cases from Crook (1995).

[52] C. Steel (2012) 261. C. Steel (2005) 40 suggests that *de Inventione* will have been the alternative to a significant early debut. See Dyck (2012) on *pro Fonteio*. Political upheaval partly delayed Cicero's debut: "With Crassus as his patron he might well have expected to enter the forum with a prosecution around 87–86 BC, if only there had been no Social War and no Marian revolution" (Fantham 2004 300). Cicero claims that the year 76 was filled with notable cases (*causas nobilis egimus*, 318), but the claim is hard to corroborate. *Pro Vareno* (lost but still published) may be meant or *pro Q. Roscio comoedo*; if so, were the two enough to justify the claim of a year's activity? Crawford (1994) 7–18 tentatively suggests 77/76 for *pro Vareno*, a vehicle of advertisement for his campaign for the quaestorship; cf. Gruen (1974) 531. On *pro Q. Roscio comoedo* see *TLRR* no. 166, usually dated to 76–68 with scholars favoring the end of that range. The term *nobilis* may be rather deceptive, suggesting not just cases of notoriety (*nobilis*) but clients of status (*nobilis*). Crawford

extortion (Fonteius and Oppius), perhaps because of his experience the previous year prosecuting *repetundae* proceedings. It was not until his praetorship in 66 that he pleaded regularly and held a contional speech (*pro Lege Manilia*), supporting Pompey's extraordinary command and eyeing the consulship of 63.[53] Hortensius by contrast first spoke at age nineteen in 95 and soon after defended Nicomedes of Bithynia, possibilities for someone of his political clout and pedigree, but unimaginable for even the most talented and ambitious equestrian upstart from Arpinum.[54] Cicero emphasizes his devotion to learning as a screen for his limited access to forensic advocacy. This reframing has been readily accepted by modern readers perhaps eager to find in him something that passes for humility: Cicero too, for all his talent, found oratory difficult to master.

Even his oratorical debut in the *Brutus* is a half-truth, as he makes no mention of the *pro Quinctio* of 81, a relatively insignificant civil case, which he in all likelihood lost to Hortensius. Instead, he notes the *pro S. Roscio Amerino* of 80, which he won, and thereby underscores the criminal trials that were far more important to his career.[55] The case offered a chance to address a larger if hazardous theme – the republic under Sulla's dictatorship – and he readily followed rhetorical injunctions to seek out a larger issue to enhance the persuasiveness of a case. Rather than focus on early defeat against his future rival, he notes an early victory and then refocuses attention onto besting Hortensius during the *Verrines* more than a decade later after his training in Rhodes, creating the illusion that they only then first clashed in the forum.[56]

Cicero also diminishes the post-consulship oratory of Hortensius after 69, citing his waning enthusiasm (*summum illud suum studium remisit*, 320). Yet Hortensius still spoke on legislative matters, such as the *lex*

(1984) nos. 1–3 lists only three trials up to 75 (*pro muliere Arretina* 79/80, *pro Titinia Cottae* 79, *pro adulescentibus Romanis in Sicilia* 75). C. Steel (2005) 22–25 on Cicero's early publication of speeches.

[53] Zetzel (2009) 73: "the first major speech in Cicero's own campaign to be elected consul."

[54] Demosthenes pled while young; Calvus, Caesar, and Pollio all handled serious cases (prosecutions) before the quaestorship (Quint. *Inst.* 12.6.1). Cicero may be stretching the truth about Hortensius' speech by stating *in foro*, in order to further align their careers, but the details are too complex to treat here. Cf. *de Orat.* 3.229 (senate speech), Quint. *Inst.* 12.6.1 (above), 12.7.4, Gruen (1966) 49–50, Dyck (2008) 144, C. Steel (2016) 215.

[55] Cicero does say that he began with both civil and criminal cases (*ad causas et privatas et publicas adire coepimus*, 311), but for a work so invested in beginnings he suppresses his own oratorical misstart. On *pro Quinctio*, see Kinsey (1971) 5–6, *TLRR* no. 126, Tempest (2011) 32. Silence about the speech in the *Brutus* may suggest that he lost. He lost but published *pro Vareno*, another overlooked case. Cf. C. Steel (2012) 258–59 on Cicero's later "suppression of failure" (259).

[56] At *Div. Caec.* 44 Cicero says they'd already met multiple times on the same and opposing sides, although, again, no other speeches are known.

Gabinia (67 BCE) and the *lex Manilia* (66 BCE) on Pompey's commands.[57]
He also pled cases; we know of three between his consulship and Cicero's,
including on behalf of Murena in November 63.[58] Hortensius, we are
told, lost interest in the art and disappeared from the forum only to
jealously return, often as co-counsel (*coniunctissime versati sumus*, 323),
after Cicero's event-filled consulship. Perhaps the real image that Cicero
wishes to suggest, in addition to intertwining their oratorical lives so
closely, comes from the relationship of Hortensius to Cotta: when
Cicero returned to Rome he noted that these two orators worked together,
with Cotta as the elder chief advocate and Hortensius as the real power-
house and younger member of the legal duo (317). Cicero inserts the idea
of the inheritance of the top spot in the forum among orators of successive
generations, and just as Cotta had yielded to Hortensius, so Hortensius
yielded to Cicero. These generational interconnections amount to an
unbroken continuity in the recent history of oratory: Brutus too will
inherit Cicero's legacy and continues the lineage back to Hortensius,
pleading alongside Hortensius in his last case, the defense of Appius
Claudius Pulcher in the spring of 50 (328).[59] Cicero's career closely tracks
Hortensius' in the natural progression of generations. He aligns them
temporally: "he flourished from the consulship of Crassus and Scaevola
to that of Paullus and Marcellus, I followed the same path from Sulla's
dictatorship to about the same consuls" (*ille a Crasso consule et Scaevola
usque ad Paullum et Marcellum consules floruit, nos in eodem cursu fuimus a
Sulla dictatore ad eosdem fere consules*, 328).[60] He equates their careers and

---

[57] Cf. *Man.* 51–53. Cicero naturally has motivations for stressing Hortensius' opposition to those laws
to bolster his own case, but Hortensius clearly played at least some role. At 302 Cicero also seems to
indulge in some rather different inventiveness, claiming that Hortensius uniquely used *partitiones*
and *conlectiones* (perhaps to follow a pattern in which speakers of generational importance should
introduce at least some technical refinement).

[58] *TLRR* nos. 202, 221, 224 (*pro Murena*). The frequency of trials in 69–63 does not deviate all that
much from the rest of Hortensius' career (with the caveat that *TLRR* cannot be complete),
especially if one considers as anomalies a year such as 54 BCE with three trials recorded for
Hortensius (*TLRR* nos. 283, 293, 295).

[59] *TLRR* no. 355. Cicero also assumes that senior senators were expected to continue pleading cases
regularly after the consulship, but this was not in fact the norm: Cicero, Hortensius, and
M. Licinius Crassus are exceptions; van der Blom (2016) 281. The expectation was that senior
senators would use their *auctoritas* to testify at trials; van der Blom (2016) 32–33; Guérin (2015)
comprehensively studies testimony in the late republic. Cicero's speeches were a better vehicle for
self-profiling, while his searing *in Vatinium* shows the pitfalls of testifying.

[60] Cicero left for Cilicia in 51 and stopped pleading slightly before Hortensius; civil war closed the
courts before Cicero's return. He does use *fere* here, a nice gesture to accuracy amidst the alignment
of careers. Exactness is especially prominent when he has nothing to lose by it.

likens their progress: "I followed Hortensius on the race-course in his very footsteps" (*simus in spatio Q. Hortensium ipsius vestigiis persecuti*, 307).[61]

Constant reference to their offices, in parallel but with Cicero a step behind, gives the impression that they followed the same oratorical and political trajectory and that great oratory naturally results in the tenure of office.[62] We may see some massaging of historical details in Cicero's desire to line up their careers so closely, as Hortensius' rise is connected to a number of crucial events: "and as he was reaching his prime Crassus died, Cotta was exiled, the war interrupted the courts, and I entered the forum" (*hoc igitur florescente Crassus est mortuus, Cotta pulsus, iudicia intermissa bello, nos in forum venimus*, 303). The alignment of events suggests contemporaneity, although Crassus died in 91, shortly before the outbreak of the war and the suspension of the courts; similarly, Cotta was not exiled until 90, when Cicero assumed the *toga virilis* ("toga of manhood") and began his *tirocinium fori* under Scaevola Pontifex.[63]

The narrative resumes with Hortensius' military service during the Social War in 91 and portrays events clustering around that year, gathering and coordinating the critical moments of Roman history, including Cicero's arrival in the forum. The connection was already anticipated by Hortensius' first speech in the forum in 95, the year Crassus and Scaevola (Pontifex) were consuls. Hortensius, as noted above, is elsewhere depicted as having spoken before the senate in that year; shifting the venue from senate to forum aligns their careers more closely, despite their vastly different debuts.[64]

Lastly, there is another near fabrication in Cicero's claims about the courts in 90. The outbreak of the Social War suspended all trials except those that fell under the *lex Varia*, whose proceedings he scrupulously attended (*exercebatur una lege iudicium Varia, ceteris propter bellum intermissis; quoi frequens aderam*, 304). We never learn that later in 90 the Varian court was probably also suspended. He also omits his service under

---

[61] The image of the race course or path follows the use of *cursus* earlier in 307 and is reiterated in 328 (*in eodem cursu*, quoted above).

[62] He notes that in 76 Cotta, Hortensius, and Cicero sought the offices of consul, aedile, and quaestor, respectively (318). During the prosecution of Verres he was aedile-elect and Hortensius consul-elect (319).

[63] See Rawson (1983) 13–14 with Plut. *Cic.* 3.1 and Cic. *Amic.* 1. Douglas (1966a) follows Fabricius and prints "Q. f." at 306, which would indicate Scaevola Augur, but Scaevola Pontifex is meant here (reading "P. f."), although Cicero first followed Scaevola Augur: see Badian (1967) 228–29, Kaster (2020) 157 n.470. To smooth the narrative Cicero omits the earlier connection.

[64] Ryan (1998) on senatorial debate; an overview in van der Blom (2016) 38–42.

Sulla and Pompeius Strabo and his absence for much of 89.[65] Again these
are not outright lies, but the omissions crucially alter the image of his
training, suggesting he spent nearly two years imbibing high-stakes
speeches in the forum.[66]

The Ciceropaideia captures several crucial details of Cicero's life while
demonstrating the selectivity, emphases, and shaping of material that so
typify the *Brutus*. Cicero repeatedly posits meaningful parallels, especially
through extended syncrises and cross-generational or cross-cultural comparisons. He deploys digressions to great effect, allowing seemingly unrelated material to serve important functions at different points in the
dialogue: the discussion of Hortensius' failure to change, for example,
makes most sense in light of Cicero's dispute with the Atticists and his
unflinching insistence on progress as a developmental principle, not only
in his own and Hortensius' lives but in the life of an artistic practice across
time. We also find Cicero carefully crafting, sometimes manipulating, the
material available in the historical record to produce a compelling
narrative.[67]

Selectivity of details in the *Brutus* gives us a glimpse into how Cicero
retrospectively represented his career. Previously published losses or smaller cases – so central to his earlier crafting of a public profile as someone
otherwise unknown – are omitted or emphasized differently, and what
emerges is a picture of a far more competent and connected advocate, one
who selectively argued more important and more successful cases that, in
the privileged view of hindsight, inevitably portended future success.[68]
And however unusual Cicero's career was, even by his own admission, he
still goes to great lengths to make it seem normal and normative. The
history of his own oratory overlooks the reality that the type of education
he had and the possibilities for remaining at Rome and involved in its
politics were relatively new in the construction of political careers.
Magistrates were in Rome more frequently at more crucial times, and

---

[65] *Phil.* 12.27, Plut. *Cic.* 3, with *Div.* 1.72, 2.65 and Cichorius (1922) 181–85, Badian (1969) 454.
Mitchell (1979) 9 has him under Sulla for the first half of 89 and under Strabo for the second.

[66] Badian (1969) 458: "It would seriously impair the picture of Cicero's assiduity in 90, if it were
known that the court only sat for a small part of the year – just as, in 89, it would do so if we were to
know that he was on military service for most of the year." Mitchell (1979) 9 n.29: "He is guilty of
distortion by omission in the *Brutus*."

[67] Although there is not space here to address the topic at length, J. Hall (2014) 50 notes that Cicero
suppresses the details of Hortensius' eccentric style of performance, barely noting them in passing
(316). Gunderson (2000) 127–32 on Hortensius' (alleged) effeminacy.

[68] C. Steel (2012) on how Cicero shapes his early career through careful publication, noting "his
constant attempt to impose, on the sometimes recalcitrant raw material of Roman politics, order
and success." Cf. Gibson and C. Steel (2010).

extensive service as a military tribune or provincial governor became less integral to a political career.[69] He also relies on assumptions about the common publication of speeches, which was far less common than one might think from reading the *Brutus*.[70]

Individually, none of Cicero's techniques of invention or presentation were new or unusual, but throughout the dialogue he deftly employs rhetorical strategies and techniques to produce a persuasive and yet seemingly artless account of his own life and of oratory's past. Drawing together the different possibilities for representing the past and for conceptualizing an art is among the dialogue's greatest contributions to intellectual history, and Cicero goes to great lengths to impress upon readers the uniqueness and novelty of his literary-historical project. His claims to innovation in the face of tradition are the subject of the next chapter.

---

[69] Military service: Harris (1979) 11–15, Rosenstein (2007) 133. Presence in Rome: Flower (2010) 67 (on the effects of moving the start of the year in 153 to 1 January from 1 March), Pina Polo (2011) on the consulship's development into a civil rather than military office after Sulla. For an overview, see Blösel (2011). Van der Blom (2016) 25–45, 280–89 details the public profiling of a career via oratory and Cicero's idiosyncratic perspective.

[70] C. Steel (2005) 22, 145 on how few great orators in the generation immediately preceding Cicero's published their speeches. Earlier orators did of course, such as the Gracchi or Cato, but the practice became more widespread in Cicero's generation.

CHAPTER 2

The Intellectual Genealogy of the Brutus

And so, I'll plant a crop as if in uncultivated and forsaken land and tend it so attentively as to be able to repay even with interest the generosity of your gift, provided that my intellect can produce as a field does, which customarily yields a greater crop when it's been fallow for many years.

seremus igitur aliquid tamquam in inculto et derelicto solo; quod ita diligenter colemus, ut impendiis etiam augere possimus largitatem tui muneris: modo idem noster animus efficere possit quod ager, qui quom multos annos quievit, uberiores efferre fruges solet. (16)

At once both bold and vague, Cicero's announcement of a new project promises repayment and hints at new opportunities. But what is the new and abundant creation that years of impatient inaction will bring to fruition? Cicero had not spoken publicly since before leaving for his proconsulship in Cilicia in 51. He had also produced no major work since around that same time, when in the 50s his dialogues *de Oratore* and *de Republica*, modeled on Plato, offered a response to his own political sidelining after the rise of the triumvirate. The *Brutus* announces Cicero's reentry into the intellectual fray (much as *pro Marcello* will announce his reentry into public speaking).[1]

Cicero's aims, however, were not solely intellectual. The preface indicates several different purposes: to repay Atticus (and Brutus), to commemorate Hortensius, and to document oratory's past. Atticus describes the dialogue's examination of orators as its central topic: "when they came into existence, as well as who and what kind they were" (*quando esse coepissent, qui etiam et quales fuissent,* 20). Seemingly neutral criteria (*quando* and *qui*) are combined with a highly subjective one (*quales*). These categories occupy the bulk of the narrative but insufficiently describe its production and examination of oratorical and literary history.

---

[1] Chapter 3 discusses the connection of the *Brutus* to the *pro Marcello* of September 46.

44

A crucial refinement rounds out the discussion of older orators and directly precedes the putatively modern age of Antonius and Crassus:

> To catalogue those who have performed this service in the city so as to rank among the orators. And in fact from what I'll recount one can judge their development and how difficult it is in any pursuit to reach the final perfection of what is best.

> conligere eos, qui hoc munere in civitate functi sint, ut tenerent oratorum locum; quorum quidem quae fuerit ascensio et quam in omnibus rebus difficilis optimi perfectio atque absolutio ex eo quod dicam existimari potest (137).

This later passage briefly yet formally outlines the evolutionary principles of the work's teleology, acknowledging its inclusive tendencies while insisting on the final aim toward the best oratory in the present. This is not the only redefinition: Brutus had already commented on "what you've undertaken, to distinguish types of orators by generation" (*id quod instituisti, oratorum genera distinguere aetatibus*, 74).[2] And yet another occurs near the end of the preface: "eloquence itself, which we're about to discuss, has grown silent" (*ea ipsa, de qua disputare ordimur, eloquentia obmutuit*, 22). The history, evolution, and quality of orators is one subject, but so too is the broader examination of the art of public speech and its continued viability: will eloquence be heard again and in what capacity? The *Brutus'* scholarly inquiries and advances come in the midst of political crisis and unquestionably respond to it.

A Preface in Crisis and Salvation (1–25)

Much of the dialogue's structure is readily discernible, and its conversational technique fairly straightforward. Discussion shifts frequently between lively digressions and the detailed historical account. The lengthy expository sections of the *Brutus* have Cicero as the main speaker – one notable exception is the discussion of Caesar and Marcellus. Atticus and Brutus offer crucial if limited interventions, the former often responding skeptically to Cicero's claims or manner of presentation, and the latter often shedding light on the pedagogical importance of those same claims and procedures. Where Atticus offers an intellectual challenge to Cicero, Brutus underscores the scholarly fruits of Cicero's labors, roles that fit well with their respective ages: Atticus older by a few years (b. 110) and Brutus

---

[2] Brutus directly responds to Cicero's enthusiasm for Atticus' *Liber Annalis*.

younger by slightly more than two decades (b. 85); Atticus the accomplished scholar of the past, Brutus envisioning his future career.[3]

The catalogue of Roman speakers begins with Lucius Brutus (53) and continues until the mention of Publius Crassus (281), the last speaker named.[4] Other than chronology there seems to be no guiding principle of organization. However, the history of orators is essentially bounded by two symmetrical yet significant sections of roughly equal length: the long preface, with the introduction (1–25) and the Greek history (26–51), on one end, and on the other end the concluding sections on Atticism (282–300) and the analysis of Hortensius and the Ciceropaideia (301–29). Chiastic arrangement reinforces the symmetry, interlacing material about Cicero/Hortensius and contemporary politics with Greek, and especially Athenian, material: Introduction : Greeks : Atticism : Conclusion.

The preface itself is conceptually rich, citing or alluding to several Roman institutions and topics that will be revisited throughout the dialogue. It is mirrored in length and complexity by the subsequent twofold excursus on the development of oratory at Greece (26–51), which is itself a template for Roman oratory.[5] The beginning of the work lavishly sets out the theoretical and practical stakes of Cicero's literary-historical enterprise.

At a first reading, however, the preface imparts a vague, almost misleading sense of the dialogue's purpose. Cicero meanders through a lengthy account of what spurred him to write it, beginning with the death of Hortensius, his chief forensic rival, nearly five years earlier – a noteworthy delay for extended homage of a figure so politically and personally significant. Next Cicero describes his own depression over the state of Rome's affairs, alluding vaguely to the violence threatening the state; then the recent writings of Atticus and Brutus, who arrive at Cicero's home, and, at long last, the main topic, an account of Rome's orators. His tale is long, rambling, and not entirely coherent on the face of it, and, for all that it contains, what it omits is likewise perplexing: Cicero dispenses with at least one traditional motif – the opening response to an imagined literary request. We might expect something at the outset such as "Often, in these troubling times of ours, you have asked me, Titus Pomponius and Marcus

---

[3] On Brutus' disputed date of birth (85 versus 78/77), see Chapter 1.
[4] Sumner's (1973) list follows the first mention of an orator. Calvus is the last orator (281–84), preceding the debate on Atticism and the final syncrisis of Hortensius and Cicero. If we count living orators, one could also argue that Brutus is the last, creating yet another connection back to Rome's first speaker, Lucius Brutus.
[5] This Greek history *en miniature* is examined fully in Chapter 5.

Junius, for an account of our Roman orators and the greatness they have brought to our republic . . ."[6] Only months later Cicero will follow this pattern in the imagined request by Brutus that results in the writing of the *Orator*. In lieu of this prefatory topos the *Brutus* offers an artful, if confusing, account(ing) of Cicero's literary exchanges and debts: Atticus and Brutus sent literary creations expecting reciprocation (13–20). The unorthodox introduction is one of the many signals – others, discussed below, are more explicit – that the preface, like the *Brutus* itself, is not just unusual but entirely *sui generis*.[7]

The dialogue begins by paying homage to Quintus Hortensius Hortalus (114–50 BCE; cos. 69). In the years since Cicero's consulship, his contemporary (older by eight years) and chief forensic rival had often joined him as co-counsel.[8] Cicero in 45 would complete the dialogue *Hortensius*, a protreptic to the study of philosophy that would greatly influence Augustine's intellectual development.[9] Its portrayal of Hortensius as interlocutor, along with Quintus Lutatius Catulus (cos. 78 with the revolutionary Marcus Aemilius Lepidus), and Lucius Licinius Lucullus (cos. 74, who lost the Mithridatic command to Pompey), gathers the bulwarks of the pro-senatorial establishment in the period between the Sullan reforms and the civil war. As the last of the three to die, Hortensius symbolizes the loss of the traditional republic:

> After arriving at Rhodes while returning from my command in Cilicia and learning there of the death of Q. Hortensius, sadness – more than most expected – overcame me. This was because, with my friend's death, I saw myself robbed of his pleasant company and of our connection through reciprocal favors, and also because I was pained at the lessened status of our college upon the demise of so great an augur. And while thinking on this I recalled that he had both nominated me to the college, professing under oath his esteem for my merit, and also inducted me into it. Because of this it was my obligation, according to the augurs' customs, to honor him as a father.

---

[6] Janson (1964) 64 outlines the shared features: "dedication, request from the dedicatee, the unwillingness of the author due to a lack of time or self-confidence, and his final submission to the dedicatee's requests." Stroup (2010) 191–202 discusses dialogue dedications, focusing on the *Brutus* and *de Oratore*. Baraz (2012) 150–86 on Ciceronian prefaces.

[7] Notably absent too is argument on each side of an issue (*in utramque partem*), prevalent in so many of Cicero's other dialogues (and the structural foundation for Tacitus' *Dialogus* and Minucius Felix's *Octavius*). Cf. Granatelli (1990).

[8] E.g. they defended Flaccus, Murena, Sestius, Scaurus, Milo. Cf. Cic. *Att.* 2.25.1 (SB 45) for their mutual praise.

[9] August. *Conf.* 8.7.17.

Cum e Cilicia decedens Rhodum venissem et eo mihi de Q. Hortensi morte
esset adlatum, opinione omnium maiorem animo cepi dolorem. nam et
amico amisso cum consuetudine iucunda tum multorum officiorum con-
iunctione me privatum videbam et interitu talis auguris dignitatem nostri
collegi deminutam dolebam; qua in cogitatione et cooptatum me ab eo in
collegium recordabar, in quo iuratus iudicium dignitatis meae fecerat, et
inauguratum ab eodem; ex quo augurum institutis in parentis eum loco
colere debebam. (1)

The increasingly somber mood of the first sentence is not fully realized
until the word that Cicero delays until its completion: *dolorem* ("pain,"
"distress"). The next sentence reiterates both mood and structure by
concluding with the verb *dolebam*.[10] Cicero focuses on their shared public
offices and cites his induction in 53 into the college of augurs, Rome's
second highest priestly office after the *pontifices*.[11] It is Cicero's priesthood
as much as his grief that dominates the paragraph: *augur* is mentioned
twice, as is *collegium*, and the verb *inauguratum* is connected lexically to
this priestly office. Cicero hints at the grandness associated with the
priesthood's name, which is related to the verb *augere* ("to grow, increase,
augment"), by emphasizing his own greatness (*dignitas*) and concern about
the college's diminishment (*dignitas deminuta*) upon Hortensius' death.
The next section picks up the semantic connection with a verb in first
position for special emphasis: *augebat* ("it increased"), a choice calculated
to heighten the rhetorical effect and smooth the transition into discussion
of the civic crisis and "conditions highly unfavorable to the republic"
(*alienissimo rei publicae tempore*, 2).

This verbal dexterity lends gravity to Cicero's tribute even as it establishes a meaningful pattern of wordplay through which he draws attention
to the language of the preface and the special resonance of key terms and
ideas. Most notably he indulges in this wordplay in connection with the
theme of salvation (*salus*) in order to align his personal return to public
affairs with the longed-for restoration of traditional order.[12] He bemoans
the inability of his contemporaries to resolve their violent disagreements
while benefiting the state (*salutariter*, 8) and then connects state well-being

[10] *Dolor* and *dolere* are used eight times across 1–8. They are then used again three times in 21–23,
though now in reference to the state of the republic rather than Cicero's grief over Hortensius.
[11] The *pontifices* perhaps had greater prestige, but the augurs, with their control of the auspices, could
be said to wield greater influence over political activities. Linderski (1986) and Driediger-Murphy
(2019) on augury and the pursuit of priestly offices.
[12] In the preface the root *salu-* is used in 8, 10, 13 (×3), 14, and 15. Cicero similarly, though to
different ends, makes a pun on a key term of the Atticist debate, *sanitas* (*sit sane ita*, 279), on which
see Chapter 7.

to his own, first by citing the battles of Cannae and Nola during the Second Punic War (218–201 BCE),[13] and then by insisting that Brutus and Atticus have rescued him:

> Then Atticus said, "We've come to you with the intention of remaining silent about the republic and to hear something from you rather than to bother you at all."
>
> I said, "The two of you, Atticus, both lighten my cares now that I'm here and also gave me great solace when I was away. Your letters first restored and called me back to my former pursuits."
>
> Then Atticus said, "I quite gladly read the letter that Brutus sent you from Asia, in which he seemed to me to advise you wisely and to console you most affectionately."
>
> I said, "That's quite right: now you should know that through Brutus' letter it's as if I'd been called back to the light of life from the protracted disturbance of my whole well-being. And, much as after the disaster at Cannae the Roman people first took heart again after Marcellus' battle at Nola, and thereafter many prosperous events took place in succession, in the same way, after my own and the state's common disasters, nothing desirable or able somehow to lessen my worries befell me before Brutus' letter."
>
> Then Brutus said, "That's indeed what I really hoped to do and I'm getting a great reward, if in fact I've achieved what I wanted in so crucial a matter. But I'd like to know, what's this letter of Atticus' that you so enjoyed?"
>
> "Well, Brutus," I said, "his letter brought me not only enjoyment but even, I hope, salvation (*salutem*)."
>
> "Salvation?" he asked. "Well, what sort of letter could be so remarkable?"
>
> "Could," I said, "any salutation (*salutatio*) be either more pleasing or more suited to the current conditions (*tempus*) than the one in that book in which he addressed me and essentially lifted me up from the ground?"

> Tum Atticus: eo, inquit, ad te animo venimus, ut de re publica esset silentium et aliquid audiremus potius ex te, quam te adficeremus ulla molestia.
>
> Vos vero, inquam, Attice, et praesentem me cura levatis et absenti magna solacia dedistis. nam vestris primum litteris recreatus me ad pristina studia revocavi.
>
> Tum ille: legi, inquit, perlubenter epistulam, quam ad te Brutus misit ex Asia, qua mihi visus est et monere te prudenter et consolari amicissume.

---

[13] In a letter to Atticus on 19 January 49, Cicero wonders about Caesar "are we talking about an *imperator* of the Roman people or Hannibal?" (*utrum de imperatore populi Romani an de Hannibale loquimur?, Att.* 7.11.1 [SB 134]).

Recte, inquam, est visus: nam me istis scito litteris ex diuturna perturba-
tione totius valetudinis tamquam ad aspiciendam lucem esse revocatum.
atque ut post Cannensem illam calamitatem primum Marcelli ad Nolam
proelio populus se Romanus erexit posteaque prosperae res deinceps multae
consecutae sunt, sic post rerum nostrarum et communium gravissimos
casus nihil ante epistulam Bruti mihi accidit, quod vellem aut quod aliqua
ex parte sollicitudines adlevaret meas.

   Tum Brutus: volui id quidem efficere certe et capio magnum fructum, si
quidem quod volui tanta in re consecutus sum. sed scire cupio, quae te
Attici litterae delectaverint.

   Istae vero, inquam, Brute, non modo delectationem mihi, sed etiam, ut
spero, salutem adtulerunt.

   Salutem? inquit ille. quodnam tandem genus istuc tam praeclarum
litterarum fuit?

   An mihi potuit, inquam, esse aut gratior ulla salutatio aut ad hoc tempus
aptior quam illius libri, quo me hic adfatus quasi iacentem excitavit?
(11–13)

The pointed comparison to the battle of Cannae could hardly paint a
grimmer picture of Rome's recent past and Cicero's political failures. The
annihilation of eight Roman legions by Hannibal at Cannae in 216 would
haunt Rome for centuries and become a virtual synonym for military
disaster. Marcellus would, in three successive years, defend the city of
Nola from Hannibal's attacks, and Cicero here reports the uplifting effects
of Marcellus' successes.[14] The simile not only establishes a close connection between state well-being and Cicero's personal well-being, but also
creates a permanent connection between the two concepts through the
term *salus*. All other uses of *salus* in the *Brutus* refer to Cicero's own well-
being, for example his recall from exile (268), or are used in contexts that
emphasize the role of oratory in the salvation of the state (256 and 330).
Salus becomes a watchword for Cicero's belief in his singular ability to save
the Roman state from its present woes.[15]

   Further wordplay strengthens these connections and gives them additional resonance, as Cicero makes a traditional pun on the terms *salus* and

---

[14] See Liv. 23.16 (the first battle in 216), where he suggests that it may have been the most significant
victory of the war (*res . . . nescio an maxima illo bello gesta sit*, 23.16.16) and 23.44–46 (the second
battle in 215) with Liv. 23.30.19 on the people's awarding of proconsular command to Marcellus
because of this first success in Italy after Cannae: *M. Marcello pro consule imperium esse populus iussit,
quod post Cannensem cladem unus Romanorum imperator in Italia prospere rem gessisset*. See
Chapter 3 on M. Claudius Marcellus (cos. 51).

[15] See Kaster (2006) 27 n.40 on *salus* in Cicero's post-exile speeches, with May (1988) 90–105,
Walters (2020) 38–44.

salutatio. It is hard to do justice in English to the play on salvation/health/ greeting (*salus*) and salutation (*salutatio*), as translators of Plautus' *Pseudolus* have long known.[16] The connection of *salus* to *salutatio* was commonplace.[17] Cicero had already noted that he greeted the interlocutors upon their arrival (*quos postquam salutavi*, 10). And the letters they had been exchanging – Atticus' and Brutus' treatises – might in themselves, or in a kind of cover letter, have included the standard well wishing, *salutem dicere*: *Cicero Attico salutem dicit* ("Cicero sends greetings [*lit.*, bids good health] to Atticus") formulaically introduces his letters to Atticus.[18] Cicero further confirms the wordplay when using *salutaris* (15) to describe the beneficial effects of Atticus' writings, thus offering in the preface a ring-composition with the initial use in 8, *salutariter*, and connecting the affairs of state to Cicero's personal status.

Another prominent and related theme is the desire for silence about the state of current affairs. That overt claim will repeatedly be unmasked as a pious hope. The dialogue returns over and again to the present crisis. Already the discussion of Hortensius referred to the troubles of the state and Hortensius' fortune in not seeing the demise of the republic. Atticus later strives to maintain the fiction of silence, repeating the injunction that they not discuss the republic: *dixeram . . . de re publica ut sileremus* (157).[19] As Jon Hall remarks, "Political allusions could easily have been omitted . . . yet Cicero evidently feels a powerful need to voice such complaints."[20] Most prominently, Caesar and Marcellus are incorporated into a long digression in which Cicero touts his own political achievements and the role of public speech (248–62). Cicero's former protégés Curio *filius*, Caelius, and Publius Crassus are criticized for their mistaken political ambitions.[21] And the speakers do in fact discuss the republic in several different ways. Brutus is moved by the mention of Torquatus, who fell in

---

[16] There are several complicated jokes at Pl. *Ps.* 41–47, 71, 707–10, 968, which involve the noun *salus* and the verb *salutare*. The puns and their relationship to the Platonic critique of writing are discussed in van den Berg (2021), with further bibliography.

[17] Cf. *salus* and *servare*; Otto (1890) 307 (s.v. *Salus*).

[18] An allusion to the formulaic opening, *si vales, bene est; ego valeo*, or to the conclusions of letters, "usually variants on the theme *cura, ut valeas, vale mi carissime*, etc." (Whitton 2013 83), may partly motivate the use of *valetudo* in this passage. Janson (1964) traces the close connection between epistolary address and literary preface.

[19] Cf. *sileamus* (256). Gowing (2000), Jacotot (2014), Kenty (2020) 120–28 on the silence's political dimensions.

[20] J. Hall (2009) 94.

[21] Chapter 3 examines in detail the political resonances in Cicero's discussion of more recent speakers.

the civil war fighting Caesar, and pained (*doleo*, 266) that Cicero's authority was insufficient to bring peace. Writings and their exchange are presented as if they were alternatives to politics but are in fact ways of
examining and discussing the republic.

Atticus and Brutus as Authors and Inspirations

Though bemoaning his political sidelining and the republic's demise,
Cicero also found inspiration for his new project in Atticus and Brutus,
and this exchange of texts signals not only the intellectual filiations of the
Brutus but also its political commitments.[22] There are several references to
texts, discussions, and even a speech as sources of inspiration for the
Brutus, and in order to get a full sense of the complexity of textual
exchanges in the preface, it will be helpful to review the several mentions
of them.

Cicero praises Brutus' (now lost) treatise "On Moral Excellence" (*de
Virtute*), the encouraging letters from Asia (11–12, quoted above).[23]
Cicero reiterates the treatise's restorative effects at the end of the dialogue:

> Though I do indeed feel pain that I've entered life a little too late, as if upon
> a road, and have fallen into the republic's nighttime before the journey was
> complete, still I am relieved by the consolation which you held out to me,
> Brutus, in your most charming letter, in which you thought that I ought to
> take heart, because I had accomplished things that would speak about me
> even were I to be silent, would live even if I were dead. And these things
> would bear witness to my counsels on behalf of the republic by the
> republic's salvation if it should survive, or even by its downfall if it
> should not.
>
> equidem etsi doleo me in vitam paulo serius tamquam in viam ingressum,
> priusquam confectum iter sit, in hanc rei publicae noctem incidisse, tamen

---

[22] Hendrickson (1962) 28. n.b thinks that this new project is some other historical work, but I see no
reason why this shouldn't be the *Brutus* itself. The preface includes the demand for repayment of
debt (and the intertwining of the two debts owed to Atticus and Brutus) as well as Atticus' claim
that he wants something now after the long period of inactivity (*longo intervallo*) because he sees
that Cicero is in better spirits (*hilarior*, 18). Hendrickson sees the work's discussion as repayment of
a debt without making the connection to the earlier description. Robinson (1951) 144 n.9 prefers
the Ἀνέκδοτα; Bringmann (1971) 13–15 argues for *de Legibus*.

[23] Hendrickson (1962) 26–27 n.a, 288–89 n.a, and Douglas (1966a) xi; Dugan (2005) 236–48; cf.
Sen. *Helv.* 8.1, 9.4–8 with *Brutus* 250. Cf. *Fin.* 1.8, *Tusc.* 5.12, and Sedley (1997). Most scholars
accept the identification of these letters with *de Virtute*, but cf. Strasburger (1990) 24, Dettenhofer
(1992) 199–201. Varro would also write about Marcellus in the *Logistorici*, but probably after
Brutus and Cicero did. On the dialogue form and content of the *Logistorici*, see Cichorius (1922)
236–48, Dahlmann and Heisterhagen (1957).

ea consolatione sustentor quam tu mihi, Brute, adhibuisti tuis suavissimis litteris, quibus me forti animo esse oportere censebas, quod ea gessissem, quae de me etiam me tacente ipsa loquerentur, mortuo viverent;[24] quae, si recte esset, salute rei publicae, sin secus, interitu ipso testimonium meorum de re publica consiliorum darent. (330)

De Virtute was among the first Latin works of philosophy in prose other than Cicero and the Epicurean writings of Amafinius and Rabirius.[25] Brutus (like the polymath Varro) followed the "Old Academy" (*vestra, Brute, vetus Academia*, 149), which Antiochus of Ascalon founded in reaction to the New Academy and his one-time teacher there, the scholarch Philo of Larissa. Brutus' treatise addressed in part how to endure civil crisis. It noted the steadfastness and *virtus* of M. Claudius Marcellus, an opponent of Caesar living in exile at Mytilene. He occupies a special place in the *Brutus* as the only living orator discussed other than Caesar.[26] Brutus seems to have offered philosophical consolation by stressing that only *virtus* ensures well-being or happiness, a prominent topic of discussion in Cicero's immense philosophical output of 46–44.[27]

While Brutus inspired Cicero to return to writing, Atticus' *Liber Annalis* turned him toward Roman history:[28]

> It had much indeed that was new to me and also a usefulness I was searching for that allowed me, with all the orders of time laid out, to see everything in one sweeping view. After I began to study it closely, the studying of the writings itself proved healthful and put me in the mindframe to take something from you, Pomponius, to reinvigorate me and to offer you if not full repayment then at least some gratitude. Still that phrase of Hesiod is praised by wise men, which instructs you to return what you've taken in equal or – if possible – greater measure.

> Ille vero et nova … mihi quidem multa et eam utilitatem quam requirebam, ut explicatis ordinibus temporum uno in conspectu omnia viderem. quae cum studiose tractare coepissem, ipsa mihi tractatio litterarum salutaris fuit admonuitque, Pomponi, ut a te ipso sumerem aliquid ad me

---

[24] Hendrickson (1962), seconded by Kaster (2020). *L* (consensus of codices based on the lost *Laudensis*) has *mortuo viverentque*, transposed by Malcovati (following Stangl and others).

[25] Cicero scorns these Epicureans at *Ac.* 1.5–6.

[26] His central importance in Cicero's catalogue is discussed in Chapter 3.

[27] Scourfield (2013) surveys the genre of *consolatio*. Cicero increasingly turned to Brutus, who becomes the "dedicatee of choice" for his philosophical works (Baraz 2012 205). Cicero dedicated to him *Parad.*, *Orat.*, *N.D.*, *Tusc.*, and *Fin.* See *Div.* 2.1–4 on the philosophical encyclopedia.

[28] On Atticus and the *Liber Annalis*, see Münzer (1905), Douglas (1966a) xii and lii, Perlwitz (1992), A. M. Marshall (1993), Welch (1996), Feeney (2007) 14–16, 20–28, *FRHist* I: 344–53, II: 718–25, III: 457–62.

reficiendum teque remunerandum si non pari, at grato tamen munere: quamquam illud Hesiodium laudatur a doctis, quod eadem mensura reddere iubet qua acceperis aut etiam cumulatiore, si possis. (15)

Cicero highlights its intellectual clarity and utility alongside Atticus' ability to encompass and represent all Roman history in a single view. Praise for the visual impression made by Atticus' book reveals Cicero's similar conceptualization of the *Brutus* as an aesthetically coherent account of literary history in the unfolding succession of time, a learned object to behold and appreciate. Indeed, the perfectly ambiguous verb *explicare* (*explicatis ordinibus temporum*) captures the simultaneously visual and intellectual experiences of such an object: the unrolling of the pages (*explicare*) reveals an explanation (*explicare*) of the ages.[29] And calling the perusal of history *salutaris* (derived from *salus*, discussed above) aligns the work's intellectual and political commitments.

This same alignment is found in the vocabulary of time (*tempus/tempora*), which contains an inherent tension in Latin. Like the English terms "time" and "times," the word can indicate both chronological progression and state of affairs.[30] Cicero capitalizes on the senses of "(current) conditions" and "(successive) times." When he earlier said that Atticus' writings are "suited to the current conditions" (*ad hoc tempus aptior*, 11), he offered both an anticipatory joke about the content of Atticus' writing and also a serious direction about the relevance of research into the past for civic circumstances in the present.

The reference to Hesiod and to the repayment of a debt with interest is likewise a brilliant means of indirect self-advertisement that allows Cicero to attribute greater significance to his own project in comparison to those of his interlocutors. He begins with deference and modesty toward Brutus and Atticus before announcing his grand project, and along the way he softens his claims and the magnitude of his ambition by placing the project squarely within the reciprocal obligations of friendship and exchange.[31]

---

[29] "Pages" is admittedly inapposite for a bookroll. See Johnson (2009), (2012) 17–31 (focusing on the early empire); Winsbury (2009), Frampton (2019) 13–32. The figurative meaning of *explicare* (as for so many Latin words) develops out of the earlier physical sense: *TLL* 5.2.1733.15–1737.78 [Hiltbrunner, 1943]; 1733.41–42 for *Brut.* 15. Cf. Catul. 1.8: *omne aevum tribus explicare cartis.*

[30] In English the singular/plural difference corresponds well to the conceptual difference, as the singular denotes temporality and the plural condition(s). In Latin the situation is reversed and less rigid: the singular typically denotes condition, though can mean (point in) time, while the plural commonly denotes temporal ages, but can mean conditions.

[31] Baraz (2012) 150–86 illuminates the workings of prefaces in other dialogues: crafting an ideal reader who is obliged to accept the terms of the work (152) and using the language of debt to draw on and reinforce the social structures of *amicitia* (165).

Atticus' interest in chronology and synchronism was anticipated by Cornelius Nepos, whose labors in the three-book *Chronica* were immortalized by Catullus. His great contribution to Latin historiography lay in expanding its scope beyond the Roman world to include the Greek world and in considering the possible synchronisms of both. As we might expect, he built on the work of a Greek scholar, the Athenian Apollodorus, who (updating the pioneering work of Eratosthenes of Cyrene) had crafted verse chronicles in the second century. In Greek prose Nepos will also have had the accounts of Polybius and Posidonius as nearer models at Rome.[32] Nepos later acknowledged the virtues of Atticus' *Liber*:

> so that he laid out all antiquity in that bookroll, in which he set out magistracies in order. In fact, there is no law or peace or war or signal event of the Roman people that is not recorded in its proper time, and – another feat of incredible difficulty – he so interwove the origins of families, that we can understand the genealogies of illustrious men from it.

> ut eam totam [*sc.* antiquitatem] in eo volumine exposuerit, quo magistratus ordinavit. nulla enim lex neque pax neque bellum neque res illustris est populi Romani, quae non in eo suo tempore sit notata, et, quod difficillimum fuit, sic familiarum originem subtexuit, ut ex eo clarorum virorum propagines possimus cognoscere. (Nepos, *Att.* 18.1–2)

Overlap with the *Brutus* is considerable: magistracies, laws, peace and war, notable events, time, and genealogies. War and peace form overarching themes: oratory thrives only in peacetime (45), the end of the First Punic War in 241 anticipates Roman literature's invention in 240 (72–73), and the contemporary civil war looms large. Laws are connected to oratory's development in Crassus' exemplary speech of 106 on the *lex Servilia* (161) and in Pompey's laws modifying the courts in 52 (324). Cicero at one point reconceptualizes familial genealogy to suggest that the republic is formed from its oratorical past and that only with this civic structure in place can noble lineages have any meaning.[33] Yet Atticus' *Liber* offered not a restrictive framework but a set of thematic emphases from which Cicero selectively drew to present the details of the past. Cicero stresses chronology but with a different structure in mind, fashioning the data of Roman

---

[32] Pfeiffer (1968) 152–70 (Eratosthenes), 255–57 (Apollodorus), Montana (2015) 111–18 (Eratosthenes), 157–59 (Apollodorus). On Nepos' *Chronica* and its contexts, see *FRHist* I: 395–401, II: 798–815, III: 497–504, *CAH*² IX.2: 711–15, Feeney (2007) 21–23, 63.

[33] Chapter 3 discusses the criticism of Publius Crassus via citation of L. Licinius Crassus (282). See A. M. Marshall (1993) on Atticus' genealogies, including Brutus' dual descent from the Junii and the Servilii. Cf. Wiseman (1974); van der Blom (2010) 97–98 on Brutus and 151–74 on Cicero's alternative genealogies. Cicero notes Brutus' dual genealogy at 331.

history into the generational groupings of orators and their public achievements.[34]

We can see Cicero's independence from Atticus in his selective use of magistracies. Magistracies connect poetry and oratory to civic power, and the consulships are used sparingly to provide a temporal framework. The *cursus honorum* of most orators remains in the background. When offices are cited it is typically because they bear some special importance, such as structuring the lifetimes of artists or because of their coincidence with another significant event.[35] Thus Cicero emphasizes Cato's quaestorship (204) and censorship (184), because they coincided with the deaths of Naevius and Plautus (60).[36] Cato's quaestorship fell in the same year as Cethegus' consulship, important not only for his role as the beginning of oratory, but because it occurred 140 years (rounded down) before Cicero's. Cicero thereby suggests a unique connection between the birth of the art and Cicero's giving of new life to Rome in his consulship by quashing the Catilinarian conspiracy (*o fortunatam natam me consule Romam*, fr. 8 Courtney).[37] Crucial figures and events are often aligned with the dates of birth and death of renowned orators or authors, information mostly available in the research of Atticus (and Varro). But as Elizabeth Rawson has observed, "Cicero's achievement was more independent than is usually thought."[38]

After the long exchange over the various textual debts that have accrued, Atticus finally presses Cicero for discussion:

> Atticus said, "And so, since he [Brutus] has declared that he'd demand as repayment what I'm owed, I'll demand from you what you owe him."
>
> "What could that be?" I asked.
>
> "That you write something," he replied. "Your writings have indeed long been silent. You know, since you produced those books *On the Republic* we haven't gotten anything from you. And I was myself spurred and

---

[34] Lintott (2008) 306: "The catalog of more or less distinguished orators that follows was perhaps to some extent a compliment to Atticus by imitation. The annotation, however, renders it more than a collection of data." Douglas (1966b), Sumner (1973) 151–54 on oratorical groupings.

[35] See Chapter 1's analysis of the Ciceropaideia for such alignments.

[36] This example of Cicero's efforts to align lives and careers is discussed in Chapter 4.

[37] *Flac.* 102 calls the famed Nones of December the salvation (*salutaris*) and birth day (*natalis*) of Rome.

[38] Rawson (1972) 42, noting that "Atticus only gave, regularly, consuls and censors, and he dated A.U.C., which Cicero does not show any sign of doing." Cf. Sumner (1973) 176, Horsfall (1989) 99–100. Douglas (1966b) argues for the use of birth dates rather than magistracies as the organizing principle for post-Gracchan orators.

impassioned by them to compose a record of our history. But I'm asking for them only whenever and however you're able to produce them. As for now, if your mind's freed up for it, explain to us what we're seeking."

"What's that?" I asked.

"That," he replied, "which you recently in your Tusculan villa began to tell me about orators: when they came into existence, as well as who and what kind they were. After I relayed our discussion to your – or our – friend Brutus, he said he really wanted to hear it. And so, we chose this day, since we knew you'd be available. For this reason, if it suits you, produce that account for me and Brutus, which you had already begun."

itaque quoniam hic quod mihi deberetur se exacturum professus est, quod huic debes, ego a te peto.

Quidnam id? inquam.

Ut scribas, inquit, aliquid; iam pridem enim conticuerunt tuae litterae. nam ut illos de re publica libros edidisti, nihil a te sane postea accepimus: eisque nosmet ipsi ad rerum nostrarum memoriam comprehendendam impulsi atque incensi sumus. sed illa, cum poteris; atque ut possis, rogo. nunc vero, inquit, si es animo vacuo, expone nobis quod quaerimus.

Quidnam est id? inquam.

Quod mihi nuper in Tusculano inchoavisti de oratoribus: quando esse coepissent, qui etiam et quales fuissent. quem ego sermonem cum ad Brutum tuum vel nostrum potius detulissem, magnopere hic audire se velle dixit. itaque hunc elegimus diem, cum te sciremus esse vacuum. quare, si tibi est commodum, ede illa quae coeperas et Bruto et mihi. (19–20)

We are again brought back to the theme of silence and the importance of writings: *conticuerunt tuae litterae*. For all the strictures against discussing the republic, the preface circles incessantly around that topic, just as Cicero's refusals to discuss himself in the dialogue only advertise the extent to which he does. In a literal sense Atticus brings up the republic when citing Cicero's dialogue by name: *ut illos de re publica libros edidisti* (19).The *de Republica* (discussed below) was the immediate precursor to the present dialogue, and citing it also aligns the *Brutus* with its focus on Roman government.

Just as the dedicatory exchange of books forges connections between the interlocutors' writings, providing sources of mutual inspiration, so too do past conversations inspire the present one (*sermo*): Atticus tells Brutus about the *sermo* that Cicero began in his Tusculan villa, which inspires in Brutus a desire for another *sermo*, the present dialogue. In Cicero's dramatic portrayal of the work's genesis the *Brutus* has a double origin: it is inspired simultaneously by written works and oral accounts, a duality replicated in the word *sermo*, as the term means both the act of talking *viva voce* ("speaking" or "a speech") and the written account of such talking in published form ("a literary dialogue").[39] Conflation of the written and the performed in the *Brutus* is even given a humorous metafictional twist when Brutus expresses concern about the orators not included in Cicero's catalogue: "I think you're worried that your discussion here might become known through us and that those whom you've omitted will be angry with you" (*vereri te . . . arbitror ne per nos hic sermo tuus emanet et ii tibi suscenseant, quos praeterieris*, 231). The written work lightheartedly trades on the fiction that it exists only in oral format.

Cicero calls attention to yet another source, Brutus' speech on behalf of King Deiotarus:

> Indeed, Pomponius, then the discussion began after I had mentioned having heard that the case of Deiotarus, a most faithful and excellent king, was defended by Brutus with remarkable adornment and fullness.

> [Atticus:] I know that the discussion began there and that you, grieving on Brutus' behalf, almost wept at the desolation of the courts and the forum.

> Nempe igitur hinc tum, Pomponi, ductus est sermo, quod erat a me mentio facta causam Deiotari fidelissimi atque optumi regis ornatissume et copiosissume a Bruto me audisse defensam.

> Scio, inquit, ab isto initio tractum esse sermonem teque Bruti dolentem vicem quasi deflevisse iudiciorum vastitatem et fori. (21)

He traces the beginning of the previous discussion with Atticus back to the speech Brutus delivered before Caesar at the town of Nicaea, near the southeastern coast of the Black Sea, in the summer of 47 BCE. Brutus defended Deiotarus, the tetrarch of Galatia (in central Asia Minor), who took Pompey's side in the civil war.[40] Again Cicero's deftness in tracing out inspirations is remarkable: a dialogue purporting to discuss and assess Roman oratory (the *Brutus*) is motivated by a discussion and assessment of an orator (Brutus). Reference to that speech again undermines claims to avoid politics. Atticus refocuses attention onto Caesar and notes Cicero's pain at the absence of forensic opportunities (again, the aforementioned

---

[39] *OLD* s.v. *sermo* 3a, "conversation, dialogue," and 3b, "a discussion on a literary, philosophic, scientific, etc., topic; a literary work cast in the form of such a discussion, a dialogue." Barwick (1963) 28–31, Zoll (1962) 105–24; on generic self-identification in Cicero's dialogues (focusing on *Tusculan Disputations*) see Gildenhard (2007) 1–88, esp. 1–34 and 63–65. Mankin (2011) 19–23 (with bibliography) reviews the conventional terminology.

[40] Hendrickson (1962) 32 n.a remarks "With the words *me audisse* Cicero observes the fiction of oral communication for knowledge derived from a written source."

key term, *dolor*). All signs indicate that the dialogue will address the immediate political crisis despite any claims to the contrary.

Though subtly presented throughout the preface, the immediate sources and inspirations cited for the *Brutus* are remarkable. If we step back and consider their content and occasions, it becomes clear that Cicero outlines an impressive range of activities and contexts: moral philosophy and ethical conduct in civic crisis (*de Virtute*); national histories and civic events (*Liber Annalis*); statehood and the "republic" (*de Republica*); public oratory and the civil war (Brutus' *pro rege Deiotaro*); learned conversational exchange (*sermo*). Reference to texts, discussion, and speech creates a complex web of cultural production and exchange, all portraying key activities of Roman elite life. Furthermore, the connections back to these works deeply implicate the dialogue in the contemporary political context, even when its ostensible subject is the past and its oratory. The new project announced by Cicero in the preface suggests that it will offer a clear alternative to political quietism and withdrawal. The possibilities for public engagement are preceded by and continue to be carried along by a torrent of writings, writings that are inspired and interconnected in a constant feedback loop of authorial performance and exchange in the service of the republic.[41]

Intellectual Traditions and the *Brutus'* Uniqueness

As should be clear from examining the preface, there is no single source, inspiration, or model for either the form or the content of the *Brutus*. Examination of the work's implicit or acknowledged debts can nevertheless shed further light on the intellectual foundations for Cicero's account. The aim in what follows is not to comprehensively document every influence or connection to earlier texts, but rather to provide an overview of the main characteristics and similarities to earlier authors, thinkers, and texts (including some of Cicero's own) that may have had the greatest intellectual affiliation with or influence on the *Brutus*.[42]

Literary dialogue at Rome was relatively new, though with a rich history of Greek precedents. Several forerunners in the Greek tradition stand out. Plato best represents (for us) the dialogue genre. Heraclides of Pontus and

---

[41] *Orator* 148 equates Cicero's new intellectual endeavors with his previous forensic and political accomplishments.

[42] I briefly address the tradition of (auto)biography in Chapters 1, 6, and the Conclusion.

Aristotle built on his legacy, although we know few direct details from their dialogues.[43] A strong nod to Plato occurs when the interlocutors sit in a grassy area near a statue of Plato (*in pratulo propter Platonis statuam consedimus*, 24).[44] Atticus later accuses Cicero of employing Socratic irony, while Cicero insists on the seriousness of his account (292–99). Heraclides of Pontus included long expository sections and interlocutors who present his own points of view, features prominent in Cicero's other dialogues. Aristotle is the closest forerunner: "but what I've written in recent years follows Aristotelian custom, in which others participate in a way that has the author taking the lead" (*quae autem his temporibus scripsi* ᾿Αριστοτέλειον *morem habent, in quo ita sermo inducitur ceterorum ut penes ipsum sit principatus, Att.* 13.19.4 [SB 326]).[45] Also important is Aristotle's Συναγωγὴ Τεχνῶν, a survey of rhetorical theorists praised in Cicero's *de Inventione* and probably drawn on in the *Brutus'* Greek history (esp. 46–48).[46] The post-Platonic rise of literary-critical and literary-historical dialogue, emerging alongside Alexandrian scholarship and Homeric philology, remains shrouded in mystery, though we do get some sense of it from the fragments of Satyrus of Callatis' lively dialogue on the life of Euripides.[47]

---

[43] Hirzel (1895) remains the seminal study of Greco-Roman dialogue. Cf. Hösle (2006), whose focus on the philosophical tradition excludes the *Brutus*. The bibliography on Ciceronian dialogue is immense. I have found the following especially useful for Cicero's relationship to Plato: Zoll (1962), Görler (1988), Schütrumpf (1988), MacKendrick (1989), Gaines (1995), Zetzel (1995) *passim*, May and Wisse (2001) 20–27, Zetzel (2003), Hösle (2008), Mankin (2011) 9–23, Stull (2011), Gildenhard (2013a), Jazdzewska (2014), Altman (2016). For Cicero's dialogue technique (with bibliography): Gildenhard (2007) 1–88, esp. 1–34 and 63–65, Schofield (2008), various essays in Schofield (2013) and Föllinger and Müller (2013). Long (1995) is illuminating on Aristotle and Cicero, as is Fox (2009) on Heraclides of Pontus and Cicero; van den Berg (2014) examines Tacitus' reuse of the inherited Ciceronian material and models for interpreting dialogue as a genre.

[44] On the motif, see Cic. *Rep.* 1.18.4 (*in aprico maxime pratuli loco*), Cic. *Att.* 12.6.2 (SB 306), and *de Orat.* 1.24, with Zetzel (2003). Plato's importance is stressed as well in the report that Demosthenes had closely read and perhaps even heard Plato (121).

[45] Cf. Cic. *Fam.* 1.9.23 (SB 20; on *de Oratore*).

[46] *Inv.* 2.6; cf. *de Orat.* 2.160. Douglas (1955b) on the Συναγωγὴ Τεχνῶν notes its distortions: "however valuable for its summaries of earlier rhetorical teaching . . . [it] was on the historical side highly tendentious" (539). Cicero will have followed Aristotle's lead. Schöpsdau (1994) is an excellent overview and analysis of sources for the material in the *Brutus*; Noël (2003) examines the remnants of the treatise found in Cicero's rhetorical works (*Inv., de Orat., Brut.*). Adamietz (1966) on Quint. *Inst.* 3.1.8–15 usefully details Quintilian's adaptations from Cicero. Chapter 5 examines Cicero's double history of Greek oratory and rhetoric (26–51).

[47] *P.Oxy.* 9.1176. Shorn (2004) for text; Leo (1960) 365–83, Jazdzewska (forthcoming). Leo (1960) 366 notes the special place of Satyrus and the lineage from Aristotle to Cicero: "wir haben auf einmal den peripatetischen Dialog litterarischen Inhalts vor uns, ein Stück der Linie, an deren Anfang Aristoteles περὶ ποιητῶν steht und am andern Ende Cicero."

Cicero had helped to forge the Roman dialogue tradition already in the 50s, although some forerunners are known. Varro's *Menippean Satires* probably contained dialogue elements, and the famed jurist Marcus Junius Brutus wrote a three-book dialogue on law addressed to his son and with villa settings.[48] The *Brutus* also criticizes a predecessor in the Roman tradition, lambasting Curio's dialogue on Caesar for its anachronisms. The objection may have been valid, although Cicero occasionally indulged in implausibility.[49] The genre, however, was still in flux and, like many genres, would continue to undergo developments and refinements of technique and presentation. Furthermore, it is essential to recognize that every dialogue, like nearly any worthwhile work of literature, contributes to its own terms of evaluation and to the shape of its tradition. While we can always speak of sources and inspirations for a given work, generic precedents can only go so far in explaining later innovations.

Cicero derives his framework for literary history from Hellenistic scholarship on arts and artists, which his contemporaries also diligently adapted.[50] Varro's *de Poetis*, written shortly before the *Brutus*, stands in this tradition and, along with the somewhat later *de Poematis*, was probably the most characteristic Roman adaptation of it. Cicero probably draws from the *de Poetis* in the *Brutus*, most prominently in dating the beginning of Latin literature to Livius Andronicus' play in 240 BCE.[51]

The differences of method and presentation, however, between (what we know of) Varro's writings and Cicero's *Brutus* suggest a limited

---

[48] *De Orat.* 2.224; Fantham (2004) 50–51 suggests that Curio's dialogue may predate *de Oratore*, but we lack evidence.

[49] E.g. Rutilius Rufus relays the opening of *de Republica*, including events that preceded his arrival. See Chapter 4 on Curio's dialogue.

[50] See *CAH²* IX.2: 689–728 for a survey of intellectual developments at Rome in the late republic, *CAH²* VIII: 422–76 on contact with Greeks. Hutchinson (2013) for an in-depth study of Greco-Roman (textual) interactions. On Hellenistic scholarship: Pfeiffer (1968), Montana (2015), and Nünlist (2015). On Greek literary historiography, see Grethlein and Rengakos (2017); Grethlein (2017) 11–22 surveys methodological questions.

[51] Varro is less visible than we might expect, in part because Cicero promotes Atticus' *Liber Annalis*, which relied on Varro's work. Cicero (surely or probably) cites Varro at 60 (contradicting him), 72–73 (Livius Andronicus), 78 (death of Ennius). At 229 Cicero cites Accius, although Dahlmann (1962) 614 claims Varro as his source. On Varro's scholarship on poetry, see also Dahlmann (1953) and (1963). Paucity of evidence obscures Varro's potential methodological influence on Cicero. See Rösch-Binde (1998) for a general overview of their intellectual relationship; Kronenberg (2009) 88–93 on (potential) parody of Cicero's philosophical self-presentation; Wiseman (2009) 107–29 on political aspects. Smith (2018) for an incisive overview of Varro's antiquarian project, with challenges to the label "Roman antiquarianism" in MacRae (2018); Momigliano (1950) and (1990) 54–79, Rawson (1985) 233–49, Moatti (1997) 97–155, Sehlmeyer (2003), Volk (2020).

influence on the *Brutus*.[52] Greek writings περὶ τέχνης and περὶ τεχνιτῶν (for Roman poetry, Varro's *de Poematis* and *de Poetis*) contained an introductory *praelocutio* defining the technical field (*ars*) and the artist (*artifex*). Hellfried Dahlmann saw in the *Brutus'* Greek history the traditional elements: εὕρησις, ἀρχή, αὔξησις, ἀκμή, that is, the early discovery (26), beginning (27–28), a period of growth (29–31), and a mature highpoint (32–38, although Demetrius initiates decline, 37–38). The *Brutus*, in his account, exemplified technographic writing (*enumeratio oratorum*, 319) and followed Varro's adaptation of the tradition.[53]

Cicero, however, goes well beyond these inherited elements. He does use some topoi also found in Varro, but the methodologically rich introduction powerfully and differently synchronizes Greek history with the Roman history that follows it and tailors that synchrony to Cicero's own aims in constructing an oratorical history (26–51; see Chapter 5).[54] The use of Varro is like his eclectic borrowing from other Greek and Roman authors to whom he explicitly or implicitly refers. Cicero drew from several sources for the account of oratorical history and the conceptual framework for writing literary history.

Ciceronian Dialogue

Cicero's own dialogues also offer crucial comparanda for the *Brutus*. Yet, as was the case with texts written by others, comparison to his own texts shows in many ways what the *Brutus* is by showing what it is not. Despite the similar focus on public speech between the *Brutus* and his other rhetorical works (e.g. *de Inventione*, *de Oratore*, *Orator*, *de Optimo Genere Oratorum*), the differences of form and subject emerge clearly. The *Brutus* is far more casual in surveying the technical explanations of the art of oratory:

> At this point it's neither necessary nor our aim to praise eloquence and to indicate its power and how much respect it brings to those who have it.

---

[52] Dahlmann (1962) 654 overstates Varro's influence. Cf. Lebek (1970) 191 n.42, Rösch-Binde (1998) 470–89, Lehmann (2004).

[53] See Chapter 4 on Accius and Porcius Licinus. Douglas (1966a) xxiii notes that Aristotle's περὶ ποιητῶν may have included dialogue elements.

[54] Leo (1901) 220 already understood the uniqueness of the *Brutus* as more than mere biographical histories. Dahlmann (1962) 565–66 n.2 unconvincingly objects to Leo's views. He argues that Cicero draws on the topoi of the *praelocutio* from Greek scholarly treatises on arts and artists, with 26–51 subsequently offering the anticipated historical overview. See Bringmann (1971) 21–24 on the shortcomings of his analysis. In particular, there is no *praelocutio* for Roman oratorical history, and the Greek history anticipates and establishes much of the intellectual framework for understanding the Roman one.

But I'll unflinchingly assert that it's the most difficult of all things, whether it's acquired by doctrine or practice of some kind or by nature. You see, it's said to consist of five departments, each of which is a great art unto itself. For this reason, it's possible to imagine the great power and difficulty in the combination of these five very great arts.

> laudare igitur eloquentiam et quanta vis sit eius expromere quantamque eis, qui sint eam consecuti, dignitatem afferat, neque propositum nobis est hoc loco neque necessarium. hoc vero sine ulla dubitatione confirmaverim, sive illa arte pariatur aliqua sive exercitatione quadam sive natura, rem unam esse omnium difficillumam. quibus enim ex quinque rebus constare dicitur, earum una quaeque est ars ipsa magna per sese. quare quinque artium concursus maxumarum quantam vim quantamque difficultatem habeat existimari potest. (25)

He rejects traditional praise for oratory's power and glances only cursorily at the traditional subject matter. The relative importance of doctrine, practice, or talent for the orator was the motivating question of *de Oratore*, and builds on earlier Greek debates, which have little place in the *Brutus*.[55] The praise of oratory also was and would remain a standard topic.[56] Perfunctory mention of rhetoric's five departments (invention, arrangement, style, memory, delivery) minimizes their individual importance and promotes instead oratory's unity.[57] Technical divisions fall by the wayside as topics of greater magnitude come to the fore, with a brief (and subsequently repeated) notice of the art's difficulty. Cicero essentially advertises: "This Is Not A Rhetorical Treatise."

Even as Cicero undertakes a different kind of project, rhetorical categories inevitably sneak back in. He compliments Brutus using the tripartite evaluation of individuals: "your admirable talent and refined learning and matchless diligence" (*tua et natura admirabilis et exquisita doctrina et singularis industria*, 22). These are the orator's individual qualities or attainments rather than areas of mastery, and they are the most common way to assess individual speakers, whom the dialogue often finds wanting in at least one area. The assessment of personal rather than technical criteria reflects the work's intense emphasis on biography. Such an emphasis reflects a deeper concern about the continued public role of the orator in Roman society, no longer just connecting oratory to great men of the past as, for example, *de Oratore*

---

[55] *De Orat.* 1.5.   [56] E.g. Cic. *Inv.* 1.5, *de Orat.* 1.34; Tac. *Dial.* 5.3–8.4.
[57] See May and Wisse (2001) 20–39 for a synopsis and history of oratory's technical divisions.

had, but seeking to judge all public figures by the standards of oratorical success.

The *Brutus* is the least overtly technical of Cicero's rhetorical works, perhaps in order to give it a distinctly Roman rather than Greek cast. Alternatively, the pursuit of simplicity and comprehensibility may explain deviations from inherited doctrine, such as neglecting the tripartite aims of oratory, *docere*, *delectare*, and *movere* (to teach, to please, and to move), in favor of the bipartite *docere* and *movere* (clearly favoring the latter). This modification was essential for the use of syncrisis to evaluate individuals. It also pigeonholed the Atticists as practitioners of elucidation (*docere*) without emotive force (*movere*). Even so, rhetorical categories are not abandoned altogether. Some figures are discussed by reference to one or more of the five departments of rhetoric, but only rarely – notably with Hortensius – do all five departments structure the judgments. The *Brutus* remains patently untechnical and avowedly historical, stressing instead individual or generational styles as embodiments of oratorical development across history.

Ciceronian Dialogue and the *Brutus*

Whatever the differences of the *Brutus* from Cicero's other dialogues, several similarities elucidate commonalities in the intellectual mindset underlying them. Examining these works can shed valuable light on the subsequent conceptual framework developed for the *Brutus*. First in the 50s and then in a feverish outpouring during 46–44, Cicero wrote on oratory, statehood, religion, and ethics. The *Brutus* would seem to have the most in common with two other works on rhetoric, *de Oratore* (the grand three-book dialogue of 55 BCE), and *Orator*, composed in the months after the *Brutus*. But the connections back to *de Republica* are just as crucial as those to the rhetorical works, and all three should be taken into account in contextualizing the *Brutus*.

Orator

The *Orator* addresses some of the main themes of the *Brutus*, especially the use of Greek role models and the debate with the Atticists. Emphasis is placed above all on the development of prose rhythm in Latin oratory and its Greek forerunners. Cicero will look back in the *Orator* to his laudatory defense of Cato the Younger, written soon after the *Brutus*: "As soon as the *Cato* was finished I began this work" (*hoc sum agressus statim Catone absoluto, Orat.* 35).[58] The *Brutus* also receives notice in *Orator* (*in illo sermone nostro qui est expositus in Bruto, Orat.* 23), and the two share a clear emphasis on the superiority of Demosthenes' forceful style. Cicero asserts that "you'd have no problem saying that Demosthenes is in fact simply perfect and lacking nothing (*plane quidem perfectum et cui nihil admodum desit Demosthenem facile dixeris,* 35).[59] Indeed, *Orator* prizes Demosthenes above all others (*recordor longe omnibus unum me anteferre Demosthenem, Orat.* 23). Isocrates also garners notice as an authority, and is as much *Orator*'s Greek hero as Demosthenes due to his perfection of prose rhythm.

Cicero also promotes the orator's role in the governance of the state and the renown that accrues from it.[60] In the debates over language and style he again targets the Atticists and dismisses Analogy in favor of Anomaly. With considerable rhetorical deftness he avoids direct mention of Caesar's *de Analogia.* Instead he transitions from discussing word-placement and hiatus to defending customary usage (*consuetudo*), which sets up a vigorous attack on the Analogists for disregarding Roman custom and the linguistic sensibilities provided by one's ears (*Orat.* 152–61). While *Orator* continues certain crucial themes and doctrinal debates of the *Brutus,* it pursues them to different ends.

Important differences between the *Orator* and *Brutus* surface as well, most immediately in the quest for the true orator in *Orator,* an ideal unattainable even for Cicero's Greek hero, Demosthenes (*Orat.* 104). Certain terms determine its emphases, especially the justification of prose rhythm through the concepts of moderation and fitting apportionment, expressed in such terms as *moderatio, moderor,* and *temperor.* The term *modus,* meaning both "measured restraint" and "rhythm," conceptually connects the judicious mixing of styles with the variation of rhythms. He partly takes his cue from the *Brutus,* in which he portrayed himself as a moderate Rhodian orator between the Atticist and Asianist extremes. *Orator* partly suggests and partly argues that the grand style consists of mixing various styles and rhythms to produce the most persuasive effects.

---

[58] C. P. Jones (1970) on *Cato,* with *Att.* 12.4.2 (SB 240), *Att.* 12.5.2 (SB 242). Caesar's response, the *Anticato,* was written in two books in March 45, during the battle of Munda; cf. Corbeill (2018a). Fabius Gallus and Brutus also wrote eulogistic *Catones,* and Aulus Hirtius and Caesar an *Anticato* (cf. Plut. *Cic.* 39 on Caesar's favorable response to Cicero's *Cato,* comparing him to Pericles and Theramenes).

[59] On defining the *perfectus orator,* see Barwick (1963) 7–13.

[60] E.g. *Orat.* 141–42 defends its superiority over jurisprudence for the Roman state in peaceful conditions.

One glaring difference is in the *Brutus'* claim that Isocrates first conceived of prose rhythm (*primus intellexit*, 32). *Orator* makes Thrasymachus the *inventor*, while Isocrates is the *perfector* (*Orat.* 174).[61]

As in the *Brutus* moderation allows Cicero to repudiate two extremes, the Atticists without rhythm and Thrasymachus without restraint: "But the discoverer was Thrasymachus, all of whose writings are even excessively rhythmic" (*sed princeps inveniendi fuit Thrasymachus, cuius omnia nimis etiam exstant scripta numerose*, *Orat.* 175). Isocrates truly embodies polished and restrained prose rhythm: he built on his predecessors and did so by applying restraint (*Orat.* 175–76), an idea captured perfectly in the phrase *moderatius temperavit* ("blended more temperately," *Orat.* 176). Despite the *Brutus'* complex evolutionary scheme and continued reverence for Atticus' *Liber Annalis* (*Orat.* 120), development in the *Orator* is far cruder.

Yet the most notable difference between the two texts is the emphasis on three styles versus two: *Orator* connects the three styles to the orator's three chief offices: "there are as many duties of the orator as there are genres of speech: the subtle for demonstrating, the middle for pleasing, the grand for persuading; and in this last one alone lies all the orator's power" (*quot officia oratoris, tot sunt genera dicendi: subtile in probando, modicum in delectando, vehemens in flectendo; in quo uno vis omnis oratoris est*, *Orat.* 69). The *Brutus*, perhaps because of its reliance on binary syncrisis, focuses on two styles and their aims, the simple to instruct and the grand to excite the listeners' susceptibilities (*cum duae summae sint in oratore laudes, una subtiliter disputandi ad docendum, altera graviter agendi ad animos audientium permovendos*, 201). It still acknowledges three chief duties (*docere, delectare, movere*, 185, 276) without schematically assigning a *genus* to each *officium* as does *Orator*.[62] While *Orator* demonstrates how the mixing of genres and blending of rhythms create the grand style, the *Brutus* insists that *vis* and *gravitas* inevitably trump the instructive simplicity of the Atticists. Even when dealing with similar material, each work pursues a distinct purpose in assessing its subject matter. While it is true that *Orator* (and probably the fragmentary *de Optimo Genere Oratorum*) was written around the same time as the *Brutus* and focuses on the Atticism debate, the

---

[61]   Gorgias' prose rhythm results from chance and diligently structured writing, which is missing in Thucydides (*in Thucydide orbem modo orationis desidero*, *Orat.* 234). Cicero seeks to associate Thucydides with the Atticists or those like them (cf. *Orat.* 30–32).

[62]   Hendrickson (1904). See Guérin (2014) for one explanation of the differences, and Chapter 7.

Brutus is quite different from these works, and we will need to look to other dialogues for further conceptual filiations and similarities.

De Republica *(and* de Oratore*)*

The *Brutus'* conceptual framework overlaps in several important ways with the *de Republica* of 54–51 BCE.[63] Its six books on statehood, written on the model of Plato's ten-book *Republic*, though quite different in scope, theme, and presentation, are not an immediately obvious source of inspiration for the *Brutus*. Yet shared themes and ideas, especially from the first two books of *de Republica*, do emerge: the condition of the state and its traditions, how Greek models and intellectual inquiry elucidate Roman achievements, a survey of earlier Roman history through prominent figures, and analogies to biological aging to explain Rome's development. *De Oratore* offers a sustained apology for the value and purpose of oratory. Drawing on prominent political figures from his youth, especially Lucius Licinius Crassus and Marcus Antonius, Cicero reworks inherited Greek theory on rhetoric into a persuasive account of Roman oratory in the service of the state.

There are several similarities (and some minor differences) in how *de Republica* and the *Brutus* portray the past, and to a lesser extent some overlap with Cicero's *de Oratore*. All three works analyze Roman institutions in a moment of crisis, signaled by the impending deaths of Scipio and Crassus, the recent death of Hortensius, and the possible death of oratory (all embodying the republic in some way). All three evince an "elegiac quality," as Catherine Steel has dubbed it, through this motif adapted from dialogues about Socrates' (impending) death.[64] The works form an intellectual trajectory that runs from *de Oratore* through *de Republica* to the *Brutus*. *De Republica* appeared soon before Cicero's departure for Cilicia in 51 and the *Brutus* is his first dialogue after returning.[65] The construction of

---

[63] Zetzel (1995) 1–3 (with bibliography) on the dating. It was publicly available shortly before his departure for Cilicia in mid-51. Zetzel (2013) for an introduction to Cicero's political philosophy, especially in *de Republica*; J. W. Atkins (2013) and (2018) for in-depth discussions.

[64] C. Steel (2013a) 229.

[65] Cicero began *de Legibus* in the 50s but (probably) never finished; the *Brutus* does not mention it. On the date see Dyck (2003) 5–7 and Zetzel (2017) xxii–xxvi. Several similar features of *de Legibus* are worth noting: a long, intricate preface; mention of or allusion to past texts (Cicero's poem *Marius* and *de Republica*, Plato's *Republic*, *Laws*, and *Phaedrus*); a request that Cicero produce some (historical) work; playful notice of the dialogue's fictional status; and intense focus on the interplay of orality and textuality; two of three interlocutors are the same (Cicero and Atticus). If the *Paradoxa Stoicorum*, which is also dedicated to Brutus and suggests Cato is living, preceded the *Brutus*, it is treated as nonexistent.

generations also connects *de Oratore* to *de Republica*: Scaevola Augur is the son-in-law of Laelius and father-in-law of Crassus; Publius Rutilius is the "source" of the *de Republica* and is the uncle of C. Cotta, Cicero's "source" for *de Oratore*. The *Brutus* succeeds *de Republica* in a different manner: *de Republica* inspired the *Liber Annalis*, which in turn inspired the *Brutus*.

Although *de Oratore*, *de Republica*, and the *Brutus* form a kind of dialogue lineage, considerable formal differences separate the first two from the *Brutus*. The earlier dialogues more closely follow Plato (and the Platonist Heraclides of Pontus). The *Brutus* is more Aristotelian: the author speaks at considerable length in his own voice. The earlier works put the dramatic setting into the past and the discussion into the mouths of political giants (the "Scipionic" and "Crassan" groups).[66] Sizeable chunks of Greek doctrine are digested into Romanized versions. Political crisis at Rome is the backdrop for aristocratic *otium* at a countryside villa, as the interlocutors break the discussion up across several days. In *de Oratore* Roman authorities offer Greek doctrine with considerable skepticism, if not discomfort, about the value and purpose of Greek theory. Such anxiety does not trouble *de Republica*'s interlocutors to the same extent; the *Brutus* openly embraces Greek examples and theory while criticizing the Atticists' philhellenism. Potential qualms about seeming too Greek are dispelled by refocusing the problem onto the Atticists and by the work's insistence on Rome's ascendancy.

The presentation of theory is leavened by the citation of historical examples. This interlacing of theory and practice also helps to minimize apparent overreliance on Greek thinkers. Across its six books *de Republica* pairs theory with history by interleaving one book on theory with another showing its application to Roman history: a theory of constitutions (1) and Rome's constitutional development (2); a debate over justice and its utility (3) and a survey of Roman morals and education (4); the *rector rei publicae*, the ideal leader (5) and the statesman in crisis, including an example of the true statesman and his everlasting rewards (6). With greater flexibility the *Brutus* alternates between methodological or technical digressions and the historical accounts of succeeding generations. The *Brutus* treats theory and doctrine briefly and informally without fretting over adapting Greek theory to Roman contexts.

---

[66] The fiction of the "Scipionic circle" has long since been debunked. See Zetzel (1972). Hodgson (2017), focusing on Sulpicius, suggests that Cicero similarly portrays a coherent group of political and intellectual figures around Antonius and Crassus in *de Oratore*.

It is unlikely that equanimity toward adaptation of Greek material in the *Brutus* reflects a substantive change in attitudes toward hellenization. Admittedly, the dialogues of the 50s hark back to the unimpeachable *exempla* of a bygone era, Scipio (d. 129) and Crassus (d. 91), while the *Brutus* is contemporary. And the instructive account of Zethus and Amphion, who represent the active and contemplative lives (*Rep.* 1.30), may serve to acknowledge and alleviate any anxiety. But political pragmatism is stressed throughout that work. Despite apparent differences, the notional separation of doctrine and history in *de Republica* and the *Brutus* is never absolute, in part because the theoretical sections structure their historical counterparts (with history often exposing the limitations of theory), and in part because abstract knowledge and practical experience are ultimately inseparable: the true statesman, like the true orator, relies on theory to foster and to explain practical success in a Roman context.[67]

Considerable stress is laid on how Romans appropriate or adapt Greek predecessors in order to fashion a superior Roman version of an art, be it government or oratory. This chauvinistic appropriation is all too evident in Scipio's unabashed claim that "things taken from elsewhere have in our hands been made better than where they first had existed and where they had been before being brought here from there" (*aliunde sumpta meliora apud nos multo esse facta quam ibi fuissent unde huc translata essent atque ubi primum extitissent*, *Rep.* 2.30).[68] With greater deference Cicero suggests that Roman oratory has outstripped its Greek forerunners: "You see, the one domain in which we were being conquered by conquered Greece we have now either taken from them or surely share with them" (*quo enim uno vincebamur a victa Graecia, id aut ereptum illis est aut certe nobis cum illis communicatum*, 254).[69]

History in *de Republica* and the *Brutus*

Both works have a shared intellectual apparatus for presenting history: Cicero structures and assesses the past, promotes synchronism across cultures, and relies on biological analogies and evolution as explanatory devices. His research into the past adopts the pose of the Greek scholar. He ostentatiously dismisses historical inaccuracy, such as the idea that Numa

---

[67] Also a central point of *de Oratore*, which criticizes the separation of philosophy from rhetoric.
[68] Cf. *de Orat.* 3.95, *Rep.* 3.18.
[69] Oratory at Rome reached maturity and rivaled the Greek canon in the age of Crassus (161); see Chapters 4 and 6. Claims about subsequent improvement are also claims of superiority over Greek oratory. Plutarch has Apollonius Molon confirm what Cicero implies (*Cic.* 4.7).

learned from Pythagoras (in *de Republica*). The *Brutus* criticizes Accius' misdating of the beginning of Roman literature to 207 BCE, which, like the refutation of Pythagoras' association with Numa, was rather low-hanging fruit and hardly original to Cicero. He also champions scrupulousness by acknowledging missing evidence rather than embellishing the gaps: the mother of Ancus Marcius is known but not the father, thus demonstrating how obscure early Roman history is (*Rep.* 2.33). Similarly, he notes missing evidence for early Roman orators whom no early records discuss (*de quibus nulla monumenta loquuntur*, 181).[70]

Most of all both dialogues explain Roman developments by drawing parallels to the Greek world. Synchronism in *de Republica* is broadly apparent in the aligning of Roman kings with Greek poets in Book 2, which Cicero adapts from Cornelius Nepos' *Chronica*.[71] The literary accomplishments of ancient Greece valorize early Roman history: Greece's contemporaneous flourishing is cited as evidence of Rome's early sophistication. Such parallels likewise justify questionable traditions, such as the story of Romulus' deification: if Rome was advanced like Greece, then such tales were not the fabrications of an uneducated and gullible people. This evidence is used as well to equate the Roman and Spartan constitutions and Romulus with Lycurgus (*Rep.* 2.18). *De Republica* gives us a glimpse of Cicero's earlier efforts at synchronizing Greeks and Romans. Such comparisons are made in order to support claims about Rome's cultural and intellectual importance. Cross-cultural comparisons of this sort receive new direction in the *Brutus*. The syncrisis of historical figures, such as the likening of Pisistratus/Solon to Servius Tullius (39), supports the idea of Rome's early political development. The likening of Coriolanus and Themistocles (41–44) implicitly argues for considerable license in the presentation and interpretation of cultural parallels generally. Most crucially, the long account of Roman orators is modeled on the miniature Greek version that precedes it (26–51).[72]

---

[70] That claim at 181 is rather deceptive. Cf. 52 on the difficulty of interpreting such records (*monumenta*).

[71] Zetzel (1995) 75–76 for summary. See above on Nepos' *Chronica*. Scholarly developments in the 50s and 40s are visible too, such as the hotly contested foundation date of Rome: 754/53 in the *Brutus*, the (now) traditional date, previously 751/50. *De Republica* follows Polybius' chronology (1.27.4) and is indebted to Nepos. By 46 Cicero trades Nepos for Varro and Atticus, helping 754/53 become the canonical date. See Fantham (1981). The *Brutus* also abandons Olympic dating and shows no interest in the *ab urbe condita* dating that Atticus presumably used. See Rawson (1972), esp. 41–42.

[72] The Greek account is discussed in Chapter 5. The examples of Coriolanus/Themistocles and Greco-Roman canons are discussed at length in Chapter 4. Parallels between stylistic decline in Demetrius of Phalerum and among the Atticists are discussed in Chapter 6.

The emphasis on synchrony is also integral to both works' temporal categories and narratives of progress. The biological analogies of *de Republica* are developed in the *Brutus*. Book 1 first mentions a state's age by noting Greece's senescence (*prope senescente iam Graecia, Rep.* 1.58.6), while Book 2 focuses on Rome.[73] We'll better understand Rome's origins, Cicero insists, "if I show you our republic being born, and growing, and mature, and finally steady and strong" (*si nostram rem publicam vobis et nascentem et crescentem et adultam et iam firmam et robustam ostendero,* 2.3.2). Similarly, in a methodological digression (2.21–22) after the account of Romulus, Scipio prompts us to see that under Romulus "not only a new people was born … but one mature already and nearly full-grown" (*non solum ortum novum populum … sed adultum iam et paene puberem,* 2.21.1). Agricultural metaphors describe "sowing the state" (*rem publicam serere,* 2.5.1) and Greek learning grafted onto native Roman stock (*insitiva quadam disciplina,* 2.34.1). The *Brutus* remarks on the birth and growth of *eloquentia* in Athens (*et nata et alta,* 39). Solon and Pisistratus are old by Roman reckoning, but young relative to Athenian history (*ut populi Romani aetas est, senes, ut Atheniensium saecla numerantur, adulescentes,* 39). The explanation uses a biological metaphor to elucidate the relative chronologies of two states.

Such analogies underpin both works' promotion of change and evolution to understand civic developments. One key phrase, *temporibus illis* ("relative to the times"), reflects an awareness that historical change requires an understanding of relative historical contexts: not only do times change, but people and customs can or must be judged relative to their times.[74] Teleology emerges in the remarks on "the republic progressing and arriving at its best condition by a kind of natural path and movement" (*progredientem rem publicam atque in optimum statum naturali quodam itinere et cursu venientem, Rep.* 2.30). Individual kings made successive contributions and improvements (*quanta in singulos reges rerum bonarum et utilium fiat accessio, Rep.* 2.37.1). Cicero credits early leaders with two signal contributions each, just as central figures early in the *Brutus* introduce lasting changes that fostered oratory. Romulus gave Romans the auspices and senate, Numa religion and mildness (*Rep.* 2.17.1, 2.27.4). In the *Brutus* Servius Sulpicius Galba (cos. 144) embellished speeches with

---

[73] Cf. *Brut.* 27: *non nascentibus Athenis sed iam adultis.*

[74] *Rep.* 2.4.4; *Brut.* 27, 102, 107, 173, 294 (all preceded by *ut,* which Cicero appears to use in the *Brutus* to distinguish from "at that time"; but cf. 57, without *ut,* although the meaning is hardly certain).

digressions, pleased and moved the audience, and introduced common-places (*loci communes*, 82). Marcus Aemilius Lepidus Porcina (cos. 137) refined style through smoothness of diction (*levitas verborum*) and periodic sentences (*comprensio verborum*, 96). Gaius Carbo (cos. 120) introduced regular training not unlike later declamatory practice (105).

Thus *de Republica* anticipates the ways in which the *Brutus* adapts biological analogies and metaphors to describe the evolution of oratory. Biological ages and aging function as an organizational principle within the *Brutus*, as Cicero employs terms such as *aetas* ("age," "lifetime") and various terms that express different stages within the lifecycle of an organism. He speaks of his own life and accomplishments by noting that "(a man of) my age had performed signal achievements" (*aetas nostra perfuncta rebus amplissimis*, 8; cf. 22). His speaking abilities have reached the final stages of the lifecycle: "just when my oratory was growing gray and achieved a kind of maturity and ripe age" (*cumque ipsa oratio iam nostra canesceret haberetque suam quandam maturitatem et quasi senectutem*, 8).

Already in Aristotle's *Poetics*, biology was one way to understand the development of a genre. Aristotle famously described a genre as an organism that contains a beginning, middle, and end, forever connecting the process of literary development to biology. Roman theorists from Cicero to Velleius Paterculus to Tacitus in his *Dialogus de Oratoribus* readily adopted and redeployed the conceit.[75] Cicero capitalizes on this conceit by using it to map his life onto the life of oratory, asserting that oratory had reached its "first flourishing" (*prima maturitas*) with Crassus' speech in defense of the *lex Servilia* of 106, the year of Cicero's birth (161).[76]

This chapter began by surveying the textual influences on the *Brutus*. The conspectus of intellectual discourses sought to illuminate the conceptual breadth of Cicero's literary history. The *Brutus'* reactionary impulses have most tended to capture scholarly attention – the way in which it mourns the loss of traditional ideas and values, such as the eminence of oratory in politics. Lost in this emphasis on Ciceronian malaise is the work's intensely progressive outlook. Intellectually it is daring, conceptualizing and explaining literary history as no work before it had. Politically its commitments are unwavering, exploring an oratorical future that contains a viable alternative to Caesarian politics. It is also hard at first to align

[75] On schemes of progress, see Dahlmann (1962) 557–79, Edelstein (1967), Novara (1982), esp. 199–270. Halliwell (1986) on the *Poetics*.
[76] The significance of this speech is discussed in Chapter 1.

the work's grander aims throughout with its stated aims in the preface. However, close attention to several contexts valuably illuminates the expansive intellectual scope and contemporary relevance of the dialogue. The *Brutus* draws on several long-standing debates, literary traditions, and contemporary discourses. The filiations and genealogies of Cicero's dialogue are impressively broad-ranging: Greek dialogue and scholarship, Cicero's own endeavors in the tradition of literary dialogue, and the contemporaries whom Cicero explicitly cites: his interlocutors – Atticus and Brutus – and the great scholar Varro. From this wealth of forerunners and influences emerges his eclectic and innovative endeavor to document an artistic tradition in all its complexity.

Cicero's reliance on Greek theory and Greek orators is undeniable, but the presence of Atticus and Brutus, and the overt allegiance to their works as inspirations, stands as a forceful reminder that this dialogue is fundamentally Roman. Cicero treats the works of his interlocutors almost as if they were filters through which scholarship and philosophy can pass, emerging in the *Brutus* as distinctly Roman products. In response Cicero will not merely repay acknowledged debts, but will offer something new to his Roman audience. And that innovation is intertwined with his unrelenting concerns over the civic crisis. His dialogue seeks to open a new entrance onto the intellectual and political stage from which he had so long been barred.

The wealth of possible influences helps us to understand the dialogue's distinct theoretical framework as well as the innovative criteria it uses to document the "literary" time of literary history.[77] Chronology is not the sole marker of progress in the account of oratorical history; rather, Cicero proposes several distinct yet interrelated criteria – analogies and metaphors – that document and explain literary progress. In addition to traditional reckoning by consular years we also encounter biological imagery, biographies, the tenure of political office, the production of artistic works as watersheds to mark development, and the discernment or alignment of meaningful coincidences between artists, states, and literary traditions.

Another crucial effect of the dialogue's explicit lineage through the *Liber Annalis* and the *de Republica* is to remind us of the fundamentally political function of oratorical history. The *Brutus* is a crucial political intervention

---

[77] On time in literary history, see Wellek and Warren (1956) 263–82, esp. 263; see also the end of Chapter 6 and the Conclusion. Cicero's criteria to explain literary development are discussed in Chapters 4, 5, and 6.

at a time when traditional forms of participation, especially forensic and deliberative oratory, had been seriously curtailed. In addition to Atticus and Brutus, another figure looms large in the literary exchange that prompted the *Brutus*: Julius Caesar. Cicero cites and discusses Caesar's *de Analogia* at length, giving it an importance similar to the works of Atticus and Brutus. Caesar dedicated *de Analogia* to Cicero even as he may have criticized *de Oratore*'s diminishment of pure Latinity as a stylistic virtue. Caesar is the only other intellectual with whom such dedicatory exchanges are mentioned in the *Brutus* (Varro is cited but remains insignificant in comparison). Caesar's intellectual contributions, and especially his role in the present crisis, are central to the *Brutus* and are the focus of the next chapter.

CHAPTER 3

Caesar and the Political Crisis

In the spring of 46 BCE there could be little question that Caesar would control Rome and thus – for Romans – the world. Rome's seemingly boundless imperial ambitions had coincided with, and for some observers seemed to culminate in, the ambitions of a single man. Caesar was at this time mopping up the remnants of the republican resistance, which was broken, symbolically if not practically, by defeat at Thapsus and Cato the Younger's suicide in the nearby north African shore-town of Utica. Years later the Neronian-era poet Lucan enshrined Cato in the republican struggle: "the victorious cause pleased the gods, but the lost cause pleased Cato."[1] His gory suicide was protracted by a failed sword-stroke and a doctor's intervention – ultimately Cato ripped out the sewn-up entrails in order to finish the task. The scene was immortalized variously: Cato's allusive reading of Socrates' forced suicide by hemlock, Plutarch's detailed narrative, and the lurid reworkings of Renaissance and Neoclassical painters: Bouchet, Le Brun, Guercino, Guérin, and Delacroix, among others, would fixate and elaborate on the image and its world-tragic potency. Cato's death signaled not only Caesar's triumph but the end of the republic.

The *Brutus* nowhere mentions Cato's demise. It even treats him as still living (118–19), which has complicated exact dating of the work. The gloomy rumblings about recent news and the mandate to avoid talking politics (10–11) intimate the defeat at Thapsus, and there can be little question about Cicero's simmering resentment, though not yet outright hostility, toward Caesar. Still, lingering hopes for a political future effectively ruled out attacking Caesar with the vehemence and venom that he would employ after the dictator's assassination by Brutus and his

[1] *victrix causa deis placuit sed victa Catoni*, Luc. 1.128. Most Americans know the phrase from the shameful appropriation on the Confederate Memorial at Arlington National Cemetery in Virginia. Only gross manipulation can make Cato's legacy justify slavery or the "Lost Cause."

co-conspirators two years later. Brave invective was postponed until after Caesar's death, while in the *Brutus* it remains unclear what Cicero thought exactly or what he felt he could state publicly. In light of the republican losses and Cato's (presumed) death, two vexing questions inevitably surface: what is Cicero's attitude toward Caesar, and what does Cicero seek to accomplish politically?

Uncertainty about the *Brutus'* dates of composition and setting complicates the answers.[2] Cicero wrote the *Brutus* in spring 46 before also completing in that year the *Paradoxa Stoicorum*, his eulogy *Cato*, and the *Orator*.[3] The dialogue seems to unfold right as news about Thapsus is arriving, and chronological indications are confusing. Because Cicero refrains from discussing living orators, mention of Cato's *summa eloquentia* without analysis suggests that he is still alive (118–19). Scipio, who perished soon after Thapsus, is treated similarly (212). Lucius Manlius Torquatus, however, is discussed among those who died during the civil war (265), and contemporary sources state that he died along with Cato.[4]

These notices and other omissions undermine any precise dating of the dialogue. The confusion may have been intentional or the product of circumstance or carelessness. Did Cicero slip when including Torquatus? Had only partial news arrived from Africa? We might excuse Cicero's inconsistency given his admission that long speeches often contain contradictions (209), but he also heavily criticizes the elder Curio's faulty recall (*memoria*) and the chronological inaccuracies of his dialogue (218–19). Brutus expresses shock at such mistakes "especially in a written work" (*in scripto praesertim*, 219). Even the dialogue's own criteria, which might help us explain the contradictory evidence, are themselves contradictory. This uncertainty about the date of the setting contributes to the very uncertainty that Cicero repeatedly manufactures – about his place in the oratorical canon, the future of oratory, and the future of Rome.

Even if we could establish the chronology of authorship with greater precision, countless obstacles make it hard to assess Cicero's attitude in the spring of 46. Like most of his contemporaries he did not know Caesar's

---

[2] On the date, see Robinson (1951), Bringmann (1971) 15–16, Gowing (2000) 62–64.

[3] Probably in that order, though uncertainty attends the *Paradoxa*: Section 5 may refer to the *Brutus*; Cato appears to still be alive. *De Optimo Genere Oratorum* is probably from 46, but a relative chronology cannot be fixed.

[4] Caes. *B. Afr.* 96.1–2; cf. Oros. 6.16.4–5. Kytzler (1970) 274 has Publius Cornelius Lentulus Spinther dying at Thapsus (and thus also confusing the *Brutus'* chronology), but Spinther probably died in 48 after Pharsalia. Similar problems are visible in the composition of *de Divinatione*, which was begun before but completed after Caesar's death.

plans – Caesar himself may not yet have formulated them – and such knowledge would not necessarily translate into Cicero's unfiltered response in a public work such as the *Brutus*. To judge from the roughly contemporary letters and public documents, Cicero's attitude is hardly single-minded.[5] Instead, it reflects the vacillations and changes of opinion that were likely to result from the rapidly changing circumstances. Still, two main imperatives emerge: first, to wait and see what the future will bring, and, second, to encourage Caesar by every means possible to reinstate traditional republican government. The *Brutus* exudes a cautious mixture of expectation, resistance, and even encouragement. Above all Cicero wanted to restore the republic – as he defined it – and the *Brutus* is the first step in realizing that desire.[6]

The uncertainty and complexity of Cicero's views in the spring of 46 have produced a range of scholarly opinion concerning the work's stated or unstated politics. Matthias Gelzer thought that Cicero wished to work alongside Caesar to renew the republic, a view that has found some supporters.[7] Cicero's desire to win Brutus away from Caesar has also remained a prominent focus.[8] Especially appealing has been the possible anti-Caesarian message, with some scholars suggesting that references to Brutus' forefathers encouraged Caesar's assassination.[9] That interpretation will already have been fostered by Brutus' portrayal of his descent from the Brutii and the Servilii, the vanquishers of tyrants.[10] Others have emphasized Cicero's difficulty in addressing Caesar critically or otherwise.[11]

The evidence from Cicero's letters does not provide a clear picture either, or at least the picture that emerges, especially near the end of the civil war, sometimes is critical and sometimes wavers between resigned, hopeful, and conciliatory. Cicero was on fairly good terms with Caesar through much of the 50s. His brother Quintus served on Caesar's military

---

[5] Lintott (2008) 310: "Cicero's attitude to the new regime ... ranged from resignation to exasperation." Gildenhard (2018) surveys the contemporary letters. Narducci (1997) 99–101 and Kurczyk (2006) 306 survey the scholarship.

[6] Jacotot (2014) 202 on Cicero's unification of "pratique rhétorique et défense de la république."

[7] E.g. Kytzler (1970) 277, but he emphasizes Brutus' connection to the tyrannicide L. Junius Brutus and sees the *Brutus* as a precursor to the actions of the Ides of March. M. Gelzer (1938).

[8] Rathofer (1986) is the fullest though not the first exponent of this idea.

[9] Jahn, Kroll, and Kytzler (1964) 34, Strasburger (1990) 29–31, Wassmann (1996) 160–72, Monteleone (2003) 107–322, Dugan (2005) 233–48 (arguing for doublespeak), Martin (2014). Heldmann (1982) 199–213, esp. 207, rejects the pro-tyrannicide thesis.

[10] *RRC* 433/1–2, dated by Crawford to 54 (probably directed at Pompey).

[11] Lowrie (2008) argues for the debilitating trauma of Caesar's rise. Bishop (2019) 173–218 argues that Cicero's preference for Demosthenes is a pattern of figured speech critical of Caesar.

staff in Gaul; via Oppius Caesar lent him money.[12] He courted Caesar's support, happily heard praise from him, and assisted Oppius with the Julian *forum* and *saepta*.[13] Nevertheless, resentment accompanied political pragmatism and was often directed in the same breath at the triumvirate (or Pompey alone) and at Cicero's own political sidelining and impotence.[14] Desperate to avoid civil war, he criticized Caesar's role in bringing it about.[15] After Caesar's march on Rome in 49, Cicero occasionally styled him a tyrant in the manner of Pisistratus.[16] In March 49 he writes of declaiming against a tyrant.[17] Disappointment with the Pompeians after Pharsalus kept him, however, from pursuing the war in Africa.[18] He returned to Italy, biding his time at Brundisium while anxiously awaiting Caesar's clemency.[19] Letters to Atticus, often critical of Caesar (and Pompey) in the lead up to Pharsalus, grow sparse as we approach the year 46, making it hard to precisely gauge his attitude.[20] Letters to his friends in 46 initially express disappointment over Caesar's victory (without necessarily praising the losing side); they also reflect sentiments familiar from the *Brutus*: Cicero's uncertainty toward Caesar and the future, and his hope that studies and writing can cure the republic of its ills (again, the key word *salus* appears).[21] By the end of 46 the once-simmering resentment of Caesar's control boils over.[22]

Amidst Cicero's varying opinions of Caesar and his desire to see the republic restored, the *Brutus* offers a subtle yet coherent challenge to Caesar. The dialogue's sweeping account of oratorical and political history opposes his rise (and the Pompeians' blind insistence on war). Yet Cicero envisions a future for the republic and its oratory. That future draws heavily on the contemporary civil context, as Cicero portrays an ideal state

---

[12] *Att.* 5.1.2 (SB 94; May 51).

[13] E.g. *Att.* 4.5 (SB 80), *Att.* 4.15 (SB 90) relations with Caesar (June/July 56, July 54); *Att.* 4.16 (SB 89) Oppius and projects (July 54).

[14] E.g. *Att.* 4.17 (SB 91; Nov. 54); *Att.* 7.3.4–5 (SB 126; Dec. 50).

[15] E.g. *Att.* 7.9, 7.11, 7.13, 7.17, 7.18, 7.20, 7.26 (SB 132, 134, 136, 141, 142, 144, 150; Dec. 50 to Feb. 49), and *Fam.* 4.2, 8.16 (SB 151, 153; both Apr. 49).

[16] E.g. *Att.* 7.20.2 (SB 144), *Att.* 8.16.2 (SB 166).   [17] *Att.* 9.4 (SB 173; Mar. 49).

[18] *Att.* 11.6 (SB 217; Nov. 48).   [19] Mitchell (1991) 263–4 summarizes it well.

[20] There is a gap from Sept. 47 to Apr. 46, and only *Att.* 12.2 (SB 238; probably Apr. 46), with little to report, before the writing of the *Brutus*. Bringmann (1971) 18–20 offers a sensible overview of Cicero's ambivalence.

[21] E.g. *Fam.* 9.3, 9.2, 9.7, 9.6 (SB 176, 177, 178, 181; mid-Apr. to June, all to Varro); *Fam.* 9.16 (SB 190; July, to Papirius Paetus).

[22] E.g. concerning the elections of 46 for 45, *Att.* 12.8 (SB 245), but with a humorous tone. To Papirius Paetus he complains of the lack of free speech, *Fam.* 9.19.4–5 (SB 194; July 46), the lack of courts, *Fam.* 9.18.1–2 (SB 191; July 46), and the autocratic passage of legislation, *Fam.* 9.15.3–5 (SB 196; fall 46).

in which oratory is the true weapon for civic action. Political oratory and its long history at Rome are to be the saving alternative to contemporary ills, especially to military success pursued for personal aggrandizement rather than for the sake of the republic. This program emerges in the course of the dialogue's preface (1–25), in the central digression on Julius Caesar, which emphasizes the value of civic oratory over military triumph (254–57), and in Cicero's carefully crafted discussions of the orators of the younger generation. Cicero pays special attention to several *exempla* of failed oratory (Curio, Caelius, Publius Crassus) in order then to shed special light on Marcellus, the key figure of the younger generation who embodies the traditional republic against the dangers posed by Julius Caesar. Marcellus' place in the dialogue, just like Caesar's, is shrouded in mystery, because Marcellus is the sole living figure Cicero discusses other than Caesar himself. The discussion of Marcellus, which can be read alongside Cicero's *pro Marcello* of September 46, reveals Cicero's hopeful resistance to Caesar, his desire to compel Caesar – with oratory – to restore the Roman republic.

The Preface at War (1–25)

Under Caesar's rule and lacking the traditional means of political opposition, Cicero's choices were compliance or innovation. He chose the latter, and the *Brutus* is the first stage in crafting and promoting political alternatives to compete with Caesar's unassailable military position. For all Cicero's positioning of the *Brutus* as repayment of literary debts to Atticus and Brutus, he also had to defend his choice to write a treatise and had to provide a larger sense of its urgency. With little delay the preface (1–25) presents the dialogue – and intellectual inquiry more generally – as a means of personal and civic salvation (*salus*).[23]

Though crafting an innovative project, Cicero turns to the rhetorical and philosophical tradition to express his vision of civic engagement. Research into the past has the twin purposes of usefulness (*utilitas*) and honorability (*honestas*). These categories, familiar from deliberative rhetoric and moral philosophy, expressed both the instrumental serviceability of oratorical history and its value as a vehicle to secure public recognition. Cicero measures his new project against what he found in Atticus' *Liber Annalis*, which produced new and useful material: *ille vero et nova, inquam,*

---

[23] Chapter 2 discusses the preface as well, focusing on grief (*dolor*) and salvation (*salus*) amidst the crisis, and the interlocutors' textual exchanges.

mihi quidem multa et eam utilitatem quam requirebam (15).[24] Utility results from the immediate view of the past that Atticus' work afforded a reader. Most of all such texts brought salvation (*salus*), for Cicero and for the republic as a whole.[25] Coupled with utility was honorability (*honestas*), the main term through which Cicero would promote his new project.[26] *Honestas* encompassed at the broadest level the honor that one could achieve by pursuing a course of action, although the abstract idea was often translated into more concrete terms with greater currency, such as authority (*auctoritas*), grandeur (*dignitas*), and renown (*fama, gloria, laus*). Cicero densely populates the preface with all of these terms, emphasizing the importance of *auctoritas* and *dignitas*.[27] *Gloria* and *laus* are cited repeatedly.[28] Leisure time should be "measured and honorable" (*otium moderatum atque honestum*, 8; see below), with *otium* understood to include the learned conversation of dialogues.[29]

This way of defining Cicero's scholarly activities surfaces against the background of traditional paths to honor: military command and triumph as a magistrate. In the 60s and 50s such recognition accrued especially to Caesar and Pompey. Special investiture with multi-year commands brought extraordinary honors, including supplication inflation – the awarding of increasing days of thanksgiving (*supplicationes*) in honor of a general's victories. The rampant pursuit of recognition, whatever its traditional aristocratic basis, culminated in civil war and spurred Cicero to remark in general terms on the opposition of glory to state well-being:

> I am deeply distressed that the republic feels no need of the weapons of counsel, talent, and authority, which I had learned to handle and had

[24] Cicero's response reiterates the terms of Atticus' preceding inquiry: *quid tandem habuit liber iste, quod tibi aut novum aut tanto usui posset esse?* (14).

[25] In older definitions of deliberative categories utility was the main focus but was divided into utility concerned with the safety or preservation of an individual or group (*utilitas tuta*) and utility deriving from the honor something could provide (*utilitas honesta*). *Salus* is closely aligned to the first of these two. *Fin.* 3.64 connects *utilitas* and *salus*. See HWRh s.v. *Utile* for discussion of *utilitas* as a rhetorical category. The consideration of *honestas* and *utilitas* was a topos in the justification of oratory, e.g. *de Orat.* 1.30–34 (Crassus) or Tac. *Dial.* 5.4–10.8 (Marcus Aper).

[26] Brutus later refers to deliberative categories by noting the *fructus et gloria* (benefit and renown) acquired through oratory (though Brutus prefers oratory in itself, *studium ipsum exercitatioque*, 23).

[27] *Auctoritas*: 2, 7 (×2), 9. *Dignitas*: 1 (×2), 25. See Hellegouarc'h (1972) 295–320 (*auctoritas*) and 388–424 (*dignitas*).

[28] *Gloria* (and related terms) at 2, 3, 8, 9, 23; *laus* (and related terms) at 2, 9, 24, 25. See Hellegouarc'h (1972) 362–87. Cf. *praestans vir* (elsewhere rendering Aristotle's πολιτικός) at 7 with Hellegouarc'h (1972) 337–38.

[29] Cf. e.g. *de Orat.* 1.1–3 with the focus on *otium cum dignitate*. On *otium* see André (1966), Stroup (2010) 43–48, and Hanchey (2013). On *otium cum dignitate*, Boyancé (1941), Wirzubski (1954), Kaster (2006) 322 (with bibliography 31–32 n.70), Altman (2016) 18.

grown accustomed to, and which befit not only a man distinguished in state service but also a community enjoying moral and civic order. But if there was any time in the republic when the speech and authority of a good citizen could snatch the arms out of the hands of raging citizens, it was surely at that time when the advocacy of peace was precluded by either the wrongheadedness or the timidity of men.

It was my own experience that, although many other things warranted lamenting, I was still pained by the fact that, at a time when a man of my age and considerable accomplishments ought to seek safe haven, not in indolence and idleness, but in restrained and honorable leisure, and just when my oratory was growing gray and achieved a kind of maturity and ripe age, then were arms taken up, and those same men who had learned to make glorious use of them could not find a way to make beneficial use of them.

equidem angor animo non consili, non ingeni, non auctoritatis armis egere rem publicam, quae didiceram tractare quibusque me adsuefeceram quae-que erant propria cum praestantis in re publica viri tum bene moratae et bene constitutae civitatis. quod si fuit in re publica tempus ullum, cum extorquere arma posset e manibus iratorum civium boni civis auctoritas et oratio, tum profecto fuit, cum patrocinium pacis exclusum est aut errore hominum aut timore. ita nobismet ipsis accidit ut, quamquam essent multo magis alia lugenda, tamen hoc doleremus quod, quo tempore aetas nostra perfuncta rebus amplissimis tamquam in portum confugere deberet non inertiae neque desidiae, sed oti moderati atque honesti, cumque ipsa oratio iam nostra canesceret haberetque suam quandam maturitatem et quasi senectutem, tum arma sunt ea sumpta, quibus illi ipsi, qui didicerant eis uti gloriose, quem ad modum salutariter uterentur non reperiebant. (7–8)

With his intellectual weapons (*arma*), Cicero (*praestantis viri, boni civis*) stands as the bulwark against rabid warmongers, presumably Pompey, Caesar, and their adherents. The conceptual distinction between figurative and actual weapons is signaled by the balanced use of *didiceram/didicerant* in the first and last sentences. Cicero consistently employs the weapons of peace: talent, authority, and especially oratory (*oratio*, used twice and reinforced by *patrocinium*).[30] The opposition of *gloriose* to *salutariter* undermines military valor because of its insalubrious effects on the body politic: Cicero stresses that individual glory in war must also benefit the republic. Cited as well is the common metaphor of the ship of state, here applied to his own career, and his own proper conduct is underlined in the

---

[30] On *arma* in connection to oratory, cf. *de Orat.* 2.72, Quint. *Inst.* 9.1.33, Assfahl (1932) 83–100, Fantham (1972) 155–58, Fox (2007) 181. Bishop (2019) 184 on *Demosthenis arma* as part of the *Nachleben* of Demosthenes' oratory.

decision to seek honorable *otium* after a political career, an idea suggestive of past political greats such as Laelius and Scipio Aemilianus (as Cicero portrayed them). The differences between such an ideal statesman and Cicero's contemporaries draw in sharpest relief the moral and political failures of those who covet power for its own sake.[31]

The conceit of oratorical weaponry recurs throughout the *Brutus* as a countervailing model to military power. Oratory deserves greater credit than martial activity, though the two resemble one another: *vis* ("forcefulness," "violence") is a key characteristic of the most accomplished orators.[32] It is the hallmark of Demosthenes, who is lionized throughout. The dialogue's other hero, Pericles, terrified his contemporaries with the forcefulness of his speech (*vim dicendi terroremque timuerunt*, 44). *Vis* is nearly an antonym of *elegantia* ("gracefulness," "charm"), best exemplified in the opposition of Galba (*vis*) to Laelius (*elegantia*, 89). Among Roman orators, only Galba, Antonius, Curio, and Cicero stand out for their forcefulness, but most of all it is the hallmark of Antonius and Cicero.[33]

Cicero aligns forcefulness (*vis*) with the arousal of emotion (*movere*), the cardinal virtue of oratory in the *Brutus*. It also defines the power that oratory has had in all historical periods, even those in which there is little or no formal evidence of great orators: "Yet still I don't doubt that oratory has always had incredible power" (*nec tamen dubito quin habuerit vim magnam semper oratio*, 39); the statement paves the way for Cicero's connection of *vis* to Odysseus and oratory's high esteem across generations (*honos eloquentiae*, 39). Romans also associated *vis* with conceptions of elite

---

[31] *De Republica, de Amicitia* and *de Senectute* are central to Cicero's idealization. Cicero bitterly contrasts enforced *otium* with the dignified retreat of Scipio Africanus after a long and honorable career (*Off.* 3.1–2).

[32] Despite its fundamental importance, *vis* as a general and unqualified character of speech occurs rarely in Cicero's catalogue: among Greeks it is used of Odysseus (40) and Pericles (44); among Romans we find it in Galba (89), Antonius (144), and it is Curio's sole saving grace (220), just as its absence is Calidius' chief shortcoming (276). The examples in connection with Pisistratus (41), Philippus (304), and Cicero himself (233) do not address an absolute judgment of style (Pisistratus has somewhat more force than his predecessors; Philippus gave testimony with the vehemence of a prosecutor; Cicero refuses to discuss his own *vis ingenii*).

[33] Cicero also notes that Philippus' passionate testimony resembled the forcefulness and fullness of a prosecutor (*cuius in testimonio contentio et vim accusatoris habebat et copiam*, 304). Cicero does hedge some in his examples in a way that suggests that only few orators truly have *vis*: the example of Galba is used to establish a dichotomy between *vis* and *elegantia* and to show that *vis* can also be lost in the transcription of speeches; Carbo is said to have *vis* and nothing else and yet still he is an *orator*, a claim Cicero makes in order to establish *vis* as a fundamental oratorical requirement. The only two orators with unqualified *vis* are Antonius and Cicero, who also have fullness of expression: *vis et copia*; these two characteristics were essential for major forensic cases (*vi atque copia quam genus illud iudici et magnitudo causae postulabat*, 15).

Roman men, through terms such as *vir* and *virtus* ("man" and "manly excellence"), and aligned oratorical power with proper male conduct.[34]

To be sure, *vis* was also a more run-of-the-mill descriptor, translating the Greek technical term δύναμις and common in more neutral phrases such as *vis dicendi*, which means little more than "the capacity to speak (well)." The association of weapons with persuasion was also nothing new, and martial metaphors are part of oratory's stock in trade. Demetrius of Phalerum is criticized for seeming to be trained in a gymnasium rather than with battle weapons (*non tam armis institutus quam palaestra*, 37).[35] Antonius will be described as perfectly disposing the elements of his speeches as "horsemen, foot-soldiers, and light infantry [are] by a general" (*ab imperatore equites, pedites, levis armatura*, 139). Even today we are prone to craft martial metaphors when wishing to lend gravity or urgency to political or social movements – think about the contemporary US slogans "fighting crime," "the war on drugs," and "the battle against cancer." The *Brutus* skillfully draws on traditional associations of rhetoric with power and violence – emphases that are not necessarily opposed to moral and civic integrity – in order to present oratory as a rival force to military power. Thus the account of oratory demonstrates its centrality to state well-being and simultaneously diminishes military achievement. Along the way, Caesar will increasingly be pulled into the center of the work's focus.

The Conquered Conquer Caesar

Since antiquity readers have traced back the events of the Ides of March 44 to the *Brutus*.[36] Reading back from later history has the tendency, however, to distort what exists in the dialogue. Without the assistance of hindsight there is little clear evidence that Cicero there encourages Caesar's assassination. References to contemporary politics remain largely oblique. Scattered allusions and touches of gloom at the outset and the conclusion are cast in language vague enough that the interlocutors seem to lament the general state of affairs, the restrictions on the courts since 52, civil war since 49, and the uncertainty of oratory's future. Explicit mention of Caesar, in connection with his style and his treatise *de Analogia*, abounds

---

[34] Gunderson (2000), Dugan (2005).

[35] Probably a pun: *palaestra* was also a covered portico for philosophers; cf. *Fam.* 7.23.2 (SB 209), *de Orat.* 1.98.

[36] Van der Blom (2010) 97–98, with Plut. *Brut.* 2.1; Cass. Dio 44.12, App. *B Civ.* 2.112.

in praise: "Toward Caesar the orator, writer, and scholar he is generous and almost excessive in flattery," says Hendrickson.[37] Yet given the pressing realities of Caesar's hold on power, we might expect much more. Instead, much of the discussion focuses on Caesar's *de Analogia*, which should be read in light of the work's claim that it was inspired by such literary exchanges between interlocutors. No other such exchanges are mentioned (Varro, for example, is cited only by name). Just as the *Brutus* settles a debt for Atticus' *Liber Annalis* and Brutus' *de Virtute*, it also indirectly repays Caesar for *de Analogia*, the treatise allegedly dedicated to Cicero.

Caesar's importance for the *Brutus* is in his ghostlike quality, haunting the dialogue without ever assuming a clear place in it. Even if Caesar is named at various points, no mention in isolation reveals a clear purpose. Yet the sum of references and allusions taken together does outline a coherent challenge to Caesar both politically and stylistically. Throughout the work Cicero directly and indirectly challenges martial authority as a source of political authority. He first likens oratory and military victory through the term *prudentia* ("knowledge," "sound thinking"): "you see, no one can speak well unless they possess sound thinking; this is why the man who strives after true eloquence also strives after sound thinking, which no one, even in the greatest battles, can calmly forgo" (*dicere enim bene nemo potest nisi qui prudenter intellegit; qua re qui eloquentiae verae dat operam, dat prudentiae, qua ne maxumis quidem in bellis aequo animo carere quisquam potest*, 23).[38] The preface concludes with strident assertions about oratory's difficulty:

> You're quite right, Brutus, and I'm all the more pleased by this praise of speaking,[39] because no one is so humble as to think that he cannot acquire or has acquired the other things that were once thought the fairest in our state; I don't know of anyone who's been made eloquent by a victory.

> Praeclare ... Brute, dicis eoque magis ista dicendi laude delector, quod cetera, quae sunt quondam habita in civitate pulcherrima, nemo est tam humilis qui se non aut posse adipisci aut adeptum putet; eloquentem neminem video factum esse victoria. (24)

---

[37] Hendrickson (1962) 8.

[38] The preface repeatedly connects the good citizen (*civis bonus*, 2, 6, and 7) with (practical) wisdom (*sapientia*, 2 and 9) and *prudentia* (2, 11, and 23 [×2]).

[39] Martha and Hendrickson understand *ista dicendi laude* as Brutus' renown. Translating it as Brutus' praise for the art of eloquence seems more sensible (cf. Kaster 2020).

The insistence that oratory is more difficult than military victory – and presumably more valuable as a consequence – is new to Cicero's rhetorical treatises.[40] This first pass at upending so traditional a hierarchy is elaborated on in one of the work's most rhetorically brilliant digressions:[41]

"Then," Brutus said, "I think it friendly and superbly complimentary that he said that you're not only the first pioneer of fullness, which was great praise, but that you even have served well the renown and excellence of the Roman people. You see, the one domain in which we were being conquered by conquered Greece we have now either taken from them or surely share with them. Although I wouldn't rank this glorious testimony of Caesar above your public thanksgiving (*supplicatio*), still I'd rank it above the triumphs of many men."

"That," I said, "is quite right, Brutus, provided that this is evidence of Caesar's true judgment and not of his goodwill. You see, whoever that man is, if he exists, who not only revealed but even gave birth to fullness of speech in our city, he certainly conferred greater dignity upon our people than those renowned conquerors of Ligurian strongholds, which, as you know, resulted in a great many triumphs. But if we want to hear the truth, disregarding those divine plans of action in which often the salvation of the state – either in war or at home – has been secured, the great orator far excels those petty commanders. 'But a commander is of greater utility,' someone will say. Who'd deny it? But still – and I'm not afraid that you'll roar in protest; on the contrary, there's room here to say what you think – I'd rather have one speech of Lucius Crassus on behalf of Manius Curius than two of those outpost triumphs. 'But it was more useful that a Ligurian outpost be captured than that Manius Curius be well defended,' someone will say. All right; but it was also of greater utility to the Athenians to have sturdy roofs over their houses than to have that most beautiful ivory statue of Minerva. I'd still rather be Phidias than the best setter of roof beams. That's why we must weigh carefully not a man's utility but his true value, especially since only a few can paint or sculpt remarkably, but you can't have a lack of workmen and heavy lifters."

Tum Brutus: amice hercule, inquit, et magnifice te laudatum puto, quem non solum principem atque inventorem copiae dixerit, quae erat magna laus, sed etiam bene meritum de populi Romani nomine et dignitate. quo

---

[40] At *de Orat.* 1.6–8 Cicero suggests the comparison without claiming oratory's superiority to military accomplishment, even if oratory is the most difficult field. The *de Officiis* (44 BCE) will, like the *Brutus*, emphasize Cicero's squelching of the Catilinarian conspiracy as an act superior to military victory, apparently regardless of size: Cicero calls on Pompey after his third triumph, in 61 BCE, as evidence for his claim (*Off.* 1.77–78). On the much-debated *cedant arma togae*, see Volk and Zetzel (2015).

[41] This hierarchical reordering is central to *pro Marcello*, which ranks civic clemency above military victory.

enim uno vincebamur a victa Graecia, id aut ereptum illis est aut certe nobis
cum illis communicatum. hanc autem, inquit, gloriam testimoniumque
Caesaris tuae quidem supplicationi non, sed triumphis multorum
antepono.

    Et recte quidem, inquam, Brute; modo sit hoc Caesaris iudici, non
benevolentiae testimonium. plus enim certe adtulit huic populo dignitatis
quisquis est ille, si modo est aliquis, qui non inlustravit modo sed etiam
genuit in hac urbe dicendi copiam, quam illi qui Ligurum castella expugna-
verunt: ex quibus multi sunt, ut scitis, triumphi. verum quidem si audire
volumus, omissis illis divinis consiliis, quibus saepe constituta est salus
civitatis aut belli aut domi, multo magnus orator praestat minutis imper-
atoribus.[42] 'at prodest plus imperator'. quis negat? sed tamen – non metuo
ne mihi adclametis; est autem quod sentias dicendi liber locus – malim mihi
L. Crassi unam pro M'. Curio dictionem quam castellanos triumphos duo.
'at plus interfuit rei publicae castellum capi Ligurum quam bene defendi
causam M'. Curi'. credo; sed Atheniensium quoque plus interfuit firma
tecta in domiciliis habere quam Minervae signum ex ebore pulcherrimum;
tamen ego me Phidiam esse mallem quam vel optumum fabrum tignuar-
ium. quare non quantum quisque prosit, sed quanti quisque sit ponder-
andum est; praesertim cum pauci pingere egregie possint aut fingere,
operarii autem aut baiuli deesse non possint. (254–57)

The passage has long been overshadowed by the surrounding highlights
in which Atticus discusses Caesar's style and his *de Analogia*. According to
Cicero (via Atticus) Caesar praised him for being essentially the first to
introduce fullness of expression as an oratorical virtue: *paene principem
copiae atque inventorem* (253). The compliment was worth hearing more
than once, as Cicero has Brutus reprise Caesar's language while omitting
the hedging adverb *paene* (254). Brutus' remark effects the transition into
this digression, whose argument proceeds in interlocked steps that lack a
clear logical progression. He boldly asserts the preeminence of Cicero's
supplicatio over the triumphs of many men, a partial but not yet complete
demotion of military victory. Cicero adapts the general idea by promoting
his own *copia* over Ligurian triumphs. In a further step he erases the
distinction between domestic and foreign affairs by claiming that the
state's preservation (*salus*) has been assured by divine counsels both at
war and at home. Cicero then imagines the objections of a fictive interlocutor only to concede the utility of triumphs (*prodesse, plus interesse*). He
concludes, however, by asserting that true achievement lies in quality
(*quanti esse*) not utility (*quantum prodesse*), citing the beauty

---

[42] I have deleted *imperatorum sapientia* before *salus civitatis* (Kaster 2020, following Fuchs).

(*pulcherrimum*) of Phidias' statue of Athena/Minerva in comparison to everyday roofs.

Cicero's strategy is not simply to devalue military success but to portray his own range of accomplishments as the preeminent contribution to the Roman state. Along the way he bridges the divide between military and civic achievement, and this conflation of two notionally distinct categories largely accounts for the ambiguity – or apparent contradictions – in the passage and for the details that Cicero selects for special emphasis. The passage begins with an abrupt transition to the justification of Cicero's *supplicatio* and its value over a triumph. We are never told which *supplicatio* is meant: for suppression of the Catilinarian conspiracy or for his military command in Cilicia? The former is the obvious choice, given that the *supplicatio* is contrasted with a triumph, which Cicero was not awarded but surely coveted. In his proconsular command of the province of Cilicia in 51–50 Cicero won some minor skirmishes near the Syrian border and was hailed by his troops as *imperator*, an exclamation that was a precursor, though no guarantee, of a formal triumph. Subsequently the senate awarded him a *supplicatio* after considerable political maneuvering at Rome and despite the recalcitrance of Cato the Younger.[43]

The coveted triumph would have partly restored his previous *dignitas*, since impaired by exile, but it never materialized and was perhaps an unrealistic expectation.[44] The recent calamity of Crassus' army at Carrhae in 53 would have been on anyone's mind in 50 BCE, and the Parthians continued to threaten the Romans in Syria, but Cicero's victory was meager, others had taken the lead in securing Rome's eastern possessions, and at least some senators opposed further honors.[45] Then again Cicero's minor success may be the reason for the faint tone of bitterness in his mention of insignificant triumphs; Lentulus Spinther, who governed Cilicia from 56 to 54, would receive a triumph in 51, and if so many others had received a triumph for so little, why not Cicero?[46] He had also done much more in the course of his career: the emphasis on the *supplicatio* and his calculated refusal to specify which one capitalizes on his having received

---

[43] See several of the essays in Rosillo-López (2017) on the backroom maneuvering and the use of intermediaries for political arm-twisting in general.

[44] Cf. *Att.* 6.6.4 (SB 121). Wistrand (1979), Beard (2007) 187–96, van der Blom (2016) 237–41, Morrell (2017) 106–16.

[45] Cicero was incensed at Cato's duplicity: Cato, promoting supplication inflation, got his son-in-law Bibulus twenty days of *supplicationes*, despite Bibulus' nearly bungled efforts to repel the Parthians and secure Syria. See Morrell (2017) 197–200 for an overview; Cic. *Att.* 7.2.7 (SB 125); Wistrand (1979) 37–40.

[46] *Att.* 5.21.4 (SB 114).

not one but two separate *supplicationes*, one for quashing the Catilinarian conspiracy in 63 and one for the Cilician victory in 50.[47]

Criticism of martial achievement emerges in various ways, most evidently in the dismissal of petty Ligurian triumphs.[48] The lengthy promotion of oratory (254–57) over martial success is structured around the deliberative opposition of *utilitas* (utility) to *honestas* (honorability), familiar from the preface (discussed above). The latter term, *honestas*, could also be expressed by other stand-ins, such as *dignitas* (254, 255). Cicero had already primed the reader to contrast oratory with military achievement in the earlier syncrisis of Laelius and Scipio (83–85). Just as Laelius was greater in learning and speaking, so Scipio was greater in war (84). The reason, we are told, is that human custom refuses men priority in more than one field (85).[49]

Cicero partly dismisses the sheer quantity of Roman triumphs as part of his attack on them: the fact that there are so many is a sign that they can be achieved easily, whereas Cicero's contribution to oratory is a singular accomplishment. This contrast of one versus many is reinforced in the subsequent example of Phidias' great statue of Athena Parthenos (Athena the maiden), partly sheathed in ivory and clad with detachable gold plates, which was the centerpiece of the Greek Parthenon.[50] The statue stands in sharp contrast to the work of countless everyday roofers. The terms Cicero here uses are important as well. In his claim that one "must weigh carefully not how much each man is beneficial, but how much he is truly worth" some careful wordplay is evident: the sheer quantity of basic objects (triumphs/roofs) would of course seem to outweigh one single object (oratory/Minerva), but this is proven false when Cicero makes the transition from physical weighing to conceptual weighing (both ideas are present in the verb *ponderare*, "to weigh" and "to ponder"). When one considers that Athena/Minerva is an immense ivory-clad statue with gold plates, her value is of course greater. Cicero has selected his image well, since one

---

[47] With a dash of humor Kaster (2005) 134–35 compares the Academy Awards' "lifetime achievement" Oscar.

[48] Several triumphs, concentrated in the second century, were awarded for defeating the disorganized if rugged Ligurians, natives inhabiting the northwestern Mediterranean basin in northern Italy, Gaul, and Spain. One might be tempted to see here indirect criticism of Caesar, whose command included the two Gauls in northern Italy and southern France, where the Ligurians, though distinct from the Gauls themselves, were based and still active.

[49] Gell. *NA* 17.21.1 catalogues men known for command or talent: *vel ingenio vel imperio nobiles insignesque*.

[50] Chapter 8 discusses Cicero's comparison of himself to Minerva and the stylistic evaluation of Caesar's *commentarii*, arguing for a much greater importance in the complex analogies of sculptor and orator/historian.

element in particular of the statue, gold, would actually be placed in the balance for weighing (*ponderare*), and the stories surrounding the statue in Plutarch focus specifically on that aspect – Pericles made the gold pieces detachable so that they could be weighed up, a fact that saved Phidias from prosecution for embezzlement of public funds.[51] Even Cicero's dismissive vocabulary draws attention to the act of weighing: it is not just any artisans that he cites, but the *tignuarius faber*, the craftsman who makes support beams (*tigna*). When he then says that there's no shortage of workers (*operarii*) he cites one specific group, the *baiuli* ("porters," "stewards"), that is, those whose job entails carrying heavy loads, small details that help sustain the image of weighing value. By contrasting lowly roofs with Minerva and the Parthenon towering above on the Athenian acropolis, Cicero suggests that military victory is merely a basic substructure holding up Rome's greatness to serviceable ends. Militarism is not truly outstanding, *praestans* or *excellens*, the evaluative terms derived from the language of spatial distinction.

Phidias' statue also marvelously straddles the divide between the distinct virtues of knowledge and military valor. The goddess embodies both wisdom and war, often simultaneously depicted with the Athenian symbol for wisdom, the owl, and a spear or sword. The statue along with the Parthenon was promoted by Pericles, the perfect example of the general, statesman, and orator, who in the *Brutus* obtains an otherwise unparalleled position among Greek orators.[52] This apparent digression from discussion of Caesar (253–57) crucially expresses the dialogue's ideological aims, redefining true accomplishment on behalf of the republic and depicting Cicero as the embodiment of that ideal. Caesar and his rise are nevertheless the immediate, if unexpressed, point of reference, and Cicero meaningfully places the digression in the middle of his discussion of Caesar. Yet Caesar's counterpart, Marcus Claudius Marcellus, is equally crucial to this larger digression.

Marcellus, the *pro Marcello*, and the *Brutus*

Alongside Caesar, Marcellus is the only other living orator who is discussed. The pairing and the praise of Marcellus are remarkable, not only

---

[51] Plut. *Per.* 31.2–3. According to Plutarch, Phidias was condemned later and died in jail for having carved a likeness of himself (and Pericles) into the depicted battle against the Amazons (31.4–5).

[52] In *de Oratore* and *Orator* his role is considerably diminished. Isoc. *Antid.* 234 makes him the height of Greek eloquence; cf. Thuc. 1.139.4.

because Cicero must invent a creative loophole in his rule against discussing the living (only Brutus and Atticus discuss the oratory of Marcellus and Caesar), but also because Marcellus is hard to imagine as an appropriate counterpart to Caesar. Somewhat younger than Caesar and considerably younger than Cicero, he was not among the finest orators, though his successful career included a consulship. There must be some reason for giving him such a place of prominence next to Caesar. Robert Kaster has asked, "Is their unexpected juxtaposition, with the highest compliments paid to both, intended to make a statement?"[53] His inclusion is central to Cicero's political aims, both as a response to Caesar and also as part of Cicero's vision for the future of the Roman republic. That vision can be discerned as well in Cicero's *pro Marcello* of September 46, a speech praising Caesar for pardoning Marcellus, and focusing on the tensions and themes of that speech will productively illuminate the politics of the *Brutus*.[54]

Marcus Claudius Marcellus came from an established plebeian family with noteworthy ancestors. Along with Servius Sulpicius Rufus, Marcellus was the consul of 51, followed in that office by Gaius (his cousin) in 50 and Gaius (his brother) in 49. He staunchly opposed Caesar before the civil war and at Pharsalus. After Pompey's defeat he went into self-imposed exile in Mytilene, on Lesbos, where he remained at the time of the *Brutus* and beyond. In September 46 the fate of Marcellus was decided at a meeting of the senate, and Caesar's pardon prompted Cicero's speech *pro Marcello*. Marcellus delayed his return and would never arrive. Servius Sulpicius Rufus reports that in May 45 he was treacherously murdered in Piraeus by his friend Magius Cilo.[55]

Contrary to what its name suggests, the *pro Marcello* was not a speech of defense or justification – as the *pro Rege Deiotaro* and *pro Ligario* were – but a political statement directed at Caesar. In this and other respects it shares a common intellectual and political framework with the *Brutus*. When Cicero mentions that Marcellus consoles himself (*consoletur se*, 250, quoted in full below), he seems to provide a reference back to the work's

[53] Kaster (2020) 17; cf. 16 "is there nonetheless a political stance to be discerned in the dialogue?" What follows seeks to answer Kaster's questions.
[54] Strasburger (1990) 30–31, Gowing (2000) 59–61, Lintott (2008) 315. Gotoff (1993) xxvi notes the similar exculpatory language of communal misfortune in 250 and in the Caesarian Orations.
[55] In *Fam.* 4.4.3–4 (SB 203) Cicero reports the senate meeting to Marcellus; in *Fam.* 4.7–9 (SB 229–31) Cicero urges Marcellus to return to Rome; *Fam.* 4.11 (SB 232) is Marcellus' thankful acknowledgment of Cicero's efforts on his behalf; in *Fam.* 4.12 (SB 253) Sulpicius reports Marcellus' murder.

preface and especially to Brutus' epistolary treatise, *de Virtute*, cited (indirectly) as a source of inspiration for Cicero and the *Brutus*. Consolation is a theme in the preface (*consolari*, 11) and the conclusion (*consolatione sustentor*, 330), the only other uses of the term in the work. As far as we can tell, Marcellus played an important role in Brutus' treatise, which offered philosophical consolation (*consolatio*) in the face of political turmoil, emphasizing *virtus* and promoting self-sufficiency as a means to individual well-being.[56]

In *pro Marcello* and the *Brutus* Cicero intertwines his own fate with that of other significant figures. The *Brutus* fixates on Hortensius in the past and Brutus in the future, oratorically and politically, and ties the fate of each to the fate of the republic. The *pro Marcello* similarly intertwines Cicero with the political fortunes of his allies:

> By restoring Marcus Marcellus to the republic at your [the senators'] instigation, Caesar restored me to myself and to the republic without anyone's intercession and restored other dignified men to themselves and their fatherland.

> cum M. Marcellum deprecantibus vobis rei publicae conservavit, me et mihi et item rei publicae, nullo deprecante, reliquos amplissimos viros et sibi ipsos et patriae reddidit. (*Marc.* 13)

Both texts announce Cicero's reentry into politics at Rome, though in different ways: the *Brutus* announces Cicero's return to written politics, the *pro Marcello* to spoken politics. In many respects the *Brutus* is the theoretical justification for the immediate practical aims of the *pro Marcello*. This explains the central tension in both texts: how to win over Caesar while offering an alternative vision of the Roman republic founded on its institutions and tradition. In this regard the aims are similar but given different weight: the *Brutus* proposes a future with oratory at the center of civic affairs. The *pro Marcello* insists on restoring order and government: "the courts must be established, credit restored, vices checked, birth rates fostered: everything that collapsed and flowed away must be bound by strict laws" (*constituenda iudicia, revocanda fides, comprimendae libidines, propaganda suboles: omnia, quae dilapsa iam diffluxerunt, severis legibus vincienda sunt, Marc.* 23).

In both works conspicuous praise of Caesar accompanies the subordination of military achievement to civic accomplishment: Cicero's civic

---

[56] On *de Virtute* see Chapter 2.

actions surpass military triumphs (254–57, discussed above). The deft rhetoric of *pro Marcello* coaxes and cajoles Caesar to accept Cicero's view of the republic. Military victory, however praiseworthy, depends on others' achievements and the gifts of fortune. Civic accomplishments, including the pardoning of Marcellus and the eventual restoration of the republic, are the true source of enduring achievement. Caesar is portrayed as a kind of ideal statesman along the lines found in Cicero's *de Republica*, and James Zetzel rightly calls the speech an "exercise in redescription."[57] Cicero redefines Caesar's actions as a partial restoration of the republic in order to promote its full restoration.

The political relevance of Marcellus, and his closeness to Cicero, emerge in the surprising insistence on the similarities between the two men:

> "Well then, what's your opinion of the man you often heard," I said.
>
> "What do you think," Brutus asked, "other than that you'd find him like yourself?"
>
> "If that's so," I responded, "I'd certainly want you to like him as much as possible."
>
> "It is," he replied, "and I like him exceedingly and for good reason. You see, he both studied and set aside other interests to pursue one thing and exercised himself arduously with daily activities. And so, he makes use of choice words and density of thought, and his speech is made attractive and brilliant by the sonorous voice and dignified movement, and all qualities attend on him so that you'd think he lacked none of the orator's virtues. And he merits praise too, since in this state of affairs he consoles himself – as much as is possible given the inevitable fate we share – with the best intentions and even a renewed commitment to learning. You know I saw the man recently in Mytilene and, as I just said, I saw a true man. And so, whereas I regarded him previously as like you in speaking, I really noticed a much greater similarity, since he's been equipped with full learning by Cratippus, an especially learned man, who, I gathered, is a close friend of yours."
>
> "Although," I responded, "I'm always happy to hear the praises of an excellent man and very good friend, still it brings me right to the thought of our shared miseries, and I'd carried on our discussion here because I sought to forget them. But I want to hear what Atticus in fact thinks of Caesar."

Quid igitur de illo iudicas quem saepe audisti?
Quid censes, inquit, nisi id quod habiturus es similem tui?

---

[57] Gotoff (1993), (2002), Gildenhard (2011) 225–43 on the Caesarian Orations. Krostenko (2005) on the protreptic function of stylistic registers in *pro Marcello*. Tempest (2013) on *de Republica* and *pro Marcello*; "redescription": Zetzel (2009) 280.

Ne ego, inquam, si ita est, velim tibi eum placere quam maxume.

Atqui et ita est, inquit, et vehementer placet; nec vero sine causa. nam et didicit et omissis ceteris studiis unum id egit seseque cotidianis commentationibus acerrume exercuit. itaque et lectis utitur verbis et frequentibus <sententiis>, splendore vocis, dignitate motus fit speciosum et inlustre quod dicitur, omniaque sic suppetunt, ut ei nullam deesse virtutem oratoris putem; maxumeque laudandus est, qui hoc tempore ipso, quod[58] liceat in hoc communi nostro et quasi fatali malo, consoletur se cum conscientia optumae mentis tum etiam usurpatione et renovatione doctrinae. vidi enim Mytilenis nuper virum atque, ut dixi, vidi plane virum. itaque cum eum antea tui similem in dicendo viderim, tum vero nunc a doctissimo viro tibique, ut intellexi, amicissimo Cratippo instructum omni copia multo videbam similiorem.

Hic ego: etsi, inquam, de optumi viri nobisque amicissimi laudibus lubenter audio, tamen incurro in memoriam communium miseriarum, quarum oblivionem quaerens hunc ipsum sermonem produxi longius. sed de Caesare cupio audire quid tandem Atticus iudicet. (249–51)

Marcellus and Cicero followed similar political paths in the civil war: supporting Pompey at Pharsalus but refusing afterward to support the republican military cause. Marcellus did not have an illustrious career as an orator, although he was active in some prominent cases in the 50s BCE.[59] Posterity had little interest in his speeches, especially compared to any number of other speakers such as Caesar, Curio, Calvus, Caelius, or Pollio. The likenesses here are calculated to remind us of basic similarities in style and especially learning (*didicit*) – Marcellus' self-imposed exile is transformed into precisely the kind of study in the East with a renowned philosopher in the service of oratory that Cicero will make so central to his autobiography; the mention of their friendship with the Peripatetic philosopher Cratippus provides a personal touch. The connection between philosophy and *copia* is likewise central to Ciceronian ideas about the relationship between philosophical knowledge and rhetorical ability. These passages underscore political action intertwined with scholarly learning as a response to civil upheaval, and the overt emphasis on *vir* and *virtus* makes it difficult not to see a repeated set of allusions to Brutus' treatise and to Marcellus' role in that treatise – again, the very document Cicero cites in the preface as having inspired him to write the *Brutus*. Indirection and

---

[58] I read *quod* for *cum* (Kaster 2020, following Peter).

[59] Milo in 56 BCE, Scaurus in 54 BCE, and Milo in 52 BCE. See *TLRR* nos. 266, 295, and 309 (in the first trial he defended Milo *apud populum*, in the last he only examined witnesses).

reference to earlier and later passages in the work integrate its political concerns with its claims to intellectual vitality and renewal.[60]

Even the ostensible desire to avoid discussion of politics only points us back to the political situation. Ironic signaling seems to underlie the wish to forget about the republic's woes: Cicero then tells Atticus, "I wish to hear about Caesar" (de Caesare cupio audire). And this later emphasis on Marcellus may also help to explain an earlier choice Cicero had made: he claims that Brutus' treatise was for him what the victory at Nola in 216 was for the Romans after the defeat of Cannae. The victorious general there was none other than Marcus Claudius Marcellus, ancestor and namesake of the Caesarian exile. The piquancy of the reference is surely reinforced by the fact that Cicero in a letter to Atticus discussed Caesar's descent through Italy and likened him to Hannibal.[61] Pressing realities, despite being kept at bay, only reinforce the parallel: Caesar was now in Africa, fighting against Rome's army only miles from the site of Hannibal's Carthage, tucked in between the battlefield at Thapsus and the spot of Cato's death at Utica.[62]

The Younger Generation

The importance of Marcellus – returned to below – emerges most clearly when set against Cicero's portrayal of the subsequent younger generation of orators. Cicero's insistence on discussing Marcellus and Caesar is inherently tied to his political aims, which he expresses indirectly by implicit comparisons with other figures. Marcellus, as a representative of the younger generation (like Brutus), is one figure in a larger tableau of younger orators once attached to Cicero and Caesar. The likening of Marcellus and Cicero to one another, and the emphasis on their adherence to traditional republican values, will soon be contrasted with the erroneous ways of the younger generation whom Cicero soon discusses. This

---

[60] Douglas (1966a) 184 remarks (on the sentence in 250 ending with renovatione doctrinae), "These words also refer by implication to Cicero himself." Another subtle similarity is their connection to Greek islands, Lesbos (Marcellus) and Rhodes (Cicero).

[61] Att. 7.11.1 (SB 134).

[62] See the beginning of Chapter 2 for discussion of Marcellus and Nola as well as the reference to Caesar as Hannibal. Connecting the two Marcelli in this way may also help us to explain the earlier choice to mention Nola and the necessary disparities in the analogy that Cicero had to overlook: Nola happened shortly after Cannae (while Cicero claims to have had nothing to uplift him for quite some time until Brutus' letter), Marcellus failed to subdue Sicily, and he ultimately died fighting the Carthaginians in Italy. Fantham (1977) argues that Cicero enlists Marcellus as an opponent of Caesar's de Analogia, but Marcellus' politics must have been crucial.

generation includes Marcus Caelius Rufus (273), Gaius Scribonius Curio (280–81), and Publius Crassus (281–82), who round out Cicero's oratorical canon. Cicero cites them for their oratorical ability, but in each case closely focuses on their political choices: their involvement with Caesar and the civil war. And as we might well expect, Cicero freely reworks the biographical material in order to produce a clear narrative that supports his own political inclinations and suggests shortcomings in the choices made by men who chose to follow Caesar and placed personal ambition before the good of the state.[63]

We first get a brief notice of Marcus Caelius Rufus, among Cicero's best-known protégés, whom he (alongside Crassus) memorably defended in April of 56. Caelius produced contional speeches, three noteworthy prosecutions, and defense speeches of lesser quality.[64] He became curule aedile in 50 BCE before siding with Caesar and instigating uprisings over debt relief in southern Italy, during which he died:

> After he had been elected curule aedile, with the greatest support of the right-thinking, somehow after my departure he abandoned himself and his downfall came after he began to copy those he had once toppled.

> hic cum summa voluntate bonorum aedilis curulis factus esset, nescio quomodo discessu meo discessit a sese ceciditque, posteaquam eos imitari coepit quos ipse perverterat. (273)[65]

On its own the example of Caelius might stand as evidence of Cicero's disappointment in a former student and friend. Yet Caelius anticipates his younger contemporaries, Gaius Scribonius Curio and Publius Licinius Crassus. They are also potent reminders of Cicero's political concerns: individuals cannot place personal ambition above the collective good of the republic without threatening its existence. Like Caelius, Curio and Crassus began as adherents of Cicero but soon struck out on their own: Curio went over to Caesar (perhaps by bribery) and Crassus followed his father into

---

[63] Gowing (2000) 54–55 reads the special attention drawn to recently dead prominent senators such as Bibulus and Appius Claudius Pulcher as a clear allusion to Caesar and the ills of the civil war (267–69).

[64] Cicero says three prosecution speeches, though five are known in the record; see Kaster (2020) 146 n.425 for details. Cicero has either misremembered or lowered the number, perhaps the latter given his distaste for prosecution (Cicero notes that Caelius prosecuted because of disagreements related to matters of state politics).

[65] It may be better, with Kaster (2020), to translate the *cum*-clause as concessive, depending on how strongly one senses a logical contrast between support of the *boni* for Caelius and his subsequent political shift away from Cicero's guidance. Hendrickson and Martha take it as a narrative *cum*-clause.

disaster against the Parthians: both men, Ronald Syme notes, represent "talent corrupted by glory of the wrong kind."[66]

Curio becomes an *exemplum* of unbridled political ambition, and Cicero connects him to his true target, Publius Crassus, son of the triumvir. This brief digression on political power and ambition, as with so many of the *Brutus'* digressions, happens because of an abrupt shift in thought. Confused by Cicero's characterization, Brutus seeks clarification:

> [Cicero:] And if he [Curio] had been willing to listen to me, as he had started to do, he would have preferred honors to power.
> [Brutus:] What do you mean by that and how do you distinguish?

> qui si me audire voluisset, ut coeperat, honores quam opes consequi maluisset. Quidnam est, inquit, istuc? et quem ad modum distinguis? (280)

Cicero is only too happy to elaborate:

> Seeing that honor is the reward for excellence conferred upon someone by the enthusiastic judgment of the citizens, the man who has obtained it by opinions, by votes, is in my judgment both honorable and honored. But when a man has gotten power by some random opportunity even though his compatriots are against it, as Curio desired to do, he has acquired not honor but merely a title. And had he been willing to listen to all this, he would have attained the highest heights with the greatest possible goodwill and reputation, climbing up the grades of offices, as his father had done, as all other men of considerable distinction had done. Indeed I think I often impressed this upon Publius Crassus, son of Marcus, after he joined my circle of friendship at a young age, insistently urging him to take the straightest path to renown, which his forefathers had followed and left for him . . .
> But some surge of glory – a new thing to young men – pulled him down as well. Because as a soldier he had served a commander (*imperator*), he wished at once to be a commander, for which duty ancestral custom has a fixed age but uncertain assignment. And so, suffering the gravest fate, while he hoped to be like Cyrus and Alexander, who had sped through their careers, he ended up being wholly unlike Lucius Crassus and many others from that family.

> cum honos sit praemium virtutis iudicio studioque civium delatum ad aliquem, qui eum sententiis, qui suffragiis adeptus est, is mihi et honestus et honoratus videtur. qui autem occasione aliqua etiam invitis suis civibus nactus est imperium, ut ille cupiebat, hunc nomen honoris adeptum, non

---

[66] Syme (1980) 407. Caes. *Civ.* 2.42 portrays Curio's devotion up to the end.

honorem puto. quae si ille audire voluisset, maxuma cum gratia et gloria ad
summam amplitudinem pervenisset, ascendens gradibus magistratuum, ut
pater eius fecerat, ut reliqui clariores viri. quae quidem etiam cum P. Crasso
M. f., <cum> initio aetatis ad amicitiam se meam contulisset, saepe egisse
me arbitror, cum eum vehementer hortarer, ut eam laudis viam rectissimam
esse duceret, quam maiores eius ei tritam reliquissent. ... sed hunc quoque
absorbuit aestus quidam insolitae adulescentibus gloriae; qui quia navarat
miles operam imperatori, imperatorem se statim esse cupiebat, cui muneri
mos maiorum aetatem certam, sortem incertam reliquit. ita gravissumo suo
casu, dum Cyri et Alexandri similis esse voluit, qui suum cursum transcur-
rerant, et L. Crassi et multorum Crassorum inventus est dissimillimus.
(281–82)

Cicero pulls no punches regarding either man, and was gravely disap-
pointed at losing protégés to Caesar. The characterization of Crassus may
well suit his actions, but has also confounded modern observers: "the harsh
judgment of Cicero is not explained by any evidence we possess" and
"nothing is known to account for these insinuations."[67]

Crassus becomes a pretext to a discussion of appropriate leadership and
the limits of traditional office. Unsurprisingly, the digression repeats
Cicero's criticisms of those who have undermined the republic by seeking
personal advantages. Publius Crassus was the son of Marcus, the triumvir,
with whom he died at Carrhae in 53. Cicero's painting of Publius closely
resembles Plutarch's portrayal of the father, which might suggest that they
were, or at least were thought to be, of similar character (or that Cicero
could interchange their descriptions easily enough).[68] Yet Cicero had not
criticized Marcus Crassus in harsh terms, instead assessing his modest
abilities and fairly successful oratorical career (236). No mention is made
of the triumvirate, much as only the briefest notice in stock terms is given
to Pompey's modest oratory and ambitious pursuit of military glory (239).

Reference to Publius does reinforce a pattern according to which several
members of the younger generation have wrongly chosen Caesar's side.
Right before the transition to the discussion of Publius Crassus, Cicero
reminds us of the relationship of sons to fathers by noting that Curio did
not wish to follow his father's path, or that of all good Romans. Curio
pater is of course present in the reader's mind as a staunch anti-Caesarian

---

[67] Hendrickson (1962) 244 n.a and Douglas (1966a) 208.
[68] Father's attributes claimed for the son: Douglas (1966a) 208. On Publius as Cicero's protegé see
Cic. *Q. fr.* 2.8.2 (SB 13). One explanation for the harsh treatment is that Cicero draws inferences
about Publius from his choice to follow his father to the East. That still does not explain why Cicero
chose to include those criticisms in an account of Publius' oratory.

for his dialogue and witty criticisms.[69] Such points make the passage applicable generally to Roman politics, given the importance of family connections in public life. In the case of Publius Crassus, however, his ambitions also brought him to Caesar. The unnamed *imperator* under whom Publius served, and who whet his ambition, was Julius Caesar himself in the Gallic campaigns. While Cicero criticizes Publius' refusal to play by the rules of the game, that is, to follow the established pattern of the *cursus honorum*, this can be just as much an indictment of the triumvirate's stranglehold on the electoral system and on the assignment of extraordinary provincial commands. While in Gaul, Publius did lead troops in battle, but received no formal title: he was neither tribune or legate, and certainly not *imperator*.[70] Upon his return to Rome he was one of the three men in charge of issuing coinage, a *triumvir monetalis*, which was often a precursory position to entrance in the *cursus honorum*. He was young when elected to the college of augurs (Cicero replaced him after his death in 53), but this hardly contradicted tradition.

His true error will have been the fatal choice to follow his father to the East, but again Cicero does not discuss the triumvir. Instead he names Lucius Licinius Crassus, inserting him in a way that suggests a family lineage among them, although the connection between these different branches of the Licinii Crassi is uncertain, if not unlikely. Glossing over this fact is all the more suspicious given that he had earlier criticized the intentional distortion of family lineages.[71] Lucius Licinius Crassus was Cicero's own role model and virtually a political surrogate for the pedigree that he lacked.[72] The remarks not only underscore the disparity between Lucius Crassus and Publius, but set criticism of the triumvir and his son against Cicero's own political and oratorical *exemplum*. Cicero essentially crafts two genealogies by discussing the Crassi in this way: L. Licinius Crassus and Cicero as saviors of the republic, and Publius Crassus (son and, perhaps, father) who subvert the state order to their own ends.

---

[69] Suet. *Jul.* 49.2; more scurrilously: "every woman's man and every man's woman" (*omnium mulierum virum et omnium virorum mulierem*, 52.3).

[70] See Caes. *Gal.* 1.52, 3.20–27. Syme (1980) and Rawson (1982) seek to explain Cicero's claims on the assumption that Cicero is not engaging in rhetorical distortion. Cf. Rawson (1982) 542: "Why should the *Brutus* be mistaken or unjust?"

[71] He dismisses inaccuracies produced by the *laudationes* (61–62), although there it should be noted that he attacks the confusion of plebeian and patrician branches and the introduction of false honors, but the principle abides.

[72] See van der Blom (2010), esp. 30–31, 177–79, 226–33, 251–54. Cf. also *Balb.* 3, *Div. Caec.* 25.

Cicero's Marcellus

Set against the failures of Caelius, Curio, and Crassus is the clear alternative: Marcellus, portrayed as almost a second Cicero, especially in the
present moment as he awaits the future of the republic and indulges in
rhetorical exercises and philosophical teachings. The pattern of failures and
successes presents a clear choice to Brutus, who is the most significant
member of the younger generation. Cicero essentially asks him, "Given all
these failed followers of Caesar (Caelius, Curio, Crassus), doesn't it make
more sense to act as Marcellus does, who, as you say, remarkably resembles
me, Cicero?" The emphasis on Marcellus, however, challenges Caesar
without attacking him. Cicero is competitive but not agonistic, since, like
Cicero, Marcellus remains an *exemplum* of moderate resistance and partial
accommodation. He refused to join the anti-Caesarian forces after
Pharsalus and did not commit unwaveringly to resistance as Cato did. In
Cicero's portrayal Marcellus represents a model of Stoic-like resistance
without the bellicose rigidity of a Cato: Stoic virtue but not Stoic extrem-
ism.[73] Indeed, Cicero's emphasis on Marcellus and his moderation may
partly explain the chronological difficulties surrounding the exclusion of
Cato, who was anything but moderate. Cicero discusses other figures who
died fighting Caesar in Africa, but the deliberately uncertain date of the
dialogue's setting allows him to plausibly exclude Cato and, more importantly, keeps him from having to judge Cato in a way that would reflect
poorly on Caesar, or the republican cause.

Lionization of Marcellus offers a prudent and compelling alternative to
Caesar. Certainly Caesar's actions and intentions will have been clear to
few observers at this point, including Cicero, who had little reason to
alienate Caesar. In the face of uncertainty, Cicero continued to champion
the good of the state over the benefit of individuals. Much of the blame for
the crisis of the civil war is directed at the personal failures of individuals
shared by the whole community.[74] To counter the crisis, Cicero seeks the
restoration of the republic, its institutions, and with these its senatorial

[73] Volk (2021), chap. 3 on philosophical allegiances in the late republic. We cannot know, but it is
tantalizing to consider whether a preference for Marcellus over Cato influenced Cicero's
chronological parameters for the dialogue's fiction: if he knew of Cato's death, might he have
excluded Cato from the dialogue's fictional world so as not to have to praise him at great length?
Marcellus certainly better represented Cicero's response to civil war. Such a suggestion must remain
speculative, and Cicero would after all write a eulogy for Cato.
[74] Lintott (2008) 315, with Cicero's (vague) blame of human error or fear in the *Brutus* (*errore
hominum aut timore*, 7). Cf. the sense of inevitable communal woe (*in hoc communi nostro et quasi
fatali malo*, 250).

class. In the early 40s he actively cultivated connections with (former) Pompeians (including Marcellus and Sulpicius Rufus).[75] No less did he court alliances with Caesar's friends, fostering social connections while avoiding, or trying to avoid, complete acquiescence to Caesar's power: Pansa, Hirtius, Balbus, Oppius, Matius, and others.[76] In particular, he promoted the younger generation, of which Brutus was the immediate example, alongside those such as Marcellus, who had already achieved political success.[77]

It is true that political calculation may partly explain Cicero's appeals for Marcellus' restoration in September 46 when he delivered *pro Marcello*. He doubtless felt isolated as one of the few former supporters of Pompey in Rome and may have feared the taint of collaboration.[78] But the appeals for Marcellus to return, whether to Caesar in *pro Marcello*, directly to Marcellus in his letters, or perhaps even implicitly in the *Brutus*, were also crucial to ensuring the involvement of leaders prominent before the civil war. The senate had lost several such men in recent years: Cato, Hortensius, and Pompey, most notably, but also Bibulus, Appius Claudius Pulcher, Domitius Ahenobarbus, and Milo.[79] As Ingo Gildenhard remarks, Cicero sought to justify, to himself no less than others, "political engagement in and with Caesar's world, in the belief that reform is a distinct possibility, best achieved through cooperation that remains devoted to a Republican vision of politics rather than sterile resistance."[80] Cicero's remaining allies were to be part of that future.

Marcellus may also have appealed to Cicero for the more immediate legacy of political pragmatism he represented. Harriet Flower has suggested that the three Claudii Marcelli may have formed a pact to help secure the plebeian consulship in succession from 51–49, right at the moment when the initial conflict with Caesar was coming to a head.[81] Marcellus in some

[75] C. Steel (2005) 101–3; Cicero's letters helped foster "a community of men who wish to find a place for themselves in the new Caesarian dispensation" (102). J. Hall (2009) 96: "his desire to work with Caesar on his arrival in Rome rather than against him." Lintott (2008) 317.

[76] Gildenhard (2018) 227.

[77] On Cicero's pursuit of the younger generation, Brutus in particular, see Rawson (1983) 211, Dyck (1996) 11. Securing Brutus' allegiance is the central topic of Rathofer (1986). On Marcellus' importance to Cicero, see C. Steel (2005) 99–101.

[78] Cf. C. Steel (2005) 101, Zetzel (2009) 279.   [79] Rawson (1983) 208 (who lists others as well).

[80] Gildenhard (2018) 224, discussing the "intellectual community" bound by the values of "elitist humanism."

[81] Flower (2010) 152, citing Gruen (1974) 155. She is seconded by van der Blom (2016) 236. The pact may have even required Cato's acquiescence to not securing the plebeian consulship for some years. He lost the elections for consul of 51 to M. Marcellus, who would be joined by Cicero's close friend Servius Sulpicius Rufus. Cato seems not to have subsequently presented his candidacy.

sense also represented pragmatic senatorial self-assertion, and promotion of Marcellus may reflect a symbolic, if wishful, turning back of the clock to a time before the woes of the civil war.

Just as Cicero thought that oratory would once again continue to develop, so did he envision the continuation of the republic, a restoration of the forum and its politics not so unlike the kind he experienced under and especially after Sulla (absent the proscriptions). There is unquestionably criticism of military force in the service of personal ambition, but it is tempered by the prospect of resolving the civic crisis. Cicero's reliance on indirection largely accounts for the conflicting messages that seem to emerge from the *Brutus*: vagueness and caution still allow him to outline political alternatives to – or perhaps for – Caesar, while recognizing Caesar's ultimate control of the republic.

Cicero's research into the literary past, how to organize, classify, and evaluate it, is beholden through and through to his vision of the Roman republic in the present. He interweaves the history of eloquence and its guiding values into the political context, implicitly arguing for the inseparability of politics and aesthetics. In examining how Cicero makes the past suit his vision of the present we gain an understanding of his mode of inquiry along with his civic aims. Cicero offers a version of the development of oratory and literature in order to prescribe a specific vision of the Roman republic – one based on the art of rhetoric and the force of persuasion in public discourse. He does not attack Caesar outright, but he does challenge much of what has brought him (no less than Pompey) power and fame: military success in the service of personal glory and ambition at the expense of the common good. In response he offers a vision of the republic in which oratory and its history are the primary vehicle of political power and its attendant renown. Oratory is also an inherited artistic tradition, opposed to conventional forms of power derived from military success and aristocratic lineage. These are not necessarily new strategies for Cicero, but in the *Brutus* they coalesce as a response to the crisis of civil war and in conjunction with new possibilities for presenting and evaluating the past.

CHAPTER 4

Truthmaking and the Past

There is little to fault in the observation that readers are made by the texts they consume. We direct the flood of lived experience into the convenient streams and reservoirs of narrative and its conventions. Paul de Man identified an underlying paradox:

> No one in his right mind will try to grow grapes by the luminosity of the word "day," but it is very difficult not to conceive the pattern of one's past and future existence as in accordance with temporal and spatial schemes that belong to fictional narratives and not to the world. This does not mean that fictional narratives are not part of the world and of reality; their impact upon the world may well be all too strong for comfort. What we call ideology is precisely the confusion of linguistic with natural reality, of reference with phenomenalism.[1]

That authors help fashion readers may seem like a quaintly postmodern phenomenon, but ancient texts participated no less in the formation of a reader's sensibilities. Readers bring interpretive equipment to bear on literary texts in the hope (or wariness) of testing and modifying settled habits. Along the way we acquire a new perspective on what it means to be a human subject in search of meaning.[2] We may also encounter authors who visibly manipulate our sympathies to self-serving ends. In such texts the most obvious and most obviously self-serving efforts amount to little more than propaganda and pamphleteering, and fall into genres such as political speeches, opinion pieces, Hallmark cards, or kitsch literature and art. In the face of undressed ideology, we may fall under the transient spell of an author with an agenda, but circumspection typically prompts an almost instinctual recalcitrance (we roll our eyes at kitsch; we thumb our noses at political evangelism). Still the two modes are interrelated; in some

---

[1] De Man (1986) 11.
[2] Burke (1973) 293–304 in his essay "Literature as Equipment for Living" discusses how literature provides frames of reference for making decisions about how to conduct our lives.

sense propaganda – persuasion with minimal concealment of one's aims – is a precursor for texts we otherwise think of as literary. An author's virtuosity can be measured by the ability to thwart resistance, not merely to persuade us but even to make us into accomplices in the construction of meaning.

Cicero's *Brutus* possesses exactly that power. But its persuasive workings have yet to be explored in detail, in part because they are complex, no less because many are novel or obscure, and especially because a key feature of the work's artistry is to conceal its ideological designs from the reader. Cicero uses indirection to disguise his aims and enlists the authority of his interlocutors and other scholars to sway readers. The overtly cautious assessment of the past makes his agenda nearly imperceptible and largely explains why the *Brutus'* vision of intellectual and political history has proved so successful. It contains a self-serving account of oratory's rise, and differing cultural responses make that self-praise more palatable to Romans than to most modern scholars, who typically bristle at perceived egotism.[3]

Yet the relentless self-promotion, including self-congratulatory gestures of hesitation or modesty, may well be a red herring. The most prominent and deceptive agenda driving the *Brutus* is Cicero's self-portrayal as a neutral recorder and arbiter of the Roman past. This feigned neutrality, which makes him look uncannily like a modern scholar, has not prompted the same distaste as his self-praise. He accomplishes this feat by aligning himself with Atticus and the recent wave of scholarship that made possible Atticus' *Liber Annalis*, Nepos' *Chronica*, and Varro's countless investigations.[4] At the same time, as has already become evident from the Ciceropaideia (Chapter 1), and as will become evident through further examination of his historical methods here, Cicero readily shapes the details of an event or account in the service of his larger historical narrative.

The potential complications in presenting an unbiased account surface already in the terms denoting the dialogue's content. After the long preface we arrive at the main topic when Atticus steers the discussion toward the historical catalogue of orators:

[ATTICUS:]   Well now, if your mind's freed up for it, explain to us what we're seeking.
[CICERO:]   What's that?
[ATTICUS:]   The discussion about orators you recently began in your Tusculan home: <u>when</u> they came into existence, as well as <u>who</u> and <u>what kind</u> they were.

---

[3] Allen (1954) explains and justifies Cicero's self-praise.
[4] *CAH*² IX.2: 689–728, *CAH*² VIII: 422–76, Rawson (1985), Volk (2021), Zetzel (2018) 31–58.

nunc vero, inquit, si es animo vacuo, expone nobis quod quaerimus. Quidnam est id? inquam. Quod mihi nuper in Tusculano inchoavisti de oratoribus: quando esse coepissent, qui etiam et quales fuissent.(20)

The topic could hardly seem more neutral at first, since to ask about the beginning of oratory and its representatives leaves little room for judgment. It is not until the third term (*quales*) that the role of judgment, quality in its basic sense, becomes evident. Ultimately the first two questions (when, who) will come to depend on the last (what kind), since Cicero must make choices about his canon.[5] The inclusions and exclusions, with whom to begin and whom to omit, are determined by his vision of how such a history can and should be structured.

Cicero excludes certain figures whom by all rights he should not. He notoriously passes over political enemies such as Catiline and Clodius without notice or scruple. The baffling choice to begin oratory with Marcus Cornelius Cethegus (*quando esse coepissent*) rather than, say, Appius Claudius Caecus or Cato the Elder, is indeed a choice and hardly a matter of fact.[6] The terms of Cicero's investigation (*quando, qui, quales*) perfectly capture the tension between ostensibly neutral criteria and those that rely on personal observation and judgment, and he manipulates this tension to great effect. It is the enabling force of the dialogue's contribution to oratorical and intellectual history, and it also ensures that his literary history reflects his views of the civic community.

Yet remarkable honesty accompanies Cicero's manipulations: he also shows us that his choices are tendentious, that literary history cannot exist without literary criticism, and that such accounts are deeply shaped by authorial choices. Literary history *must* be constructed according to criteria that are anything but disinterested: the biases and emphases of the literary historian are an intrinsic part of the account. Yet he does not stop at that basic theoretical insight, instead building on it by acknowledging crucial "extraliterary" considerations: his ideological aims ultimately shape his history of oratory.[7] We may be tempted to see in this a flaw in Cicero's

[5] Douglas (1966a) xvi: "In applying [his] standards, Cicero is remarkably free of partisanship." This is mostly true, but fails to address the underlying issue: isn't application of his standards already a form of partisanship in constructing a canon?
[6] Chapter 5 discusses the preference of Cethegus over Caecus.
[7] Hayden White's thought is especially useful in thinking through Cicero's presentation of the past and the relationship between the form of the dialogue and its account of the past. See White (1987), especially chaps. 1, 2, and 8. Paul (2011) is a sensible introduction to White's ideas (which, it is worth noting, have not infrequently been used for purposes to which they are ill-suited). Dench (2009) provides a reasonable prospectus and analysis of some approaches to Roman historiography in

methodology: the modern scholar might, with the limiting prejudices of modern scholarship, claim that accuracy and comprehensiveness are paramount. Cicero has made a quite different and deliberate choice in that he anticipates and seeks to overcome the inevitability that any account will be biased. Rather than dwell on that fact, he embraces the possibilities it creates, since there are considerable advantages to a necessarily imperfect account – foremost among them to show that Roman literary history is inextricable from its political history and therefore from a vision of Rome in the present. Cicero does not so much argue that oratory culminated in his triumphant values as show, little by little and in the guise of curiosity and circumspection, that Rome's true triumph is the greatness of its oratorical past, that Rome in fact cannot be great without oratory, whether in the past or present. If, in turn, the reader is disposed to see Cicero as the culmination of a great tradition, all the better.

Now, this argument is certainly a lot to place on one adverb and two pronouns (*quando, qui, quales*), but confirmation of Cicero's aims will become evident as the dialogue progresses. Cicero allows the tension between factual accuracy and plausible presentation to play out visibly throughout the discussion, making it a central theme of the work and constantly staging an examination of the veracity of his or others' accounts. The larger question in the *Brutus* is not *What are the facts?* but *Which facts are significant enough to appear in the record and why?* Cicero complicates this question by assuming rather than arguing for the significance of the figures and events he includes and by leaving it to the reader to puzzle out why and in what way those facts are meaningful. He thereby makes readers into accomplices for his vision of literary history.

In trying to assess the full scope of Cicero's project, the emphasis here will fall in the first instance on statements about factual accuracy and on the presentation of material. It will then consider the arrangement of traditional markers of time and historical examples. Cicero offers a framework for interpreting history that is interwoven with the presentation of historical details – a procedure perhaps akin to building a car while driving it. A related yet no less essential focus will be on the ways in which Cicero guides his readers in the new method. This instructional technique not only underlies the pedagogical function of the *Brutus*, by which Cicero

---

the last hundred (or so) years of classical studies. On the value of perspectivalism in literary history, see Grethlein (2017).

details for readers the necessity of Roman *antiquitas et litterae*; it is also calculated to fashion a legacy of literary thinkers who will come to share his historical and rhetorical sensibilities. The dialogue pursues that aim by inserting Atticus and Brutus as willing yet nonetheless resistant disciples of Cicero's techniques, modeling through them possible responses for readers.

Lessons in Syncrisis

The experience of the *Brutus* involves accepting two potentially contradictory ideas: we are made aware of how it tendentiously represents the past even as Cicero overtly manipulates our sympathies and undermines our resistance. No technique is more appealing or readily employed than syncrisis, which over and again serves as a guiding technique of analysis. The comparisons and parallels vary widely in content and complexity. The basic syncritic model involves the comparison of two elements, although the binary comparanda are drawn liberally from diverse groups and generations: the orators of Greece and Rome in general or the specific instance of Lysias and Cato the Elder; of Antonius and Crassus in a single generation, or the jurists Quintus Mucius Scaevola and Servius Sulpicius Rufus in succeeding ones.

The necessity of such comparisons would seem obvious in a work of criticism as a way to organize individuals, ages, or cultures, but binarism comes to define even the criteria by which judgments can be made. Doctrinal scruple did not keep Cicero from claiming that there are two paramount virtues in the orator (*duae summae laudes*, 89), to instruct (*docere*) and to move (*permovere* or *inflammare*).[8] There are similarly not three but two "characters of style" (*duo genera sunt*, 201), the plain and the grand, leaving out the middle style dutifully noted a decade earlier in *de Oratore* and returned to so adamantly in *Orator*. Cicero reflects on the difficulty of oratory and the consequent paucity of skilled orators to ask, "Don't we observe that scarcely two praiseworthy orators stood out in any given age?" (*nonne cernimus vix singulis aetatibus binos oratores laudabilis constitisse?*, 333). The pull of binary thinking has even distorted the *paucitas oratorum* motif in the *Brutus*, the only version of the topos to

---

[8] See Chapter 7 on the "two styles." Chris Trinacty suggests to me an analogous sharpening of an opposition in Aristophanes' *Frogs*. Aeschylus and Euripides are the play's focus in part because they differ more from one another than either does from Sophocles. Cf. Gutzwiller (2014) 15–16, 24.

emphasize the rarity of two orators in each age.[9] Comparison is so essential to assessing and categorizing oratory and its history that absolute judgments can prove deceptive, hence the otherwise out-of-place remark about Quintus Lutatius Catulus, the noted philhellene and a character in Cicero's *de Oratore*: put up against contemporaries his shortcomings were clear, yet he seemed like a perfect orator "when, however, you heard only him speaking in the absence of comparison" (*cum autem ipsum audires sine comparatione*, 134). This local judgment – as so often in the *Brutus* – reveals an underlying theoretical premise: literary criticism and history are inherently dependent on syncrisis, because, even if we can accurately describe an author or text, such a description has little meaning unless contrasted with another speaker or text and placed into a larger narrative.

The various syncrises cannot stand on their own, however, and here the dramatic exchanges in the dialogue establish how comparisons serve as the basis for complex interpretation.

> Brutus said, "I think that I've gotten to know Crassus and Scaevola well from your speech, and when I think about you and Servius Sulpicius I conclude that you have a kind of similarity to them."
>
> "In what way?" I asked.
>
> "Well," he replied, "you seem to me to have aimed to know as much about the civil law as was necessary for an orator, and Servius took on as much eloquence as was needed to be able to defend the law with ease; and your ages, like theirs, differ little or not at all."

> cum ex tua oratione mihi videor, inquit, bene Crassum et Scaevolam cognovisse, tum de te et de Ser. Sulpicio cogitans esse quandam vobis cum illis similitudinem iudico.
>
> Quonam, inquam, istuc modo?
>
> Quia mihi et tu videris, inquit, tantum iuris civilis scire voluisse quantum satis esset oratori et Servius eloquentiae tantum adsumpsisse, ut ius civile facile possit tueri; aetatesque vostrae ut illorum nihil aut non fere multum differunt. (150)

On display is a methodological feature of dialogue: the interlocutors outline different interpretive models for the material presented. Such exchanges encourage a reader to work through the possible similarities among the different ages – in this case the obvious parallels and similarities between successful orators and jurists, including Cicero's tendency to connect the two areas of knowledge even as he still prioritizes *eloquentia*

---

[9] On *paucitas oratorum* ("scarcity of orators") in rhetorical dialogues, see van den Berg (2014) 208–12 with *de Orat.* 1.6, 1.8, 1.11, 1.16, 1.19, *Orat.* 20, Tac. *Dial.* 1.1.

over *ius*. The dramatic interjection by Brutus places interpretive expectations on the audience: to draw inferences from the material, to puzzle out the parallels among individuals and ages, and to evaluate transgenerational syncrisis for the patterns of similarity and difference that emerge.[10]

Yet the dramatized interpretation may not necessarily match the complexity of the material under discussion. Cicero by this point has already walked us through the better part of a remarkably elaborate scheme.[11] First two Greek orators, Demosthenes and Hyperides (138), were compared to Antonius and Crassus; the latter then to Scaevola (145). Brutus makes the further connection between Crassus/Scaevola and Cicero/Servius Sulpicius Rufus. Intervening between these generations are Gaius Aurelius Cotta and Publius Sulpicius Rufus (203), the inheritors of the oratorical legacy and its transmitters, both figuratively and literally: *de Oratore*'s fiction had Cotta recount to Cicero the conversation among Rome's oratorical luminaries in 91 BCE.[12] Cicero will even add three more Greeks to bring the number to twelve: Isocrates dampened the vigor of Theopompus and fostered that of Euphorus by "applying the goad to one and the brake to the other" (*alteri se calcaria adhibere alteri frenos*, 204).[13] The elaboration covers some seventy chapters of the *Brutus* on its way across cultures, generations, fields of expertise, and pedagogical authority.

The series of parallels, however, offers more than just direct analogies or oppositions. The comparisons prime the reader to be alert to parallels, to respond as Cicero has Brutus do. Yet however helpful Brutus is as a surrogate reader, in his hands the nested syncrises yield little more than a labyrinthine chain of connections, a mystery investigated but never solved. While Cicero models the forging of such connections, he still leaves considerable interpretive latitude for a reader to draw inferences independently from the assertions of the dialogue participants. That is, significant events and individuals are set side by side, but Cicero does not complete the interpretive work that is made possible by the posited comparisons and analogies. Although Brutus connects the pairs Crassus/Scaevola and

---

[10] Feeney (2007) 39–40 on synchronism of cultures as "an exercise in correspondence" as well as "an exercise in disparity" (39).

[11] On this complex syncrisis see Kytzler (1970) 292–94.

[12] On citation of oral sources for written material, see Hendrickson (1906), with demurrals at Douglas (1966a) l (mistakenly citing Hendrickson 1926).

[13] Kytzler (1970) 293 tallies eleven figures, but the didactic role of Isocrates and Cicero's similar position in the *Brutus* make Isocrates no less essential to the "chain of comparisons" ("Kette von Vergleichungen"). Cf. the discussion of the dozen Roman orators of the late republic in C. Steel (2002).

Cicero/Sulpicius, he does not draw the most obvious conclusion of the comparison: just as Crassus surpassed Scaevola in eloquence, so too does Cicero surpass Sulpicius as the great orator of his generation. And working further back into the various syncrises, another set of parallels emerges: Sulpicius had two teachers, Lucius Lucilius Balbus and Gaius Aquilius Gallus, whom he surpassed and whose shortcomings he supplemented. The relevance to Cicero is not directly stated, but it must be apparent: Cicero also devoted himself to two figures of a previous generation (even if he did not study under them at great length), Antonius and Crassus.[14]

The presentation of these orators, including Brutus' complex comparison, implicitly asserts what could not be said: Cicero too combined and supplemented what Antonius and Crassus lacked, merging the forcefulness of one and the elegance of the other, and outdoing both. When speaking about them directly Cicero instead shows deference: little could be added to their generation's accomplishments, except by someone better prepared in philosophy, law, and history (*ut eo nihil ferme quisquam addere posset, nisi qui a philosophia a iure civili ab historia fuisset instructior*, 161). When Brutus seeks an example (*iam est iste quem exspectas?*), Cicero defers (*nescio*, 162). The response is neither true ignorance nor false modesty: leaving things uncertain only redirects onto the reader the search for this knowledge, as if to say "*I* don't know, but *you* might." We are encouraged to find connections across generations and, eventually, in Cicero's biography: philosophy, jurisprudence, and history were all part of his education (322).

We are also under no obligation to accept and interpret the happy coincidences as Brutus does by likening Cicero to Sulpicius. It's possible to resist their surface allure, as Atticus does when pointing up the historical distortions of Cicero's likening of Themistocles and Coriolanus (41–44, further discussed below). Indeed, the two interlocutors are so valuable precisely for their different responses. Brutus accepts Cicero's claims and advances the lines of interpretation. Atticus assists the dialogue's conceptual progression, but often by challenging its claims or unstated assumptions. Cicero's elaborate game of show-don't-tell instructs readers even as it leaves them to their own speculative impulses: we are fashioned into independent readers of syncrisis.[15] Nevertheless, that independence may still come at the price of becoming subject unwittingly to Cicero's own aims in other matters. He also posits far less innocent parallels that are

---

[14] And of course he also emulated Cotta and Hortensius later on (317, discussed in Chapter 1).

[15] Barchiesi (1962) 21–38 makes groundbreaking observations about the pedagogical shaping of readers in the *Brutus*, although the scholarship has often neglected his insights.

equally irresistible and involve the crafting of historical details to suit his own narrative.

History and Veracity in the *Brutus*

As the chronology progresses Cicero interweaves countless digressions into its catalogue of speakers.[16] Just as there are nested syncrises of considerable sophistication, Cicero recursively handles concepts and ideas in the work's examples and digressions. Part of its elaborate artistry involves fleshing out a topic or theme by revisiting it at intervals.[17] One central topic is the accurate presentation of the past, which the interlocutors address at various points and often at length: the "beginning of Latin literature" in 240 (72–73), the potential distortions of the *laudatio funebris* (62), Curio's dialogue on the conduct of Julius Caesar (218–19), and fictional syncrisis of the lives of Themistocles and Coriolanus (41–44). Although these digressions in isolation appear to be little more than scattered vignettes on tangential topics, taken together they programmatically outline the limits and latitude for presentation that Cicero accords himself in the *Brutus*. The evaluation of truthful narratives throughout the dialogue reveals Cicero's attitude toward the dual – and sometimes rival – expectations of accuracy and plausibility in his account.

Livius Andronicus and the Beginning of Roman Literature in 240 BCE

Few passages of the *Brutus* have received more attention than the discussion of Livius Andronicus' play of 240 BCE.

> And yet this Livius first produced a play when Gaius Claudius, son of Caecus, and Marcus Tuditanus were consuls in the very year before Ennius' birth, and 514 years after Rome's foundation, as Atticus says, and we concur. You know, writers dispute the number of years. Accius wrote that Livius was taken prisoner at Tarentum by Quintus Maximus while consul for the fifth time, thirty years after he had produced a play – this is not only

---

[16] Barchiesi (1962) 21–38 first noticed that the progressivist evaluation of Livius–Naevius–Ennius, pulled along by an inherently modernizing and Enniocentric momentum, can only be understood in connection to the parallel narrative about Cato's place in early oratorical history.

[17] E.g. the lasting merits of older artists (in poetry or oratory), biography, the role of Greek culture in shaping Roman literature, the difficulty of oratory, and effective persuasion as the main aim of oratory. Even the work's subject is defined on four separate occasions (20, 22, 74, 137; see Chapter 2).

what Atticus writes but also what I've found in ancient registers. Yet Accius wrote that Livius produced the play eleven years later in the consulship of Gaius Cornelius and Quintus Minucius during the Ludi Iuventatis, which Livius Salinator had vowed at the battle of Sena. And in this matter Accius was so far off that Ennius was forty years old when they were consuls; if Livius were his contemporary then the man who first produced a play was a little younger than both Plautus and Naevius, the men who had already produced many plays before those consuls.

atqui hic Livius [qui] primus fabulam C. Claudio Caeci filio et M. Tuditano consulibus docuit anno ipso ante quam natus est Ennius, post Romam conditam autem quarto decumo et quingentesimo, ut hic ait, quem nos sequimur. est enim inter scriptores de numero annorum controversia. Accius autem a Q. Maxumo quintum consule captum Tarento scripsit Livium annis xxx post quam eum fabulam docuisse et Atticus scribit et nos in antiquis commentariis invenimus; docuisse autem fabulam annis post xi, C. Cornelio Q. Minucio consulibus ludis Iuventatis, quos Salinator Senensi proelio voverat. in quo tantus error Acci fuit, ut his consulibus xl annos natus Ennius fuerit: quoi aequalis fuerit Livius, minor fuit aliquanto is, qui primus fabulam dedit, quam ii, qui multas docuerant ante hos consules, et Plautus et Naevius. (72–73)

This passage has cemented for posterity – both ancient and modern – the beginning of Latin literature, when Livius Andronicus produced a *fabula* for the *ludi Romani* in September 240.[18] The story behind the establishment of this date is far more complex than the smooth account of Greek-to-Latin translation on offer here, both in terms of what had to happen in Rome's relationship to Greek and Italian powers and traditions, and also in terms of the scholarly jockeying that for some time had been seeking to fix a firm date. The Greco-Roman reflex to focus on individuals and their actions, to seek out first creators or adaptors of institutions, runs counter to modern emphases on impersonal cultural and linguistic contexts or on the competing agents and documenters of literary change.[19]

The traditional story has it that "Andronikos" hailed from Greek-speaking Taras (Tarentum in Latin), one of many Greek colonies in Magna Graecia, the region of Italy that Rome subdued piecemeal in the

---

[18] In addition to 72–73, see Cic. *Sen.* 50, *Tusc.* 1.3 with Gruen (1990) 80–92 and Bernstein (1998) 234–51. On the debates over 240 see Suerbaum (2002) 51–57, Manuwald (2011) 30–40, Welsh (2011). See now Feeney (2016) for a larger contextualization; D'Anna (1984). The establishment of Livius as the beginning was not certain but would win out: Liv. 7.2.8, V. Max. 2.4.4, Gell. *NA* 17.21.42, Euanth. *de Com.* 4.3, Diom. *Gramm.* 1.489, Cassiod. *Chron.* 128 M.

[19] Habinek (1998) emphasizes the determining role of Roman elites in their attempts to secure and maintain power.

wake of the expulsion of the invading Macedonian king Pyrrhus in 275. Tarentum fell into Roman hands in 272 and Andronikos would have been one of the enslaved in the city's settlement with its new masters.[20] He acquired, upon later manumission by one of the *Livii*, the name Livius Andronicus (a praenomen, Lucius, attested for example in Gellius, is uncertain), a name that perfectly reflects the Greek and Latin halves of his poetic output, such as his Latin *Odyssia* and Latin plays based on Greek models.[21] Centuries later Suetonius dubbed him (and Ennius) a "half Greek" (*semigraecus*, *Gram. et rhet.* 1.2), no doubt a nod to his ethnic background as much as to his cultural production. Livius was also an ideal choice to translate and produce a Latin play because of his background as an actor and playwright (the two were closely allied in the early history of Roman drama), because of Tarentum's renowned theater, and because Romans grew to appreciate dramatic performances after experiencing them during the First Punic War (264–241).

A play at the *ludi Romani* capped Rome's military success with a cultural flourish, as the event marked in public performance all that Rome had accomplished in defeating Carthage the year before. Rome was now a major military power in the Mediterranean, and a Greek play in Latin on a Roman stage would showcase its simultaneous assertion to cultural relevance on the international stage. As Erich Gruen has written, "The accomplishment would be marked by elevation of the ludi to a cultural event that announced Rome's participation in the intellectual world of the Greeks."[22] Hiero, ruler of the powerful Greek town of Syracuse, would draw the right conclusion, attending the festival in 239 and bringing a large gift of grain, Sicily's prize crop. The visit and the gesture were not so unlike the embassy of amity from the Hellenistic kingdom that was dispatched when the Romans expelled King Pyrrhus a few decades before.[23]

The *ludi Romani* were the quintessentially Roman state festival, honoring Jupiter Optimus Maximus and serving as a venue for the powerful to display significant changes in the *res publica*. According to legend the festival – originally just circus races (*ludi circenses*) without theatrical performances (*ludi scaenici*) – was established near the beginning of the republic. Livy and Valerius Maximus claim that the *ludi scaenici* were

---

[20] Suerbaum (2002) 94–95 notes the possibility that he may have (just like Ennius in 184) come to Rome as a professional author and eventually gained citizenship.
[21] See Feeney (2016) 62–63 on variant spellings of *Odyssia* (and the now commonly adopted form *Odusia*); I follow Cicero's spelling here.
[22] Gruen (1990) 84.   [23] Eutr. 3.1.

added as part of a religious expiation in 364 BCE.[24] These would have been Etruscan dancers and nothing like the later unified dramas based on Greek models. Around this time, a fourth day was added to recognize the reconciliation of the patricians and plebeians after the Aventine Secession in 367. By the end of the republic the games had expanded considerably: the *ludi scaenici* would occupy 15–18 September, with the *circenses* beginning already on 5 September. The centerpiece of the whole event remained the feast in honor of Jupiter (*epulum Iovis*) on 13 September, the day of the dedication of the Capitoline temple of Jupiter in 509. The continuing political importance of this festival is seen in examples that postdate Livius' play. Marc Antony brilliantly sought to trade on the festival's political and religious relevance by passing a law that added a fifth day in Caesar's honor in 44 (19 September). Probably not coincidentally, Augustus' deification in 14 CE fell on the middle day of the five days of *scaenici* (17 September). Augustus thereby left a lasting and regular impress on Roman events even in death, as he came to occupy the middle of the *scaenici* just as Jupiter occupied the middle of the whole festival.[25] In light of this larger continuum, the choice of the venue (*ludi Romani*) and the year 240 BCE, the year after the defeat of the greatest power in the western Mediterranean, were thus freighted with immense symbolic meaning, and to choose this date as the beginning of literature at Rome was also to suggest an intimate relationship between Roman letters and Roman dominion.

One can thus see the attraction of this event not only to its originators, but also to the likes of Varro, Atticus, and Cicero, who conspired to overrule the beginning that Accius, (probably) following Porcius Licinus, had provided a century earlier. Cicero, as Jarrett Welsh has persuasively shown, hardly gives a fair account of what these second-century researchers were doing or what their motivations were. Accius (170 – ca. 85) was a prominent poet, primarily of tragedies, and an innovative figure in the writing of literary history. He was a freeborn Roman citizen who came to Rome from his native Pisaurum, probably to teach grammar. He must have been trained in rhetoric as well, but probably avoided the forum, since, as Quintilian tells us, he once quipped that he could not (as he could in the theater) get his opponents to say what he wanted in order to craft a snappy comeback (*Inst.* 5.13.43).[26] Accius penned the *Didascalica*, a work

---

[24] Liv. 7.2.1–13, V. Max. 2.4.4.   [25] Discussed in van den Berg (2008) 265–66.

[26] The anonymous *Rhetorica ad Herennium*, once thought to be Cicero's, does report that Accius successfully prosecuted a mime for slandering him on stage (*Accius iniuriarum agit*, *Rhet. Her.* 1.24, cf. 2.19). If Accius did speak on his own behalf, as *agit* would seem to suggest, it is perplexing that

of prose perhaps mixed with poetry in nine books, perhaps a precursor of
Latin Menippean satire.[27] It was, by all accounts, the first major work on
literary history in Latin, although he will have followed Porcius Licinus'
earlier attempts, starting from Livius' hymn to Juno Regina of 207 and
noting his play of 197.

In the *Didascalica* Accius may have sought to cultivate a more general
audience, and his work included dialogue in its exposition. He covered
poetic genres, chronology, and questions of authenticity. In this regard he
is not only the most prominent representative of the pre-Varronian chronology, but also the most significant precursor to Cicero's *Brutus* in the
Roman tradition of literary history and criticism.[28] The *Didascalica*, probably for lack of adequate access to reliable records, put Livius Andronicus'
first drama in 197. This date was corrected to 240 by Varro and Atticus, a
redating that Cicero ostentatiously defends even as he conceals the good
reasons Accius would have had for such a choice. Accius probably still put
Livius at the beginning of literary history, but in a different genre, and
dated other early authors, Naevius and Plautus, to a later time that would
have still allowed for internal consistency in his chronology. His posited
beginning would have been in 207 during the consulship of Marcus Livius
Salinator and Gaius Claudius Nero. Livius was commissioned to write a
hymn to Juno Regina, to be sung by a procession of twenty-seven girls.
Rome continued to struggle during the Second Punic War (218–201), and
after this hymn's performance the Roman forces won the crucial battle of
the Metaurus against the Carthaginian forces under the leadership of
Hannibal's brother, Hasdrubal Barca. This was a major turning point,
and the hymn and its author were recognized as having contributed to
Rome's success.[29]

We have so internalized Cicero's correction of Accius that it is worth
spelling out the assumptions and silences that it has imposed on our sense

Cicero fails to mention his oratory, choosing instead exclusively to note his poetry. The anonymous
author's report may be apocryphal – perhaps derived and adapted from a rhetorical exercise?
[27] Courtney (2003) 60–62 questions the poetic elements against Leo (1913) 386. On the *Didascalica*
see Degl'Innocenti Pierini (1980) 58–67, Dangel (1995) 49–50, 252–55, 382–86, Schwindt (2000)
52–59, Suerbaum (2002) 163, with bibliography, Feeney (2016) 160–63. We know less about
Accius' *Pragmatica*, which discussed aspects of stage performance and language: Degl'Innocenti
Pierini (1980) 68–73, Dangel (1995) 51, 256–60, 386–89, Suerbaum (2002) 164.
[28] A potentially chastening point should at least be acknowledged: without Accius' account it is hard
to know if he may have anticipated some issues and problems that Cicero seems to be the first to
consider (much the same could be said for Varro). Leo (1913) 386–91 on the several similarities.
See also the Conclusion.
[29] On the establishment of the *collegium scribarum histrionumque* (and the *collegium poetarum*) and
possible, if murky, connections to Livius' hymn, see Horsfall (1976).

of literary history. Jarrett Welsh takes issue with Cicero's claim that Accius dated Livius' first play to 197, which Cicero says is eleven (or ten) years after Livius' capture in 209 (*annis post xi*). We might expect a Roman to have described the twelve years from 209 to 197 as *annis post xiii* (inclusive counting). This may not simply be Cicero's mathematical mistake, but rather a less-than-graceful obfuscation of what Accius, following Porcius Licinus, wrote: the hymn to Juno Regina in 207 was his first production, followed *xi* (i.e. ten with inclusive counting) years later in 197 by a dramatic production. Cicero distorts the chronology and introduces a mathematical error.[30]

Varro, Atticus, and Cicero dated Livius' play to 240, having uncovered new information to share with their audience. They also endowed literature's debut at Rome with new meaning, as Welsh notes: "elevating a different narrative that made Latin literature begin in times of peace, only occupying Roman attentions when they were not engaged in more pressing matters of war."[31] Cicero distorts Accius' reconstruction of literature's beginnings even as he is correcting it: he hides what were probably reasonable inferences and reconstructions based on the evidence Porcius Licinus and Accius had and magnifies Accius' mistake (*tantus error*) by cherry-picking those details that make Accius seem grossly inconsistent. Cicero not only follows the corrections of Atticus and Varro, he does so ostentatiously. The passage – on the surface at least – makes Cicero too seem like a prudent scrutinizer of events and their records.

The portrayal of Accius also diminishes his role as a literary historian and has two further effects. First, it allows Cicero to claim that he and his contemporaries have gotten it right because of their careful attention to detail. He unfairly suggests that Accius' whole chronology was not only mistaken but implausible even on its own terms, which was likely not true, as traces of a pre-Varronian chronology continued through antiquity. Porcius Licinus and Accius probably offered internally coherent, if factually questionable, accounts. Second, in decrying these predecessors Cicero repeats a rhetorical move that he made in discussing

---

[30] Again, Welsh (2011) 32–38 is invaluable. This may also be an example in which Cicero's hastiness serves his penchant for distortion. Rather than produce an internally coherent version he allows mathematical inaccuracies to stand. This manicured chaos enhances the impression that Accius had so confused matters.

[31] Welsh (2011) 32. The Conclusion discusses the relationship between peace and the development of oratory.

Ennius' documentation of Marcus Cornelius Cethegus (57–60).[32] Ennius becomes a reliable literary historian, for oratory at least, and Cicero follows in Ennius' literary-historical footsteps. The demotion of Accius as a literary historian goes hand in hand with the elevation of Ennius to a prominence in the field that he neither sought nor probably would have recognized. Much has been made of the distorting effects of Cicero's reconstructions of Ennius generally,[33] but to what extent he does so with Accius in the field of literary history is also important, not least because his criticisms of Accius, building on Varro and Atticus, contributed to the demise of Accius' reputation and hence the neglect of his texts.[34]

To have literature begin in 240 rather than 207 also affects the relative chronologies of oratory and poetry. Livius' hymn to Juno Regina in 207 would have provided a virtually simultaneous dating with Cicero's first orator, Marcus Cornelius Cethegus, which would confuse the beginnings of literary history by making oratory and poetry debut at roughly the same time. Yet only poetry is accorded a fixed beginning. Why doesn't oratory have a precise start date when such great hay is made of poetry's? Oratory does reach its *prima maturitas* in 106, the year of Crassus' speech on the *lex Servilia* and Cicero's birth (161), and it seems to be nearing old age along with Cicero. Oratory has a life and yet no date of birth.

This should seem far stranger to us than it usually does, as should the lack of any reference to emulation of Greek models in oratory's rise. It is baffling that a work so motivated by chronological exactness in determining or highlighting the key moments of a tradition or genre should give no date whatsoever for oratory's inauguration other than suggesting something like 204. That Latin poetic texts were first produced from Greek models is important because oratory, though eventually influenced by Greek models, could be considered Roman from the beginning. Reconstructing the early tradition in this way makes oratory a kind of native practice, which is quite different from the art of Livius and Ennius, who were "both poets and also semi-Greeks" (*et poetae et semigraeci*, Suet. *Gram. et rhet.* 1.2).[35]

---

[32] Chapter 5 discusses Cicero's manipulations of Ennian material to bolster his claims to accuracy and neutrality.

[33] Discussed in Chapter 5.

[34] All the more ironic given Cicero's insistence on recognizing older Roman poets and orators. Earlier literary historians are not granted the same indulgence, which conveniently supports Cicero's role as literary historian.

[35] It is undoubtedly true that public speech isn't limited to a single culture and does not require a formal theory of rhetoric. But most cultures also have some form of poetic or song culture, the Romans included. And yet in the version that they (and we, following them) have produced, that

One consequence of having a Roman origin for oratory (shared with the Greeks rather than merely taken over from them; cf. 254) is that the account of its origin is shrouded in the mists of time and the great Roman figures there. Cicero may cite Ennius on Cethegus, but he avoids an account that says "in the year X early orator Y produced a speech modeled on Greek orator Z, much as in 240 Livius adapted Greek poets." He might have claimed that "Appius Claudius Caecus inaugurated oratory after hearing Cineas, Demosthenes' greatest student, thereby furnishing the first monument of Latin oratory inspired by a Greek model."[36] Such an account would require some imaginative reconstruction, but tracing oratory's beginning through Cineas to Demosthenes would also provide yet another support for the work's Demosthenic bent and is at least as plausible as other fanciful unions across disciplines and cultures, such as Demosthenes' association with Plato or Numa's with Pythagoras.[37]

Admittedly, oratorical education modeled on Greek authors experienced a marked upturn in the middle of the second century, with Rome's eastern conquests and the subsequent importation of Greek disciplines and their teachers: Macedonia in 168, Achaia proper in 146, and the Pergamene kingdom in 133. Cicero cautiously labors to find the appropriate beginnings for oratorical adaptations of Greek material. Despite Cato's obscure position in the pre-hellenized phase of the *Brutus*, he still has a patently Greek cast: the only orator directly compared with a Greek model (Lysias) and described with technical terminology in Greek. He is also the figure whose lifetime (234–149) bridges the first significant watershed (168) in the pre- and post-hellenizing phases of oratory. It is not until after Lucius Licinius Crassus that Greek influence on orators comes fully into its own, although a good dose of skepticism will serve us well when facing the public anti-hellenism of the likes of Cato, and especially of Crassus and Antonius in *de Oratore*.

---

native version has been supplanted by a hellenizing account. See Habinek (2005) and Feeney (2016) for (quite different) takes on poetry's beginnings at Rome. Nothing prevented Romans or Cicero from producing an account for oratory that was also based on the imitation or adaptation of Greek models, even if it could not have been based on the translation of Greek models in the way that Livius Andronicus invented Roman poetry. Cicero's version involves choices and what matters for our purposes is not their correctness but their consequences for conceptualizing literary history and the beginning of an artistic tradition.

[36] On Cineas see Lévêque (1957) 346–50 with Plut. *Pyrrh.* 14–15 (Cineas) and 18–19 (Caecus). See also Chapter 5 for Cineas' connection to Appius Claudius Caecus.

[37] Demosthenes and Plato: 121, *de Orat.* 1.89, *Orat.* 15, Plut. *Dem.* 5.5. Numa and Pythagoras: Humm (2004).

That poetry began in 240 while oratory has designedly obscure beginnings may result from a desire to emphasize negligible imitation of Greeks
in the early tradition and how this characterizes the oratorical tradition.
Cicero attacks the Roman Atticists for subservience to Greek models and
makes the early tradition fit his own hellenizing-but-not-philhellenizing
commitments. It surely cannot be a coincidence that Atticus' objection to
older orators involves not just Cato but also Crassus (294–96), who, in
Cicero's depictions, publicly avoided ostentatious Greek learning, whatever his private activities and intellectual preferences. The line Atticus
draws between outdated and modern orators is about stylistic differences,
but also about attitudes toward Greek learning and emulating Greek
orators.[38] The need to counter Atticist philhellenism may have prompted
Cicero to reject early Roman dependency on Greek oratory. In that case
what we have is yet another example of a seemingly ingenuous and
unbiased account of origins and developments that are nevertheless shaped
by Cicero's partisan aims.

The *Laudatio Funebris* and Curio's Dialogue

In criticizing the *laudatio funebris* ("funeral praise," "eulogy") Cicero yet
again trumpets factual accuracy as a screen for his own motivations:

> our history has been compromised by these speeches. Many things were
> written in them that didn't happen: false triumphs, excessive consulships,
> even made-up lineages and transfers to a plebeian branch, mingling men of
> lower birth with a different branch of the same family name, much as if
> I were to claim descent from Manius Tullius, patrician consul with Servius
> Sulpicius a decade after the expulsion of the kings.

> his laudationibus historia rerum nostrarum est facta mendosior. multa enim
> scripta sunt in eis quae facta non sunt: falsi triumphi, plures consulatus,
> genera etiam falsa et ad plebem transitiones, cum homines humiliores in
> alienum eiusdem nominis infunderentur genus; ut si ego me a M'. Tullio
> esse dicerem, qui patricius cum Ser. Sulpicio consul anno x post exactos
> reges fuit. (62)

Though aware of the potential for misrepresentation in *laudationes*, Cicero
does not dismiss them wholesale. The main emphasis falls on the skewing
of content – retrospectively conjuring up details that misrepresent and
therefore permanently confuse the historical record. Just before Cicero

---

[38] Gruen (1992) 52–83, 223–71, Eckert (2018) on (hostile) attitudes toward Greek learning.

rejected them for aesthetic reasons (61), but here pivots to their distorting potential, a criticism emerging from his deliberate confusion of aesthetic and historical criteria.

Despite the declared allegiance to factual accuracy, the passage does not square with the realities of oratorical practice. Any trained speaker courted possibilities for the invention and arrangement of details, an oratorical principle also applicable to dialogues. Another telling point against the passage's conclusiveness is the characterization of the *Brutus* itself as a *laudatio* for Hortensius, which, ironically, suggests what the evidence of the dialogue bears out: similar distortions might make their way into Cicero's history of oratory. At the end of the dialogue he promotes Brutus' familial descent from the Junii Bruti, presumably going back to Lucius Junius Brutus (331), from whom Brutus could not have descended directly.[39] Cicero may also have had an axe to grind, since the *laudationes* were restricted to the *nobilitas* and its families and thus were the one area of public oratory closed to him. In stark contrast stands the likes of a Caesar, who in his quaestorship held a *laudatio* at the *rostra* for his aunt Julia (the widow of Marius) and his wife Cornelia. Caesar there traced his family's lineage back to Ancus Marcius and to Venus, that is to the Roman kings and to the gods.[40]

Cicero similarly insists on factual accuracy when he castigates Curio *pater* for an anachronism in his dialogue criticizing Caesar's administration of Gaul, which featured Gaius Vibius Pansa and Curio *filius* as interlocutors (218–19). Curio set the dialogue in 59 BCE, the year of Caesar's consulship and before his near-decade-long conquest of Gaul (58 to 50). The passage underscores the dangers of artistic license for plausibly ordering events, although the dialogue's fictional elements are never criticized. The fabrication of a conversation with Pansa and Curio, for example, like the *Brutus'* made-up meeting with Brutus and Atticus, is never challenged.[41] The fiction's plausibility, chronologically or otherwise, must be maintained.

---

[39] Kierdorf (1980), Flower (1996) 128–50 on the *laudatio*. Wiseman (1974) on legendary genealogies. Gildenhard (2013b) 248 on Cicero's flirtations with regal descent; on Romulus, *Catil.* 3.2, on Servius Tullius, *Tusc.* 1.38 (perhaps in jest).

[40] Suet. *Jul.* 6.1. Wiseman (1974) 159: "the highest historical standards were not to be expected, but that does not mean that these semi-fictional family trees were not taken seriously at their own level."

[41] *Fam.* 9.8.1 (SB 254), discussing the inclusion of Scaevola in *de Oratore*, emphasizes verisimilitude over truth: Varro should not be surprised to read about conversations that never actually took place. Cf. R. E. Jones (1939) for Cicero's latitude in portraying individuals, Hendrickson (1906) for Cicero's freedom with sources. Frisch (1985) reads the discussion of Curio's dialogue as a covert

The singling out of anachronisms may not be so innocent or common-sense for two quite different reasons. Cicero was hardly a friend of Curio, who not only had a successful political career but also clashed with Cicero, probably acquitting himself well.[42] He seems to have persuaded the jury to overlook Cicero's testimony at the *Bona Dea* trial and they sparred publicly afterwards.[43] The overt criticism of Curio's faulty memory, and thus his oratorical skills, may be calculated to mask a covert dismissal of his politics. Yet most of all Curio's purported failures are a foil to Cicero's own circumspection in writing a dialogue so invested in the accuracy of its chronology. Whether the criticisms are warranted is another matter. It is not clear that Curio's anachronism was necessarily suspect or that his fiction violated the conventions of the genre, which was still quite new at Rome.[44] The conversations staged by Plato, Cicero, or in Tacitus' *Dialogus* had some latitude for authorial inventiveness, and modern criteria would situate these works into the category of (historical) fiction. As with the refutation of Accius' beginning of literature, the criticism of Curio highlights Cicero's commitment to accuracy even as his use of the dialogue form and rhetorical presentation does not commit him absolutely to factual accuracy.

Coriolanus and Cultural Syncrisis

While the passages concerning Accius' dating of Livius, the *laudationes*, and Curio's dialogue bolster Cicero's persona as a seeker of truth, this is not the case throughout the *Brutus*. Other passages call attention to Cicero's creative license in reconstructing or judging the past. The syncrisis

---

attack on Caesar. See also the brief discussion of Curio's dialogue in Chapter 2, which notes a minor anachronism in Cicero's staging of *de Republica*.

[42] Curio was consul in 76, triumphed in 72, and was censor possibly in 61 (cf. *MRR* 2.92–93, 2.119, 3.186, respectively), with Moreau (1982) 157–67. W. J. Tatum (1991) on their antagonism and how it colored Cicero's judgment of Curio.

[43] Testimony: Moreau (1982) 194–226. Invective: The details surrounding dates and actual publication are disputed and need not concern us. See Geffcken (1973), Crawford (1994) 233–69 on *in P. Clodium et C. Curionem*, circulated without Cicero's permission in 58; *Att.* 1.16.8–10 (SB 16), *Att.* 3.12.2 (SB 57). McDermott (1972) 407–9 thinks Cicero published a separate attack on Curio, rejected by Crawford (1984) 108–9 n.10, (1994) 236 n.9.

[44] The earliest known example is from the jurist Marcus Junius Brutus, a didactic treatise on Roman law written to his son, discussed at Cic. *de Orat.* 2.224. Fantham (2004) 50–51 suggests that Curio's dialogue may precede Cicero's *de Oratore*. However, it is not certain that Curio wrote the dialogue before *de Oratore*, given that he criticizes Caesar's later policies – how much of Caesar did he criticize, i.e. how late could it have been written?

of Themistocles and Coriolanus reveals Cicero's potential to shape facts, ideas, and arguments:

> I said, "In the next generation Themistocles followed him [Pisistratus], a very old figure for us but not so old for the Athenians. He lived in fact when the Greek state dominated but our state had only recently been freed from regal domination. You see, that terrible war against the Volsci, which the exiled Coriolanus was in, took place at about the same time as the Persian war, and the fortune of these two illustrious men was similar. Each in fact, though being a noteworthy citizen, was expelled by the wrongdoing of an ungrateful populace and went over to the enemy side and settled with voluntary death their wrathful intention. Now although you write differently about Coriolanus, Atticus, still grant me my preference for this manner of death."
>
> Atticus smiled and said, "As you wish, since it's in fact permissible for rhetoricians to invent things in their narratives (*in historiis*) in order to render a more compelling account. Clitarchus and Stratocles made up the same story about Themistocles as you're doing now with Coriolanus. Now Thucydides, a noble Athenian and a very great man, was born only a bit later and wrote that he [Themistocles] died merely from an illness and was buried secretly in Attica, but added that there was suspicion of suicide by poison: your models [Clitarchus and Stratocles] say that after he had sacrificed a bull he caught the blood in a bowl and fell dead upon drinking it. While they were able to adorn this death rhetorically and tragically, that basic account offered no material to embellish. And so, since it so suits you that everything was the same for Themistocles and Coriolanus, you can have the drinking bowl from me too and I'll even give you the sacrificial animal, so that Coriolanus can fully be a second Themistocles."
>
> "As for that matter," I responded, "let it be settled: I'll be more careful now when treating history in earshot of someone whom I can adduce as an extremely scrupulous authority on Roman events."

hunc proximo saeculo Themistocles insecutus est, ut apud nos, peranti-quus, ut apud Athenienses, non ita sane vetus. fuit enim regnante iam Graeca,[45] nostra autem civitate non ita pridem dominatu regio liberata. nam bellum Volscorum illud gravissimum, cui Coriolanus exsul interfuit, eodem fere tempore quo Persarum bellum fuit, similisque fortuna clarorum virorum; si quidem uterque, cum civis egregius fuisset, populi ingrati pulsus iniuria se ad hostes contulit conatumque iracundiae suae morte sedavit. nam etsi aliter apud te est, Attice, de Coriolano, concede tamen ut huic generi mortis potius adsentiar.

---

[45] *Graeca* for *Graecia* (Kaster 2020, following Jahn; discussed at Badian 1967 225).

At ille ridens: tuo vero, inquit, arbitratu; quoniam quidem concessum est
rhetoribus ementiri in historiis, ut aliquid dicere possint argutius. ut enim
tu nunc de Coriolano, sic Clitarchus, sic Stratocles de Themistocle finxit.
nam quem Thucydides, qui et Atheniensis erat et summo loco natus
summusque vir et paulo aetate posterior, tantum <morbo> mortuum
scripsit et in Attica clam humatum, addidit fuisse suspicionem veneno sibi
conscivisse mortem: hunc isti aiunt, cum taurum immolavisset, excepisse
sanguinem patera et eo poto mortuum concidisse. hanc enim mortem
rhetorice et tragice ornare potuerunt; illa mors vulgaris nullam praebebat
materiem ad ornatum. quare quoniam tibi ita quadrat, omnia fuisse
Themistocli paria et Coriolano, pateram quoque a me sumas licet, praebebo
etiam hostiam, ut Coriolanus sit plane alter Themistocles.

Sit sane, inquam, ut lubet, de isto; et ego cautius posthac historiam
attingam te audiente, quem rerum Romanarum auctorem laudare possum
religiosissumum. (41–44)

Cicero pleads with Atticus for indulgence in aligning Coriolanus' death
with that of Themistocles, seeking to make the details match in each
account (*similis*, *uterque*).[46] Atticus emphasizes precisely this alignment
of the two historical figures (*omnia paria*). This playful sparring challenges
gross historical distortion while supporting the parallels produced by
syncritic comparison. Cicero may be chary of inventing a blatantly erroneous scenario with obvious chronological flaws, such as he found in
Curio's dialogue. He will, however, embellish lives or align careers to
enhance the plausibility of a given narrative, and here, as elsewhere, he
draws attention to these embellishments. Cicero is at liberty to select,
emphasize, and even create similarities between distinct individuals or
events.[47]

For this reason, Atticus comments, rhetoricians have latitude for inventiveness when producing a better account (*concessum est rhetoribus ementiri
in historiis, ut aliquid dicere possint argutius*). This is not the same as
falsification of the past, since the embellishment of facts must serve the
coherent aims of the narrative. Atticus will subsequently adduce alternative
evidence from Thucydides, who reports Themistocles' death, his secret
burial in Attica, and the rumors of suicide by poison, which he

---

[46] Cicero repeats the parallel at *Amic.* 42. Liv. 2.40.10–11, Plut. *Cor.* 39.1–9, and Dion. Hal. *Ant.
Rom.* 8.59 offer alternative accounts. See Berthold (1965) on Cicero's varying depictions of
Themistocles; Marr (1995) on the genesis of Themistocles' suicide. Cf. Boyancé (1940), Bréguet
(1967) 607–8, Rawson (1972) 33 n.4.

[47] At *Amic.* 42 Themistocles postdates Coriolanus by twenty years. Cf. *Att.* 9.10.3 (SB 177), where
both are mentioned but the similarities are not emphasized. *De Oratore*, *de Republica*, and *de Legibus*
all draw attention to their fictional status and potential for distortion.

acknowledges but rejects. Rhetoricians can elaborate accounts rhetorically and tragically (*hanc enim mortem rhetorice et tragice ornare potuerunt*, 43).[48] Furthermore, Cicero can at least cite sources for his version, even if the alternatives are less venerable than Thucydides (*ut enim tu nunc de Coriolano, sic Clitarchus, sic Stratocles de Themistocle finxit*, 42).[49] Cicero lays bare the procedures for the embellishment of inherited material (*ornare*), which is justified provided that it enhances similarities and patterns of a narrative.

Embellishment of details was standard practice among orators, who seek out the best material for a case (*inventio*) but with considerable license to fill in gaps with details that can be plausibly attributed or inferred. Imperial Roman declaimers formalized this artistic technique, exploring fully the power of its fictive tendencies for moral and ethical speculation. From a broader perspective Cicero's methodological reflections in the *Brutus* are of a piece with the general practice of ancient historians, who incorporated the data of history into embellished scenarios in order to produce the most coherent and plausible narrative.[50] It is noteworthy that the *Brutus*, a dialogue surveying the past rather than an annalistic account, nonetheless defines *historia* as the inventive artistic production of historical narrative.[51]

Cicero is by no means deaf to the substantive point underlying Atticus' objections. He concedes the need for circumspection in the presence of a historical authority as scrupulous as Atticus (*ego cautius posthac historiam attingam te audiente, quem rerum Romanarum auctorem laudare possum religiosissimum*, 44). The need for caution, however, only heightens attention to possible fictions without ruling them out. Through Atticus Cicero will later call into question his own pledge to be more cautious, as *religiosissimum* ("most punctilious," 44) anticipates Atticus' later

[48] The term *rhetorice* in the light of the norms of declamation may help to elucidate the procedures of factual embellishment. Declaimers had considerable license with the invention or supposition of facts, motives, or reasons provided that they did not contradict what was known or widely believed to be known.
[49] Citation of alternative precedents is crucial to his dating of Naevius' death, discussed below.
[50] The remarks at Lintott (2008) 3 are instructive: "most accounts of past history in his works have a persuasive element that tends to overshadow his devotion to the truth as he knows it."
[51] The study of historiography in classics is now well established, with a considerable scholarship on the theoretical questions and countless studies of ancient historians' literary approaches. In addition to Cicero's discussions (Cic. *Fam.* 5.12 [SB 22], *Att.* 1.19, 2.1.1–2 [SB 19, SB 21], *de Orat.* 2.51–64, *Leg.* 1.1–5), see also several essays in Kraus (1999), and the Introduction, chaps. 1–3 and chap. 25 in Feldherr (2009). Wiseman (1979) and Woodman (1988) esp. 70–126 are seminal. There are still holdouts, most notably Lendon (2009, chap. 3 in Feldherr 2009). On the material from *de Oratore* see further Leeman (1963) 168–74, Fantham (2004) 146–52, and Fox (2007) 134–41.

questioning of Cicero's *religio* ("scrupulousness," "accuracy") in the likening of Cato's rhetorical ability to that of Lysias (293). The frequent gestures to scruple and accuracy ultimately throw into relief Cicero's considerable license to evaluate and manipulate the available material.[52]

The *Brutus* does not insist on absolute truth in organizing the past, and references to distinctions such as fact/fiction or history/rhetoric provide only so much guidance for understanding Cicero's historiographical methods. Over and again the interest in exemplarity depicts later actors and events in harmony with preexisting models in an effort to search out repetitions and to make sense of later events through similarities to earlier ones. Most broadly, for example, Roman oratory develops similarly to Greek oratory and even to early Roman poetry on a number of scores (as this and other chapters discuss). The positing and analysis of parallels involve not so much passively comparing inert facts as actively organizing them so that they acquire explanatory meaning. Cicero eschews thoroughly implausible and contradictory ideas (as with Curio's anachronism), but the judicious selection and elucidation of details guide the narrative and its arguments throughout the dialogue. Cicero's duty is to persuade readers of the validity of his literary history, not to demonstrate its absolute factual accuracy.[53]

Chronology and the Making of the Past

Cicero orders his material with an eye to the significance of watershed events, coincidences in the lives of individuals that often rely on but are not explicitly tied to syncritic judgment and are, nonetheless, essential to the larger image of literary history that emerges. These events include births and deaths of poets and orators, literary production alongside the tenure of office (often but not always the consulship), important literary works, or key stages of an orator's career.[54] A number of these details, to be sure, are traditional and therefore seem relatively innocent – the use of consular dating, for example. Indeed, scarcely a page of the *Brutus* fails to

---

[52] Boyancé (1940) goes too far in reading the passage as granting Cicero carte blanche. We must also infer his attitude from his treatment of historical data.

[53] As Moatti (1997) 310 notes, for late republican scholars illuminating the past was equivalent to getting it right: "la clarification valait bien la vérité." Zetzel (2007) 11 on the chronology of Atticus, Nepos, and Varro notes that "it is firm only in the sense that it became generally accepted, not that it was true." Cf. Fox (2007) 195.

[54] My section on the Ciceropaideia in Chapter 1 also discusses Cicero's alignment of biographical data, literary creations, and political events.

increase Cicero's debt to the annalistic tradition. Yet biographical details are essential to constructing a meaningful history, not as mere data points within a sequential narrative, but as "chronological hooks," which give meaning to that narrative.[55]

Cicero only selectively draws on the traditional annalistic framework, the dating of years by reference to the two consuls. The consulships do not create a predictable linear trajectory; rather, select consulships populate his history with meaningful coordinates onto which the development of literature can be plotted. Other events, including individual births and deaths, lesser magistracies, periods of war, and the production of literary texts, whether poetry or oratory, are then plotted onto this grid of offices in order to provide a different sense of literary development in time.[56] Cicero lays out before the reader a "chronoscape" of meaningful literary events and their crafters. Rather than present smooth continuities of linear, annual, or cyclical regularity, he details instead a landscape of temporal progression from which emerge the key markers of literary-historical significance, artists and artworks of special distinction.[57]

This history begins with his documentation of poetic events and deaths, which, because poetry precedes oratory at Rome, provides a model for later developments in the field of oratory. Cicero notes that Gaius Sulpicius Galus

> was the most devoted to Greek letters of all noble men; and he was both ranked as an orator and was distinguished and elegant in other matters. By now the general manner of speech was rather rich and remarkable: you see, he was the praetor in charge of the games to Apollo at which Ennius had staged a *Thyestes* and then died, in the consulship of Quintus Marcius and Gnaeus Servilius.

---

[55] Douglas (1966b) 291: "Few pages, apart from the digressions into literary criticism and polemic, lack chronological indications." On "chronological hooks" cf. Feeney (2007) 13: "What eventually comes to underpin the entire ancient project of organizing historical time is precisely the use of such canonical events as hooks from which intervals forwards or backwards could be counted." Sumner (1973) 158, refining the arguments of Douglas (1966b), first conclusively established the importance of birth dates generally as a structuring principle: "Cicero used as his chronological foundation (a) dates of birth where known and (b) the evidence on dates of birth afforded by his orators' public careers." Sumner (1973) 3–5 and 159–60 takes an intermediate position between Douglas (1966b) and Badian (1964) 241 n.11, noting that "Douglas's theory is overstated rather than fundamentally mistaken" (5), while Badian's criticism of Douglas and characterization of the *Brutus* were "unduly severe and uncompromising" (160).

[56] Mazzarino (1966) 412–61 (one long note) discusses time in historiography, including the plotting of events onto conceptual space.

[57] "Chronoscape" is an adaptation of what Bakhtin (1981) 84 calls the "chronotope" to describe "the intrinsic connectedness of temporal and spatial relationships that are artistically expressed in literature." For a cognitive approach to physical representations of time, see Zerubavel (2003).

maxume omnium nobilium Graecis litteris studuit; isque et oratorum in
numero est habitus et fuit reliquis rebus ornatus atque elegans. iam enim
erat unctior quaedam splendidiorque consuetudo loquendi. nam hoc prae-
tore ludos Apollini faciente cum Thyesten fabulam docuisset, Q. Marcio
Cn. Servilio consulibus mortem obiit Ennius. (78)

Cicero cites Ennius' play as a marker of contemporary style, much as
Naevius' writings reflect the speech of his age (*illius autem aetatis qui sermo
fuerit ex Naevianis scriptis intellegi potest*, 60, discussed below).

Key elements, however, surface here and will resurface at other crucial
points: a specific office (not necessarily the consulship) is connected to a
piece of literature and the death of an author. This pattern aligns developments in literary history with the tenure of office and the birth or death
of a significant figure. This is a lot to attribute to a single example, but the
connection of Galus' praetorship to Ennius' *Thyestes* and his death in the
same year endows these otherwise random events with explanatory force.
The account is not one of strict causality, but it does explain and document aesthetic change. The simultaneity of events becomes a landmark in
the chronoscape of literary history, confirming through coincidence the
validity of Cicero's claims about oratorical progress. It may initially seem
that Cicero treats these data much as he does the chronological hooks of
the annual consulships, that is, as markers of temporal progress. Yet there
is a crucial difference: the consulship provides a structure of regular
intervals, while notable clusters of events allow a significant development
in literary history to stand out against the background of the consulships.

Cicero will later draw on this pattern to explain his own place in literary
history. The most obvious – and obviously self-serving – attempt to
meaningfully populate this chronoscape is the presentation of his own
birth:

> But at the time when Crassus' speech was published, which I know you've
> often read, he was thirty-four and as many years older than me. He argued
> for the law in the year of my birth, whereas he was born in the consulship of
> Quintus Caepio and Gaius Laelius, three years younger than Antonius. I've
> set this out so it could be observed in which age the first maturity of Latin
> oratory had come into being and understood that it had been brought then
> nearly to its summit, so that virtually no one could enhance it, except
> someone better trained in philosophy, civil law, and history.

> sed haec Crassi cum edita oratio est, quam te saepe legisse certo scio,
> quattuor et triginta tum habebat annos totidemque annis mihi aetate
> praestabat. his enim consulibus eam legem suasit quibus nati sumus, cum
> ipse esset Q. Caepione consule natus et C. Laelio, triennio ipso minor

quam Antonius. quod idcirco posui, ut dicendi Latine prima maturitas in qua aetate exstitisset posset notari et intellegeretur iam ad summum paene esse perductam, ut eo nihil ferme quisquam addere posset, nisi qui a philosophia a iure civili ab historia fuisse instructior. (161)

Cicero's birth coincides with Crassus' speech in defense of the Servilian law (106 BCE), and Crassus himself came to the world in the consulship of C. Laelius (140 BCE), a significant figure in the *Brutus'* pairing of him with Africanus; Galba in turn outranks both men. Cicero provides not only the chronology but its interpretation, or at least part of it. He draws attention to what initially seem to be innocent parallels: his birth coincides with a formative speech by Crassus, who is born during the consulship of an eminent figure. Careful selection and interpretation, however, turns brute chronology and Roman habits of timekeeping into a meaningful narrative. Cicero forgoes any aesthetic argument about Crassus' speech or why oratory has attained maturity, assuming rather than seeking the reader's acknowledgment of the speech's status as a marker of oratory's florescence (we would do well to remember that Atticus later derides it, 296). Causality emerges from the established pattern, the interconnection of significant office, birth, and the production of a literary work. No argument is made about the specific historical or aesthetic developments that somehow demonstrate that oratory has reached maturity. Instead oratory's *prima maturitas* arises from the inevitable collusion of historical events: major figures in an interconnected sequence producing meaningful works of literature.

Cicero's birth is hardly the first instance in which ulterior motives underlie his artful construal of apparently inert facts. He repeatedly selects and then inserts specific events into his narrative in such a way that meaningful patterns emerge from the raw data of biography, as when he maps his and Hortensius' careers onto the life of Crassus in order to make those careers align more closely and to highlight their rivalry.[58] We first hear of Hortensius' debut in the forum in 95:

> he first spoke in the forum when Lucius Crassus and Quintus Scaevola were consuls and even before the consuls themselves, and he left with the approval of those present and of the consuls themselves, who excelled all others in understanding.

> is L. Crasso Q. Scaevola consulibus primum in foro dixit et apud hos ipsos quidem consules, et cum eorum qui adfuerunt tum ipsorum consulum, qui omnibus intellegentia anteibant, iudicio discessit probatus. (229)

---

[58] Chapter 1 discusses this aspect of the Ciceropaideia and Crassus' speech on the *lex Servilia*.

It is not until some seventy chapters later in the *Brutus*, after a long series of digressions, that Hortensius will return, now at the peak of his powers: "and so he was reaching his height when Crassus died, Cotta was exiled, the courts suspended, and I entered the forum" (*hoc igitur florescente Crassus est mortuus, Cotta pulsus, iudicia intermissa bello, nos in forum venimus*, 303). Cicero's career follows closely on Hortensius', but the determining points for their debuts are connected to quite different aspects of Crassus' life: for Hortensius Crassus' consulship, for Cicero Crassus' death.

The details are useful for what they reveal as much as for what they omit, and small differences show how ingeniously Cicero labors to craft a seamless narrative. Cicero did not deliver a speech in 91/90 as Hortensius had in his debut "in the forum" in 95.[59] Cicero would only first take up cases, both private (Quinctius, 81 BCE) and public (Roscius of Ameria, 80 BCE), nearly a decade later (311). Unlike Hortensius, his entry into the forum was not a speech but the *tirocinium fori*, the introduction of an aspiring orator to public life. The details of Crassus' life and death are not simply neutral chronological points on a timeline. Crassus' biography is used to create the image of Cicero as the natural rival to Hortensius and, more importantly, as the natural successor to Crassus. References to these stages in Crassus' life are all the more important because along the way in the *Brutus* Cicero endows events such as these, as well as births, deaths, offices, or literary productions, with meaning greater than their factual dates.

Inventing the Death of Naevius

The history of early poetry is riddled with confusion in the historical record, but some of it can be better understood by recognizing how Cicero interconnects biographical and political details within the development of an *ars*. One notorious example demonstrates well the transformation of raw data into a meaningful pattern: the date of Naevius' death. It remains one of the riddles of the *Brutus*.[60] Barring new evidence his date of birth will remain unknown, and his death, Cicero claims, fell in the consulship of Cethegus (204 BCE):

---

[59] There are two separate issues in Cicero's presentation here: first, he combines the events of 91/90 to make them seem contemporaneous and massages the details to make his career follow that of Hortensius. Hortensius likely did not speak in the forum but in the senate, and Hortensius' participation in the forum (whatever it was) fundamentally differs from Cicero's *tirocinium fori*. These are both discussed in Chapter 1.

[60] On this passage and the dates for the deaths of Plautus and Naevius, see Dahlmann (1962) 605–13, Schaaf (1979), D'Anna (1996), Rösch-Binde (1998) 470–89, Lehmann (2002) 102–7.

This Cethegus was consul with Publius Tuditanus during the Second Punic War and Marcus Cato was quaestor when they were consul, clearly just 140 years before I was consul… When these men were consuls, Naevius died, as was written in the old records (although our friend Varro, an extremely careful researcher of antiquity, thinks this wrong and extends the life of Naevius). You see, Plautus died in the consulship of Publius Claudius and Lucius Porcius, when Cato was censor, twenty years after those consuls I mentioned.

At hic Cethegus consul cum P. Tuditano fuit bello Punico secundo quaestorque his consulibus M. Cato modo plane annis clx ante me consulem… his enim consulibus, ut in veteribus commentariis scriptum est, Naevius est mortuus,[61] quamquam Varro noster diligentissumus investigator antiquitatis putat in hoc erratum vitamque Naevi producit longius. nam Plautus P. Claudio L. Porcio viginti annis post illos quos ante dixi consulibus mortuus est Catone censore. (60)

Once again Cicero perfectly unites the appeal to diligent accuracy with what is likely a distortion in the service of his own aims, insisting on 204 BCE as the death date of Naevius and citing *veteres commentarii* as an alternative source. He also shows a markedly independent attitude toward Varro, again suggesting his scholarly circumspection by not appearing beholden to either Varro or even Atticus. That impression is misleading: he praises Varro's scrupulousness and notes the later date, but does not refute Varro in detail as he had refuted Accius for misdating the beginning of literature (72–73).

We are privy here to the attempted establishment of a chronological tradition based less on indisputable evidence than on a consensus of authorities or sources. One can compare disagreements over Rome's foundation, which years earlier Polybius, Varro, and Cicero had agreed upon as 751/50 BCE. By the time of the writing of the *Brutus* new evidence made compelling the revised and (now) traditional 754/53. Neither date is correct in any absolute sense. Cicero and his contemporaries were still sorting out precisely these kinds of questions while facing considerable material limitations in the historical record. Determinations were often made by assessing which date, in the absence of conclusive evidence, offered the best narrative; that narrative could, in a circular fashion, then also help to explain the choice of date.

What exactly is Cicero up to in this passage on Naevius' death? Two separate yet interrelated issues are involved: the insistence on 204 as the

---

[61] I punctuate here with a comma for Malcovati's semicolon. The reasons are given below.

year of Naevius' death and the attribution of the sentence beginning with *nam* (is this Cicero's or Varro's reason?). One reading of Cicero's statement is as follows: Plautus died in the censorship of Cato (184); Plautus is Naevius' contemporary; therefore (Varro claims), Naevius lived longer than 204. As Douglas notes, the logic is senseless.[62] The reasoning is coherent, however, if we see that Cicero recalls and reinforces a pattern he noted in the cases of Gaius Sulpicius Galus and Crassus/Hortensius/Cicero (discussed above). He prefers 204 because it has a canonical author dying during the tenure of office of a significant orator.

Producing that alignment involves some scholarly contortions. Cicero's reference to *veteres commentarii* is vague and warrants circumspection. The choice of 204 probably refers to notice of Naevius' last known dramatic production. Varro was almost certainly right in choosing a later date for Naevius' death, and Cicero probably knew so. Jerome claims that Naevius died while exiled in Utica in 201 (did Varro use similar details for his dating?). Cicero makes convenient use of conflicting but equally plausible evidence in the sources. While feeling obliged to signal his differences with Varro, he still insists on 204.[63]

We can follow Cicero's train of thought to the end if we attribute the *nam*-clause to him rather than Varro.[64] Cicero does not say something like *nam, ut dixit Varro noster*, or cast the sentence as indirect statement to signal Varro's explanation. The notice of Plautus' death in 184 is Cicero's, and he provides it because he has been highlighting the career of Cato the Elder, who held office in 204 and 184. Mention of Cato's censorship might make sense, but the quaestorship is surprising. It is true that in 204 Cethegus, the first *orator*, held the consulship, but the synchrony of Cato's quaestorship with Cethegus' consulship cannot alone have motivated the

---

[62] Douglas (1966a) 51.

[63] Jer. *Chron.* 1816 = Olymp. 144.4 = 201 BCE (*Uticae moritur, pulsus Roma*). Cf. Badian (1972) 160–61, Marmorale (1967) 31 and 132; Jocelyn (1969) 41–42 questions Jerome's reasons, but not a later dating. I suspect that Cicero omits details from Varro's account and not, as Jocelyn thinks, that Cicero found in Varro only the conjecture of a later date. Plautus' death in 184, it must be noted, is also only conjecture from the last known performance; see Leo (1912) 70. What records Cicero consulted remains a mystery, but these were presumably privately held documents rather than state archives; see Culham (1989).

[64] Schaaf (1979) 30, Rösch-Binde (1998) 478 n.2; D'Anna (1996) 100 n.31 attributes it to Varro. In the translation above I have made *quamquam* parenthetically concessive ("although"). Placing a half or full stop before it, as Malcovati does, shifts the focalization to Varro's viewpoint ("And yet"). Cicero does not switch to Varro's view but continues to present his own to the end of the section, merely noting Varro's different claim in passing.

notice.[65] Inclusion of the detail makes sense in conjunction with the later mention of Cato's censorship of 184 (when Plautus died). The *nam*-clause states that Plautus lived until the censorship of Cato not to argue that Naevius therefore lived longer but to underscore the alignments with Cato's career. Cato, of course, will usher in the next major stage in the development of oratory at Rome after Cethegus. The deaths of Naevius and Plautus meaningfully bracket each end of his *cursus*: his first major office (*quaestor*) and the final and most famous one (*censor*). Cicero contrives to make the dates line up in order to suggest a meaningful pattern: the tenure of office by one significant literary figure (Cato) coincides with the death of another – in this case, with two others, Naevius and Plautus.

Cicero invents (in the ancient and modern senses) meaningful parallels in the biographies of Naevius, Plautus, and Cato, insisting that Naevius died in 204 in order to connect those deaths to the careers of the first two figures of oratorical history, and to the *cursus* of Cato the Elder in particular.[66] Just as Cicero aligned significant events for himself and Hortensius with the biographical data of Crassus, so does he contrive to organize the deaths and careers of Naevius/Plautus and Cethegus/Cato. This is yet another example of Cicero's impulse to find or craft meaningful patterns and synchronies in the historical account.

Now, this way of conducting the business of literary history may not sit well with modern scholars, who would probably throw up their hands at Cicero's emphasis on a coherent narrative over the better facts of chronology. But his interest is in selecting the right chronology for the purposes of his account, and not, as the modern scholar does, seeking to get the chronology right and then building the account from the data points. Cicero labors to create a larger sense of literary history that is interconnected and coherent, formed from patterns, repetitions, and coincidences in chronology and lives that suggest a unity and inevitability in the history.

A theoretical basis for plotting the deaths of Naevius/Plautus onto the careers of Cethegus/Cato had already surfaced in Cicero's exchange with Atticus over Coriolanus and Themistocles (discussed above). Cicero had

---

[65] Badian (1972) 155 and 201 remarks that no other quaestorship is mentioned in this way in the *Brutus*. Cf. Jocelyn *apud* Badian (1972) 201 with Badian's response. Of the four uses of *quaestor*, the closest example denotes C. Gracchus, but to indicate the age difference between Gracchus and Brutus' kinsman M. Junius Pennus (109).

[66] Plautus/Naevius make a convenient pair (apparently coevals at *Tusc.* 1.3; cf. *de Orat.* 3.45, Gell. *NA* 3.3). Schaaf (1979) argues that they indicate generational differences in style, rightly rejected by Rösch-Binde (1998) 480–81.

used the deaths of those two figures as a way to associate them and suggest their conceptual affinities within a larger narrative.[67] And just as he demonstrated free use of sources in selecting between Thucydides and the *rhetores*, Clitarchus and Stratocles, so too does he reject Varro's account concerning the death of Naevius in favor of unspecified *commentarii*. The presumably less reliable sources – which probably gave no other information than that Naevius last produced a play in 204 – are preferred because they provide better parallels. Cicero does not permit the evidence to drive the narrative; rather, as we might expect from someone alert to the latitude accorded to ancient rhetoric and historiography, he allows the narrative to shape the selection and presentation of plausible facts to support the grander design.[68]

To be sure, he cannot willy-nilly manufacture the raw data of history, even if, in the face of competing sources, he can choose those he suspects or even knows are wrong. When turning to the biographies of early Roman poets, for example, it is largely coincidence that the significant dates of the poets' lives yield a fairly neat succession: Livius Andronicus first put on a play in 240, Ennius was born in 239 and lived until 169, and Accius was born in 170. If one overlooks other contemporaries such as Naevius or Pacuvius, then the material forms a neat, though not perfect, lineage of authors. One can imagine the physical impression of continuity all the more vividly when keeping in mind a visual representation such as Atticus' *Liber Annalis*, with all events laid out in a single sweeping view (*ut explicatis ordinibus temporum uno in conspectu omnia viderem*, 15).[69] One can further imagine Cicero gazing hopefully at the exact parallels that could have been – why could not Ennius have been born a year earlier and Accius a year later, a perfect sequence of deaths and births in the poetic succession of Livius–Ennius–Accius? Setting aside what Cicero saw or might have hoped to see in Atticus' *Liber*, a partial caveat must be issued in the case of Naevius, for whose death Cicero visibly selects the evidence that matches his own sense of the workings of literary history in the *Brutus*.

---

[67] Cicero's choice of Coriolanus/Themistocles in the "theoretical" discussion of syncrisis and historical distortion may have been motivated not only by their similar fates while alive but also specifically for their similar deaths; only later in the dating of Naevius/Plautus does the focus on their deaths obtain its full importance.

[68] Jastrow (1900) 132 gets at the underlying psychology: "Create a belief in the theory, and the facts will create themselves."

[69] Münzer (1905) on the *Liber Annalis* with Feeney (2007) 7–42, who emphasizes the physical layout of synchronistic works across and within cultural histories. Again, it is worth noting that the death of Ennius does become a significant marker for the presentation of Gaius Sulpicius Galus. As for Plautus and Naevius, circumspection is warranted.

This is not outright falsification, however, since he remains true to his methodological principles: he cites an alternative source for his claims; and the orator's commitment to *inventio* mandates the presentation or suppression of details to support an argument.

The tendentiousness in Cicero's literary history emerges not so much in the evolutionary scheme that culminates in Cicero, however important that feature is. To be sure, it is self-serving, but transparently so, leading most modern readers to question its assumptions. Less apparent and more compelling is the way it organizes literary history to suggest inevitability. Cicero adverts to the accurate presentation of factual details, but discerning a meaningful pattern in those details requires both the literary historian's arrangement of that material and the reader's willingness to accept it. The allure in this way of conducting business lies in providing surface gestures to reliability and plausibility on the one hand and then selecting and presenting those details to suggest a consequential pattern on the other. Cicero naturalizes the historical relationship of cause and effect, helping readers to forget that he, as much as history, is the organizing force behind the patterns that emerge.

The emphasis on meaningful coincidences powerfully reminds us that the plausibility of Cicero's literary history is sustained as much by its overall aesthetic impression as by any facts it may contain.[70] But all the scholarly energy devoted to biographical alignments must amount to more than simply an exercise in conveniently matching up dates or establishing patterns. Indeed, it cannot be merely coincidental that Cicero documents the beginning of orators by looking to poets. Just as Roman oratorical history maps onto Greek oratorical history, so too do Rome's oratorical beginnings map onto an early phase of the poetic tradition. Here early – but not earliest – is the operative word, since oratory's start necessarily postdates poetry's. Naevius and Plautus postdate Livius Andronicus, and so pairing them at their deaths with the careers of Cethegus and Cato juxtaposes the representatives of two different arts while keeping us in mind of the chronological sequence: oratory follows poetry.[71]

---

[70] Perkins (1992) 110: "Yet after they have constructed their narratives, most literary historians believe them. Their sense of conviction rests, I believe, on grounds that may broadly be called aesthetic. They have integrated many events into a pattern, and the sense of totality and coherence transforms itself into a sense of truth."

[71] Literary historiography similarly passes from poetry to prose. Ennius and Accius, poets and literary historians (in Cicero's portrayal), give way to Varro and Cicero, prose authors of literary history. This shift is anticipated by the mention of poetic laments for dead colleagues – typically understood as Sophocles' tribute to Euripides – through which Cicero defends the *Brutus'* mourning of Hortensius (3).

The aesthetic impression of the neat sequence of facts lined up so perfectly also justifies yet another choice that ancient and modern readers have struggled with: making Cato not the first but the second orator. Yet having Cato come right after Cethegus fittingly unites the two through their simultaneous tenure of office (quaestor and consul, respectively) at the death of Naevius, a coincidence that neatly paves the way for Cato's censorship at the death of Plautus.

The alignment of Roman office holders and poetic deaths also brings us back to the discussion above of Galus' praetorship, his superintendence of the *ludi Apollinares*, and Ennius' death after producing his *Thyestes* there. That account also interconnects Roman literature and Roman office, conceiving of literary texts in the light of official duties and civic institutions and likening poetic performance to oratorical practice. And it is all the more meaningful that Galus' stylistic achievements are attributed to Greek learning and that he is affiliated with Roman games for Apollo – the divine sponsor, of course, of music, song, and poetry.

All these careful juxtapositions underscore what we can think of as the literariness of oratory. They are yet another pragmatic step in likening one literary genre to another literary genre by association. This is not the same as strictly or theoretically equating poetry and oratory, of course. It is rather the crafting of a persuasive web of cultural associations between early authors irrespective of genre, not to discount or ignore generic differences, but to fit each genre into a larger conception of a literary network. And it is for this reason that the *Brutus* – purportedly a history of oratory – initially focuses so intently on poetry and poets. Poetry began as an adaptation of Greek models, while oratory is a native tradition that evolved to rely on Greek texts while still rivaling or perhaps surpassing the best of them. If poetry is part of an established, recognizable, and evolving literary system, then, Cicero show us, it is a system to which oratory too must belong.

CHAPTER 5

Beginning (and) Literary History

No passage from Roman antiquity has so determined the shape of Latin literary history as Cicero's discussion (72–73) of Livius Andronicus' dramatic production of 240 BCE.[1] In the year following the successful conclusion of the first of three wars against Carthage (the First Punic War, 264–241), Livius adapted a Greek play into Latin to be put on at the Great or Roman Games (*ludi magni* or *Romani*). Likewise, no event of Latin literary history has received such sustained attention from scholars since: Aulus Gellius in the Roman empire, Vasari and Bruni in the Renaissance, Friedrich Leo's marvelous literary history (1913), and on up to Denis Feeney's 2016 *Beyond Greek*. The moment described was itself not a first but (at least) a second beginning for Latin literature, as Cicero, with the assistance of Varro and Atticus, ostentatiously refutes Accius' proposed starting point, Livius' *Hymn to Juno Regina* of 207 BCE. The terms Cicero laid out, in conjunction with the bare facts of history and the refined inquiries of his contemporaries, have been the subject of endless fascination and dispute, and the values and prejudices that brought him to this beginning have been equally questioned and embraced by scholars ever since.

It is not this book's aim to insist on a different beginning of Latin literature. It will suggest, however, that Cicero – and all of us who have since followed him – must have seriously considered at least one other possibility: Appius Claudius Caecus and his *Speech against the Peace with Pyrrhus* in (roughly) 280. Still, even a better beginning would be a failure of sorts, for Cicero as for any literary historian. That hard skepticism results not so much from the paucity and complexity of the Roman evidence as from the acknowledgment that seeking out such beginnings is akin to tracking unicorns: a better unicorn trap cannot yield better prey. Such beginnings are serviceable fictions that reveal as much about their

---

[1] Quoted and discussed at length in Chapter 4.

authors' intellectual assumptions and limits as they do about the literary tradition. As Eviatar Zerubavel remarks, "offering a fair historical account may very well require some willingness to actually consider multiple narratives with *multiple beginnings*."[2] Consideration of Cicero's beginnings illuminates his guiding assumptions and innovations in literary historiography. It also reveals his political and intellectual aims: what motivated him in 46, as Caesar was winding down the civil war, to write a dialogue on the history of Roman oratory and literature? Why look to the past when the present and future were so in doubt?

There was nothing new in this nostalgic reflex, to intervene in the present and future by looking backward. In creatively reworked accounts, Roman historians had made an entire historiographical category out of *exempla* – great men and women of the past who exemplified communal values through singular actions.[3] And even the most past of past authors for Greeks and Romans, Homer, conjures up a world in which the fascination of a bygone era reveals the shortcomings and hopes of the present, a world in which the great heroes in and around Troy are categorically unreachable and worthy of poetic recollection and heroic emulation. This is one of the great and inevitable manipulations of historical accounts – to shape the present by claiming a particular shape for the past, because however much the past is factual and did happen in a particular way (that has never been in dispute), what determines our understandings of those facts, and therefore our future actions, is not the raw past but the memory we impose on it.

Such rewritings of the past continue to animate political interventions. Reactionary political groups active in the United States since the 2010s, from the Tea Party to #MAGA to Identity Evropa, have so eagerly reenvisioned the past in order to sideline new possibilities made urgent by demographic and social change. To imagine or long for prerevolutionary America (Tea Party), the United States in the 1950s (#MAGA), or a long-gone ideal of Western Whiteness (Identity Evropa) is hardly mere nostalgia for a bygone era. It is a dictate about what and who in the past merits remembrance, and such claims are so attractive and so powerful precisely because they easily and almost imperceptibly omit, ignore, or quell the counterclaims that others have on the past and its meaning for

---

[2] Zerubavel (2003) 100; cf. 109 on "entertaining multiple perspectives on the past."

[3] For valuable surveys of Roman *exempla*, see Langlands (2018) and Roller (2018), the former addressing larger conceptual issues and the latter focusing on a select but significant group of figures.

the present. Whether today or for Cicero and his contemporaries, such remembering is almost always a political act.[4]

Even as modern scholars have scrutinized Cicero's newfound emphasis on 240 as the beginning of Rome's literary tradition, those same inquiries have yet to consider the relationship of that date and its event to other possibilities in the *Brutus*. His decision to settle on 240 is inextricably connected to the foregone alternatives, which all in turn reveal his methods and motivations. Insistence on Livius Andronicus' play as literature's beginning is inseparable from insistence on Marcus Cornelius Cethegus (cos. 204) as the beginning of oratory (57–58).[5] Even more so, these decisions are inextricable from the remarkable, even perplexing, refusal to set Appius Claudius Caecus at the beginning of oratory and therefore literature. Cicero's choices, it will become clear, have at least as much to do with his various aims in the dialogue as with any sense of obligation to factual accuracy in narrating a beginning of literature. He goes to great lengths to depict literary history as a valid discipline of scholarly inquiry, providing it with Greek and Roman forerunners who justify his own appropriative and hellenizing tendencies. Unsurprisingly (for students of Cicero, at least), the narrative presented is as much about Cicero as it is about the origins of Roman literature.[6]

Oratory's Hard Beginnings

"Every beginning is hard" ("Aller Anfang ist schwer") according to the German proverb, and Cicero's beginning of oratory is no exception. He hardly makes matters any easier by choosing Marcus Cornelius Cethegus

---

[4] By contrast, leftist agendas tend to look to the future in a way that is also a kind of reflected nostalgia: progressivism and the vocabulary that goes with it, "hope" in aspirational moments, or neo-liberal salvation by the eventuality of demographics in others; in this regard Lin-Manuel Miranda's musical *Hamilton* is a rare exception. The difficulty for the progressive view is that few ideologies, however justified their ideals, can live on without appropriating and valorizing the past, even if only in a distorted version. This is, in many respects, the great insight that concludes Sander Goldberg's (1995) explanation of the failure of first-century epic before the advent of the *Aeneid*: late republican epic, including Cicero's own verses, could no longer adapt inherited forms to the ideologies and pressures of the inherited context. That would require an emperor and his bard.

[5] Chapter 4 contextualizes 240 BCE and Livius' play in addition to considering the perplexing fact that Roman oratory – unlike Roman poetry and despite a wealth of possible options – begins with neither a fixed date nor a fixed text.

[6] While the *Brutus* is a history of oratory, Cicero's account is based on the evaluation of other literary genres, such as poetry of various types, dialogue, or biography. He treats speeches as if they function like literature, and thus his oratorical history does explain what we call literary history. See Schwindt (2000) 96 on "Rhetorikgeschichte" in the *Brutus* as "Literaturgeschichte" and the end of Chapter 4 on oratory's literariness. On (Latin) "literature," see Feeney (2016) 152–78, esp. 152–55.

(cos. 204) as the first orator at Rome (57–58, quoted and discussed further below). The choice is justified not by judgment of Cethegus' speeches but by citing the judgment of the epic poet Ennius and by dismissing earlier orators, most notably Appius Claudius Caecus (cos. 307, 296). There are several problems in beginning the history with Cethegus, both because of Caecus' achievements and because of Cicero's otherwise inclusive tendencies. As Henriette van der Blom remarks, "Cicero operates with two criteria for inclusion into his history of Roman orators: oratorical activity and no longer living at the time of writing (46 BC)."[7] Caecus was probably the best choice for the beginning of (prose) literature at Rome, and Cicero struggles with Caecus' inevitable presence in his account.[8]

I propose here first to make the strongest possible case that Cicero on his own terms should have set Caecus at the beginning of Roman oratorical (and literary prose) history and, second, to defend Cicero's choice with an eye to the dialogue's literary-historical enterprise. The point of reconstructing Appius Claudius Caecus as the fount of oratorical history (and perhaps of published literature at Rome) is not merely to point up Cicero's logic. His choices, along with their inconsistencies and justifications, will contribute once more to the methodological insight that literary history is skewed by its authors' needs and perspectives and by the nature of literary history itself.[9] Cicero provides just enough information in the *Brutus* to demonstrate how arbitrary his construction of oratorical history is, and that arbitrariness suggests ulterior motives in the construction of his, or any, literary history. Furthermore, in offering one – visibly biased – version of literary history, Cicero also equips the reader with the means to consider and to construct alternative and equally valid versions.

Given his public prominence, Appius Claudius Caecus (ca. 343 – ca. 275 BCE) must have been a candidate to lead off Cicero's oratorical history. Caecus' renown well outlasted his own generation, as literary and political history would grant him a considerable afterlife.[10] Two inscriptions, one from Rome and the other found at Arretium (modern Arezzo, in eastern Tuscany), document a litany of remarkable achievements:[11] thrice a military tribune, quaestor (by 316?), twice curule aedile (by 313? and 305?), twice praetor (by 297? and 295), twice interrex

---

[7] Van der Blom (2016) 5.
[8] Cf. Suerbaum (2002) 80–83; at 81 he calls Caecus' speech the oldest datable document of Latin literature (although its dating is not exactly fixed).
[9] Perkins (1992) is the seminal study on the problems of literary history, which I address in greater detail below.
[10] Roller (2018) 95–133 on Caecus as an *exemplum*.   [11] *CIL* 6.40943, 11.1827.

(298, 291?), dictator, twice consul (307, 296), and censor (312). The censorship brought crucial building projects, a major roadway and aqueduct (see below), and the temple of Bellona, the Roman goddess of war, a meeting place outside the *pomerium* for the senate and foreign ambassadors. He boasted victories over Samnites, Sabines, and Etruscans. Livy, even despite apparent hostility to the *Appii Claudii*, finds him outstanding in law, eloquence, and the civil arts.[12]

Plutarch's *Life of Pyrrhus* memorably portrays Caecus' speech. King Pyrrhus of Epirus invaded Italy after the Greek colony Tarentum (Taras), in Magna Graecia and on the inner "heel" of Italy's "boot," requested aid against Roman encroachment. The conflict was cast into a well-conceived global and historical mold: Pyrrhus claimed descent not only from Alexander the Great, but from Achilles. Set against this lineage was the parallel backstory of the Romans, who claimed descent from the Trojans via Aeneas, who fled Troy's destruction to found what would become the Roman state. Alert to the historical parallels, Pyrrhus aligned the mythical past so as to arrange a conflict between two great nations, Greece and Rome, whose intertwined histories stretched back to the beginnings of warfare and literature: the descendants of Aeneas against the descendants of Achilles.[13]

Pyrrhus won successive battles, first at Heraclea (280) and then at Asculum (279). His response to this latter event secured his renown for millennia: after Asculum he quipped, "If we beat the Romans in one more battle, we'll be wholly ruined" (Ἂν ἔτι μίαν μάχην Ῥωμαίους νικήσωμεν, ἀπολούμεθα παντελῶς, Plut. *Pyrrh.* 21.9). Thus "Pyrrhic victory" would come to mean something far different from just "the victory of Pyrrhus." Cineas, Pyrrhus' ambassador, soon came to Rome to negotiate with the Romans, who seriously considered the offer of peace until the appearance of Appius Claudius Caecus ("the Blind"). A litter carried by attendants brought Caecus, now suffering the effects of age, to upbraid the senate.

---

[12] Livy 9.42.4, 10.15.12, 10.19.6, 10.22.7. Cf. *ORF*⁴ no. 1, Humm (2005) 510. Hostility is likely too simplistic a formulation; see Vasaly (1987) on the *Appii Claudii* in Livy's first pentad. The hypothesis that Cicero excluded Caecus because of distaste for his former nemesis, Clodius the tribune, should be discarded. Cicero could malign Clodius all the more by conferring distinction upon Caecus and excluding Clodius. He includes three different Appii Claudii Pulchri (coss. 143, 79, 54 – the brother of the tribune), and three Gaii Claudii Pulchri (cos. 177, cos. 92, pr. 56). Cicero's beginning, Cethegus, is an ancestor of an executed Catilinarian conspirator: the struggles of the 60s and 50s pale in comparison to those of the 40s.
[13] *CAH*² VII.2: 464–65, with the marvelous didrachm issued by Pyrrhus; the coin depicts Achilles on the obverse and on the reverse Thetis bringing him armor.

He railed against peace with the invading Greek general. Ever on the alert for the perfect bon mot, Plutarch perfectly ramps up the rhetoric:

> "Previously, Romans, I bore as an affliction the misfortune to my eyes, but now it pains me not to be blind *and* deaf as I hear your shameful deliberations and decrees that debase Rome's glory."

> Πρότερον μέν ... τὴν περὶ τὰ ὄμματα τύχην ἀνιαρῶς ἔφερον, ὦ Ῥωμαῖοι, νῦν δὲ ἄχθομαι πρὸς τῷ τυφλὸς εἶναι μὴ καὶ κωφὸς ὤν, ἀλλ᾽ ἀκούων αἰσχρὰ βουλεύματα καὶ δόγματα ὑμῶν ἀνατρέποντα τῆς Ῥώμης τὸ κλέος. (Plut. *Pyrrh.* 18.1)

Plutarch notes the speech's immediate effectiveness.[14] It is hard to know what Latin word for "glory" Caecus might have used in concluding the memorable retort (*fama, gloria, laus, nomen?*), but Plutarch, or even Caecus himself, with the wryness reserved for *sententia*, may have crafted a recognizably Achillean response in arguing against the Achilles-like invader: κλέος, of course, is the value that so animated Achilles in the *Iliad* and ultimately led to his death at Troy.

If we were seeking out a forerunner for the combined civic and literary enterprises of a Cato or a Cicero, it would seem to be Caecus. He emerges from the mists of Roman history as the first political personality of recognizable depth and is tied to the invention of written publication as a means of public self-profiling in the republic.[15] His reputed predilection for intervocalic "r" probably helped to formalize Latin rhotacism in written records, a preference matched by his ardent displeasure at the sound of the letter "z".[16] Traces of his larger cultural interests would also endure, such as the enduring tag *faber est suae quisque fortunae* ("each man is craftsman of his own fortune"), one of the *sententiae* or *carmina* for which he was known and for which Cicero himself praises Caecus in the *Tusculan*

---

[14] Plut. *Pyrrh.* 18.5–19.5. Cf. App. *Sam.* 10.2 on the speech, 10.1–3 on the Roman prisoners taken at Heraclea.

[15] Humm (2005) marshals the primary evidence and secondary literature: 1–12, 61–73 (on Appius' speech), 508–40 (on his eloquence and *carmina*), and 666–70 (conspectus of sources); cf. Suerbaum (2002) 80–83. Tacitus' Aper can still quip that some prefer Caecus to Cato (*num dubitamus inventos, qui pro Catone Appium Caecum magis mirarentur, Dial.* 18.2). Centuries later Isidore of Seville would place Caecus at the beginning of Latin prose (oratory): "and among the Romans Appius Caecus speaking against Pyrrhus first used speech without meter. And since then others vied in prose eloquence" (*apud Romanos autem Appius Caecus adversus Pyrrhum solutam orationem primus exercuit. Iam exhinc et ceteri prosae eloquentia contenderunt,* Isid. *Orig.* 1.38.2 = Varro GRF 319). Van den Berg (2019) 575–76 erroneously attributed Isidore's claim to Varro (whom Isidore cites shortly before).

[16] Pompon. 1.2.2.36, Mart. Cap. 3.261.

Disputations.[17] His maxims in the native Saturnian meter were – or for an observer of the first century BCE could be thought to be – based on Greek (Pythagorean) models. In 304 (or thereabouts) he prompted the curule aedile Gnaeus Flavius to publicize the *legis actiones* and calendar days for court proceedings, precedents that Cicero notes in *pro Murena* were essential to ensuring the prestige of oratory over the prestige of law.[18] No longer was knowledge of juridical formulas or calendrical restrictions on legal procedures the sole purview of patricians and priests, which opened advocacy to other social groups.

Civic achievements such as the *Via Appia* and the *Aqua Appia* also ensured a material legacy in Rome and Italy. Michel Humm has well demonstrated that Caecus was a catalyst in Rome's hellenizing process, a core feature of Cicero's literary history: like Livius' adaptation of a Greek play (72–73), Caecus offers the prospect of a literary beginning inspired by Greek models.[19] Caecus equally suited a narrative for oratory's rise that celebrated Roman militarism along with the adoption of Greek culture, as was the case when Livius initiated Latin poetry.

Given Cicero's interest in the synchrony of cultural and military developments, he could, for example, have considered a very different organization: the classical Athenian canon, from Lysias to Demosthenes,[20] begins to decline with Demetrius of Phalerum, the moment at which Caecus inaugurates a crude stage of Roman oratory. Cato the Elder makes subsequent refinements that shore up oratory's essential place in the history of the art and of political life, without yet raising oratory to the level of the Greek masters. Romans finally begin to compete with their canonical Greek forerunners in the generation of Crassus and Antonius.[21] Caecus was a near coeval of Demetrius of Phalerum, the "beginning of the end" of Greek oratory (37–38), and their simultaneous presence as political and

---

[17] *Tusc.* 4.4: Cicero uses it as an example of early learning, specifically of Pythagorean influence. He notes that Panaetius praised Caecus' *carmen*. Dupraz (2007) on the *sententiae* as literature.

[18] Cic. *Mur.* 25; cf. *Att.* 6.1.8 (SB 115), Liv. 9.46.1–6; V. Max. 2.5.2, Macr. *Sat.* 1.15.9; Humm (2005) 441–55, Rüpke (2011) 44–67.

[19] See esp. Humm (2005) 483–540 on Caecus' hellenism. Cicero will not have excluded Caecus from the canon because he was insufficiently trained in Greek, since that is not a *sine qua non*: Gaius Titius lacked Greek learning and yet was an exemplar of Latin style (167), in both oratory and drama.

[20] Cf. [Plut.] *X orat.* 836a, 848c for the story (probably apocryphal) that the young Demosthenes once saw Lysias. The topos may motivate Cicero's possibly invented claim to have heard Accius (107) or Ovid's to have seen Vergil (*Tr.* 4.10.51).

[21] Cf. the second of Quintilian's four groups at *Inst.* 12.10.10–11, which spans Crassus through Hortensius. Quintilian singles Cicero out for special treatment at *Inst.* 12.10.12–15. Quintilian's modernism allows him to begin with Cato and to extend the classical period into the empire.

oratorical figures would serve well the synchronies courted by Greek and Roman thinkers. This imaginary scheme emphasizes that oratory in Greece reached dusk just as it found first light at Rome, an idea in consonance with the *Graecia capta* motif, by which Rome's imperial assertions against Greece go hand in hand with enthrallment to and adoption of its cultural acquirements.[22] Cicero's penchant for cultural parallels is evident in the cases of Pisistratus/Solon and Servius Tullius (39), or Coriolanus and Themistocles (41–43), exactly the synchronism so essential to Roman habits of mind.[23] The Pyrrhic War heralded Rome's emergence onto the world stage:[24] Pyrrhus was repelled and Greek hegemony in the colonies of Magna Graecia became uncertain; Rome was recognized as a player on the Mediterranean scene, as evidenced by the opening of an embassy of amity by the Macedonian king of Egypt in Rome in 273 BCE.

Despite the alluring imperial context into which Caecus' speech could have been placed, Cicero astonishingly resists what must have been a nearly instinctual reflex to map Roman cultural achievement onto Roman power. Livius Andronicus and 240 are emphasized precisely because of Carthage's defeat in 241 (72–73). Why not align the debut of oratory – an art so associated in Cicero's eyes with political greatness – with Rome's debut on the Mediterranean scene? Instead Cicero aligns the emergence of poetry with a later stage of Rome's dominance in the Mediterranean after the First Punic War; the beginning of oratory is pushed forward well into the Second. Even in the dispute over whether to make Livius' hymn of 207 or his play of 240 the beginning of literature, the same pattern emerges: a significant event is associated with a specific piece of literature marking that event, just as Caecus' speech is a significant literary monument of the eventual expulsion of Pyrrhus.[25]

---

[22] *Brut.* 254 and Hor. *Ep.* 2.1.156–57. The topos of captive conquerors is not original to Cicero; cf. Aesch. *Ag.* 340: οὔ τἂν ἑλόντες αὖθις ἀνθαλοῖεν ἄν.

[23] See Feeney (2007), esp. 7–67, with bibliography. Humm (2005) 519 n.148 stresses the similarities of the two both chronologically and in the *artes civiles*. The syncrisis of Coriolanus/Themistocles is discussed in Chapter 4.

[24] Cf. *CAH²* VIII: 83: The defeat of Pyrrhus "put Rome on the map for the Greek world. Ptolemy II Philadelphus was sufficiently impressed to choose this time to send presents to the Senate and to form an informal friendship; the Romans returned the diplomatic gesture." Cf. Cass. Dio 10.41.1 and Dion. Hal. *Ant. Rom.* 20.14.1 with *CAH²* VII.2: 456–85. Consider the similar embassy sent to Rome in 239 to mark the victory over the Carthaginians, which also led to Livius' first Latin play at the *ludi Romani* of 240.

[25] Feeney (2007) 38 discusses how ancient scholars (Apollodorus, Eratosthenes, Gellius, Trogus) used Pyrrhus' expulsion to mark Rome's emergence and to synchronize Greece and Rome. On the reading of Humm (2009) Caecus' speech also reflects a newly formed sense of Roman–Italian identity.

It is worth remembering as well that Rome's defeat of Pyrrhus was a victory over Greeks, whereas in the Punic War Rome defeated Carthaginians (even if control of Greek Sicily was in play), and the Carthaginians, though perhaps underestimated in the field of letters, were hardly potential rivals in the cultural domains of eloquence and poetry. Pyrrhus offered a conceptual advantage that Hannibal could not, since Pyrrhus represented the legacy of Alexander and the height of Greek imperialism, which was also a legacy of lost freedom. Cicero could have presented the Roman victory over Pyrrhus as an assertion of Roman *libertas*, both "freedom" and "frankness," contrasted with Greece's succumbing to the Macedonian kings. Given the Caesarian context of the *Brutus*, with its constant anxiety over the silencing of eloquence, so topical a reference must have been tantalizing.

The embassy of Cineas to Rome, which was the occasion for Caecus' speech, presents yet another scenario thoroughly apt for rhetorical and conceptual embellishment. The orator and quasi-philosopher Cineas represented Pyrrhus in the embassy. This pupil of Demosthenes was thought by many to reflect the master's greatness "as a statue does" (οἷον ἐν εἰκόνι), says Plutarch (although Cicero ignores Cineas in the *Brutus*). He exemplified the greater power of rhetoric over military command, an idea dear to Cicero in the current crisis (255–57): "Pyrrhus, you see, would say that more cities had been won for him by the words of Cineas than by his own weapons" (ὁ γοῦν Πύρρος ἔλεγε πλείονας πόλεις ὑπὸ Κινέου τοῖς λόγοις ἢ τοῖς ὅπλοις ὑφ' ἑαυτοῦ προσῆχθαι, Plut. *Pyrrh.* 14.2). Cineas also represented the prospect of cultural translation and transfer that nicely complements the parallels represented by Demetrius of Phalerum (discussed above). He was Demosthenes' greatest student, and his words link directly back to the Greek master. He embodies *translatio eloquentiae* between two empires: Greek eloquence literally came to Rome.[26]

Synchrony and historical figureheads were hardly Cicero's only concern, however, and inclusion of Caecus would require some justification that his oratory could earn him the title *orator*.[27] Cicero at first feigns a lack of evidence with which to judge Caecus, shrouding him amidst a cloud of political greats who are nothing more than names and achievements from

---

[26] Cineas and Pyrrhus: *Fam.* 9.25.1 (SB 114), *Sen.* 43.1, *Tusc.* 1.59.

[27] Welsh (2011) argues that 240 reflects Cicero's desire to have literature begin in times of peace. Cicero, then, may have excluded Caecus to avoid having oratory/literature begin in wartime. However, these two reasons are not mutually exclusive: Cicero's choice of Livius Andronicus' play both created a peacetime beginning for literature and still allowed Cicero to exclude Caecus. 240 offered more than one advantage.

the past: "we can suppose that Appius Claudius was well-spoken since he pulled back the senate from the brink of peace with Pyrrhus" (*possumus Appium Claudium suspicari disertum, quia senatum iamiam inclinatum a Pyrrhi pace revocaverit*, 55). The criterion for exclusion is that Caecus was *disertus* ("fluent") but not *eloquens* ("eloquent"); the latter judgment would qualify him to be included in Cicero's canon. This initial statement is part and parcel of Cicero's rather deceptive treatment, since language such as *possumus suspicari* recognizes the memory of his deeds (persuasion of the senate) even as it suggests a total absence of his words (the speech). Cicero further minimizes Caecus by burying his name in a litany of quasi-mythical statesmen from the sixth to the third centuries (53–57). Yet we later learn of the renown of Caecus' speech when Cicero ostentatiously excludes Caecus in the discussion of Marcus Cornelius Cethegus and Cato the Elder:

> In fact, I know no one more ancient [than Cato] whose writings I'd think need citing, unless someone happens to take pleasure in the speech I mentioned about Pyrrhus by Appius Caecus or the numerous funeral laudations.

> nec vero habeo quemquam antiquiorem, cuius quidem scripta proferenda putem, nisi quem Appi Caeci oratio haec ipsa de Pyrrho et nonnullae mortuorum laudationes forte delectant. (61).

Cicero's judgments and the criteria he initially uses to exclude Caecus seem plausible enough for the account he presents. Yet his logic becomes increasingly suspect as the dialogue progresses, and indeed the most compelling reasons to include Caecus come from the inclusive criteria that Cicero sets forth in the *Brutus* itself. Building on Aristotle and in consonance with Greek critics, Cicero noted that nothing is both discovered and perfected at a single stroke (*nihil est enim simul et inventum et perfectum*, 71).[28] And while he scorns Livius Andronicus' *Odyssia* and claims that his plays are not worth a second read (*non satis dignae quae iterum legantur*, 71), Livian drama still inaugurates Latin poetry. Aesthetic objections, for poetry at least, are insufficient in determining who begins a tradition. Elsewhere the catalogue of orators contains as many figures as possible, even those Cicero deems undeserving. Over-inclusiveness is a leitmotif of the work, tied to claims about the difficulty of the *ars*.[29] Cicero elsewhere

[28] Cf. Arist. *Poet.* 1449a7–15, Cic. *de Orat.* 1.13, and (later) Dion. Hal. *Din.* 1.
[29] On over-inclusiveness see, e.g., 137, 176, 181, 244, 269–70, 299. On the difficulty of the *ars*: *rem unam esse omnium difficillimam* (25); cf. e.g. 137, 199.

labors to include and to praise speakers who might be thought old-fashioned. Forced to refute charges of irony or poor judgment for including Cato and Crassus, he responds that both speakers must be seen in the contexts of their accomplishments. The willingness to assess works in light of their own times left open the possibility of arguing, as he often does for others, that Caecus' speech was eloquent *ut illis temporibus* ("relative to the times"), according him a place while registering misgivings.[30]

At the same time, Cicero's logic for the inclusion of Cethegus has two somewhat unexpected consequences. On the one hand, he sheds light on the methodology of his literary history, implicitly outlining how the literary historian should operate and the guidelines and limitations in crafting his account. On the other, his reasons for beginning with Cethegus turn out to be equally valid reasons for beginning with Caecus:

> But record exists that Marcus Cornelius Cethegus was the first man memorialized as eloquent and also judged to be so; the authority for his eloquence – and an ideal one in my opinion – is Quintus Ennius, in particular because he both heard Cethegus in person and writes about him posthumously; consequently, there's no suspicion that he lied on account of partisanship. Here's what's in Ennius' ninth book, I think, of the *Annales*:
> "Joined to Tuditanus as colleague is *orator* Marcus
> Cornelius Cethegus of agreeable speech,
> son of Marcus."
> He both calls him *orator* and confers agreeable speech on him.
>
> quem vero exstet et de quo sit memoriae proditum eloquentem fuisse et ita esse habitum, primus est M. Cornelius Cethegus, cuius eloquentiae est auctor et idoneus quidem mea sententia Q. Ennius, praesertim cum et ipse eum audiverit et scribat de mortuo; ex quo nulla suspicio est amicitiae causa esse mentitum. est igitur sic apud illum in nono ut opinor annali:
> 'additur orator Cornelius suaviloquenti
> ore Cethegus Marcus Tuditano conlega
> Marci filius':
> et oratorem appellat et suaviloquentiam tribuit. (57–58)

Placement of Cethegus at the head of the list comes with reflections on his memorialization. He is both eloquent and has been judged so (by Ennius).

---

[30] *Pace* Suerbaum (2002), who assumes that Cicero rejects Caecus' speech as spurious (62 confirms its existence but rejects its aesthetic). Humm (2005) 65–71 defends its authenticity (at least in the eyes of second- and first-century BCE audiences) and considers its afterlife.

Cicero implies that the memory of an orator requires that someone document that memory fairly, which is an uncontroversial statement on the face of it. Yet Cicero also takes Ennius' assertion as proof of Cethegus' status and ignores the fact that, while memory of Cethegus' oratory persisted, his speeches did not: "the passage of time would have condemned him to be forgotten, like perhaps many others, without Ennius' singular testimony to his ability" (*id ipsum nisi unius esset Enni testimonio cognitum, hunc vetustas, ut alios fortasse multos, oblivione obruisset*, 60).[31] The interest is less in whether one could actually determine that Cethegus was eloquent – how could Cicero judge in the absence of concrete evidence? – but in the fact that Ennius had already made such an assertion. Here Cicero appeals to autopsy as a source of authoritative statement (though Ennius, not Cicero, bears witness).

The citation of Ennius also evokes the historiographical topos *sine ira et studio* ("without animosity or sympathy"), which validates a judgment or account by noting an author's lack of immediate bias for the dead.[32] An appeal to disinterested judgment underlay the discussion of older orators: "But I don't think I've ever read that these men were regarded as orators or that there was then any reward at all for eloquence: I am led simply by conjecture to infer it" (*sed eos oratores habitos esse aut omnino tum ullum eloquentiae praemium fuisse nihil sane mihi legisse videor: tantummodo coniectura ducor ad suspicandum*, 56). Cicero is not merely taking a stab at retrodiction; this earlier reluctance makes him seem as if he diligently meets a duty to scrupulousness. The appeal to historiographical norms contributes to the perception of Cicero's impartiality in his history of oratory, which will become especially important later in the dialogue when he takes his cue from Ennius in reliably documenting orators of a later age. With Ennius as his model, Cicero reviews at length the now-dead orators of the late republic whom he once heard. When Cicero refuses to speak of living orators, it is in light of the earlier discussion of Ennius that such forbearance becomes the mark of impartiality and redounds to his credit.[33]

Once again comparison with Cicero's view of poetry is instructive, since in that case documented approval by an older authority, just like aesthetic

---

[31] At 61 (quoted and discussed above) Cicero says that no speech earlier than Cato exists, other than the funeral *laudationes* and the speech of Appius Claudius Caecus.

[32] Luce (1989) is germane on the topic. Cf. Piras (2012), Elliott (2013) 54–57, 156–61, 382–84 on this passage.

[33] It would be more accurate to say that Cicero takes his cue from the version of Ennius he has managed to construct – see below on Cicero's manipulation of Ennius.

quality generally, matters little in establishing the beginning of a tradition. When disparaging Livius Andronicus' lackluster poetry (71, quoted above), Cicero approvingly cites Ennius' self-serving claim to be the first poet of significance, a claim that seems to exclude Livius from Ennius' canon. Cicero shows us that Livius fails to meet both his criteria: he was neither a good poet (Cicero) nor was he held to be one by a past authority (Ennius). Despite failure on both scores, Livius still inaugurates Latin literature. The criteria to begin one literary tradition (oratory) are dismantled in the case of another (poetry).

There are other clear indications that Cicero's history is hardly as artless as he would have us believe. Despite Ennius' compliment, *suaviloquens*, Cicero is heavy-handed in pressing the evidence for Cethegus: he probably manipulates the semantic breadth of the term *orator* to make a case for Cethegus' inclusion into the history of great speakers.[34] And even the term *suaviloquens* involves some sleight of hand, as Cicero introduces the passage by stating that Ennius had judged Cethegus to be *eloquens*.[35] This is, at best, stretching the truth, since Ennius nowhere uses the words *eloquens* or *eloquentia*. Cicero seems to suggest that Ennius' term, *suaviloquens*, is a compound of *suavis* and *eloquens* (rather than *suavis* and *loquens*).[36] Cicero's coinage of the term *suaviloquentia* only works to underscore the connection, given the formal likeness to what was (in Cicero's day) a well-worn term, *eloquentia* ("eloquence"). All this verbal

---

[34] In early and poetic usage *orator* typically meant "envoy" or "ambassador" as much as "(great) speaker." At 55 Cicero clearly uses *orator* in the older sense when speaking of C. Fabricius' mission as envoy to Pyrrhus (*ad Pyrrhum de captivis recuperandis missus orator*). Douglas (1966a) and Skutsch (1985) take the usage here to mean "orator," but Cicero trades on the ambiguities; see *Var. L.* 7.41, Elliott (2013) 160 n.74. What Cicero cites from Ennius about Cethegus does emphasize his speaking abilities (which is still no guarantee that *orator* necessarily means "orator" in the strong sense that Cicero seems to require in other cases). Sander Goldberg *per litteras* suggests another example: Ennius' *spernitur orator bonus, horridus miles amatur* (Enn. *Ann.* fr. 249 Skutsch) probably refers to a context of diplomacy. Cicero takes *orator* at *Mur.* 30 to mean "orator" because that meaning suits his context while disregarding the initial Ennian context.

[35] Nor is *suavis* a cardinal virtue in the *Brutus* when contrasted with *gravis*. See Cic. *Cat.* 16 and below on Appius' speech (*gravissime*). See Cic. *N.D.* 1.60, Nepos *Att.* 18.5 on *suavitas* as characteristic of poetry. Ennius also used alliteration, assonance, and a *figura etymologica* (*orator Cornelius / ore Cethegus*) to adorn the depiction of Cethegus' eloquence (not unlike Cicero's frequent praise of others' language to offer self-praise); Piras (2012) 50.

[36] The terms *suaviloquens/-ntia* are not connected to *eloquens/-ntia* by Roman etymologists. *Eloquentia* is connected to full (rather than sweet or pleasing) speech. See Maltby (1991) 203: "eloquens, -ntis. *Var. L.* 6.57: hinc (*sc. a loquendo*) eloquens qui copiose loquitur. Isid. *Orig.* 10.81: eloquens, profusus eloquio."

magic stands in stark contrast to his lapidary claim that Caecus could be assumed to be merely *disertus* ("fluent," "well-spoken").[37]

Further arguments supporting Caecus' inclusion emerge. Cethegus (or any early orator) could be criticized as Cato will be later on: "a (great) man ... but an orator?" (*virum ... sed oratorem?*, 293). Cicero defends Cato in terms that also support according Caecus a place in his canon:

> And I know full well that I'm spending time recalling men who neither were thought to be nor were orators, and that I'm omitting some ancients who merit commemoration or praise. But this is from lack of knowledge about an earlier age. What then can be written concerning men about whom no records speak, neither others' or their own?

> Atque ego praeclare intellego me in eorum commemoratione versari qui nec habiti sint oratores neque fuerint, praeteririque a me aliquot ex veteribus commemoratione aut laude dignos. Sed hoc quidem ignoratione superioris aetatis;[38] quid enim est quod scribi possit de eis, de quibus nulla monumenta loquuntur nec aliorum nec ipsorum? (181)

The pair of verbs, *esse* and *habitum esse*, repeat the criteria used to include Cethegus (Ennius' documentation), but the criteria cited to include someone in the historical record (commemoration and the existence of material) would logically dictate that Caecus must be included as well. Cicero is being visibly inconsistent. Caecus' speech (or versions of it) existed alongside a tradition honoring his achievements.[39] Indeed, after his exile Cicero frequently turns to Caecus to attack his archenemy Clodius.[40] And Caecus, like Cethegus, had been memorialized by Ennius, as Cicero knew. In *de Senectute*, Cicero cites Ennius' praise of Caecus and goes on to note the renown of his speech, a speech that Cicero may well have pressed into service years earlier in the *pro Caelio*.[41]

---

[37] At 55 (quoted above). Cicero goes on to state that Ennius called Cethegus the "marrow of Persuasion" (*Suadai medulla*, 59), which certainly suggests Ennius' approbation. Cicero's citation is convoluted and examined at length below.

[38] I follow Mommsen, Douglas, and Kaster in moving *superioris aetatis* after *ignoratione* from its transmitted position before *quod* (which requires extreme hyperbaton with *eis*).

[39] Suerbaum (1996/1997) rightly questions Cicero's choice to begin with Cethegus but wrongly assumes that Cicero excluded Caecus' speech on the grounds of inauthenticity; contra, Humm (2005) 65. Suerbaum claims that Cicero's choices cannot be explained; the following section offers an explanation.

[40] Cic. *Dom.* 105, *Har.* 38, *Cael.* 33–35, *Mil.* 17. For other notices: *Div. Caec.* 54, *Phil.* 1.11, *Tusc.* 5.112, *Sen.* 37.

[41] Osgood (2005); on Ennius see Skutsch (1985) 360–62, J. G. F. Powell (1988) 136–39, 278, Elliott (2013) 161–63. Cf. Cic. *Phil.* 1.11, V. Max. 8.13.5, Quint. *Inst.* 2.16.7. Piras (2017) 64 connects the summoning of Caecus in the *pro Caelio* to mention of the technique at 322.

The old age of Appius Claudius was accompanied no less by blindness; nevertheless, when the senate's opinion tended toward making a peace treaty with Pyrrhus, he didn't shy away from saying those famous words that Ennius expressed well in verse:

"Where have your minds wandered off to
in madness, which before this used to stand firm?"

and so forth with great authority. I'm sure you know the poem, and anyway Appius' own speech survives.

ad Appi Claudi senectutem accedebat etiam, ut caecus esset; tamen is cum sententia senatus inclinaret ad pacem cum Pyrrho foedusque faciendum, non dubitavit dicere illa quae versibus persecutus est Ennius:

quo vobis mentes, rectae quae stare solebant
antehac, dementes sese flexere viai ... ?

ceteraque gravissime; notum enim vobis carmen est, et tamen ipsius Appi exstat oratio. (Cic. *Sen.* 16; Enn. *Ann.* fr. 199–200 Skutsch)

In the *Brutus*, by contrast, the very kind of evidence used to bring Cethegus into oratorical history is suppressed in the case of Caecus. Cicero presents Ennius as a transparent witness to oratory's beginnings, but then manipulates his version of Ennius to produce the account he needs.[42]

Caecus' literary afterlife is remarkably persistent and only considerable misdirection and special pleading by Cicero create the illusion that Caecus could be gotten rid of. Caecus is the zombie that Cicero can't quite seem to put away. This is not to say that valid reasons for including Cethegus could not be found. He was born about a century after Caecus, around 240 BCE, and his career, mostly during the Second Punic War, is impressive even if it is overshadowed by greater figures such as Quintus Fabius Maximus or Quintus Caecilius Metellus. Cethegus was curule aedile (213), praetor (211), censor (209), and consul (204). He was also a pontifex, and as censor had a historic quarrel with his colleague, Publius Sempronius Tuditanus, that undermined traditional criteria for the office of *Princeps Senatus*. As proconsul of upper Italy in 203 he helped the praetor, Publius Quintilius Varus, defeat Mago Barca and force him out of Italy.[43]

---

[42] Elliott (2013) 159 captures Cicero's distortions: "he turns to the work that suggests the information that he would like and treats it as if it were of the type he requires." See also Gildenhard (2003) 98–100.

[43] *MRR* I: 263, 266, 267 n.4, 273, 277 n.3, 285, 305, 306. Livy: 25.2.2 (pontifex), 25.2.6 (curule aedile), 25.41.12 (praetor), 27.11.7 (censor), 30.18.1–15 (proconsul, defeat of Mago).

As a literary figure Cethegus receives some notice beyond the *Brutus*. Cicero mentions him again in *de Senectute*, again along with Ennius' memorable tag *Suadai medulla* (*Sen.* 50). Cato there remarks that he even saw Cethegus training his oratory into old age (*quanto studio exerceri in dicendo videbamus etiam senem*). Yet Cicero's motivations for citing Cethegus seem to extend little beyond the probative value of the *exemplum* for Cato's claim that there's a history of eminent men speaking in old age. No speech by Cethegus is cited, whereas Quintus Fabius Maximus at *Sen.* 10, for example, is at least said to have spoken concerning the *lex Cincia* (in 204, a year before his death). Basic questions abide: What did Cethegus speak about and what made him a great speaker? Did Cicero even know much about his oratory beyond Ennius' few words? Cethegus left no oratorical legacy beyond what Cicero has reconstructed out of self-interest, and by the time we reach Horace and Quintilian, he is little more than a quaint example of old-time speech.[44]

This is a remarkably poor foundation on which to build a literary history. One might, however, look to material production to explain Cicero's choice of Cethegus over Caecus. Denis Feeney, drawing on Jörg Rüpke, has taken the terms of Cicero's narrative and reverse-engineered the technical conditions to support them, suggesting that Caecus doesn't become the beginning of literature because the promulgation of prose texts as literary monuments in the early third century did not catch on as a cultural trend and would not until Cato the Elder in the second century.[45] For this reason it is poetry in the mid-third century that begins literary history in Cicero's account.

The explanation, grounded in social and bibliographic history, is well attuned to the nascent publication of written media in third-century Rome. In Cicero's first-century Rome, however, third-century technical or material constraints need not have been his primary concern (nor is it clear how much he knew about Caecus' constraints). It was certainly possible to craft a narrative that ignored or discarded the realities of mid-republican textual dissemination. Again, whereas Caecus left behind a speech that was still widely available – and this despite the technical constraints on publication – Cethegus had at best a meager afterlife: we know of no speech circulated among his contemporaries, and Cicero never

---

[44] On his language: Hor. *Ars* 50; *Ep.* 2.2.117 (probably indebted to the *Brutus*; paired with Cato, but without indicating extant texts by Cethegus).

[45] Feeney (2016) 210–12; Rüpke (2012) 26: "what we see here is a break with tradition, but not a trend," and 86: "Whatever the historicity of this text, it remains an isolated datum. Larger numbers of speeches were transmitted only later, from the time of Cato the Elder onward."

claims to have read anything by him. Cethegus is at best a ghost to Caecus' zombie.

In summary, Cicero gives us ample reason to question his decision to begin oratorical history with Cethegus at the expense of Caecus. The rival possibility of Caecus, however, need not invalidate the choice on which Cicero ultimately settled. Beginning oratorical history with Caecus might be the better option without being more true in an absolute sense. In refusing to put Caecus at the head of oratorical history, Cicero reveals the extent to which the ascription of any art's beginning to a single individual is arbitrary, potentially subject to revision, and tailored to the local purposes of a given text. It is worth emphasizing that Cicero generally remains scrupulous with factual details – or at least contrives to give that appearance – even as he deftly manipulates the presentation of those details in line with the purpose of his narrative.[46] In light of the material at hand, Cicero faced essentially three choices for the beginnings of literature and the genre that inaugurated it: (1) ca. 280 vs. 240/207 (literature begins with oratory); (2) 207/204 (virtually simultaneous origins for poetry/ oratory; (3) 240 vs. 204 (literature begins with poetry). One chief advantage of the third scheme, on which he settled, is that it validates another repeated assumption for which he never argues: oratory, because of its difficulty, develops later than the other arts.[47] Nothing, however, required a literary history to take this course, just as nothing requires us to take the claims about oratory's retardation at face value.[48]

First Beginnings among the Greeks (26–51)

Cicero had prepared us for the choices he would make about the beginnings of literature and oratory at Rome. Before turning to Roman oratory he offered a survey of oratory in Greece, or at least what purports to be such a survey (26–51). It soon becomes evident, however, that this is

---

[46] Cicero's prejudices against the *laudatio funebris* obviated other possible beginnings: the *laudatio* of Quintus Caecilius Metellus (cos. 206) in 221 had the advantage of taking place outside of the context of war; see *ORF*⁴ no. 6, Kierdorf (1980) 10–21. One could also make a case for Quintus Fabius Maximus, *ORF*⁴ no. 3. He gave a *laudatio* in 213 (Kierdorf 1980 83–85) and spoke in support of the *lex Cincia* in 204 (Cic. *Sen.* 10). Cicero's dismissal of the *laudationes* obscures more of the literary-historical record than one might initially think.

[47] Roman biography does develop after oratory. Philosophy postdated other arts while oratory was adopted quickly, according to *Tusc.* 1.5: Cato is the first example of the orator influenced by learning; cf. Gruen (1992) 52–83 on Cato's hellenism in Cicero.

[48] Scholars have taken great interest in the peculiar fact that Rome even developed a vernacular tradition of national literature at all, much less one based on Greek models: see Habinek (1998) 15–68, Goldberg (2005), Feeney (2005, 2016).

hardly a historical synopsis. Structurally and thematically the synopsis of Greek oratory is unusual, but its idiosyncrasies shed light on the dialogue's methodological and organizational principles. Cicero's interest in two different aspects of oratorical history, that history itself and those who document it, explains the perplexing "double history" of the art in Greece. He first provides a synopsis of the chief practitioners (26–38) followed by a synopsis focusing on theorists and cataloguers (39–51).[49] The second section is less a chronology than a methodological justification of Cicero's literary history.[50]

Despite the differences, several parallels of structure and presentation do emerge in the two accounts, and basic details reveal some sense of an attempt to craft the narratives in parallel to one another, like a diptych, in which both comparison and contrast contribute to the total effect. The two halves are of roughly equal length, with the second a bit longer.[51] The first account contains 31 citations of 28 names, the second 38 citations of 28 names; of these, 9 figures appear in both.[52] Structural repetitions reinforce the parallels. Ring-composition in the first half (Pericles at 27 and 38) recurs in the second (Homer at 40 and 50) and across both halves in the geographical emphasis on Athens.[53] Philosophers appear in both (Socrates, 31; Anaxagoras, 44). The list of *magistri* (30) balances a list of theoreticians (46–47), with Gorgias and Protagoras in both lists. Isocrates assumes a prominent place, first as an innovator (32) and then as an author-theorist whose career inversely parallels that of Lysias (48). Stylistic decline concludes each version: the first chronologically initiated by Demetrius of Phalerum and the second conceptually initiated by

---

[49] Compare Horace's double history for Roman literature in *Epistles* 2.1: 139–55 (native verses) and 156–81 (adaptation of Greeks).

[50] Douglas (1966a) *ad loc.* calls it "hesitant and digressive." Compare his general rejection of the two synopses in xliv–xlv. Douglas' insistence that Cicero write a chronology requires him to misunderstand the point of the catalogue and to reject it with severity. Cf. Douglas (1973) 103–4. Objections to the scheme also take aim at the repetitions, e.g. Pericles (29, 38, 44), Gorgias (30, 47), Lysias (35, 48), and Isocrates (32–33, 48). Rathofer (1986) 51–88 makes numerous valuable observations, especially about Cicero's chronological distortions, although his division of the two histories into a history of the *ars* and a history of non-artistic political actors is less convincing. Schöpsdau (1969) 113–34 assesses Cicero's freedom with several sources and the originality of his Greek history.

[51] Each is thirteen chapters in modern editions (26–38, 39–51), although the second catalogue has a higher word count (~720 versus ~840 words).

[52] Atticus, Gorgias, Isocrates, Lysias, Pericles, Pisistratus, Protagoras, Themistocles, Thucydides. Lycurgus is in each but refers to different people (the Athenian orator and the early ruler).

[53] The parallel geography is further emphasized by the names cited: *Atticus* (the interlocutor) is the first example and *Attici* (the Athenians) are the last. Athens is, however, so prominent in each account that the appearance of ring-composition may be inevitable rather than intentional.

stylistic tendencies (the allegorical wanderings of *eloquentia*). Geography receives constant emphasis, as the first half intently focuses on Athens to the exclusion of other locales; Cicero signals this focus by citing Atticus before anyone else, proclaiming Athens as his city (*Athenae tuae*), and balancing the reference with the concluding allegory of *eloquentia* departing from Athens.

Similarly, conceptual parallels abound. A loose and simplistic scheme of development offers a handful of technical refinements (Isocrates and rhythm, 32; Pericles and *doctrina*, 44), a general sense of progress, and conclusions that schematically outline oratorical decline. The vocabulary of ages is prominent,[54] as are references to theory and technical aspects of the *ars*, via teachers (30),[55] theorists (46–47), and philosophers (31, 44). Two significant groupings emerge, first canonical orators (35–36) and then canonical theorists (46–47). Strong emphasis is placed on how to write about the past, including the use of other authors as sources for information and as a means by which to judge the style of those they document or as representatives of their age. Atticus and Thucydides are the central prose sources for constructing Greek literary history. They are the main Roman and Greek models of historical inquiry, though Aristotle has a moment too as a documenter of theorists, and the poets Eupolis and Homer are important witnesses of oratory. The similarities, differences, and general patterns of historical progress give the impression of a loosely organized whole, a generally coherent group of Greek practitioners and theorists who serve as forerunners for Cicero's own project. In the spirit of competitive emulation, Cicero seeks inspiration from his predecessors even as he seeks to outdo their modes of research.

Encapsulated in the dual histories is a model for how to write literary history, but one with a specific purpose: to calibrate the audience's expectations by offering miniature versions of what such histories could contain and the ideas they could explore. The Greek history draws attention to central ideas and patterns in order to underscore their relevance for the subsequent Roman version. While it might be easy to attribute too much significance to any single parallel, coincidence, or theme, synchrony and parallelism do much of the conceptual heavy lifting. Cicero also exploits the potential flexibility in the presentation of details to create histories that align with his own preferences and prejudices.

---

[54] E.g. *aetas*, 28, 29, 36 (×2), 39 (×2), 43, 45; *senes/adulescens*, 37 and 39.
[55] Cf. *de Orat.* 3.127–29 for the same group (along with Socrates).

The first account (26–38) contains a relatively straightforward catalogue of the major speakers of the Greek world and the sources of innovation, including prominent figures in the training and education of orators – essentially a discussion of oratory, its development, and the means by which to acquire fluency.[56] As is the case for early Roman history, the early Greek history names political greats who leave no trace of their oratory. For Pisistratus, Solon, and Clisthenes, Cicero must surmise on the basis of widespread belief (*opinio*, 27). We then move through central figures such as Themistocles and Pericles, before arriving at the instructors of rhetoric (*magistri dicendi*) and their most notable detractor, Socrates. The narrative then reaches a seminal stylistic innovator, Isocrates, who introduced innovations in the periodic sentence and prose rhythm and paved the way for Athens' golden age: Lysias, Demosthenes, and the likes of Hyperides and Aeschines. From this highpoint rhetoric descended to the less vigorous style of Demetrius of Phalerum, who went into battle "not as though from the soldier's tent, but as though from the shady retreats of the very learned Theophrastus" (*non ut e militari tabernaculo, sed ut e Theophrasti doctissimi hominis umbraculis*, 37). The modern division of the two catalogues into "orators" and "theorists" has rightly been questioned. Apart from the *magistri* of the first catalogue, the most prominent figure speaking against such a distinction is Demetrius of Phalerum, who wrote extensively on history and rhetoric (Diog. Laert. 5.80); yet in the first account Cicero reduces him to nothing more than an orator.

While the first history offers a veneer of neutrality and circumspection, it is guided by several crucial principles, some unstated, which become evident in Cicero's arrangement of the material. It is explicitly about Athens, as all the people mentioned are Athenian, except for the small number of foreigners who were nonetheless active in Athens as sophists (30). Atticus is highlighted in terms of both his nickname and his residence, and Thucydides becomes his Greek counterpart in many respects. Unquestionably important to the first panel is its intense Periclean emphasis. Pericles begins the catalogue of orators literally and canonically: he is the first Greek mentioned and begins Greek oratory. Ring-composition also underscores his importance: he concludes the panel, with Eupolis mentioned as the very last name, but because he documented Pericles'

---

[56] Cf. *de Orat.* 2.93–95. Douglas (1966a) xliv–xlv rightly rejects dividing the two catalogues into "speakers" and "theorists," but his subsequent explanation is unsatisfactory, citing hasty or negligent composition as the cause of the separate accounts.

powerful oratory. He assumes the most important role in each half of the Greek digression (his only competition, really, would be Isocrates).

The account also offers a fairly simple scheme of development and then decline. Cicero documents Athenian intellectual life almost exclusively in connection to oratory's development. We get *magistri, philosophi,* and Isocrates, who crucially discovers prose rhythm and periodic structures. But Cicero organizes the material chronologically to suit his own ends. Isocrates discovered prose rhythm, although months later in *Orator* Cicero would credit Thrasymachus with the discovery.[57] He notes Isocrates' innovations (32–34) and then places Lysias after Isocrates in the chronology (*tum fuit Lysias,* 35). Lysias was a slightly older contemporary of Isocrates, yet their reversed order in the narrative suggests that Lysias should have benefited from Isocrates' innovations. Placement of Lysias immediately next to Demosthenes only highlights his inadequacy: Demosthenes powerfully employed prose rhythm.[58] While the importance of this distortion is not immediately apparent, it will become all the more crucial in the subsequent debate over Atticism and Asianism. Cicero holds up Demosthenes as the model of the powerfully effective oratory against the smoother refined style of Lysias. This is an early shot across the bow in one of the work's central debates.

Further choices, emphases, or distortions enable Cicero to meaningfully craft the account, in particular to make Pericles the first orator of record. His questionable beginning of oratory at Greece anticipates his questionable beginning for Rome (with Cethegus, discussed above). A group of early figures (Solon, Pisistratus, Clisthenes) are recognized as probably having some facility, and reluctance in the face of missing evidence allows Cicero to seem circumspect and therefore reliable. He refers to Atticus' inclusion in the *Liber Annalis* of Themistocles. Although he allegedly possessed wisdom and eloquence, Cicero excludes him from the Greek history (28). Instead Pericles begins oratory because his writings are extant, along with those of Thucydides (27). The status of these writings has been variously disputed since antiquity; their mention is vague and tentative.[59] In the second history Pericles is credited with a significant innovation, that of having first applied *doctrina* to oratory (44). This results from his association with Anaxagoras, otherwise known more for natural

---

[57] *De Orat.* 3.173 also credits Isocrates. What prompted the change remains unclear.
[58] Rathofer (1986) 76.
[59] Cic. *de Orat.* 2.93 speaks of them as among the earliest available. Quint. *Inst.* 3.1.12 is far more skeptical of their value; Plut. *Per.* 8 of their existence at all.

philosophy than ethics or dialectic. How he benefited Pericles is unclear, given Cicero's privileging of moral philosophy and logic to help the orator best craft persuasive arguments. The idea that Anaxagoras provided Pericles with learning beyond mere physics appears to be taken from Plato's *Phaedrus* (269e–70a). Cicero may also have read of their connection in Isocrates' *Antidosis*, the justification of Isocrates' civic career, teaching, and works.[60]

Related to the promotion of Pericles is the exclusion of Antiphon from the canon of Athenian orators. He only appears in the list of theorists (46–47); most other accounts cite him as the beginning of artistic oratory at Greece. His writings are still extant, and he receives considerable praise from Thucydides, who classified Antiphon's defense of himself as the best delivered up to his own day.[61] The choice brought with it several advantages. Excluding Antiphon (ca. 480–411) helps to "modernize" the Athenian canon, which is largely populated by figures active in the fourth century. The later and denser canon of Athenian orators supports Cicero's narrative of improvement that then begins to decline with Demetrius of Phalerum. Pericles, somewhat earlier, stands out as the premier oratorical figure of his own generation. Thus an adjustment as minor as excluding one early canonical figure reshapes the center of the canon and allows a lesser-known figure (Pericles) to obtain a new importance. The exclusion of Antiphon reveals yet another virtue of the double history for Greece: surely Antiphon must appear somewhere, and relegating him to the second catalogue makes possible his absence from the canon of Athenian orators.

Although it loosely follows chronology, the second catalogue (39–51) contains individuals and ideas of programmatic import. It offers indirect reflections on writing literary history and the structure of the *Brutus*. Similarities and differences between the two renditions make clear the different emphases. We begin with what seems like a repetition, Solon and Pisistratus (39), but the emphasis turns to explaining the lateness of oratory by comparative chronology across cultures. The Greek politicians are set against Rome's sixth king, Servius Tullius, allowing for metaphors on the relative old-age and youth (*senes, adulescentes*) in the lifetime (*aetas*) of Greek and Roman worlds.[62] Rome's late development will offer an

---

[60] Isoc. *Antid.* 235, also listing Damon; Plut. *Per.* 4.4 on Anaxagoras' influence.

[61] Thuc. 8.68. Gagarin (2002) surveys Antiphon's speeches and career.

[62] *Aetas* is used throughout to describe the ages of individuals, generations, and cultures, but this is the only point at which the *Brutus* uses *senex* and *adulescens* with metaphorical application to Greek or Roman oratory. The terms were first used together for the actual difference in age between orators of the "classical" period at Athens and Demetrius, who was a young man in their old age (37).

entrée into the early documentation of oratory in Greece by Homer. Homer was, significantly, a contemporary of the "first" Lycurgus, thereby connecting significant rulers with the documenters of oratory, a scheme we will later encounter with finer granularity in the Roman world. Homer stands as the first poetic witness to oratory, with a reference to the fact that Nestor and Odysseus possessed force and sweetness (40).[63] Mention of Homer and the Homeric heroes in some sense undermines the claim that oratory follows other arts in time and that it is incompatible with kings and war, but it most importantly sets out the idea that poets document oratory. As an epic poet Homer is a kind of "first Ennius," establishing a pattern that will make sense fully once Cicero comes to the early oratory of Cethegus as documented by Ennius.

Themistocles and Coriolanus provide an opportunity for more elaborate syncrisis, including an interest in the limits and distorting potential of dealing with history (41–43).[64] The carefully planned digression, with Atticus' strained acquiescence, highlights the potential of cross-cultural comparison throughout the *Brutus*. The next stage only elliptically suggests a relevance to method, as the introduction of Pericles emphasizes his reliance on the philosophy of Anaxagoras for the improvement of oratory. It resembles an entry from the earlier catalogue, and even refers back to his inclusion in it: *de quo ante dixi* (44). Earlier, however, Pericles was mentioned in two contexts, as the first figure of considerable fame whose writings are extant (28–29), and again at the conclusion as a short addendum to the judgment of Demetrius, who failed to attain what Eupolis praised in Pericles: leaving a sting in the audience's mind (*aculeos etiam relinqueret in animis*, 38).[65] Discussion of Pericles in the later catalogue emphasizes his application of learning to oratory (*doctrina*) and refers back to Eupolis' documentation of him. The later pairing of Pericles with Eupolis will be essential to Cicero's review of literary historians (59, discussed below), and special mention of him anticipates the prominence he ultimately obtains.

Subsequent notice of the *aetas prima* of oratory at Athens stresses, though in abstract terms, the historical determinants of eloquence, connecting the flourishing of oratory with tranquil statehood. The universal claim of the passage is difficult to apply without reservation to circumstances at Rome, and it makes most sense in reference to the Golden Age

---

[63] *Il.* 1.248–49 on Nestor and *Il.* 3.221–22 on Odysseus.

[64] The passage is discussed in Chapter 4.

[65] Although it may be simply coincidence, assonance seems to highlight the contrast between Demetrius and Pericles (*tabernaculis* and *umbraculis* in 38 versus *aculeos* in 39).

of peace between the Persian and Peloponnesian Wars, which roughly coincides with Pericles' adult life. The relationship between state order and judicial procedure effects a transition into the subsequent group of theorist-practitioners (46–48), all of whom fall under the documentation of Artistotle's Συναγωγὴ Τεχνῶν. Significant here is that Cicero provides details not from a rhetorical treatise but from a historical survey of rhetorical theory. In some sense Aristotle's treatise was one significant forerunner for the *Brutus*, and the selection from Aristotle's catalogue importantly includes individuals who significantly altered oratory through doctrinal reflections or teaching, including those who, like Cicero, were also active as pleaders. The most telling indication that we do not have here a second chronology of orators is the absence of Demosthenes, who will remain for Cicero the pinnacle of Greek achievement and the stylistic countermodel to the restrained Atticism of Lysias.

Lysias will make a second appearance in the catalogue but in order to express a larger set of problems, namely that experts in oratory and its theory respond to one another and that this determines in many ways their interest in an art, whether as practitioner or theorist. Lysias first focused on theory but then, in response to Theodorus' abilities in that area, began to write speeches for others instead. His career parallels in reverse that of Isocrates, who first wrote speeches before dedicating himself to theoretical questions. The parallels, like those of Coriolanus and Themistocles but without the cross-cultural element, emphasize the ways in which two figures can be read against one another. Cicero, unless he follows material from Aristotle, goes to great lengths to liken Isocrates and Lysias to each other.[66]

The concluding panel (49–51) transforms a chronologically vague explanation into a geographical allegory on the wanderings of *eloquentia*. The conceptual travelogue takes us from Athens to Asia and then back to Rhodes, with an implicit set of values attached to each of the regions. The description foreshadows a range of central arguments in the work: the ultimate passing of eloquence from the Greek to the Roman world, the polemics concerning Atticism and Asianism, the significance of the Aristotelian golden mean as category of explanation, and lastly Cicero's mapping of the narrative of eloquence onto the details of his own life.[67]

---

[66] Douglas (1966a) places the blame on Aristotle, but much of the material and the explanation seems to come from Cicero as well, including the detail outlawing misuse of court procedures, which is distinctly Roman. At the very least, the depiction of Isocrates hardly matches his biography.

[67] Dugan (2005) 214 and 226. Stroup (2010) 237–68 on the personification of *eloquentia*. Chapter 1 discusses the allegory in relation to the Ciceropaideia.

The second catalogue is a farrago of ideas and images in comparison to the simpler chronology of the first. We have two sections of comparable length but considerably different character. These are entirely different ways to approach the history of oratory at Greece, the first a relatively transparent and seemingly artless rendering of names and developments, the second a series of repetitions and insertions that outline key methodological principles for literary history. The crucial difference lies not in whom the catalogues introduce, but in the distinct conceptual frameworks produced by each account. Cicero offers two versions of Greek development, each of which sheds light on his aims and instructs the reader in the principles of his method.

An understanding of these two narratives will also help to clarify apparent problems in the teleology of orators and in the principles underlying how Cicero structures oratorical history in the *Brutus*. Themes, ideas, and strategies of representation from the two Greek histories will resurface in various ways throughout the longer Roman version. Pericles will continue to play an outsize role at the beginning of Roman oratory (59) and in connection with Phidias' famed statue of Athena/Minerva on the Acropolis in Periclean Athens (257). Poets crucially document oratory: Ennius first documents Cethegus just as Eupolis documents Pericles. Syncrisis across cultures or of individuals and groups within Roman oratorical history is among the most important – perhaps the single most important – conceptual technique for evaluating the past and creating a canon of orators. With this habit comes the license to find and take advantage of actual or possible parallels to create a more persuasive narrative. The developmental scheme, with individual figures making identifiable contributions, will be the mainstay of oratorical evolution up to Cicero's day. Politics and oratory will be connected to one another over and again. Geography, especially the role of Athens and Atticism, will become a central concern, centered on the question of how best to appropriate Greek intellectual culture in a Roman context.

The second catalogue, when juxtaposed with the first, suggests that the writing of literary history, at least in Cicero's version, will necessarily be shaped by the metaphors, habits of mind, and cultural reflexes of the documenter. Far from denying these factors, as the modern literary historian might wish to do, Cicero signals their importance early on. Yet the two styles of history are simultaneously employed throughout the work, often in a dialectical relationship. Presentation of both in succession at the outset does not mean that Cicero prefers one of the two perspectives on history, but that he will blend them into one another in the subsequent

Roman account. And it is precisely this need to move back and forth between the basic chronological account and the conceptual digressions that makes the dialogue so conceptually and intellectually powerful. Throughout the text Cicero indirectly reflects on the values underlying his construction of literary history.

Because Cicero's catalogue of orators is teleological, we have often been lulled into reading its conceptual development as a forward-driven narrative as well. Yet this is to confuse the work's stated aim to document rhetorical history with Cicero's further aim to document how such a history is possible and why it is meaningful. Assembling the different sections into a coherent picture illuminates Cicero's own conception of literary history. Although there are necessary distortions in the literary history, it does not follow that we therefore must reject Cicero's theoretical framework. Doubtless, modern accounts of Roman literature should strive to resist Cicero's tendentiousness.[68] Yet resistance alone cannot explain why Cicero chose to be tendentious in the way he has. By demonstrating the arbitrary nature of literary history, and by visibly distorting the material, he prompts us to consider closely his criteria and motivations: why did Cicero choose these beginnings for Greek and Roman oratory, and are they connected?

Poetic Historians

A determining factor in Cicero's literary history is the repeated assertion of oratory's late development. Acceptance of Appius Claudius Caecus' speech (ca. 280 BCE) into the canon would, of course, overthrow the sequence of poetry (240 BCE) and oratory (ca. 204 BCE) at Rome (discussed above). This account requires that poetry reach Rome earlier than oratory and develop long enough for Ennius to supplant his uncouth forerunners such as Naevius and Livius Andronicus in order then to bear first witness to the rise of Roman oratory.[69] That construction allows Cicero to reflect on his literary-historical predecessors and to insert himself programmatically into a recognizable lineage of literary historians. To create his own version of literary history, Cicero invents a genealogy of significant forerunners that goes back to Eupolis in Greece (59, quoted below). There are three main

---

[68] As Goldberg (1995) 3–12 and Hinds (1998) 52–98 remind us. Cicero's prejudices seem still to hold sway, for example, over the terms of the revised first volume of the *Handbuch der lateinischen Literatur*, with its serene embrace of the label "archaic" (Suerbaum 2002); see Feeney (2005).

[69] Citroni (2001) on Livius–Naevius–Ennius and claims to firstness.

stages in the lineage of literary historians and orators: Eupolis documents Pericles in Greece; Ennius follows by documenting Cethegus at Rome. Cicero and all other Romans are third. Along the way Cicero ingeniously works across both culture and genre: the citation of poetic authorities is accompanied by the repositioning of literary history from Greece to Rome and from poetry to prose.[70]

Cicero had already likened his own project to the transfer of authority among successive poets, taking his cue from rival poets, presumably Sophocles and Euripides, to honor Hortensius: "if tradition has it that renowned poets had grieved the loss of their peers, how should I in fact react to the death of the man with whom it was more glorious to compete than to be utterly without a rival?" (*si ... memoriae proditum est poetas nobilis poetarum aequalium morte doluisse, quo tandem animo eius interitum ferre debui, cum quo certare erat gloriosius quam omnino adversarium non habere?*, 3).[71] Cicero will return to the poetic tradition in order to align himself with a legacy of literary historians. Eupolis appears at the end of the first catalogue of Greek speakers (38) and reappears in conjunction with Ennius:

> But surely the greatest praise is the following:
> "He was called once by those people,
> Who lived and passed their years then,
> Select flower of the people."
> Well said, since talent distinguishes a man just as eloquence illuminates his genius; because he excelled marvelously in eloquence, men at that time pronounced him "flower of the people" and
> "Of Suasion ... the marrow."

> The thing the Greeks call *Peitho* and whose creator is the orator, Ennius called *Suada* and he means that Cethegus was the very marrow of it, such that he claims that our orator was the marrow of that goddess who, in what Eupolis wrote, had sat upon the lips of Pericles.

> sed est ea laus eloquentiae certe maxuma:
> 'is dictust ollis popularibus olim,
> qui tum vivebant homines atque aevum agitabant,
> flos delibatus populi:'

---

[70] The scheme is anticipated as well by Homer's "documentation" of Nestor and Odysseus (40). Cf. Hinds (1998) 82: "it is clear that his narratives are implicitly teleological and appropriative, tending towards a characterization and defence of his own philhellenism."
[71] Cf. *Vit. Eurip.* 10. The background gives further point to the metaphor of the forum as the theater of Hortensius' talent: *theatrum illius ingeni* (6).

probe vero; ut enim hominis decus ingenium, sic ingeni ipsius lumen est eloquentia, qua virum excellentem praeclare tum illi homines florem populi esse dixerunt:

'Suadai medulla'.

Πειθώ quam vocant Graeci, cuius effector est orator, hanc Suadam appellavit Ennius; eius autem Cethegum medullam fuisse vult, ut, quam deam in Pericli labris scripsit Eupolis sessitavisse, huius hic medullam nostrum oratorem fuisse dixerit. (58–59)

This seems to punctiliously relay Ennius' depiction of Cethegus, while actually obscuring Ennius' words in the guise of paraphrase and philological elucidation. Cicero seamlessly integrates the Ennian passage into his own discussion, even imitating and naturalizing Ennius' artificiality by turning the adjective *suaviloquens* into the noun *suaviloquentia* (discussed above).[72] He translates ἐπεκάθιζεν in Eupolis with *sessitavisse*. And the phrase *effector Suadai* adds a further twist by recalling the πειθοῦς δημιουργός, a nod to Plato as a documenter of rhetoric.[73]

The alignment with Plato is bemusing, given Aristotle's importance as a dialogue model, the numerous references to his texts, and the Peripatetic teleology of artistic progress. Allusion to the *Gorgias* here, however, would help to explain the initial symbolic nod to Plato in a work so Aristotelian on the face of it: "we sat in a meadow next to a statue of Plato" (*in pratulo propter Platonis statuam consedimus*, 24), a detail reminiscent of the *Phaedrus* and Cicero's dialogues of the 50s.[74] The citation of Ennius shows an intense awareness of Greek forerunners across genres, and the Platonic touch is highly programmatic.

A Roman poet casting around for Latin equivalents to Πειθώ may well have considered *Suada*. Yet it is entirely Cicero's suggestion – made without Ennian evidence – that Ennius translated and transposed Eupolis' description of Pericles. It would be all too easy to accept this assertion, but having the goddess *Peitho* sitting on Pericles' lips is hardly

---

[72] Douglas (1966a) 48, Elliott (2013) 56–57 (with n.130) and 160.

[73] Quintilian confirms the connection by "reading" Plato's *Gorgias* onto the *Brutus* at *Inst.* 2.15.4. He casts aspersions on Ennius' *Suadai medulla*.

[74] Kytzler (1970) 280 and 286–88 suggests a connection to the *Phaedrus* here and throughout by emphasizing the triad *ars, natura, ingenium*. However, those traditional terms in the *Brutus* need not indicate exclusive reference to *Phaedrus*; see Shorey (1909). Kytzler (1970) 280 on the "Aristotelian orientation"; Dugan (2005) 172–250 on the Aristotelian aspects alongside the Platonic ones. The reference is also crucial to the role that statuary plays in the *Brutus*, on which see Chapter 8.

consonant with the idea that Cethegus was the *Suadai medulla*. A. E. Douglas rightly called the connection "very far-fetched, and its expression cumbrous."[75] Over a century ago Friedrich Leo elucidated Ennius' meaning: the "flower" of oratory is contrasted with its "marrow" as a careful conceit relying on contrast to make its point: Cethegus was both the most externalized and most internalized expression of eloquence.[76]

Cicero has invented the connection because of the crucial lineage it creates.[77] Eupolis documents Pericles, the first Greek orator, just as Ennius documents Cethegus, the first Latin orator. Such a tradition of firsts in Greece and Rome offers remarkably persuasive parallels and synchronies. By distorting Ennius' poetry Cicero makes him participate in a process of appropriating Greeks: Ennius' account of Cethegus copied Eupolis' account of Pericles. Eupolis and Ennius are cultural precedents created by Cicero to bolster his own authority as a scholar of the rhetorical and literary past.[78] For prose literary history he engages in what, for Roman poets, Stephen Hinds memorably dubbed "do-it-yourself tradition."[79] He triumphantly steps into a literary-historical legacy of his own making. The alignments also reflect the celebration of Periclean Athens and Cicero's self-portrayal as a Roman Pericles.[80] He has brilliantly crafted a lineage that does double-duty, highlighting his twin roles in the *Brutus* as both documenter and documented, literary historian and orator.

---

[75] Douglas (1966a) 50.   [76] Leo (1913) 181: "das Äußerste und Innerste vom Besten."

[77] Recent studies have well demonstrated Cicero's distortions of Ennius the poet as well as the subjects of Ennian poetry, e.g. Goldberg (2006), Zetzel (2007), Elliott (2013). Zetzel (2007) 10 notes of Cicero's version of Ennius in the *pro Archia* that "Cicero is constructing Ennius on the basis of Archias, in order to defend Archias on the grounds that he is like Ennius." Cicero likewise manipulates Ennius to make the case for Cethegus.

[78] A better citation would be Aristophanes' *Acharnians* 530–31, used only months later: "he is said by Aristophanes the poet to have blazed, thundered, and shaken up Greece" (*ab Aristophane poeta fulgere tonare permiscere Graeciam dictus, Orat.* 29). While the passage more ably demonstrates effective forcefulness, it would not support Cicero's construction of Ennius' hellenizing literary history.

[79] Hinds (1998) 123–44. Cicero's remark that he often heard Accius' judgments of Decimus Brutus (107) draws on a potentially agonistic topos, making Cicero the most recent member in a triumphant genealogy of literary historians. See Leo (1913) 386–91 on several similarities of Greco-Roman subject matter, audience, and authorial position in Accius' *Didascalica* and Cicero's *Brutus*. Dahlmann (1962) 587–88 n.2 implausibly claims that the choice of Cethegus is taken from Varro.

[80] Though named only six times, Pericles is central to the *Brutus'* history and ideology. He begins oratory at Greece, or at least, oratory with written memorialization (27, although Cicero's assertion there lacks corroboration – have the facts about Pericles been fudged to give him the first record of oratory?). Pericles otherwise does not play the same role in Cicero's theorizing, and Cicero's later references to Phidias and Minerva are part and parcel of the *Brutus'* intensely Periclean moment (257); cf. Chapter 8, Noël (2014).

Crafting this succession from Eupolis and Ennius is also part of the larger strategy to claim superiority in the tradition of Greco-Roman literary historians. Cicero ostentatiously diminished the role of Accius and accords Varro a lesser place among literary historiographers.[81] On this score Accius and Varro are the biggest losers in the *Brutus*. After using Varro (via Atticus) to dispense with Accius, Cicero turns on him, relegating Varro to a lineage of learned researchers through the laudatory comparison to Aelius Stilo: "And our friend Varro, a man eminent in talent and universal learning, laid out in several brilliant writings what he had taken from him and independently supplemented" (*quam scientiam Varro noster acceptam ab illo auctamque per sese, vir ingenio praestans omnique doctrina, pluribus et inlustrioribus litteris explicavit*, 205).[82] The portrayal is an object lesson in the manipulative magic of panegyric. As a contest for primacy in literary historiography Cicero damns Varro with fulsome praise: elevating – or demoting – him to the position of mere scholar while wresting away the mantle of literary historian.[83] Cicero's alternative lineage of literary history, leading triumphantly from Ennius via Accius to himself, makes him Rome's premier, though not its first, literary historian, ignoring, adapting, and vanquishing predecessors as he crafts an as-yet-unknown model of literary history.

---

[81] The nod to the *Phaedrus* in the elucidation of the Ennian passage may also be Cicero's attempt to upstage Ennius by aligning himself and his dialogue with Plato's august legacy and by translating his Greek.

[82] On Stilo see *ORF*⁴ no. 74, Cic. *Ac.* 1.8, Suet. *Gram. et rhet.* 3.1–2, Varro *L.* 7.2, Gell. *NA* 1.18.2; Leo (1913) 362–68, Zetzel (1981) 10–26, Rawson (1985) 269–77, Kaster (1995) 68–70, Suerbaum (2002) 552–57, Goldberg (2005) 60–62.

[83] Concealing reliance on Varro involves obscuring and mediating his contributions through Atticus and his *Liber Annalis* – although the triangulation of the three men, including oral and not just textual sharing, should not be ruled out; R. M. A. Marshall (2017). Other literary historians, Volcacius Sedigitus (Gell. *NA* 15.24, fr. 1 Courtney) and Porcius Licinus (Gell. *NA* 17.21.44, fr. 1 Courtney), are nowhere to be found (Aurelius Opillus and Ateius Praetextatus wouldn't have been worth mentioning).

CHAPTER 6

Perfecting Literary History

By beginning his oratorical history with Marcus Cornelius Cethegus (cos. 204) rather than Appius Claudius Caecus (cos. 307, 296), Cicero shows that several sometimes contradictory criteria are required to craft a literary history. As Chapter 5 has just discussed, Caecus is rejected because his speeches are outdated. At the same time, no direct evidence supports the favorable judgment of Cethegus' oratory, and Cicero's stated criteria should have logically led to Caecus' inclusion. By being so visibly inconsistent, Cicero forces the reader to closely examine how he constructs literary history and what self-interested reasons are at play. He also confronts a much larger problem: if literary history is skewed by its author's predilections, then what place can he rightfully assume in his history of Roman orators? Beyond this lies another less evident problem: how can Cicero secure a place not only in his own account but also in future oratorical histories? Cicero's choices, including all the wrangling over Appius Claudius Caecus versus Marcus Cornelius Cethegus, are inherently tied to concerns about securing a lasting place within oratorical history. This is a serious problem, for if Caecus (or any "outdated" orator, such as Cato or Crassus, as Atticus claims) could be excluded from such a history, what prevents the same fate from befalling Cicero?

An answer to this question exists, but it is complex and extends across the length of the dialogue, including the dramatic exchanges, which constructively challenge Cicero's assumptions and methods. As I noted in the previous chapter, Cicero indirectly reflects on the values that underlie his construction of literary history; moreover, the work's different sections can be assembled to create a coherent statement about his own conception of literary history. Cicero crafts a normative historiographical framework for literary history, and also composes a literary history in which he assumes pride of place and which ensures his inclusion in all future histories.

Teleology is central to understanding literary change: orators in successive generations made changes to oratory that contribute to the state of the

art. While relying on a teleological model, Cicero does not fully endorse it
and in fact shows its serious limitations. One main concern is how to keep
alive the contributions made by authors who now seem outdated – how to
appreciate the past without succumbing to its aesthetic criteria. In the
dialogue he examines and ultimately rejects both antiquarianism and
presentism, which requires him to face the related problem of using
absolutist versus relativist standards: when judging an author should we
use today's standards or those of the author's own age? He knows that the
absolutist and the relativist perspectives cannot be reconciled – the antithesis remains even today a fundamental problem in the writing of literary
history. The different steps of the problem and his innovative solution
merit examination in detail, since his solution, which amounts to a kind of
historicism, continues to determine how literary history is and can be
written.

As one of Rome's premier orators, Cicero would seem to be the natural
endpoint of his own teleological history. The forward movement involving
the gradual improvement and refinement of oratory passes through recognizable stages. Cato's speeches provide a baseline of sorts, filled with the
required virtues (*omnes oratoriae virtutes in eis reperientur*, 65), with the
τρόποι and σχήματα classified by the Greeks, and yet still wanting polish
and refinement (69). Servius Sulpicius Galba (cos. 144) first introduced
embellished digressions, pleased and moved his audience, and employed
the *loci communes* (82). Marcus Aemilius Lepidus Porcina (cos. 137) first
mastered smooth diction (*levitas verborum*), periodic sentence structure
(*comprensio verborum*, 96), and skillful writing. Gaius Carbo (cos. 120)
made regular practice a virtue as a precursor to the later institution of
declamation (105). The virtues of erudition can be read in the likes of
Quintus Catulus, philhellene interlocutor of *de Oratore* and consul of 102
(132). Antonius and Crassus finally usher in an age to rival the great age of
Greeks such as Demosthenes and Hyperides, and this Roman pair attained
a fullness comparable to that of the Greek canon (*in his primum cum
Graecorum gloria Latine dicendi copia aequatam*, 138). Crassus is singled
out for his terse and compact periodic structure (162). This age also takes
us up to Cicero's lifetime, and further developments are elaborated in the
Ciceropaideia and perhaps best summed up by Caesar's reported remark
that Cicero was the pioneer of full eloquence (*principem copiae atque
inventorem*, 253).[1] But the voyage to the present day is not without
challenges and detours. Even as the narrative relentlessly gravitates toward

---

[1] See Chapter 1 on the Ciceropaideia.

Cicero, questions surface about the final trajectory: is the contemporary teleology open or closed, which is essentially to ask, has oratory reached a final stage of perfection? This concern bears directly on Cicero's uncertain place in the forward progress of his history, an uncertainty that he manufactures by omitting judgment on the living in general and on his own accomplishments in particular.

The work's concluding exhortation of Brutus suggests that another stage might develop, a continuation of the teleology that would seem incumbent upon any literary historian hoping to preserve the integrity of the larger narrative. Yet it also raises questions about Cicero's position in the sequence.[2] Cicero first praises Brutus' own accomplishments:

> That was your forum and your trajectory, you alone arrived there not only having sharpened your tongue by training but even having enriched eloquence itself with an array of weightier disciplines, and by them joined all distinction of excellence with utmost renown in eloquence.
>
> tuum enim forum, tuum erat illud curriculum, tu illuc veneras unus, qui non linguam modo acuisses exercitatione dicendi sed et ipsam eloquentiam locupletavisses graviorum artium instrumento et isdem artibus decus omne virtutis cum summa eloquentiae laude iunxisses. (331)

He then aligns his and Brutus' achievements by suggesting that each must escape being numbered among the mediocre speakers: *numerari in vulgo patronorum* (332). Although he abjures self-praise to the end, he also hopefully exempts himself from the throng of everyday orators: "if it had happened to me to be counted merely among the many" (*si mihi accidisset, ut numerarer in multis ...,* 333).[3] The parallel between Cicero's and Brutus' accomplishments allows the viewpoint to shift from orators of the past to orators of the present and future. From a literary-historical perspective, Cicero's oratorical success depends not only on his achievements but also on the prospect that Brutus will embody a subsequent stage of development that builds on his accomplishments. For this reason, Cicero gives Brutus a patently Ciceronian cast, pointing to Brutus' daily practice and his enrichment of oratory through "weightier disciplines" (presumably philosophy) in order to create a fuller style of eloquence.

Once again Cicero makes thoroughly plausible claims even as he distorts the evidence. He does not deny but rather ignores Brutus'

---

[2] His concern about looking forward in this way is confirmed by *de Oratore*'s prediction of Hortensius' rise to prominence (3.228–30; cf. *Orat.* 41), modeled on Plato's prediction of Isocrates' greatness (*Phdr.* 279a).

[3] The text is lost at this point, but the larger thought can be reconstructed.

shortcomings.[4] Rather than lie outright, Cicero focuses instead on daily practice (*exercitatio*) and the influence of adjacent disciplines (*artes*) that were so essential to oratorical preparation in *de Oratore*. The reader is prompted to infer that such preparation necessarily resulted in the full eloquence that was Cicero's hallmark. Alternatives are not countenanced here; for example, that Brutus' real strength was in logical argument rather than oratory, or that philosophical devotion could have a deleterious effect on oratory, exemplified by a dyed-in-the-wool Stoic, Rutilius Rufus.[5] As so often in the dialogue, this masterstroke of indirection will pay off in spades. This praise of Brutus is a marvelous form of indirect self-praise, highlighting the aspects of Brutus that best support Cicero's own habits and values.[6] Most importantly, Cicero creates continuity between his innovations and the established practices of the next generation, suggesting that oratory will move forward and will do so along Ciceronian lines. The teleology is not yet complete in the technical sense, nor has it come to an end in the historical sense.

Cicero's reluctance to include himself in his history of oratory is related to another problem: how serious is Cicero in his critical accounting of the past? The challenges to his interpretation of the history of oratory come from his interlocutors, as in Atticus' demurrals at the likening of Cato to Lysias: "I could hardly contain myself when you were comparing the Athenian Lysias to our Cato, a great man, by Hercules, or rather a uniquely outstanding man – no one will say otherwise – but an orator?" (*risum vix tenebam, cum Attico Lysiae Catonem nostrum comparabas, magnum me hercule hominem vel potius summum et singularem virum – nemo dicet secus – ; sed oratorem?*, 293). The criticism comes in the middle of Atticus' sweeping dismissal of orators prior to Cicero's generation (294–96). It is, of course, Cicero who drives this inquiry and the conflict underlying it, even if he puts the objection into the mouth of an

---

[4] Cf. Quint. *Inst.* 10.1.23, Tac. *Dial.* 21.5–6. Martin (2014) argues that Brutus is portrayed in an especially negative light in the *Brutus*, but the analysis seems to misread the pedagogical function of the ignorance that Cicero ascribes to Brutus. Cicero portrays Brutus as a student who comes to appreciate the history of oratory as he learns from Cicero's illuminating catalogue. I discuss further below an example of Brutus' pedagogical role in the dialogue.

[5] Cicero earlier noted the insufficiency of Stoic and Academic/Peripatetic philosophy for oratorical training, even while praising Cato as an exception (118–120). On Cato's style see Stem (2005) and van der Blom (2016) 204–47. On Rutilius Rufus, see 110–18 (part of a syncrisis with M. Aemilius Scaurus), *de Orat.* 1.227–30, Cic. *Off.* 3.10; Aubert-Baillot (2014); D'Alton (1931) 163, 217 notes Cicero's terminological overlap in describing Stoics and Atticists. Moretti (1995) 71–138 discusses (Cicero's take on) Stoic style.

[6] Just as the praise of Brutus' speech *pro Rege Deiotaro* early in the dialogue advertises Cicero's values: *ornatissume et copiosissume* (21).

interlocutor. The underlying question of how to appreciate the past is crucial to how a literary history can be constructed. To an orator of the 40s BCE, what good are Cato the Elder's speeches, nearly 150 in number and dating back almost as many years?

To ask about Lysias versus Cato, apart from the significant (if different) difficulty of cross-cultural comparison, is ultimately to bring into conflict the dual commitments to aesthetic absolutism and aesthetic relativism. Absolutism dictates that we use only today's standards, while relativism requires that we judge a style by its contemporary criteria. The two possibilities are crucial to writing literary history, largely irreconcilable, and the Achilles heel of any such project: should authors be judged only by the standards of their day, and, conversely, why are today's standards better than those of yesterday? The antithesis between absolute and relative judgments is not small and not transient, since it abides even today as a central problem of literary history.[7] Cicero offers a solution (discussed in the next section), but it is worthwhile to outline first in greater detail what is at stake. It will also be necessary first to counter one common suggestion – offered in the *Brutus* itself by Atticus and accepted by some modern readers – that Cicero is merely being ironic in his support for older authors and that he actually believes only in the absolute standards of the present day.

Initially Cicero might seem to sidestep the question of how to appreciate past authors, either by excusing it as a problem beyond the scope of the present discussion or by retreating into an ironic pose.[8] Atticus criticizes as ironic Cicero's support for Crassus' speech on the Servilian law of 106 BCE, both suggesting that Cicero is at heart an absolutist and pinpointing the very problem of what standards to use when judging past ages. Atticus' charge amounts to little more than disbelief at the prospect that Cicero actually appreciates older authors. Cicero again goes to great lengths to manufacture this and other objections in order to draw attention to fundamental problems of the construction of literary history. Behind the interlocutors' objections lies not a rejection of Cicero's literary-historical principles but rather an indication of the theoretical issues at stake.[9] Atticus remarks that Cicero's ironic pose may be acceptable in a Socratic

---

[7] Perkins (1992) again is the seminal study of the tensions, esp. 46 and 175–86.
[8] "You've brought up a matter worthy of a new discussion" (*remque commovisti nova disputatione dignam*, 297). Another suggestion is that the scheme falls apart when pressure is placed on it: Goldberg (1995) 6–7.
[9] *Pace* Dugan (2005) 208 and Fox (2007) 188. Suerbaum (1997) 417–18 n.20 rejects the ironic reading. Desmouliez (1982) offers the most astute reading of Cicero's irony in the *Brutus*.

dialogue, "but in historical matters, which you've drawn on throughout the discussion, . . . perhaps irony should be censured as much as when giving evidence" (*sed in historia, qua tu es usus in omni sermone . . . vide . . . ne tam reprehendenda sit ironia quam in testimonio*, 292). Irony and aporia are inherent features of the dialogue genre, familiar from the Greek tradition, yet recognition of the well-known Socratic ploy does not entail acceptance of it, and Cicero pointedly rejects the suggestion:

> We must scroll through the works of others and especially of Cato. You'll see that only the floridity and brightness of not yet discovered pigments were wanting from his general features. And I do think that Crassus himself perhaps could have written a better speech, but I don't think anyone else could have. Don't think I'm being ironic because I said this speech was my teacher. You see, although you might seem to think better of whatever ability I may now have, still when I was young there wasn't a Latin model to imitate instead.

> volvendi enim sunt libri cum aliorum tum in primis Catonis. intelleges nihil illius liniamentis nisi eorum pigmentorum, quae inventa nondum erant, florem et colorem defuisse. nam de Crassi oratione sic existumo, ipsum fortasse melius potuisse scribere, alium, ut arbitror, neminem. nec in hoc εἴρωνα me duxeris esse, quod eam orationem mihi magistram fuisse dixerim. nam etsi [ut] tu melius existumare videris de ea, si quam nunc habemus, facultate, tamen adulescentes quid in Latinis potius imitaremur non habebamus. (298)

Cicero adamantly defends the formative significance of Crassus' speech on the Servilian law.[10] Older authors, including Cato, still merit study, despite their unquestionable shortcomings. Atticus doubts the value of Cato's speeches and takes a more extreme position than that of Cicero's reserved judgments on Cato earlier in the work (61–76, esp. 63). Atticus will not yet concede the point at issue (is Cato worth reading?). Brutus ultimately settles the matter when he asks to examine these older texts under Cicero's guidance (*orationes nobis veteres explicabis?*), a prospect Cicero saves for a future conversation (300).

Cicero neither avoids the question at hand nor concedes that older texts have no value. With Brutus' assistance he overcomes the underlying problem in what amounts to ingenious question-begging. Rather than explain why older texts must be read, he dramatizes a solution based on his own authority, showing how Brutus, and presumably any other student of oratory, should accept the reading of older texts under the guidance of

---

[10] C. Steel (2002) 208 stresses its importance. Cf. *de Orat.* 1.225.

an experienced orator. Although the evaluation of such texts is postponed to some other occasion, the work's dramatic fiction justifies Cicero's inclusion of older orators in the first place, because Brutus will eventually read their texts.[11] Cicero's point here is not, nor is it anywhere in the *Brutus*, to insist that ancient orators will satisfy the stylistic criteria of any era, but rather to insist that older texts remain valuable resources for study, appraisal, and excerption even when, and at times because, their faults are apparent.[12]

The interlocutors' objections undoubtedly undermine Cicero's insistent praise for Crassus' speech and isolate weaknesses in his evolutionary model. Yet it would be futile to construct so long a history in full cognizance of its shortcomings, only then to let that entire construction collapse. And there would be little intellectual benefit in Cicero's advancing positions to which such easy responses can be offered – why put himself in the position of being such a crude and refutable advocate? To read Cicero's sparring with Atticus or Brutus as a disguised dismissal of models like Cato or Crassus is to deny him the acknowledgment of a complex challenge requiring a complex answer: how to benefit from the teleological perspective and yet escape its inherent, and inherently destructive, limitations.[13]

The answer to this challenge has typically been to argue that Cicero must be using either absolute or relative criteria in judging style.[14] Neither alternative is satisfactory. Indeed, he shows the value, limitations, and irreconcilability of the two categories before turning to historical context as the means to escape the antithesis. Cicero undoubtedly emphasizes the value of past innovations as a stage of development. But when assessing older speeches, he insists on honoring not the final product as an eternal artifact but rather the intelligence and artistry that led to its initial creation. For this reason, he observes that ancient writers would nowadays

---

[11] To postpone the discussion is not to concede the point. The examination of mechanics has no place in the *Brutus*. How to read ancient authors is a significant, if different, technical question from the fundamental question of whether to read them at all. Brutus will revisit older material (*multa legenda ... quae antea contemnebam*, 123).

[12] *Orat.* 169 reprises the balancing act: "I don't demand what antiquity lacks but praise what it has" (*nec ego id quod deest antiquitati flagito potius quam laudo quod est*). Gaius Gracchus' imperfect speeches still sharpen and enhance one's talent (*non enim solum acuere, sed etiam alere ingenium*, 126).

[13] Valuable analysis in Goldberg (1995) 3–12 and Hinds (1998) 52–98, but Barchiesi (1962) 21–38 best adumbrates the relativist perspective and its consequences.

[14] Douglas (1966a) xl–xli believes that Cicero holds absolute standards and rejects the analysis of J. W. H. Atkins (1934), who argues that Cicero defends relativism. Douglas must, however, make an exception for Cato. Hendrickson (1962) 254 n.a suggests that Cicero has Atticus voice the absolutist perspective, which Cicero shares, despite his earlier support for relativism.

update their works if given the opportunity: Crassus would not only rewrite his own speeches, he would rewrite them better than anyone else could (298).[15]

Cicero must maintain an open teleology because oratory will continue apace.[16] The focus on Brutus' future prospects makes no sense otherwise, and that future is indistinguishable from the reception of Cicero, who implicitly predicts that he will himself become one stage in a long development. The preface uses political imagery to underscore the difference in age and the transfer of authority to the next generation: "since at my age I am now making way for you and lowering the fasces" (*cum tibi aetas nostra iam cederet fascisque submitteret*, 22).[17] Recognition of this inevitability enhances rather than diminishes Cicero's oratorical achievements, since crafting a literary history in this way frames his reception and ensures a place for his speeches, even when their aesthetic values will show the inevitable wear of time.[18] He relies not solely on the perspective of the present, but acknowledges the different perspectives that can be brought to bear on texts both in the past and also in the future.

Later authors would take up Cicero's terms, focusing on his innovations while bringing their own revised expectations. This is why Quintilian can praise Cicero (but not only Cicero), why Pliny can still hope to rival his achievements, and why Marcus Aper of the *Dialogus* can criticize Cicero's lumbering digressions and outmoded fullness of language, all from viewpoints that are neither utterly beholden to Cicero nor wholly irreconcilable to one another.[19] Neither Cicero nor any other classical author (to my knowledge) suggests the converse and necessary conclusion that dawned

---

[15] Horace portrays Lucilius in Cicero's terms (*S.* 1.4, 1.10, 2.1).

[16] A crucial historiographical insight, even if non-teleological models are certainly possible; cf. Gadamer (1989) 201: "The ontological structure of history itself, then, is teleological, although without a telos." It is worth considering the alternative framing of artistic development, namely that the telos has been reached from a presentist and biological perspective, but that this does not exclude the possibility of future development. Cf. Edelstein (1967) 124 n.145: "it does not follow that, once this τέλος is apprehended, nothing further can be added"; Citroni (2001), esp. 309–10, Cavarzere (2012).

[17] The striking image *fasces submittere* ("to lower the fasces") refers to the lictors' symbolic recognition of the authority of the people or of another magistrate's greater *imperium*. See A. J. Marshall (1984), Bell (1997) 11–13, Goltz (2000), Hölkeskamp (2011b), with Livy 2.7.7, Plut. *Publ.* 10.7; Cic. *Rep.* 2.53; V. Max. 4.1.1.

[18] See Dugan (2005) and Stroup (2010, 237–68) on Cicero's textual afterlife. My interest here is in how Cicero crafts a normative historiographical framework through which posterity could place him into a literary history.

[19] Quint. *Inst.* 10.1 and 10.2 impress upon students the need to know many styles, to improve on the past, and to recognize the inevitable shortcomings of even the best speakers. Pliny remarks: "You see, I too rival Cicero" (*est enim … mihi cum Cicerone aemulatio, Ep.* 1.5.12). Marcus Aper details Cicero's flaws at *Dial.* 22–23.

on Erasmus centuries later in his *Ciceronianus*: Cicero spoke as best he could for his own day, but would have spoken differently if born in an earlier age, since his style would have cloyed earlier tastes.[20] What Erasmus lays out clearly and emphatically is given a rather obscure form at the conclusion of Tacitus' *Dialogus* by Maternus, who notes that different ages produce different eloquence and "that each man should enjoy the good in his own age without the detraction of another" (*bono saeculi sui quisque citra obtrectationem alterius utatur, Dial.* 41.5). Tacitus reads backward into history and brilliantly captures Cicero's evolutionary logic; he justifies stylistic change and yet still appreciates the oratorical merits of distinct generations.

Saving the Past

A general principle about the value of past authors emerges from Cicero's discussion of Ennius' rivalry with Naevius, in which Cicero notes the crucial dependence of the former on the latter:

> Grant that Ennius is clearly more polished: yet if Ennius scorns him as he pretends, he wouldn't have left out that fiercely contested First Punic War when he treated all wars. But he explains his actions: "others wrote about the event in verses." They did write brilliantly, even if with less refinement than you. And in fact it shouldn't seem otherwise to you, who either borrowed much from Naevius, if you admit it, or stole much, if you deny it.

> sit Ennius sane, ut est certe, perfectior: qui si illum, ut simulat, contemneret, non omnia bella persequens primum illud Punicum acerrimum bellum reliquisset. sed ipse dicit cur id faciat. 'scripsere' inquit 'alii rem vorsibus'; et luculente quidem scripserunt, etiam si minus quam tu polite. nec vero tibi aliter videri debet, qui a Naevio vel sumpsisti multa, si fateris, vel, si negas, surripuisti. (76)

The portrayal of this rivalry reflects a disposition toward early oratory as well as early poetry. Mandating that Ennius must recognize his debt to Naevius makes a general argument on the need to value literary

---

[20] Erasmus (1528 [1986]) 381: Bulephorus notes, "Cicero spoke in the best possible way in the age he lived in. Would he still have spoken in the best possible way if he had adopted the same style in the age of Cato the Censor, Scipio, or Ennius?" Nosoponus replies, "No. The ears of his audience would have rejected that polish and rhythm of his, being accustomed of course to a more rugged form of speech. Their language matched the customs of the age they lived in." Cf. Bulephorus at Erasmus (1528 [1986]) 404: "Cicero's style would not have met with approval in the time of Cato the Censor, as it was too elaborate and fancy to suit the standards of that age." I am grateful to David Quint for first suggesting the usefulness of the *Ciceronianus*.

predecessors. Later authors may be more refined (*perfectior, polite*), but that does not acquit posterity of its standing debt or the need to acknowledge it.[21] The remark typically has been connected to ideas about poetic *imitatio*, a tendency already fostered in antiquity by Seneca the Elder's oft-cited reprisal of the opposition "borrow" and "steal" to describe Ovid's transparent reworking of Vergil.[22] The claim serves no less as an oblique response to the detractors of the early oratorical tradition – to an Atticus or a Brutus disparaging the dusty pleadings of a Cato or a Crassus. Once again, part of the brilliance of the *Brutus* consists in Cicero's ability to offer such indirect reflections on literary history within the shaping of that history and its polemical assertions. Through such indirection, theory is integrated seamlessly into the historical picture advanced throughout.

It is equally important not to misconstrue partial approval of older authors for antiquarianism. Orators cannot live solely for the virtues of the past, hence the muted criticism of antiquarian style in the case of Laelius (83). Similarly, Lucius Aurelius Cotta was a middling orator who attained only limited fame for his rustic and antiquated manner (137).[23] A penchant for the outdated may have some merit, but blind appreciation of older material can sever the live connection to the present. On this score Cicero undermines his Atticist detractors by suggesting that they admire outdated Greeks, such as Thucydides, and yet overlook the native equivalents (287–88). He caps his diatribe at 284–88 with an oenological analogy, recommending that one should neither search out the vintages of Lucius Opimius (121 BCE) and Lucius Anicius (160 BCE) nor draw from a fresh vat. The analogy distinguishes appreciation of the past from being trapped in it: how can we walk the divide between antiquarian escapism and presentist solipsism (doubtless an antithesis familiar to modern classicists)?

Absolutism and Relativism

The need to honor the achievements of the past comes out most prominently in the evaluation of Cato early on (61–76). Cicero likens Cato to Lysias but notes the latter's universal preeminence: "in these [speeches]

---

[21] Cicero's *sumpsisti* and *surripuisti* were broadly applicable to discussions of literary borrowing, as Terence's prologues show. Goldberg (2005) 48–51 and McGill (2012), esp. 115–45.

[22] Seneca's opposition is *surripere* and *mutuo(r)*: Sen. *Con.* 3.3.7. See D. A. Russell (1979) 12, McGill (2012), Peirano (2013).

[23] Dihle (1957) 200 rightly distinguishes – as does Cicero – between contemporary antiquarianism and the dated style of an eminent speaker from the past such as Cato.

there's some likeness between the two men: they are pointed, elegant, clever, terse; but that famous Greek has fared better in all manner of praise" (*est nonnulla in iis etiam inter ipsos similitudo: acuti sunt, elegantes faceti breves; sed ille Graecus ab omni laude felicior*, 63). Readers must be on guard against Cato's acknowledged imperfections: "let men choose the parts worthy of being marked out for distinction" (*licet ex his eligant ea quae notatione et laude digna sint*, 65). Cicero implicitly and crucially shows the differences between literary criticism with an eye to the needs of the present and literary history with its eye on the horizons of the past.

The evaluation of a style for imitation in the present requires some measure of absolutism, insofar as we must keep in mind present-day expectations when choosing what to imitate. This absolutist tendency is fundamentally different from the decisions governing the inclusion of a given author within a literary history, which requires a relativist sensibility: how are texts valuable in their own day and how might they be written differently now? Like Crassus (discussed above), Cato could be brought up to date, since his style necessarily lacks modern refinement:

> His speech is rather dated and certain words are pretty rough. That's how they spoke then. Change what he couldn't at the time and add rhythms, arrange and join (as it were) the words so that the speech has a better fit – which even the old Greeks didn't do – then you'll prefer no one to Cato.

> antiquior est huius sermo et quaedam horridiora verba. ita enim tum loquebantur. id muta, quod tum ille non potuit, et adde numeros et, <ut> aptior sit oratio, ipsa verba compone et quasi coagmenta, quod ne Graeci quidem veteres factitaverunt: iam neminem antepones Catoni. (68)

The true danger lies in the tendency of later innovators to overshadow earlier authors: "and so this style of later men, heaped up (as it were) to the sky, has blocked out Cato's brilliant features" (*sic Catonis luminibus obstruxit haec posteriorum quasi exaggerata altius oratio*, 66). The problem would affect more than a few luminaries in older generations: the speeches of Servius Galba "are now scarcely visible" (82), and Cicero recognizes, with some prompting from Brutus, that his own rise has contributed to the fall in popularity of older authors (123–24).[24] Even as Cicero admires the innovations that have cast a pall on preceding generations, he still works to highlight past contributions: although their brilliance has been "cut off" by subsequent authors, the later eclipse should not discredit the earlier

---

[24] Lebek (1970) notes that Cicero's contemporaries weren't reading older orators (but rather historians and poets).

luminaries. Cicero carefully balances the conflicting criteria that result from his teleology, discerning key developments in successive stages without losing sight of past achievements. He is wedded to neither the relativist nor the absolutist approach.

That ambivalence, though not yet a solution to the problems posed by each alternative, does show his alertness to the competing, and potentially irreconcilable, perspectives. At stake are larger questions: to what extent is historical context essential to understanding texts? How do texts relate to their contexts? The mindsets of absolutism and relativism cannot offer adequate responses: absolutism fails to appreciate the past or account for future developments, while relativism can excuse any style and thus render aesthetic judgments useless. Yet if neither approach sufficiently captures history's relationship to literature, how will Cicero arrange a marriage between text and context?

Greek Evolution, Roman Evolution, and the Problems of Atticism

That Cicero connected literature to history is partly visible in the Greek formalization of rhetorical methods after the abolishment of the Sicilian tyrants (46). Much later at Rome, Livius Andronicus' dramatic performance in 240 BCE is a literary response to military victory over the Carthaginians a year before. However, the connection of the play to the event is too thin to offer a satisfactory causal narrative of how Livius' play became a piece of literature. In literary terms, the Roman victory was the occasion but not the artistic cause of the literary drama that Livius produced.[25] Elsewhere Cicero does offer a more nuanced consideration of how aesthetic developments are connected to historical circumstance. His connection of text to context is related to the acknowledged problems of his teleology and his attempt to find solutions. Foremost among the problems is that the teleology can elucidate artistic changes in successive generations, yet often cannot explain why certain changes were made or why they were meaningful and necessary.

Powerful evidence for Cicero's attachment to historical understanding emerges from comparing the trajectories of oratory at Greece and Rome. Cicero only occasionally looks back to Greek developments to assess

[25] Crane (1971) is the seminal modern work on literary-historical principles and the complexity of ascribing causes to final products. *CAH*[2] VIII: 422–76 and Feeney (2016) on the contexts of the rise of Roman literature.

Roman ones, but the most prominent similarity exists between the great ages of the Greeks and the Romans:

> Just as a while back we arrived at Demosthenes and Hyperides; now we've come to Antonius and Crassus. You see, I think that these men were supreme orators and that in them the fullness of Latin oratory first came to equal the renown of the Greeks.

> ut dudum ad Demosthenen et Hyperiden, sic nunc ad Antonium Crassumque pervenimus. nam ego sic existimo, hos oratores fuisse maximos et in his primum cum Graecorum gloria Latine dicendi copiam aequatam. (138)

Perhaps surprisingly, that great age does not coincide with Cicero's generation – even if an exemplary speech by Crassus coincided with Cicero's birth (161). This cross-cultural analogy of Greeks and Romans raises the question of how to interpret subsequent oratorical history at Rome against the Greek model. If Rome equaled Greece in the generation of Antonius and Crassus, then what changes have befallen Roman oratory and do they parallel those in Greece? The next Greek stage was its "endpoint" or "decline" in Demetrius of Phalerum, who succeeded the older generation of great Athenians while a young man (37). The negative portrayal of Demetrius as the endpoint of Greek oratory conflicts with some positive portrayals in other works, and this different account meaningfully suits the local purposes of the *Brutus*.[26]

The parallel developments suggest that Rome has surpassed – or at least has the potential to surpass – the accomplishments of Greece's canonical figures. While Greece has declined, Roman oratory culminates in Cicero's triumphant values, *vis* and *copia* (forcefulness and fullness) in the service of *movere* (emotive persuasion). Even as Cicero promotes these values, he must also refute his Atticist detractors. Syncrisis of Greece and Rome shows that Cicero advances oratory while the Atticists blindly follow Greece's downward trajectory. Aesthetic similarities liken the notionally classical periods to one another: at Greece "this age poured forth its bounty and, in my opinion, that noteworthy sap and blood maintained its integrity up to this age of orators, whose splendor was natural and not made-up" (*haec enim aetas effudit hanc copiam; et, ut opinio mea fert, sucus ille et sanguis incorruptus usque ad hanc aetatem oratorum fuit, in qua naturalis inesset, non fucatus nitor*, 36). At Rome the same features first arise with Crassus and Antonius: "in all these exists a remarkable shade of

---

[26] I differ here from Chiron (2014), who suggests that Demetrius parallels Cicero.

reality without any rouge" (*in his omnibus inest quidam sine ullo fuco veritatis color*, 162).

The post-classical generations also share certain key characteristics of style. At Athens:

> You see, Demetrius succeeded the old generation, surely the most learned of all these, but practiced less in real weaponry than in wrestling. He would entertain rather than inflame the Athenians, since he had ventured out to the sun and dust of action not as though from the soldier's tent but as though from the shady retreats of the very learned Theophrastus. He was the first to bend speech and render it soft and tender; he preferred to seem charming, as was his nature, rather than formidable, but with a charm that flooded rather than broke through their susceptibilities, so that he left but a memory of his refinement and not also, as Eupolis wrote about Pericles, pleasurable stings in the audience's minds.

> Phalereus enim successit eis senibus adulescens eruditissimus ille quidem horum omnium, sed non tam armis institutus quam palaestra. itaque delectabat magis Atheniensis quam inflammabat. processerat enim in solem et pulverem non ut e militari tabernaculo, sed ut e Theophrasti doctissumi hominis umbraculis. hic primus inflexit orationem et eam mollem teneramque reddidit et suavis, sicut fuit, videri maluit quam gravis, sed suavitate ea, qua perfunderet animos, non qua perfringeret; [et] tantum ut memoriam concinnitatis suae, non, quemadmodum de Pericle scripsit Eupolis, cum delectatione aculeos etiam relinqueret in animis eorum, a quibus esset auditus. (37–38)

The contrast of Demetrius with Pericles is slightly different from but related to the later distinction of the two primary oratorical virtues in the *Brutus*: the grand style aimed at forceful persuasion, *movere*, and the sparse style, *docere*, aimed at instruction (89 and *passim*).[27] Cicero's insistence on *movere* is part and parcel of his attack on Atticism, and his ambivalence here about refinement based on excessive learning is part of

---

[27] Narducci (1997) 114–24 on the "two kinds of eloquence." Fantham (1979) 450 suggests Cicero's argumentative motivations for suppressing *delectare* in the *Brutus*. Traces of the three aims remain (cf. *delectare*, 185, replacing *conciliare* from *de Oratore*). Cicero criticizes Demetrius' pleasing qualities (*delectare*) and the Atticists' focus on explication (*docere*). The common criticism is lack of emotional force (*movere*) because of excessive devotion to (Greek) learning. Guérin (2014) sees the binary system of the *Brutus* as the remnants of a separate tradition and as Cicero's first steps toward the definition of ideal style and the connection of *officia* to *genera* in *Orator*. For him the *Brutus* only temporarily suspends the tripartite understanding of the *genera dicendi*. Crucial for my purposes is that the binary abides: grand style aimed at forceful persuasion versus sparse style aimed at instruction. Cf. C. Steel (2002) 209–10 and Dugan (2005) 196–203. Fortenbaugh (1988) discusses how Cicero's divisions differ from Aristotle's tripartite *logos*, *ethos*, and *pathos*. May (1988) 1–11 valuably summarizes the centrality of ethos as argument at Rome. Wisse (1989) examines *ethos* and *pathos* in rhetorical works.

the weaponry in his arsenal. Demetrius, like the Atticists at Rome, ignored the needs of the audience in favor of his own standards of learning: *eruditissimus* (along with Theophrastus' *doctissimus*) sounds complimentary, but ultimately results in feebler oratory. The earlier evolution toward the great generation of classical Athenian orators is depicted in retrograde, a decline in the ability to fulfill the orator's chief duty to persuasion (*movere*).

In the case of the Roman Atticists, Cicero similarly faults their precious attention to learned detail. Their fastidious style is a result of the surrender to the dogma of learned refinement, yet overly precious oratory fails to captivate the masses, as in the case of Calvus (283). Cicero evokes Demetrius' wanting innovations through linguistic parallels to the "proto-Atticist" Calidius, who is soft, delicate, and pleasing (*mollis, tener,* and *suavis*), all virtues to be sure, but insufficient in the absence of emotional forcefulness.[28] Calidius becomes the Roman counterpart to Demetrius, and both are similarly flawed.[29] Cicero quotes liberally from his defense of Quintus Gallius, when he chided Calidius: "far from having you fire our emotions, we nearly fell asleep on the spot" (*tantum afuit ut inflammares nostros animos, somnum isto loco vix tenebamus,* 278).[30] Like Demetrius and Calidius, the Atticists in general cannot rouse their audience (279), which soon abandons them (289).

The Atticists' failures stem from their indifference to the expectations of the audience:

> It follows that a speaker approved by the masses is also approved by the learned. You see, I'll judge what's right or wrong in speaking, provided I'm a capable speaker or can judge; but it'll be possible to understand what sort of orator a man is from his effectiveness in speaking.

---

[28] "Supple and transparent speech would clothe his profound and extraordinary thoughts" (*reconditas exquisitasque sententias mollis et pellucens vestiebat oratio. Nihil tam tenerum quam illius comprensio verborum,* 274); "If the best thing is to speak pleasingly, you wouldn't think it necessary to search out anything better than this" (*si est optimum suaviter dicere, nihil est quod melius hoc quaerendum putes,* 276). The parallels are reinforced by the fact that Cicero uses *inflammare* strategically: to describe Demetrius (37), to draw the fundamental distinction between *movere* and *docere* (89), and to discuss Calidius (278–79). Cicero also remarks that Atticus has fired his mind (*inflammavit*) with the passion to write the *Brutus* (74).

[29] Douglas (1955a) emphasizes that Calidius was not an Atticist. However, Cicero represents Calidius as though his style were essentially Attic. On Calvus see *Fam.* 15.21.7 (SB 207) with Hendrickson (1926) 237; cf. Chapter 7.

[30] A passage that Tacitus' Marcus Aper brilliantly turns against contemporary aficionados of late republican orators (Tac. *Dial.* 21.1).

necesse est, qui ita dicat ut a multitudine probetur, eundem doctis probari. nam quid in dicendo rectum sit aut pravum ego iudicabo, si modo is sum qui id possim aut sciam iudicare; qualis vero sit orator ex eo, quod is dicendo efficiet, poterit intellegi. (184)

The distinction drawn between the learned and unlearned audience anticipates the later claims about Atticism's failure to adapt their style to large-scale public oratory.[31] The underlying assumption is clear: aesthetics must be anchored in immediate realities. This is neither relativism nor absolutism in aesthetic terms. Rather, Cicero here makes a fundamental point about the role of context in determining how literature works: aesthetic change is only meaningful and necessary if it is effective in its own context.

While the larger historical thrust of oratory at Rome proceeds through stages of progressive refinement, the Atticists exemplify the reality that formal refinements are pointless if they cannot captivate the public. Authors in any genre must to some extent accommodate the needs and expectations of their audience. Cicero has anticipated what literary historians of late have so strongly emphasized: literature evolves in consonance with changing standards and expectations in the extraliterary world. Although modern scholars have faulted ancient critics for failing to account for extraliterary influences, the *Brutus* will show that cultural and historical contexts can and must shape literary values. Cicero makes this conclusion inevitable in those parts of the *Brutus* that document the relationship between text and context.

Anti-Philhellenism and Cicero's Culture Wars

Nowhere is Cicero's historical sensibility on display more than in his attack on Atticism, which is in fact part of a much larger consideration of one significant influence on literature: Greek culture, and specifically Greek oratory. Cicero's historical mindset is inextricable from the portrayal of Greek culture. Roman oratory has not only equaled the Greeks but surpassed them. If Antonius and Crassus rivaled Greek orators (138, discussed above), Brutus will propose Rome's superiority: "the one domain in which we were being conquered by conquered Greece we have now either taken from them or surely share with them" (*quo enim uno vincebamur a victa Graecia, id aut ereptum illis est aut certe nobis cum illis communicatum*, 254).[32]

---

[31] Schenkeveld (1988) and Bolonyai (1993) on judgments by *docti* and *indocti*.
[32] Consider Cicero's subsequent exhortation to snatch philosophical glory from the Greeks, since Romans had already conquered all the other arts (*Tusc.* 2.5, with Gildenhard and Zissos 2004).

For all the brazen assertions about Rome's oratory, contemporary philhellenism still posed a threat, and we should take Cicero's anti-hellenism
seriously, as James Zetzel has argued: "Greek learning, which had been
deracinated by excessive cleverness from its own society, could only be
rescued, or even understood, by anchoring it once more in a social and
moral context – in the service of Roman tradition and Roman values."[33]
Cicero acknowledges the Greek forerunners of Roman oratory, championing the *doctus orator* while subordinating the meaning of being *doctus* to the
practical aims of being a public *orator*. Oratory's developmental narrative is
grounded in a distinctly Roman past, which is contrasted with competing
threats to Roman cultural production. He instances various forms of contemporary philhellenism and faults their failure to appreciate the history of
intellectual activity at Rome: the jejune Lysianic refinement of the Atticists,
Caesar's overly systematic *de Analogia*, and even the writing of biography.

Hints of the problem surface in the discussion of biography and
autobiography – hardly the most prominent theme in the work, but an
area in which philhellenism undermines Roman achievements and their
documentation:

> There exist speeches of his [Scaurus] and also three very useful books of
> autobiography addressed to Lucius Fufidius, which no one reads; yet they
> read *The Education of Cyrus*, which, though illustrious, neither befits our
> circumstances much nor yet merits being preferred to the praises
> of Scaurus.

> huius et orationes sunt et tres ad L. Fufidium libri scripti de vita ipsius acta
> sane utiles, quos nemo legit; at Cyri vitam et disciplinam legunt, praeclaram
> illam quidem, sed neque tam nostris rebus aptam nec tamen Scauri
> laudibus anteponendam. (112)

Cicero undoubtedly appreciated both the style and the content of
Xenophon's *Cyropaideia* (as his letters repeatedly show), but emphasis on
practical applicability to Roman circumstances (*utiles*; *nostris rebus aptam*)
lends the Roman biography a pragmatic authority that cannot exist in the
Greek version.[34] This is not in any case a rejection of Greek authors but
rather a call to appreciate them with due measure. Cicero opposes not
Greek culture but his contemporary philhellenes who admire Greek

---

[33] Zetzel (2003) 137.
[34] Cf. Cic. *Fam.* 9.25.1 (SB 114) on the *Cyropaideia*. M. Aemilius Scaurus is the consul of 115. Dugan
(2005) 213 n.125 offers suggestive observations on biography in the *Brutus*; see Chapter 1 for brief
discussion and further references to the development of (auto)biography.

culture to the detriment of the Roman tradition. Gaius Memmius, praetor in 58 and immortalized in the poetry of Catullus and Lucretius, was surely not the only senator enamored of Greek rather than Latin literature (247). Such attitudes meant the neglect of Roman contributions:

> Quintus Catulus was educated not in that old but in our new way, or perhaps more perfectly, if that's possible: he possessed wide reading, the utmost grace not only of his life and disposition but even of his speech, and an untainted soundness of Latin speech; this can be seen both in his speeches and most readily in that book he wrote about his consulship and accomplishments, composed in a smooth Xenophontean style and addressed to his friend Aulus Furius, the poet. Yet this book is no more known than those three by Scaurus I mentioned.

> Q. Catulus non antiquo illo more sed hoc nostro, nisi quid fieri potest perfectius, eruditus. multae litterae, summa non vitae solum atque naturae sed orationis etiam comitas, incorrupta quaedam Latini sermonis integritas; quae perspici cum ex orationibus eius potest tum facillime ex eo libro, quem de consulatu et de rebus gestis suis conscriptum molli et Xenophonteo genere sermonis misit ad A. Furium poetam familiarem suum; qui liber nihilo notior est quam illi tres, de quibus ante dixi, Scauri libri. (132)

The mentions of Xenophon – here noted only as a stylistic accomplishment – and Scaurus connect the later passage to the earlier one. The favorable comparison of Catulus' language to Xenophon's smoothness has the added bonus of documenting Roman stylistic achievements, comparable to Greek models but focusing on Roman events. Brutus will draw the appropriate conclusion as a surrogate student for the audience: "I'll search them out more diligently in the future" (*conquiram ista posthac curiosius*, 133). The mention of two stages in Roman biography mirrors on a miniature level the grander evolution of oratory and anticipates Cicero's own autobiography at the end of the *Brutus*. Again, the objection is not to Greek literature, but to Greek literature when it eclipses native texts.

In moving from biography to the study of language and grammar, a similar criticism of philhellenism emerges in the discussion of Caesar's *de Analogia*. Cicero is our first witness to Caesar's work, called here *de ratione Latine loquendi* (253), of which a few dozen fragments survive, partly from Cicero, often from Gellius, but mostly through citation from later grammarians such as Charisius, Pompeius, and Priscian.[35] The shortcomings of

---

[35] See Garcea (2012) on *de Analogia*. Schironi (2007) 333–34 on Cicero's "paraphrasing" title. By necessity the account here limits itself to examining Cicero's anti-philhellenism in relation to Caesar's (alleged) views on language. I should make it clear, once again, that this book's analysis reflects Cicero's representation in the *Brutus*. I am not suggesting that Cicero's picture is accurate.

analogy are visible in the entertaining story of Gaius Rusius and Sisenna. Rusius once mocked Sisenna's fondness for neologism when Sisenna coined the term *sputatilica* ("spittlicious," 260). Sisenna had said that accusations made against his client, Gaius Hirtuleius, were *sputatilica*.[36] Rusius countered with a marvelous stroke of sarcasm: "Unless you help me, judges, I'm done for. I don't get what Sisenna's saying. I'm worried it's a trap. Spittlicious – what *is* that? I get 'spit' (*sputa*) but not 'tlicious' (*tilica*)" (*circumvenior . . . iudices, nisi subvenitis. Sisenna quid dicat nescio; metuo insidias. sputatilica, quid est hoc? sputa quid sit scio, tilica nescio,* 260).

The humorous anecdote may at first seem to have little to do with Cicero's arguments against philhellenism or even Caesar's *de Analogia*, but it contains an indirect jibe against Roman appropriation of Greeks. Cicero takes aim not merely and not wholly at analogy, but at analogy that results from untrammeled philhellenism, that is, from the brute imposition of Greek morphological forms onto the Latin language: As Alessandro Garcea notes, Sisenna's *sputatilica* is derived from "a formally correct but wholly unused calque of *πτυαλιστικός*."[37] The barbarous neologism is patently Greek, as is the linguistic competence required to produce it. Most crucially for an audience-directed art such as oratory, expertise in Greek is also necessary to understand it.

Caesar may have backed some poor alternatives in theory, but the occasional peccadillos in his system hardly matched the exuberance of Sisenna's *sputatilica* in a Roman court of law. It is true that Caesar recommended analogical forms unused by his contemporaries or himself, such as the nominative pronoun *isdem* or the participle *ens*. Cicero objects to the former in the *Orator*, and in the eyes of posterity (and probably many contemporaries) Cicero had the more sensible argument. But Cicero's discussion of Caesar is all the more powerful (and tendentious) because of the false opposition it creates, suggesting that the alternatives are either forms produced by the mastery of a Greek system or native habits of speech that have developed as Rome itself has. Cicero champions *consuetudo* over Caesar's analogical *ratio* in part because analogy derives from a Greek scientific model, but especially because strict application of its methodology excludes the authority and diversity of Latin's native evolution.

His deft citation of Sisenna seems to ignore the fact that Caesar was probably not an extreme analogist. Cf. Pezzini (2018).

[36] I read *Hirtuleium* for *Hirtilium* (Kaster 2020, following Reis).

[37] Garcea (2012) 103 n.80. Compare Lucian's similar figure, Lexiphanes, who is so taken with linguistic novelty that he cannot be understood (*Lex.* 22–25). On Sisenna see Rawson (1979).

Cicero's criticisms throughout the *Brutus* are directed at visible appropriations of Greek intellectual matter that either have no history at Rome or are too obviously Greek. This would partly explain the odd analogy – one that has yet to find a full scholarly explanation – of *eloquentia* as a maiden who should be guarded at home as an *adulta virgo*, both mature and also a product of domestic tutelage.[38] Cicero argues on behalf of a distinctly *Roman* oratorical history. However much the Greeks are valuable, it is ultimately the best of the Romans who merit the limelight. Greek intellectual achievement must help Romans move forward, an idea already prominent in Cicero's rewriting of Platonic dialogue in the 50s: "The end result," William Stull observes, "is not a return to earlier models but the attainment of new possibilities."[39] Despite his continued support for the *doctus orator*, Cicero deftly manipulates the tension between Roman *auctoritas* and Greek *paideia* in order to place himself squarely on the Roman side.[40] Greek oratory remains valuable as a model for comparison and emulation or as a template for the stages of artistic improvement but not as the ultimate authority on aesthetic standards. Only with this assumption in mind can Cicero simultaneously admit Cato's stylistic inferiority to Lysias and yet still insist on Cato's exemplary status for Roman orators.

Oratorical Development and Roman History

The interdependence of literature and history, however significant a theme in the *Brutus*, has been overshadowed by historical interest in the context of Caesar's rule.[41] The changes in legal advocacy are one aspect of the work's intermittent interest in how historical change produces aesthetic change: changes in court procedure are linked to changes in oratorical practice. As an aspect of literary historiography, the notices about legal procedure, while not a strong emphasis, nevertheless show that the development of a literary form depends on factors extrinsic to the art alone.

A century before the writing of the *Brutus*, numerous changes in court procedure placed greater demands on orators – and intertwined politics

---

[38] See Stroup (2010) 237–68. Cf. Dion. Hal. *Orat. Vett.* 2–3.   [39] Stull (2011) 252 n.10.
[40] I draw the opposition from Wallace-Hadrill (1997) 14: "social authority and academic learning pull in opposite directions."
[41] Haenni (1905) is seminal but brief. He balances the competing influences of history, theory and doctrine, and personal elements. M. Gelzer (1938) emphasizes Cicero's reentry into political life. Rathofer (1986) examines how Cicero's *auctoritas* influences Brutus in the face of Caesar's dictatorship. Cf. Narducci (1997) 98–101, Dugan (2005) 244–46, Lowrie (2008), and Chapter 3.

and advocacy ever more tightly. The *lex Calpurnia de repetundis* of 149 BCE (106) saw to the establishment of the *quaestiones perpetuae* for cases of *repetundae* (extortion). Later struggles to fortify the laws included the addition of *equites* to the panels of juries and an increase in the severity and nature of penalties.[42] These developments, along with introduction of the secret ballot for courts and legislation, shifted the center of gravity from aristocratic control toward a socially diverse group of advocates.[43]

The *lex Pompeia de vi et ambitu* of 52 BCE, which allotted speakers three hours for defense and two for prosecution and limited the number of advocates, reduced the opportunities for lengthy speeches (324). The date and the effects would become a watershed for later authors gauging oratorical change in what we commonly think of as the transition from republic to principate.[44] The limitations on the length of speeches also presumably curtailed the orator's ability to overwhelm an audience. Cicero remarks that the changes to forensic procedure could only be endured by those whose extensive training had prepared them for it. Speakers almost daily had to prepare fresh arguments for several often similar cases (*ad causas simillimas inter se vel potius easdem novi veniebamus cotidie*, 324). Cicero, somewhat counterintuitively, adduces the restrictions on time as a cause for the increase in the orator's daily workload. Most important, however, are the law's effects: Brutus and Cicero could endure the changes because their training had prepared them for it (*exercitatio*, 324). The same changes ruined the likes of Arrius, who lacked sufficient training and succumbed to the new rigors of the new forum: "he couldn't endure the severity of that judicial year" (*illius iudicialis anni severitatem . . . non tulit*, 243).[45]

---

[42] On the development of the courts, see *CAH²* IX.2: 491–530, Kunkel (1962), Nicolet (1972), Gruen (1968), Lintott (1992). On the Sullan reforms, compare the different takes in Brunt (1988) 194–239 and Hantos (1988) 63–68, 154–61. On legal and court procedure in Cicero's day, see Greenidge (1901), Lintott (2004), J. G. F. Powell (2010a).

[43] The democratizing effects remain a matter of debate. Pro-democratizing: Yakobson (1995) and (1999) 116–33; anti-democratizing: Gruen (1991) 257–61, Jehne (1993), U. Hall (1998), and Morstein-Marx (2004) 286, with an overview and further bibliography; U. Hall (1990) offers a more intermediate position. Secret ballot was introduced by the *lex Gabinia* (139 BCE), *lex Cassia* (137 BCE), *lex Papiria* (131 BCE), and *lex Coelia* (106 BCE), which covered elections, non-capital trials, legislation, and capital trials, respectively. For an overview, see Lintott (1999) 47–48, Brennan (2000) II: 365–71, Flower (2010) 72–75, Cic. *Leg.* 3.34–39. Salerno (1999) is a general study.

[44] Cf. Asc. *Mil.* 31, 34, Cass. Dio 40.52.2, Tac. *Dial.* 38.1, Plin. *Ep.* 2.14, Syme (1939) 28–46, Taylor (1949) 148–52, Gruen (1974) 458–60, Lintott (1974), Ramsey (2016), Morrell (2018). This watershed event in ancient accounts is cited more readily than the institution of the principate and, as Tacitus' *Dialogus* demonstrates, complicates the separation of republican from imperial orators. Cf. Kennedy (1972) 16.

[45] *Pace* Douglas (1966a) 180, it is unlikely that Cicero means that Arrius was convicted of a crime.

The true significance of this later development becomes evident only in light of the earlier discussion of oratorical training in the *Brutus*. Gaius Carbo (cos. 120) "was industrious ... and painstaking and would typically put considerable effort into exercises and compositions" (*industrium ... et diligentem et in exercitationibus commentationibusque multum operae solitum esse ponere*, 105).[46] Carbo grew up under the new set of prosecutions in the wake of the *quaestiones perpetuae* established in 149 BCE; he also introduced the habit of regular practice and declamatory-style exercises (105–6). No direct dependence is initially posited between regular practice and the orator's ability to manage a heavy workload. Carbo's dedication is connected to his abilities and hence his popularity: through constant training and advocacy he became the best orator of his generation. Carbo's assiduous reliance on oratorical exercises would prove essential to later generations, when extensive pedagogy and training prepared speakers to endure the new burdens. However, Carbo had initially introduced these changes for the sake of his own stylistic improvement. What was at an earlier point a matter of aesthetics would subsequently become a means of survival.

Historical change and aesthetic change are involved in a circular process of cause and effect: pedagogical techniques derived from Greek rhetoric and an emphasis on formal training were initially introduced to improve eloquence, but would later equip orators for the stress of forensic advocacy, which in turn allowed the best orators to become better pleaders. Cicero marvelously demonstrates the close interplay of intrinsic and extrinsic factors in shaping literature and therefore how to write literary history: an educational development initially meant to promote a speaker's style acquires new meaning in the light of historical factors that loomed well over the horizon.[47] He delivers a remarkably successful account of the mystifying relationship of text to context, what David Perkins calls "mediation," adequate explanations for which remain the greatest obstacle to the writing of literary history.[48] Cicero's version of oratorical history is put into the service of the orator's need for extensive preparation, championing broad learning in all fields and regular practice with diverse training. This

---

[46] A generation after the *Brutus* Cassius Severus would become the standard-bearer of the orator's increased workload, usually getting up one criminal or two civil cases per day (Sen. *Con.* 3 *pr.* 5). Cassius and the aesthetic changes he introduced could later be cited to demonstrate the interdependence of style and historical circumstance (Tac. *Dial.* 19.1–2).

[47] Gadamer (1989) 201: "success or failure causes a whole series of actions and events to be meaningful or meaningless."

[48] Perkins (1991) 5: "Mediation, the paths leading from the alleged context to the text, is an insurmountable problem. The paths can never be fully known, and if this were possible, a book could not be long enough to trace them."

historical justification is an important and compelling advance over the persuasive, yet largely dogmatic, justification first presented in *de Oratore*.[49]

The Ciceronian Futures of Oratory and Literary History

Several interrelated questions and consequences emerge from Cicero's framework for literary history. One practical question is whether Cicero believed that oratory had come to an end, either in the evolutionary terms he sketches out or in absolute terms in light of Caesar's rule. The presentation of his career, along with meaningful parallels in that career, point the way to an answer. Sylvie Charrier examines the temporary halt of oratory under Sulla's domination as a parallel for oratory's abeyance under Caesar's and has argued that it suggests that oratory has a viable future.[50] Just as Cicero previously developed under political constraints, so too can Brutus (and other orators) in present circumstances. Furthermore, Cicero's reluctance to write himself explicitly into his canon of orators nonetheless suggests his inevitable inclusion in oratorical history as well as the prospect that oratory will continue to develop as an art.[51] Actual history confirms what Cicero might have hoped or even expected: he would subsequently return to the dust and sun of the forum to deliver the *Philippics*.

Accounts sympathetic to the thesis of the "death of oratory" rely on *post hoc ergo propter hoc* assumptions. They tend to read the *Brutus* by superimposing later history and the rise of the principate onto the Cicero of the mid-40s and his staged retreat from public life. Such pessimism cannot be reconciled with the elaborate simile of *eloquentia* (330), which depicts the art of speech as a maiden bereft of her protector, Hortensius, and in need of a new *tutor*, Cicero and Brutus in the immediate sense, but also the future inheritors of the Ciceronian legacy.[52] What matters most is trying to

---

[49] This argument supplements that made in Chapter 7 about Cicero's insistence on having a historically diverse canon to emulate. How and to what extent Cicero agrees with Crassus' maximalist position in *de Oratore* is less certain than has often been assumed; see Görler (1974) 27–45.

[50] See Charrier (2003) on the parallels of the decade of the 80s to the period 49–46 (erroneously attributed to Catherine Steel at van den Berg 2019 598).

[51] C. Steel (2002) notes six pairs of orators, although the last pair includes only Hortensius, with Cicero understood as the implicit other half. Cf. C. Steel (2005) 131–36, 140; Gildenhard (2011) 381 n.21. Kytzler (1970) 293 similarly counts a key group of Greek orators (discussed in Chapter 4).

[52] Zetzel (1995) 205–6 notes the political significance of *tutor* as a citizen watching over the state in crisis. C. Steel (2005) 137 on Cicero's writings as "an aspect of, and not a substitute for, political activity."

recapture Cicero's perspective in this period, and that was likely – in unison
with historical circumstances – to be far more in flux and subject to far more
volatile judgments than are likely to result from the clearer perspective of
later hindsight, when the dust in the republican forum had settled, and the
sun shone on a new generation of speakers born to the principate.[53] In the
meantime, and despite Caesar, oratory must move forward.

Modern readers have faulted Cicero and the Roman epigones for failing
to acknowledge the relationship of history to literature. As D. A. Russell
put it some decades ago, "the historical study of literature in antiquity was
very rudimentary by modern standards."[54] Admittedly, unlike its modern
counterparts in literary historiography, the *Brutus* eschews laborious explanations of cause and effect or the protracted weighing up of one developmental factor over another. Yet in a few instances – the development of the
quaestiones perpetuae, Carbo's innovations in training, or the effects of
Pompey's laws in 52 – he does demonstrate how historical change can
be a catalyst for aesthetic change. Other seemingly crucial elements are
nevertheless overlooked. We do not, for example, hear of the fundamental
change in the *contio* introduced by C. Licinius Crassus in 145 as tribune of
the plebs, when he turned around and faced outward on the *rostra*, thus
addressing the Roman forum and the much larger crowds that could be
assembled there.[55] Nonetheless Cicero's account shows that literature can
be a product and catalyst of history.[56]

His apparent silence on matters of method has caused modern readers
wrongly to regard Roman criticism as a still brutish stage in the long
development of literary history. Still, he foresaw the difficulties inherent in
writing literary history and innovatively examined several interrelated
problems: presentism and antiquarianism, the difficulty of contextual
mediation, the benefits and dangers of the evolutionary model, and the
necessity of intellectual and aesthetic appropriation tempered by the

---

[53] David (2014) 38: "Certes, l'époque était difficile. Mais l'Histoire n'était pas close." C. Steel (2002)
211. *Tusc.* 2.5 posits oratory's decline, but must be read in light of its local justification of
philosophy and Cicero's subsequent reemergence with the *Philippics*.

[54] D. A. Russell (1981) 159, although scholars are coming to acknowledge the complexity of ancient
literary history and criticism: cf. Goldberg (1995) 3–12, Hinds (1998) 52–98, Feeney (2002), Ford
(2002), Farrell (2003), Levene (2004), Feeney (2005), Goldberg (2005), Laird (2006).

[55] Morstein-Marx (2004) 271–72 examines this change in the context of the emergence of populist
rhetoric and (soon after) of its premier representatives, the Gracchi. Were Cicero devoted to
extrinsic history, he might have cited the role of the *lex Cincia* of 204 in regulating legal
advocacy, the same year as Cethegus' consulship.

[56] Even the main figures of new historicism, the scholarly movement most devoted to tracing
mediation, have forsaken claims to methodological coherence. See Gallagher and Greenblatt
(2000) 1–19.

realization that alien influences can overwhelm a native tradition. Cicero offered compromises and workarounds when faced with these competing or irreconcilable demands. The inability to craft a perfect system only makes him resemble subsequent thinkers: solutions still have yet to be found, and all the guilty avowals of recent literary historians have brought at best penance without absolution.[57]

The arguments made thus far have tended toward the conclusion that the *Brutus'* scheme of oratorical development confounds our ability to "slot" Cicero with absolute certainty into the picture of literary history advanced throughout.[58] Yet some calculated misdirection is at work here as well: to prompt us to place Cicero, or even Brutus, into the work's teleology already requires complicity with the vision of evolution that Cicero creates. The open-endedness of the historical development gives readers latitude to read into the narrative the details and trajectory they prefer; such latitude accounts for the differing modern opinions about Cicero's own place in the *Brutus'* history and his belief in oratory's continued viability. Perhaps modern disagreements exist not because we don't get Cicero but because we do. Cicero gestures toward himself as the endpoint but refuses to make the claim overtly. He secures a place for himself and for future orators within his canon, and yet this openness exists not because of uncertainty about oratory's future but as a meaningful feature of the entire system of literary history he has created.

This explains as well why he insists on preserving the contributions of past *ingenia* and yet notes the necessary changes to artistry and training. For the individual craftsmen of a tradition, *ars* and *labor* can always be applied with greater rigor and finesse, but *ingenium* is the foundation for the history of an artistic practice. It is a sort of natural substrate of human accomplishment, outlasting revised artistic and pedagogical standards: "as talent adorns the man, so does eloquence illuminate genius" (*ut enim hominis decus ingenium, sic ingeni ipsius eloquentia*, 59).[59] Cicero could not become the final endpoint of his telos, because doing so would derail the entire historical thrust of his literary history. The teleological framework would devolve into a defense of technical ability based on contemporary aesthetics, what George Saintsbury considered to be the aim of

---

[57] For all his hand-wringing and optimism Perkins (1992) ultimately concedes failure.
[58] I have borrowed the idea of "slotting" in literary history from Levene (2004).
[59] Authors leave behind writings as proof of their *ingenium* (93); at Tac. *Dial.* 1.1 orators are judged for the reputation (*laus*) of their *ingenia*. Gell. *NA* 17.21.1 divides in terms of talent and command: *vel ingenio vel imperio nobiles insignesque*. Cf. Plin. *Nat.* 7.117; Kaster (1998) on Cicero's *ingenium* in Seneca the Elder.

literary criticism: "the reasoned exercise of Literary Taste – the attempt, by examination of literature, to find out what it is that makes literature pleasant, and therefore good."[60] Cicero had already grasped what Saintsbury could not, that a belletristic endeavor, whatever its appeal, would be literary history without history and the end of Cicero's entire project.

The impressive prosopographical labors of the last century have shown that Cicero uses not the consulships but (essentially) dates of birth to determine the sequential presentation of Roman orators.[61] Despite Atticus' presence, the dialogue is not a purely annalistic account, perhaps in recognition of the reality that artistic practices like human lives do not develop solely in chronological terms.[62] In some sense, then, a partial answer exists to the still pertinent question posed in the mid-twentieth century by Wellek and Warren: "Is it possible to write literary history, that is, to write that which will be both literary and a history?"[63] Their concern was not a chronology of texts and authors but the entire cultural system in which texts were produced across time, something that would be both literature and history. Cicero anticipated this question with an answer that was artistically feasible and free from belabored quibbling over method, even if we might challenge his final answer or object to his manipulation of the record. To write literary history requires the careful discernment of meaningful patterns no less than it entails distortions of the material and acknowledgment of the chronicler's inevitable influence; to write successful literary history requires that our misgivings remain *sotto voce*.

---

[60] Saintsbury (1900) 4.
[61] Sumner (1973): dates of birth when known or those surmised by offices held. Cf. Douglas (1966b), David (1992), Fogel (2007) 45 n.6. Badian (1964) 241 n.11 remarked, "the order in the *Brutus* will not help in fixing the chronology of a man or an event not otherwise chronologically anchored."
[62] On Atticus' *Liber Annalis*, see Chapter 2.
[63] Wellek and Warren (1956) 263. Crane (1971) elaborates the underlying principles of what this might be, while Perkins (1992) considers whether literary-historical principles can ever produce a successful account. Cf. Citroni (2005).

CHAPTER 7

Cicero's Attici

It is both expected and also surprising that Cicero's history of Roman orators begins with a survey of the craft in Greece (26–51). Greece had long been the cultural *exemplum* against which to measure artistic achievement at Rome. Surprising, however, is the length, range, and structure of the twofold digression, the first of many in the dialogue. It might seem superfluous for a critical history of speakers at Rome. Yet Cicero's vision of Roman oratory requires looking to, emulating, and evolving beyond Greek achievements. The survey concludes with an embedded joke, a wink and a nudge for those who have paid close attention through the entire digression. *Brevitas* is commendable in certain parts of speaking but not in eloquence as a whole (*brevitas autem laus est interdum in aliqua parte dicendi, in universa eloquentia laudem non habet*, 50). Cicero then wonders if the synopsis of Greeks was all that necessary (*forsitan fuerint non necessaria*, 52). Brutus hesitates, with a touch of coyness, given that the digression announces several programmatic emphases. If anything the opening was pleasing and perhaps shorter than he would have liked (*ista vero, inquit, quam necessaria fuerint non facile dixerim; iucunda certe mihi fuerunt neque solum non longa, sed etiam breviora quam vellem*, 52). The response draws attention to the digression's importance and reaffirms the rhetorical principle that Cicero had proposed earlier: brevity, though not a universal virtue, still suits certain rhetorical contexts.

The passage exudes polite urbanity but accomplishes much more, since the exchange relies on an important feature of Roman dialogue technique. It fulfills argumentative and persuasive functions, even in the case of apparently anodyne banter crafted to break up the monotony of sustained exposition. By confirming the pleasurable brevity of the synopsis, Brutus implicitly endorses the rhetoric that Cicero employs for the dialogue itself. Moreover, Cicero sets himself in good stead by showing that he appreciates and has mastered one aspect of rhetorical – and ultimately Atticist – values before challenging the fundamental tenets of brevity and Atticism as he perceives them.[1] He also forestalls potential criticism that he has simply made a virtue of necessity because his preference for fullness arose from the inability or unwillingness to be terse. Cicero's shunning embrace of *brevitas* reflects the dialogue's treatment of the Atticists and the rhetorical strategies that constantly undermine them. He does not closely analyze stylistic differences or demonstrate his principles at length, as he will do months later in the *Orator*, which closely examines prose rhythm as a stylistic necessity for the grand oratory espoused by Cicero and spurned by his Atticist detractors.[2] Instead, the arguments are largely rhetorical, rejecting Roman Atticism with a definitional quibble over the term *Atticus* before attempting to redefine and coopt Atticism in the service of his own rhetorical ideals.

For all the similarities of the *Brutus* to the *Orator*, the prevalent assumption has been that Cicero's anti-Atticism is uniform and coherent across the works, a more or less stable and independent doctrine that finds its way into both dialogues.[3] Yet to understand Atticism as doctrine requires considering how it appears in each text, which for our purposes means asking how Cicero adapts the portrayal of it to the local considerations of the *Brutus*. The discussion of Atticism surfaces in a range of passages in addition to Cicero's famous diatribe (284–91). The long section beginning with Calidius and running through Atticus' objections are crucial to it (274–300). No less relevant is the Ciceropaideia (301–29, see Chapter 1), which contains his educational biography and a syncrisis with his great rival Hortensius. These passages challenge Atticism and Asianism and offer an intermediate alternative to the geographical binary Athens/Asia: Rhodes. Rhodianism is the stylistic tendency espoused in the *Brutus*, even if Cicero never illustrates what it entails.

The discussion of Atticism is intertwined with two tangential issues: the historical evaluation of early Roman orators, including the perplexing problem of antiquarianism (Cato and Lysias as stylistic models, 66–69, 292–300), and the best means by which to appropriate Greek culture, and,

---

[1] *Brevitas* is often used in two senses without a clear distinction: treatment of subject matter and linguistic compression. Brevity was especially important for *narratio* and valued along with lucidity and realism (the three features at Quint. *Inst.* 4.1.31; cf. *Rhet. Her.* 1.14; Lausberg (1998) §§294–314; *HWRh* s.v. *brevitas* [Kallendorf, 1994]. Cicero ascribes it to Lysias and Cato (63).

[2] I write the following discussion of Atticism from the perspective that Cicero provides, which is neither endorsement nor corroboration, historical or logical, of that perspective (its tendentiousness will soon be apparent). As this book's prefatory note indicates, I avoid repeated disclaimers such as "according to Cicero" or "as Cicero claims." *Caveat lector.*

[3] The other major text is *de Optimo Genere Oratorum*; *Tusc.* 2.3–4 is also illuminating but should be read with its own ends in mind (justifying philosophy).

specifically, the emulation of Greek oratorical greats. Cicero crafts a grand narrative that attacks the so-called Atticists but then coopts their values with arguments that range from specious to spectacular. The terminology of the Atticism debate has its origins in Hellenistic thinkers, but Cicero reworks it in line with his own vision of grand oratory. Ultimately, he argues that only a diversity of Greek and Roman models can ensure the forceful and persuasive style required for the forensic (and therefore political) sphere.

An Overview of Atticism

The stylistic tendencies and debates transmitted along with the labels "Atticism" and "Asianism" have a fraught and uncertain history. In Greek letters the key terms, the verb ἀττικίζειν and the noun ἀττικισμός, originally indicated military allegiance to the Athenian *polis*, but the meaning gradually migrated from the military to the linguistic sphere, denoting the speaking of the Attic dialect rather than a neighboring one. With the establishment of Greek *koine* in the wake of Alexander the Great's conquests, and with the natural linguistic evolution of speakers in Athens and the Greek world, the terms eventually came to denote the speaking of proper classical Attic, a mobile literary ideal rather than a fixed spoken reality.[4]

Atticism also could denote a rhetorical (rather than linguistic) tendency. And in this sense it was opposed to Asianism (or the Asians, *Asiani*), which is even more of a conceptual unicorn, because it was only used in a negative sense to criticize the stylistic exuberance of someone else.[5] Authors never claimed that their own style was Asian. What's more, the term had only a brief lifespan at Rome, lasting from Cicero's writings in the 40s to the Greek Augustan critic and historian Dionysius of Halicarnassus in the 20s. Later discussions refer to these earlier debates

---

[4] The bibliography on Atticism/Asianism is considerable (the list is hardly exhaustive): Norden (1898), Wilamowitz (1900), Desmouliez (1952), Dihle (1957), Leeman (1963) 97–111 and 136–67, Lebek (1970), Bringmann (1971) 21–24, Douglas (1973) 119–31, Dihle (1977), Bowersock (1979), T. Gelzer (1979), Delarue (1982), Wisse (1995), O'Sullivan (1997), Hose (1999), Narducci (2002) 408–12, Dugan (2005) 214–32, Aubert (2010), Kim (2010), Guérin (2011) 342–49, O'Sullivan (2015), Kim (2017), *HWRh* s.vv. *Asianism* [Robling and Adamietz, 1992] and *Atticism* [Dihle, 1992]. Kim (2017) offers the best concise overview for Greek authors. Wilamowitz (1900) challenged the thesis of Norden (1898) that the Atticism/Asianism debate at Rome was part of a long-standing well-defined conflict between the traditional Attic and the new Asian styles.

[5] The order of my presentation is not intended to stake a position in the debate over the precedence of linguistic/grammatical and stylistic Atticism. See O'Sullivan (2015) for arguments against the common view that stylistic Atticism preceded grammatical Atticism and for complications in such a distinction.

and have little independent life beyond them. The originator of the decadent Asian style was allegedly Hegesias of Magnesia-on-Sipylus, a third-century BCE writer from Asia Minor.[6] The stylistic faults of Asian speakers typically included short, choppy sentences without subordination (parataxis rather than hypotaxis), similar word endings (homoioteleuton), sing-song rhythms (especially the ditrochee) or lack of rhythmic variation, clauses of equal syllables (isocolon), and a penchant for extravagance and bombast.

Most evidence for the Atticism controversy comes (or is derived) from Cicero. The debate had yet to emerge, in the extant record, when Cicero wrote *de Oratore* (ca. 55 BCE). This fact, along with the claim that Gaius Licinius Calvus misled others in his stylistic preferences and wanted to be called *Atticus orator* (284), has prompted the conclusion that Calvus spear-headed the movement of Roman Atticism among a younger generation of orators in the years before his untimely death at some point before 47 BCE.[7] Cicero's criticisms of Atticism are coherent unto themselves, yet the accuracy of his portrayal has been challenged, especially his assessment of Calvus (see below). Given the polemical tone of the debate, he most assuredly obscures as much as elucidates its terms. Later authors claim or suggest that detractors accused Cicero of Asianist tendencies, although he never cites such attacks in the *Brutus* or *Orator*, and instead ridicules the jejune weakness of the Atticists and criticizes the unreformed Asianism of his biographical foil Hortensius. If ancient authors never called themselves Asianists, Cicero extends the taboo by never claiming that his rivals had pinned the label on him. We do learn of his exuberant delivery as a young man (discussed in Chapter 1). He dampened his excesses while in Rhodes, but nowhere mentions being called *Asianus/Asiaticus*. He consistently and doggedly aligns his developing talent with Rhodianism, the stylistic middle ground between these two extremes.[8]

[6] Cic. *Orat.* 231; Str. 14.1.41; cf. Dion. Hal. *Comp.* 4 and 18. Larry Kim (*per litteras*) urges caution: no one before Strabo explicitly cites Hegesias as the first Asianist, although Cicero groups him with other Asian orators and criticizes his use of ditrochee in *Orator*. It is hard not to imagine Hegesias as, if not the founder, then at least an infamous representative of Asianism in the eyes of later critics, including Cicero.

[7] "Jungattiker" is a favored term in the German scholarship. Wisse (1995) suggests 60 BCE as a starting point; *de Oratore* nowhere mentions Atticism.

[8] See Chapter 1 on Cicero's biography, abandonment of his early style, and depiction of Hortensius (Asian) and himself (Rhodian). Quint. 12.10.18–19 discusses a Rhodian school and the categories for it, but his summary and lack of specificity suggest that he largely draws inferences from Cicero's texts.

Criticisms of the Atticists in the *Orator* are fairly straightforward and familiar from the *Brutus*:[9] their overly simplistic style barely merits the title Attic (*Orat.* 23–32; cf. *Orat.* 231, 234–35); they prefer the simplest of three styles, the *genus tenue*, which receives extensive treatment (*Orat.* 75–90). The *Orator* focuses on prose rhythm and consequently portrays the Atticists' neglect of its persuasive potential. The simple style is restrained and lacks *ornatus* ("embellishment," *Orat.* 79), but requires considerable skill to master. It has a studied, carefree quality, nicely summed up with etymological wordplay as "a kind of diligent neglect" (*quaedam etiam neglegentia est diligens*, *Orat.* 78). It is likened to a woman who stands out for natural rather than made-up beauty (*Orat.* 79). Ornamental devices are used sparingly and with an eye toward propriety. Humor, especially wit, should be part of the stylistic repertoire, a virtue mastered by the Athenians but ignored by the Roman *Attici* (*Orat.* 89–90).

While the *Orator* discusses Atticism more directly and coherently, the *Brutus* integrates the debate into various issues spread across the length of the dialogue. Oratorical decline – as much a possibility of stylistic development as continued progress – beset Greek oratory after the classical period and is described in geographical terms as movement from Athens to Asia (51). The exemplary role that Lysias plays for the Atticists is tied to the early history of Roman oratory through the unbalanced and murky comparison with Cato the Elder (63–69). Linguistic purism, a crucial feature of Greek Atticism, especially among later Greek imperial authors, has a parallel in the discussion of Caesar and his treatise on language regulation, *de Analogia* (251–62), but plays only an indirect part in the attack on Atticism.[10] The core discussion of Atticism (283–91) is intertwined with a discussion of Calvus, itself one of the digressions built into the discussion of Hortensius, as we are intermittently reminded (e.g. *sed redeamus rursus ad Hortensium*, 291).[11] The diatribe against the Atticists is framed by Atticus' adamant objections against Cato and older orators as a

---

[9] Although this chapter focuses on the *Brutus*, it still occasionally draws on the *Orator* for clarification (as here). The rhetoric in each work is tailored to the local text, which does not preclude examining parallels to understand the workings of that rhetoric.

[10] But see below on Gaius Titius for a pointed example. For Greek Atticizers linguistic purism mandated copying classical Attic by appealing to canonical authors, which is considerably closer to the Latin criterion *auctoritas* ("authoritative usage"). The criterion, *ratio* or *analogia*, quite differently regulates morphology through systematization. The closest Roman equivalent to the purist strand of Greek Atticism was the vogue of Latin archaism in the second century CE.

[11] He begins to outline Hortensius' career at 229. On the marking of digressions, cf. 232, 279.

stylistic model, which touches on the core questions of canon building and the value of older authors for literary history and criticism (292–300).[12]

The Atticists employed a restrained and (overly) learned style, as in the case of Calvus:

> And he was an orator more learned in matters of theory than Curio and even wielded a more meticulous and refined style. Although he handled it in a knowledgeable and discriminating manner, still he was too given to self-examination and, while scrutinizing himself and worrying that he might make a mistake, ultimately lost true vigor. As a result, his speaking style, reduced by excessive scruple, shined for the learned and those paying close attention, but would be swallowed down whole by the masses in the forum, for whom true eloquence was created.

> qui orator fuit cum litteris eruditior quam Curio tum etiam accuratius quoddam dicendi et exquisitius adferebat genus; quod quamquam scienter eleganterque tractabat, nimium tamen inquirens in se atque ipse sese observans metuensque, ne vitiosum conligeret, etiam verum sanguinem deperdebat. itaque eius oratio nimia religione attenuata doctis et attente audientibus erat inlustris, \<a\> multitudine autem et a foro, cui nata eloquentia est, devorabatur. (283)

Cicero will go on to call it thinness or dryness (*exilitas*, 284) and will remark that the proper admirer of the Attic style "despises tastelessness and arrogance as though some kind of illness of speech, but approves of the orator's health and wholeness as though it were scrupulous respectfulness" (*insulsitatem ... et insolentiam tamquam insaniam quandam orationis odit, sanitatem autem et integritatem quasi religionem et verecundiam oratoris probat*, 284). Cicero provides both negative and positive versions of Atticism, which establishes a tension that will remain important throughout the discussion: he does not reject Atticism wholesale, but rather begins to redefine what Atticism should mean in order to suggest that it is one crucial element within the true orator's full stylistic repertoire.[13] We can bracket this ambiguity for now and revisit it in conjunction with Cicero's other challenges to the meaning of *Attici* in his attacks on the Roman Atticists.

The Distortion of Calvus

The main orator Cicero aligns with Atticism is Calvus, but circumspection is warranted, since the criticisms do not match what little we possess of his

---

[12] Discussion of the *Attici oratores* occurs as well at 51, 67–68, 167, 172, 284, 289, 315.

[13] This aspect of the argument is common to the three works of 46 that discuss Atticism (*Orator* and *De Optimo Genere Oratorum* being the other two). Its rhetorical purpose, to minimize and thus coopt Atticism, has received less attention than Cicero's quibbling over *Atticus*.

speeches or later testimony about them.[14] References in the later tradition outline a dispute between Calvus, Cicero, and Brutus. Seneca the Elder, Quintilian, Tacitus, and Pliny, variously contradict the *Brutus*.[15] Seneca notes that Calvus took Demosthenes as a model for his *compositio* and possessed a lively style (*Con.* 7.4.8). Pliny set him alongside Demosthenes as a model for imitation, highlighting the forcefulness of both speakers (*vim tantorum virorum, Ep.* 1.2.2).[16] Seneca quotes Calvus playing to the audience's emotions in the epilogue of the third speech in defense of Messius: "believe me, there's no shame in taking pity" (*credite mihi, non est turpe misereri, Con.* 7.4.8). The emotional appeal concludes with the powerful – and notoriously Ciceronian – rhythm: resolved cretic plus trochee. A fragment from Calvus' second speech against Vatinius, whom Cicero defended at the urging of Caesar and Pompey (and to his own chagrin), has likely been modeled on the famous *climax* from Demosthenes' speech *On the Crown* (18.179).[17]

In Tacitus' *Dialogus* Aper criticizes Cicero's generation for being outdated:

> the prosecution speeches "Against Vatinius" are in the hands of all the students, especially the second speech. You see, it's embellished in words and thoughts, accommodating the tastes of the judges, so that you know that even Calvus himself knew what was better, and he lacked not the will to speak in a loftier and more refined manner, but the talent and strength.

> in omnium studiosorum manibus versantur accusationes quae in Vatinium inscribuntur, ac praecipue secunda ex his oratio; est enim verbis ornata et sententiis, auribus iudicum accommodata, ut scias ipsum quoque Calvum intellexisse quid melius esset, nec voluntatem ei, quo <minus> sublimius et cultius diceret, sed ingenium ac vires defuisse. (*Dial.* 21.2)

---

[14] On Calidius see Douglas (1955a), who argues that he was not an Atticist, and the discussion of him in Chapter 6. On Calvus, including Cicero's distortions, see Leeman (1963) 138–42, Gruen (1967), Lebek (1970) 84–97, Fairweather (1981) 96–98, Aubert (2010) 92–93 n.26, Guérin (2011) 342–49, and below.

[15] Cic. *Fam.* 15.21.4 (SB 207): "he pursued a certain style and, although his normally strong judgment failed him, still attained what he approved; there was much deep learning, but no force" (*genus quoddam sequebatur, in quo iudicio lapsus, quo valebat, tamen adsequebatur quod probaret; multae erant et reconditae litterae, vis non erat*). The obvious opposition learned/forceful matches the criticism of Calvus in the *Brutus*, as does the general criticism that Calvus achieved what he pursued.

[16] Is Cicero's claim about the sleep-inducing style of the Atticists (Calidius) echoed in Pliny's arousal (*me longae desidiae indormientem excitavit, Ep.* 1.2.3)? He then names Cicero (*Marci nostri*, 1.2.4.).

[17] Lebek (1970) 86–87, with *ORF*[4] no. 165 fr. 25, Quint. *Inst.* 3.9.56, and Aquila Romanus (*RLM* 35 Halm). For Quintilian *gradatio/climax* "possesses more obvious and studied artistry" (*apertiorem habe artem et magis adfectatam, Inst.* 9.3.54); Cicero insists that the Attic *genus tenue* avoid obvious artistry (*Orat.* 75–90, esp. 78, 82, 84).

Even this staunch critic accords Calvus some virtues that Cicero found wanting: accommodation to the audience and embellishment (*ornatus*) of words and thoughts; both men do cite Calvus' lack of forcefulness.[18] Twenty-one of Calvus' speeches still existed for Aper to heap scorn on (*cum unum et viginti, ut puto, libros reliquerit, vix in una aut altera oratiuncula satis facit*, 21.1). If Calvus was as deficient as Cicero claims, his impressive afterlife seems unlikely. Quintilian happily praises him: "his style is venerable and serious, it is also restrained and often vigorous" (*est et sancta et gravis oratio et castigata et frequenter vehemens quoque*, Quint. *Inst.* 10.115). Vatinius himself was moved in court to interrupt Calvus: "I implore you, judges: surely I don't deserve to be condemned just because this man speaks well?" (*rogo vos, iudices: num, si iste disertus est, ideo me damnari oportet?*).[19] Calvus seems to have emerged as a challenge to Cicero's supremacy, and criticizing his one-sided adherence to Atticism is steeped in concerns about the appropriate models to imitate. It is only speculation, but perhaps Cicero already feared losing the reception wars – were younger contemporaries, including Brutus, in the thrall of his recently dead rival?

Lysias, Cato, and History

Cicero returns to the complex questions about what to imitate and how to assess Greeks versus Romans, and his answers invariably reflect his evolutionary understanding. The desire to integrate the stylistic debate into the larger historical thrust of the *Brutus* explains the perplexing, if crucial, syncrisis of Cato and Lysias (63–69), revisited in Atticus' later charges of antiquarianism (293–300). The first similarity cited is their prolific production of speeches (*Catonis autem orationes non minus multae fere sunt quam Attici Lysiae*, 63), an oddly superficial similarity, which becomes the springboard for several others (*non nulla similitudo*, 63).[20] Emphasis on their productivity may foreground Lysias' primary activity as a *logographos*, a professional speech writer. He was born in Athens, but because his father was not an Athenian he was a metic without full citizen rights and could not have spoken in the courts or public

---

[18] It's tempting to see Aper's faulting of Calvus' talent as a response to Cicero's claims that it was a question of choice (284), perhaps suggested too in the ambivalence about whether Demetrius had a milder style by nature or by choice, *natura quaedam aut voluntas*, 285). Aper places his response squarely in the binary opposition of *ingenium/iudicium* that Cicero first develops in his dialogues of the 40s BCE and that would become central to stylistic judgment soon after, especially in Seneca the Elder and in Quintilian's reading canon in Book 10.

[19] Sen. *Con.* 7.4.6; cf. V. Max. 9.12.7, Apul. *Apol.* 95.5.

[20] Lebek (1970) 179. Dion. Hal. *Lys.* 17 lists 200; [Plut.] *X orat.* 836a lists 425.

assemblies (although he did fulfill numerous public duties, as Cicero notes).[21] This is an important distinction, since Cato's speeches presumably all had a specific political or juridical occasion to explain their existence, and for Cicero eloquence is nearly unimaginable outside of a specific civic context. Cicero here may allude to a fundamental difference between the two: one active only as a kind of Greek intellectual for hire, the other as a dyed-in-the-wool public figure of the middle republic.[22]

In terms of style "they are pointed, elegant, clever, terse; but that famous Greek has fared better in all manner of praise" (*acuti sunt, elegantes faceti breves; sed ille Graecus ab omni laude felicior*, 63). *Subtilitas*, unobtrusive exactness, above all is Lysias' chief virtue, but Cato has several too: "who is weightier in praise or harsher in criticism, more acute in thoughts, more exact in demonstrating and explaining?" (*quis illo gravior in laudando, acerbior in vituperando, in sententiis argutior, in docendo edisserendoque subtilior?*, 65). The differences from Lysias, especially weight and sharpness, along with the later claim that Cato excels in the various *schemata*, suggest an orator much more like Cicero than like a contemporary Atticist (or even Lysias himself). Despite Cato's antiquity and acknowledgment that his speeches could be updated (68), Cicero presents him as the ideal starting point for substantive oratory, the first stage in a trajectory toward Cicero. Cato also has a remarkable stylistic range.[23] For this reason he inaugurates the evolution of the art at Rome, much as Crassus' speech of 106 inaugurates the evolution of modern style.[24]

Diatribe against the Atticists (285–91)

The ultimate purpose of this syncrisis becomes clear some two hundred chapters later, when Cicero revisits Atticism in a diatribe that targets its

---

[21] Even Lysias' most widely read speech, *Against Eratosthenes*, may not have been delivered (like Cicero's *Second Philippic*). See Todd (2000) 114. Lysias notes his liberality in carrying out public duties (Lys. 12.20).

[22] The *Orator* singles out Lysias as a *scriptor* (*Orat.* 29), but treats him like other oratorical models.

[23] Lebek (1970) 179–80 and 190, although the self-serving nature of Cicero's history is evident throughout. The schemata (later termed *lumina*) are essential to *ornatus*: *ea maxume ornant oratorem* (141); *et verborum et sententiarum illa lumina, quae vocant Graeci schemata, quibus tamquam insignibus in ornatu distinguebatur omnis oratio* (275). The crucial feature of the *genus grave* is reflected in *laudando/vituperando*, parts of emotionally charged *amplificatio*, especially in a peroration (cf. *de Orat.* 3.105, *Part.* 52–58). Plut. *Cat. Mai.* 7.2 rejects the comparison of Cato to Lysias.

[24] To inaugurate evolution is not to be the beginning (Cethegus). Crassus' speech was the best Latin speech available in his youth (*adulescentes quid in Latinis potius imitaremur non habebamus*, 298); the mature Cicero sees its shortcomings.

unnamed adherents – presumably detractors of Cicero – and the models they imitate. As critics have observed, this "notable example of monologistic dialogue" is "initiated by the author with an imaginary interlocutor whose objections and comments the author in turn snatches up and refutes."[25]

Imitation of Lysias alone might seem to be the main purpose of his dispute with the Atticists, since Cicero insists on Demosthenes' superiority and proposes the imitation of several models.[26] The syncrisis of Cato and Lysias and the heroization of Demosthenes suggest that Cicero attacks the Lysianic predilections of Roman neo-Atticists. Yet the *Brutus* and the *Orator* only imply but never confirm that exclusive preference.[27] Lysias was named, along with Hyperides, as a model for the Atticists in the earlier discussion of Cato.[28] The emphasis on Lysias emerges clearly only in the *Orator*, and even there it is only part of Cicero's arguments.[29] We have no evidence, for example, that Calvus followed Lysias alone; Quintilian calls him an "imitator of Attic speakers" (*imitator . . . Atticorum, Inst.* 10.115), the plural suggesting more than one model.

Uncertainty about the extent of Lysianic imitation reflects the larger impossibility of distilling clear arguments from Cicero's criticisms, not least because the diatribe style tends to locate inconsistencies or catch out naiveté attributed to an imaginary interlocutor without then fleshing out the terms and logical consequences of the questions or answers. Confusion is compounded by Cicero's failure to propose clear criteria or to indicate how multifaceted imitation works. He also refuses to clearly define *Atticus*: quite to the contrary, as I noted earlier, he variously deploys the term, allowing it to mean different things at different points to best suit each argument. These conspiring factors have led scholars to varying

---

[25] First quotation: Hendrickson (1962) 250–51 n.b; second: May (1990) 177, comparing Hor. *Ep.* 2.1. Quintilian imitates with his own diatribe against Atticism (*Inst.* 12.10.22–26).

[26] Guérin (2011) 341: "La façon qu'eut Cicéron de critiquer ce choix est connue. Elle consiste à défendre l'extension maximale du qualificatif d'attique: Démosthène et les orateurs de sa génération étant tout aussi attiques que Lysias, il n'est pas possible de limiter la remontée vers les classiques au seul logographe athénien."

[27] *Pace* Lebek (1970) 90. He asserts that Lysias and Hyperides are paired at 68–69 but that Lysias is the real focus for the remainder of the work; he overlooks other references to Hyperides (e.g. 285). Cf. Aubert (2010) 92–93 n.26.

[28] Admiration for Lysias is discussed at 64, but there is no indication that it is for him alone. Hyperides is also mentioned at 67 (*Hyperidae volunt esse et Lysiae*) and again at 68.

[29] At *Orat.* 28, 30 (*qui Lysiam sequuntur*), though the evidence for Atticists' adherence to Lysias as their primary model is not as strong as has often been assumed, e.g. by Lebek (1970) 90, although he also argues that there is a group of Demosthenic imitators manqués.

interpretations. Yet recognizing rather than dismissing the shortcomings and ambiguities will better illuminate his arguments.

The first claim, "I wish to imitate the *Attici*" (*Atticos … volo imitari*, 285), is easily demolished. Cicero asks which *Attici*, since the term, taken literally, indicates a diverse group of classical Athenian speakers: Demosthenes, Lysias, Hyperides, Aeschines, etc. But one can't imitate fundamentally different styles simultaneously:

> Now what's more different than Demosthenes and Lysias, or Lysias and Hyperides, or than all of these and Aeschines? Whom then do you imitate? If you choose one, did the others therefore not speak in the Attic style? If you choose all, how can you imitate them, since they're so different?

> nam quid est tam dissimile quam Demosthenes et Lysias, quam idem et Hyperides, quam horum omnium Aeschines? quem igitur imitaris? si aliquem: ceteri ergo Attice non dicebant? si omnis: qui potes, cum sint ipsi dissimillumi inter se? (285)

His unstated target is the Roman Atticists' allegiance to a single "Attic" norm, the misguided belief in a notional essence of style dominant in the city of Athens and its canon of speakers. The emphasis on dissimilarity also allows Cicero to respond to a later claim from his fictive interlocutor: "We want to be like the Attic speakers" (*Atticorum similes esse volumus*, 287). Having already made the case for dissimilarity, he swiftly discards the attendant possibility of imitation: "how can you [imitate men] who are different from one another and from others too" (*quo modo, qui sunt et inter se dissimiles et aliorum?*, 287).

The absurdity of the fictive response is brought out fully when Cicero moves from the classical models to Demetrius of Phalerum. Cicero trades on the geographical ambiguity of the term *Atticus* by focusing on Demetrius' association with Athens: "Athens itself seems to waft from his speeches; yet he's what you might call more flowery than Hyperides or Lysias" (*ex illius orationibus redolere ipsae Athenae videntur. at est floridior, ut ita dicam, quam Hyperides, quam Lysias*, 285). The implicit argument is that no one (including the classicizing *Attici*) will want to imitate Demetrius' pleasant, learned, and yet impractical style, which Cicero earlier slighted (37). The term *floridior* also emphasizes that Demetrius, a practitioner of the middle style, embellished his speeches, unlike the Atticists with their smooth, simple leanness.[30]

---

[30] Cf. the description of Cato's *Origines* (66, 298) and the connection of *flos* to ornament (*lumen*).

Cicero undermines the notional ideal of "Atticism" by adducing the diversity of styles among Athenians and then offering a geographical argument *ad absurdum* – shouldn't anything produced in Athens be called *Atticus*?[31] The Atticists presumably emphasized certain qualities and authors while overlooking other valid details and styles, as any movement based on a collection of models invariably must. This does not mean that its adherents failed to find in Atticism a coherent and recognizable program, and catching out fictive interlocutors should not be confused with sound argument. To isolate a weak spot in the movement's self-portrayal by quibbling over an ambiguous term is hardly a masterstroke of logic or criticism.

Instead, his strongest arguments are integrated into the larger intellectual framework of the *Brutus*. We next get a historical example of Greeks who imitated classical speakers:

> And in fact there were two contemporaries who were different from each other but still Attic: Charisius wrote numerous speeches for others, since he seemed to want to imitate Lysias; Demochares, the nephew of Demosthenes, wrote several speeches and a history of contemporary events of Athens, less in a historical than in an oratorical manner. But then Hegesias wanted to be like Charisius and thought himself so Attic that he considered those real Attic forerunners almost uncouth. Yet what is so broken, so minced, so childish as that very refinement he sought?

> Et quidem duo fuerunt per idem tempus dissimiles inter se, sed Attici tamen; quorum Charisius multarum orationum, quas scribebat aliis, cum cupere videretur imitari Lysiam; Demochares autem, qui fuit Demostheni sororis filius, et orationes scripsit aliquot et earum rerum historiam, quae erant Athenis ipsius aetate gestae, non tam historico quam oratorio genere perscripsit. at Charisi vult Hegesias esse similis, isque se ita putat Atticum, ut veros illos prae se paene agrestes putet. At quid est tam fractum, tam minutum, tam in ipsa, quam tamen consequitur, concinnitate puerile? (286–87)

In essence, Cicero says: "Let's put your idea to the test and consider a Greek example of what it means to 'imitate the *Attici*,' now that it's become clear that there's such a diversity of models." Pointedly, the two models are Lysias and Demosthenes. Charisius imitated Lysias by writing speeches for others, a rather weak connection, since it entails copying a practice rather than emulating a style. Demochares follows Demosthenes, although Cicero will not claim that explicitly, relying instead on family

---

[31] Cicero's undermining of the term *Atticus/Attici* is discussed below.

lineage as a surrogate for artistic allegiance. It's hardly a ringing endorsement, and little is known of Demochares' speeches and rhetorical afterlife beyond what Cicero tells us. The emphasis on a style of history appropriate to oratory anticipates that later claim that Thucydides' speeches possessed an inimitable – often incomprehensible – denseness (287–88, discussed below), as modern students of the speeches in his history readily attest.[32] Both examples make clear the impossibility of imitating fundamentally different styles.

Yet that point had already been made, and its true purpose is the withering criticism of Hegesias. Hegesias believed that earlier, notionally classical orators were uncouth (*paene agrestes*); he sounds like Cicero's contemporary *Attici*, who similarly criticized earlier Roman authors. Most importantly, Hegesias allegedly "invented" Asianism, a crucial detail passed over in blaring silence.[33] These lineages are a rhetorical masterstroke, aligning the *Attici* with the origins of Asianism and suggesting that veneration of Lysias is not at all Atticism, but a false version of Atticism that is ultimately revealed, through recourse to historical proofs, to be Asianism. The concluding stylistic bravado (*tam fractum, tam minutum, tam in ipsa, quam tamen consequitur, concinnitate puerile?*) reinforces in form the content of the argument: the tricolon crescendo concludes with the quintessentially Ciceronian rhythm, resolved cretic plus trochee. These metrical fireworks are made possible by not one but two instances of "long-range" hyperbaton, postponing *concinnitate* after the relative clause and *puerile* to the end.[34] Such hyperbaton, Jonathan Powell notes, tends to mark passages "with a somewhat higher than usual rhetorical or emotional 'temperature.'"[35]

Thucydides, Lysias, Cato

Notice of Demochares' histories paved the way for discussion of Thucydides (287–88), whose speeches in his history have no place in the courtroom despite their grandeur. Cicero admires and dismisses them at a

---

[32] Demochares also famously attacked Demetrius of Phalerum (again, a suggestion that is in line with the *Brutus*' negative view of Demetrius). His histories also criticized the Macedonian cause.

[33] Cicero lambasts him (*Orat.* 226, 230), as does Dionysius of Halicarnassus (*Comp.* 4.11, 18.21–29).

[34] Note that *concinnitas* could, perhaps should, result in good *compositio* or rhythm, as in Gorgias' case: "symmetry on its own often created the rhythm" (*plerumque efficit numerum ipsa concinnitas, Orat.* 167; cf. *Orat.* 165, 175). Cicero here tantalizingly literalizes the possibility that *concinnitas* produces moving rhythms. Does he coyly draw our attention to word placement by making *consequitur* ("pursue, obtain, follow") precede *concinnitas*?

[35] "Long-range" is from J. G. F. Powell (2010b) 179, who illuminates prose hyperbaton in Cicero. He further notes that "Cicero cultivates this type of hyperbaton partly for rhythmical reasons" (179; see the preceding note).

stroke; he has neither the talent nor the desire to imitate them: *imitari neque possim, si velim, nec velim fortasse, si possim* (287). Most striking is the abrupt segue into the odd, and seemingly unjustified, claim that Thucydides' inapposite oratory results from his antiquated style:

> As in the case of a man who likes Falernian wine, but not wine so new that he'd want last year's vintage or in turn so old as to search out the vintages of Opimius [121 BCE] or Anicius [160 BCE]. "But those are great vintages." True, but excessive age has neither the smoothness we're seeking nor is it tolerable any longer. A man who thinks this way surely won't therefore suppose, when he craves wine, that he should drink from a fresh vat. "Of course not." Let him seek out wine of a certain age. I think then that your friends should shun this newfangled style, seething in ferment like must in a vat, and that renowned Thucydidean style, too old just like the Anician vintage. Thucydides himself, if he had come later, would have been much better aged and milder.

> ut si quis Falerno vino delectetur, sed eo nec ita novo ut proximis con-sulibus natum velit, nec rursus ita vetere ut Opimium aut Anicium con-sulem quaerat – 'atqui hae notae sunt optumae': credo; sed nimia vetustas nec habet eam, quam quaerimus, suavitatem nec est iam sane tolerabilis – : num igitur, qui hoc sentiat, si is potare velit, de dolio sibi hauriendum putet? minime; sed quandam sequatur aetatem. sic ego istis censuerim et novam istam quasi de musto ac lacu fervidam orationem fugiendam nec illam praeclaram Thucydidi nimis veterem tamquam Anicianam notam persequendam. ipse enim Thucydides, si posterius fuisset, multo maturior fuisset et mitior. (287–88)

Cicero here relies on several unstated arguments.[36] Denseness and harshness mark Thucydides as outdated, which essentially reverses cause and effect: not "Thucydides is antiquated and therefore harsh" but "Thucydides is harsh and therefore antiquated." Cicero seeks to explain a signal feature of Thucydidean style that might have little to do with his antiquity – Cicero readily admits that his historical works are not appropriate for the courts, but this is surely a question of genre and personal style as much as age. The contrastingly fulsome praise in *de Oratore* may also give us pause.[37]

---

[36] For Lebek (1970) 155 Thucydides' antiquity is "die als bekannt vorausgesetzte Prämisse seiner Argumentation."

[37] *De Orat.* 2.56. Philistus is said to be an imitator of Thucydides, and the genre culminates in Theopompus and Ephorus (2.57). In the *Orator* the (unnamed) followers of Thucydides (*se Thucydidios esse profitentur*, *Orat.* 30) are chastised for preferring his abrupt, dense style, but antiquated style is not cited. He is paired with Herodotus and both are compared favorably to Thrasymachus and Gorgias (*Orat.* 39), but also likened to Crassus, classified as *vetus*, and praised for careful word order leading to serendipitous rhythms (*Orat.* 219).

The arguments about his antiquity are crafted with the Atticists in mind. The emphasis on the age of a suitable model does not seem to have a place elsewhere in the discussion of Attic style. It does, however, anticipate Atticus' objections about relative standards (292–97). This preemptive strike allows Cicero to turn the tables on the Atticists. Atticus, having bided his time, challenges Cicero's attachment to Cato (and Crassus) and charges him with Socratic irony. Cicero – and we would do well to believe him – rejects any suggestion that he was employing irony: his qualified admiration for Cato and Crassus was sincere.[38]

Atticus levels criticism at the outdated speakers up to and including Crassus' generation. He rejects the comparison of Cato to Lysias because of the latter's unquestionable polished acuity and chides the likening of Cato's *Origines* to Thucydides and Philistus:

> But when you said the *Origines* were filled with all the orator's virtues and compared Cato with Philistus and Thucydides, did you think you'd convince Brutus and me?

> Origines vero cum omnibus oratoris laudibus refertas diceres et Catonem cum Philisto et Thucydide comparares, Brutone te id censebas an mihi probaturum? (294)[39]

Atticus cites the appraisal of Cato (66, discussed below), but mention of Thucydides also sends us back to the immediately preceding discussion of him. The placement of Atticus' objections has been engineered perfectly to follow on Cicero's Thucydidean digression, which, unlike Atticus' false dilemma – either presentism or antiquarianism – proposes a middle ground in the assessment and imitation of stylistic models of the past. In line with Atticist positions, Atticus essentially argues that a style is either modern (contemporary) or antiquated (the generation of Crassus and older) and that Cicero unreasonably defends outdated style. Through Atticus, Cicero has his detractors claim that he is on the wrong side of a dilemma, an antiquarian to their presentism. This is, however, a false dilemma, and having manufactured it Cicero manages in advance, through

---

[38] See Lebek (1970) 178 n.7 (not ironic) and n.8 (ironic) for older literature, and his valuable discussion, 176–93, which I differ from on several points. Desmouliez (1982) remains the best argument against irony (cf. Chapter 6). For revival of the ironic position, see, e.g., Dugan (2005) and (2012), Fox (2007).

[39] The *Origines* reflects Cato's abilities not as a writer of history but as a speaker, reinforced by Atticus' surprise: "you're comparing a man from Tusculum to these men, even though he didn't yet have a sense of what it means to speak fully and elaborately" (*his tu comparas hominem Tusculanum nondum suspicantem quale esset copiose et ornate dicere*, 294). Historiography, no less than poetry, reveals the style of an orator or age.

his criticism of Thucydides, to move beyond its straitjacketed terms, presenting himself instead as a happy adherent of a mature stylistic mean, neither too old nor too young.[40] The arguments here accord well with Cicero's avowed "golden mean," which figures so prominently in the narrative of his own development toward a tempered "Rhodian" style between the extremes of Atticism and Asianism.[41] Cicero has carefully preempted any charge of antiquarianism.

Atticus' claim that Cicero compared Cato to Thucydides and Philistus is important as well because Atticus misunderstands Cicero's earlier comments, a meaningful error that redirects our focus onto the earlier statements:[42]

> As for his *Origines*, what flower or embellishment of eloquence do they not have? He lacks admirers, just as the Syracusan Philistus and Thucydides himself did many centuries ago. You see, just as Theopompus, with the height and grandeur of his style, blocked out their thoughts, which were terse and even sometimes made obscure by brevity and intricacy – Demosthenes had the same effect on Lysias – so too the style of later orators, heaped up (as it were) to the sky, has blocked out Cato's brilliant features.

> iam vero Origines eius quem florem aut quod lumen eloquentiae non habent? amatores huic desunt, sicuti multis iam ante saeclis et Philisto Syracusio et ipsi Thucydidi. nam ut horum concisis sententiis, interdum etiam non satis apertis [autem] cum brevitate tum nimio acumine, officit Theopompus elatione atque altitudine orationis suae – quod idem Lysiae Demosthenes – , sic Catonis luminibus obstruxit haec posteriorum quasi exaggerata altius oratio. (66)

Theopompus overshadowed Philistus and Thucydides, just as recent authors overshadow older ones; Cicero nowhere claims that Cato rivaled these Greeks.[43] Chronology is the crucial issue, and Cicero draws attention to it in Atticus' later remarks in order to impose his own interpretation of what is antiquated and what is modern. He achieves this precisely through

---

[40] Chapter 6 examines Atticus' objections in light of the conflict between absolute and relative standards in literary history.

[41] Cicero's choice of a middle ground will virtually become *the* guiding value of the *Orator* through the use of terms such as *moderatio*, *temperatio*, etc. See below for discussion of this passage in light of Atticus' later objections and the relative chronologies of historians and orators.

[42] Such "errors" are often meaningful and productive features in the genre of dialogue, because they invite closer scrutiny of the arguments under discussion. It is worth comparing interpretations of Tacitus' *Dialogus de Oratoribus*, which is filled with these kinds of errors. Tacitus' insertion of them has often been a pretext for modern readers to disqualify one or another speaker. However, it is more fruitful to look at such flaws or inconsistencies as a way for the author to promote the reader's close involvement with the terms and arguments of the text.

[43] Lebek (1970) 185–86.

the complex analogy of historians and orators. That extended comparison is already hinted at with the passing notice that Demosthenes overshadowed Lysias.[44] Thucydides (ca. 460–ca. 400) was a rough contemporary of Lysias (ca. 460/445–ca. 380)[45] and appears in the *Brutus* at the origins of Greek oratory, first named alongside Pericles (27) as the oldest extant record of oratory and then also associated with one of the early generations of speakers: Alcibiades, Critias, and Theramenes (29). Theopompus (ca. 400/380–ca. 320), by contrast, was a later near-contemporary of Demosthenes (384–322). Cicero has crafted a fairly rough analogy of older and younger historians in parallel to older and younger orators in the Greek world.[46]

Cicero, as so often, makes his arguments not through close stylistic analysis, but by relying on cross-generic developments and patterns that plausibly organize the past into a coherent order. Atticus does not object to the claim that later authors eclipsed their forerunners; he focuses instead on the problem of cross-cultural syncrisis between Lysias and Cato.[47] Cicero had earlier remarked that "the same men who delight in the Greeks' antiquity and in that preciseness they call Attic, do not even recognize it in Cato" (*hi ipsi, qui in Graecis antiquitate delectantur eaque subtilitate, quam Atticam appellant, hanc in Catone ne noverunt quidem*, 67). He manufactures

---

[44] Attention is also drawn to this claim when one considers that Lysias' *Nachleben* was surely more secure than Cato the Elder's at this time, and Demosthenes' overshadowing of him is a forced analogy. Lebek (1970) 96 n.53 remarks that there's no clear connection between Demosthenes' overshadowing of Lysias and the Atticist controversy, but the comment does make sense if we see it as part of the careful chronological scheme that Cicero establishes throughout sections 66, 287–88, and 294.

[45] Most modern scholars place his birthdate near 445 BCE (see *OCD*[4]). Dion. Hal. *Lys.* 1.12 and [Plut.] *Vit. Lys.* 835c, 836a put it with the foundation of Thurii (459/8). If Cicero followed that tradition, then Lysias and Thucydides were essentially coevals. In *de Oratore* Cicero aligns Thucydides with Pericles, and describes them as *subtiles, acuti, breves* (*de Orat.* 2.93), quite similar to Cato and Lysias (*acuti sunt, elegantes faceti breves*, 63). Still, Cicero does place Lysias in the next generation of orators (*de Orat.* 2.93–95), and Lebek (1970) 154–55 notes that Thucydides "vertritt ... das älteste noch faßbare Stadium in der griechischen Eloquenz." Cf. Lebek (1970) 155 n.12 (for historiography Herodotus represents an older stage; *de Orat.* 2.55).

[46] The earlier contrast between Charisius and Demochares also suggests a difference in style based not on imitation, but on chronology: Demochares imitated a modern model, Demosthenes, whereas Charisius imitated an outdated model, Lysias, which also caused the outlandish decadence of Hegesias.

[47] Cicero's interest in this chronology may help to explain why Herodotus, the "father of history," is conspicuously absent in the *Brutus* from any discussion of historiography at Greece, whereas Cicero elsewhere acknowledges his foundational role, and in the *Orator* twice pairs him with Thucydides (39, 219). Cf. *Herodotum patrem historiae* (*Leg.* 1.5) and *princeps genus hoc ornavit* (*de Orat.* 2.55). Thucydides is close in age to Lysias, and thus represents "antiquated" history in the *Brutus*, just as Lysias represents "antiquated" oratory. Herodotus (ca. 480 – ca. 425), at least a full generation before Thucydides, offers a less compelling chronology, and Cicero astutely ignores him in the *Brutus*.

a dilemma for his opponents: either you accept Demosthenes' superiority over Lysias, or you choose to value Lysias, despite his antiquity, in which case you must appreciate the merits of Cato as well.[48]

With Thucydides out of the way, the fictive interlocutors finally cite Cicero's hero:

> "Let's imitate Demosthenes, then." Good god, yes! What else, I ask you, do I pursue and hope for? Even so, we don't obtain our goal. Of course, our Atticist friends here surely do obtain what they want.

> 'Demosthenem igitur imitemur'. o di boni! quid, quaeso, nos aliud agimus aut quid aliud optamus? at non adsequimur. isti enim videlicet Attici nostri quod volunt adsequuntur. (289)

The idea quickly advances from selecting appropriate models to recognizing Demosthenes' inimitable virtuosity, as Cicero admits.[49] This is in stark contrast to the Atticists, who can acquire the limited and restrained style that they pursue. This might at first seem like defeat, but Cicero offers two crucial points, which again rest on several unstated assumptions. That Demosthenes is hard, indeed impossible, to imitate is precisely a reason in favor of emulating him. The essential nature of oratory is its difficulty because of all that it demands, and Cicero here turns that difficulty into a virtue. It is crucial, however, not to imitate the style of a single individual but to emulate an ideal possessing all the requisite stylistic virtues. Imitation of Demosthenes implies ceaseless striving after an unattainable goal, which requires constant improvement, in individuals and across the history of the art. We are reminded too that Demosthenes may be the best model but cannot be the only model. Cicero's elevation of Demosthenes anticipates the classicizing attitude that Quintilian will take toward Cicero: he is a preeminent model, but diverse authors must be read and emulated for their distinctive virtues.

At the heart of this ideal lies a paradox that is also a justification of Cicero's literary history: one model is best and yet also unattainable. As a result, contemporary orators must look to the long history of Greek and Roman style with all its potential resources. The complexity and difficulty of oratory make *varietas* not just an aesthetic – but also a historical – ideal: diversity must be sought from past models. For the Greek tradition this means appreciating the ranks, differences, forcefulness, and variety of the

---

[48] Craig (1993) on dilemma in Cicero.
[49] The suggestion (Castorina 1952 212 n.1, cited at Lebek 1970 93 n.44) that *at non adsequimur* is a response by Cicero's interlocutors has merits (but would not affect my argument).

Attic canon (*videat ne ignoret et gradus et dissimilitudines et vim et varietatem Atticorum*, 285).[50]

Cicero also enlists help from his own history of Roman oratory against the Atticists. The seemingly artless comparison of Gaius Titius, a Roman *eques* contemporary with Lucilius, is devastating:

> At about the same time there was the Roman equestrian Gaius Titius, who seems in my opinion to have progressed about as far as any Latin orator could without Greek learning and much activity. His speeches have so many clever refinements, so many historical precedents, and so much sophistication that they seem almost to have been written with an Attic pen.

> eiusdem fere temporis fuit eques Romanus C. Titius, qui meo iudicio eo pervenisse videtur quo potuit fere Latinus orator sine Graecis litteris et sine multo usu pervenire. huius orationes tantum argutiarum tantum exemplorum tantum urbanitatis habent, ut paene Attico stilo scriptae esse videantur. (167)

The comparison to Attic style, matched with Titius' lack of education and training, is hardly innocent. Clever refinement, historical precedents, and sophistication could be mastered by an *eques* without the support of Greek learning or significant practice.[51] To equate his Latin with an Attic style lacking adornment is a backhanded way to suggest that Roman Atticists have no genuine connection to Greek intellectual culture or forensic practice. Yet such learning was a defining characteristic of Roman *Attici*. The description places the style of Roman Atticism far back on the trajectory of stylistic development at Rome (second half of the second century BCE), reinforcing the claim that Atticism is outdated. The analogy surely contains a social and political dig as well: great oratory is the province of senators, not mere equestrians, yet Titius must have avoided a political career and regular activity as a *patronus*.[52]

Recognition of diverse styles begins with the contrast of Crassus and Scaevola (148) but comes to fruition with Cotta and Sulpicius: "And we should notice in these orators the fact that those who are different from

---

[50] Lebek (1970) 91–93 implausibly suggests that the Atticists also imitated Demosthenes but did so incorrectly, and that this explains Cicero's criticisms here and of Lysianic tendencies among the Atticists in 46 BCE. The point of the passage, rather, is that no one can completely imitate (we should perhaps say, copy) Demosthenes because he represents an ideal. May (1990) 178 says that Cicero "tricks" the interlocutor into agreeing with his Demosthenic viewpoint, but that overlooks Cicero's own remarks on the difficulty of imitating Demosthenes, and so tells only half the story. Again, the point isn't just to imitate Demosthenes, but to take him as a model of the heights to which multifaceted imitation can bring you. On *varietas* see Fantham (1988) and Fitzgerald (2016).

[51] There is considerable overlap between his style and that of the Atticists at *Orator* 75–90.

[52] Cf. Macr. *Sat.* 3.16.14–16; Cavarzere (2018), Dugan (2018).

one another can still be the best. You see, nothing was so different as Cotta from Sulpicius" (*Atque in his oratoribus illud animadvertendum est, posse esse summos qui inter se sint dissimiles. nihil enim tam dissimile quam Cotta Sulpicio*, 204). Historical depth in the Roman tradition allows for stylistic breadth, as later authors build on their predecessors, whose relevance abides even as their stylistic flaws may grow increasingly evident and in need of updating. The number of authors drawn on can thus always increase, precisely because literary history, by its nature, must incessantly accommodate as-yet-unknown innovations.

The wealth of possible options would be overwhelming, and Cicero offers an ingenious workaround to the problem of knowing which authors to imitate and how, especially if one's true model (Demosthenes) is inimitable. His discussion unexpectedly shifts from stylistic achievements to pragmatic considerations: emulate not individual styles but rather successful orators in large public venues. The abrupt shift in logic depends on an unstated assumption he argued for earlier: the paramount criterion is the orator's effect on the audience.[53] And the greatest cases demand large crowds. Unsurprisingly, Demosthenes enthralls a crowd of enthusiastic onlookers, while the circle of onlookers (*corona*) and supporters (*advocati*) abandon the Atticists (289).[54] The Roman *Attici* attain the stylistic refinement they seek out, but also render their speech unsuitable for all but the smallest venues, such as civil trials before a praetor in the *comitium*. When emphasizing effectiveness over aesthetic refinement, Cicero names Attic speakers politically active in grand venues: Pericles, Hyperides, Aeschines, and Demosthenes (290). Conspicuously, Lysias is left off the list.[55]

Redefining and Coopting Atticism

Another crucial line of attack against the Atticists is the complex and casuistic redefinition of *Atticus*. This strategy goes well beyond questioning the movement's learned simplicity or its canon of imitation. Cicero destabilizes the meaning of *Atticus* in order to question the legitimacy of Atticism. True Atticism should embrace all rhetorical virtues, but Roman Atticism aspires only to the simple style (*genus tenue*). Cicero, in turn, defines this as a minimum baseline of oratorical propriety. Once he has

---

[53] Cicero had already made this case in the digression on the judgment of the masses (*volgi iudicium*, 183–200).

[54] The idea is marvelously adapted and updated by Tacitus' Aper (*Dial.* 23.3).

[55] Of course, Lysias was a metic and logographer, which Cicero overlooks. Cicero can exclude Lysias but cannot offer proof that audiences abandoned him.

argued for this restricted definition of Roman Atticism, he can then subsume it under the full panoply of requisite oratorical values: the *genus tenue* is but one register that the true orator masters. Cicero thereby defines and appropriates the Greek oratorical tradition in order to privilege his own comprehensive program for Roman oratory.

This attack on Atticism is carried out partly in the diatribe and partly elsewhere, and it is largely indirect. Nowhere does Cicero engage in an extended abstract debate over the precise technical or doctrinal meaning of *Attikismos*, even if he occasionally touches on its closest analogues, *urbanitas* (170–72) or *Latinitas* (140, 252–62). He focuses instead on the polyvalent terms *Atticus/Attici*.[56] This might seem the weaker strategy, but it allows him to manipulate the flexibility and ambiguity of *Atticus* to craft rhetorical arguments that are more compelling than logical or doctrinal arguments. Cicero crucially redefines Atticism in order to coopt the stylistic precedent of Attic orators and through them the political and artistic authority of Athens. He begins by exploiting ambiguities of geography and identity inherent in the term *Atticus* in order to undermine the stylistic claims of Atticism.

The discussion of Lysias is the first part of a continuous strategy to destabilize the term *Atticus*. It begins with identity: is he Athenian or Syracusan?

> Yet there are about as many of Cato's speeches as there are of the Attic speaker Lysias, which are, I think, very many – you know, he is Attic, since he certainly was born and died at Athens and performed every civic duty, although Timaeus reclaims him for Syracuse as if under the Licinian-Mucian law.[57]

> Catonis autem orationes non minus multae fere sunt quam Attici Lysiae, cuius arbitror plurumas esse – est enim Atticus, quoniam certe Athenis est et natus et mortuus et functus omni civium munere, quamquam Timaeus eum quasi Licinia et Mucia lege repetit Syracusas. (63)

Cicero cannot seriously entertain the prospect that Lysias might be considered Sicilian, but inclusion of Timaeus' claim does point up the weak conventionality of the label *Atticus*.[58] More than just the learned insertion

---

[56] In what follows I use *Atticus* as shorthand for *Atticus/Attici/Attice* (singular and plural cases and the adverb).

[57] *MRR* 3.118 on the Licinian-Mucian law of 95 BCE. It was aimed at false claims of Roman citizenship.

[58] Cf. *Attico Lysiae* (293). Cicero surely is not challenging Lysias' status as an Attic model on the grounds of citizenship.

of a stray detail, it is the first salvo in a terminological battle. The notice anticipates crucial questions of definition: what does *Atticus* really mean, and if no clear answer exists, what use is the term?

Certainly in several cases the term maintains its conventional sense: as a substantival adjective in the plural it essentially means "Athenians" or "Athenian speakers."[59] As an adjective it also denotes "Attic" style.[60] The semantic ambiguity of *Atticus* comes to the fore when it serves as a stylistic label with a restricted scope ("[good] Attic speakers" or "[good] Attic style") or indicates the term's geographical meaning. In the example of Demetrius of Phalerum, Cicero exploits the polyvalence of the term:

> Didn't Demetrius of Phalerum speak Attic?[61] Athens itself seems to me to breathe from his speeches. But he's more flowery (so to speak) than Hyperides, than Lysias.

> Phalereus ille Demetrius Atticene dixerit? mihi quidem ex illius orationibus redolere ipsae Athenae videntur. at est floridior, ut ita dicam, quam Hyperides, quam Lysias. (285)

Reference to Athens makes clear the term's geographical aspect. Demetrius is unquestionably Attic, both geographically and lexically (presumably what Cicero means is that he used recognizably Attic language), but as a stylist he differs considerably from the classical generation of Attic speakers whom the Roman Atticists presumably took as their models.

A similar point but from a different perspective emerges from the mention of Theophrastus in the discussion of *urbanitas*:

> So I don't now wonder about what allegedly happened to Theophrastus: he asked some old woman the price of something and she responded and added "you can't go lower, stranger"; he took it badly that he couldn't evade seeming a visitor, although he lived his life at Athens and spoke better than everyone. So, I think, there's a distinct sound among us of Romans just as of Athenians there.

> ut ego iam non mirer illud Theophrasto accidisse, quod dicitur, cum percontaretur ex anicula quadam quanti aliquid venderet et respondisset illa atque addidisset 'hospes, non pote minoris', tulisse eum moleste se non effugere hospitis speciem, cum aetatem ageret Athenis optumeque loqueretur

---

[59] E.g. 51 (Attic speakers); it means "Athenians" at 254, probably to avoid repetition after *Atheniensis Hyperboli*.

[60] In the singular accompanied by a noun indicating style, e.g. *Atticae dictionis* (51); *Attico genere dicendi* (68).

[61] Or "in [an] Attic style." Cicero trades on the semantic flexibility of the adverb.

omnium. sic, ut opinor, in nostris est quidam urbanorum sicut illic
Atticorum sonus. (172)

Cicero likens Attic speech to Roman *Latinitas*, and the anecdote does
double duty: undermining the definition of *Atticus* and showing that
qualitative speech is independent of geographical origin. Theophrastus, a
native of Lesbos, lived in Athens and became the premier speaker of his
day. Quintilian's version brings out Theophrastus' hypercorrectness: he
gave away his foreign origin by seeming to be too Attic (*Inst.* 8.1.2–3).[62]

Cicero had already begun to undermine *Atticus* earlier in the syncrisis of
Lysias and Cato: "The same men, who delight in the Greeks' antiquity and
that subtlety they call Attic, do not even recognize it in Cato" (*hi ipsi, qui
in Graecis antiquitate delectantur eaque subtilitate, quam Atticam appellant,
hanc in Catone ne noverunt quidem*, 67). He objects to the Atticists'
attempts to make a stylistic feature the province of one group alone.
While defending Cato he shows up the conventionality of *Atticus*. Like
most designations of national or group identity, the term and its legitimizing assumptions are contingent and malleable. *Atticus* is not a fixed
essence, but rather an identity that is performatively constructed in the
process of naming and in the term's subsequent reception. The conventional instability allows Cicero to question its meaning, to suggest alternative ones, and to associate the term with a different set of values.

This revaluation is also achieved in a less perceptible fashion, by drawing
on his interlocutor's authority and the name he bears, Atticus. The words
Atticus/Attici/Attice pervade the *Brutus*, and the virtual ubiquity of 'Attic-
ness' is carefully manufactured by Cicero.[63] The presence of Titus
Pomponius Atticus as an interlocutor calls special attention to the term
and its polyvalence. His cognomen, we are reminded, derives from his
adopted city: "And whenever I consider Greece, your Athens especially,
Atticus, meets my gaze and shines forth" (*in quam cum intueor, maxime
mihi occurrunt, Attice, et quasi lucent Athenae tuae*, 26).

---

[62] Hendrickson (1962) 148 n.a calls Quintilian's detail an "inept addition." A different perspective
might suggest that Cicero suppresses the detail of hyperatticism to suit the needs of the *Brutus*: a
geographically non-Attic speaker can still be a great Athenian speaker. Quintilian's version would
undermine this point. Perhaps Quintilian includes a detail Cicero needed to omit.
[63] Cicero's interlocutor is addressed as Atticus (×26), Pomponius (×6), and Titus (×1). *Atticus/Attici*
(the style or its adherents) appears 33 times in *Brutus*. *Atticus* appears 24 times in *Orator* (plus 1 for
T. Pomponius Atticus). Cicero enjoyed puns in his letters on Atticus' cognomen, Athens, and
Atticism. Cf. *Att.* 1.13.5 (SB 13), 6.5.4 (SB 119), 15.1a.2 (SB 378). *De Senectute* opens with double
nameplay, citing a passage from Ennius that addresses Titus Flaminius (*O Tite . . .*) and then noting
that Atticus had taken his cognomen from Athens (*cognomen . . . Athenis deportasse, Sen.* 1); cf. *Leg.*
1.2. See Baraz (2012) 173–82.

Set against Atticus and his cognomen are the aspirations of Calvus: "Attic[us] is what our friend Calvus wanted to be called as an orator" (*Atticum se ... Calvus noster dici oratorem volebat*, 284). Named for his adopted home, "your Athens" (*Athenae tuae*, 26) as Cicero calls it with an imperialist touch, Atticus adapts Greek scholarship and new knowledge to Roman ends in the production of the *Liber Annalis*. This activity sharply contrasts with Calvus' failure to adapt his philhellenism to a Roman context.[64] We are reminded of another failure, Hegesias, who similarly courted the label (*se ita putat Atticum*, 286). Geographically and stylistically he was Asian, and the language of the *exemplum* contributes to the widespread undermining of the label *Atticus*. The absurdity of the term's geographical denotation similarly emerges in the Ciceropaideia: Menippus of Stratonicea, the most eloquent man of Asia, garners a place among the *Attici* based on his faultless style (315).

Cicero traverses several stages of his argument in order to make the claim that faultlessness is the primary quality of Roman Atticism. After challenging *Atticus* as a label for geography or identity ("Athenian [speakers]") and then criticizing the Atticists for their meager style, he begins to redefine *Atticus* as a stylistic tendency. Of the successful orators who attract a crowd, Cicero says: "to whomever this happens, know that he is speaking in the Attic fashion, as we have heard for Pericles, Hyperides, Aeschines, and especially Demosthenes" (*haec cui contingant, eum scito Attice dicere, ut de Pericle audimus, ut de Hyperide, ut de Aeschine, de ipso quidem Demosthene maxume*, 290). This maximalistic ideal, based on a principle of effectiveness through a diversity of styles (as discussed above), is thoroughly opposed to the Roman Atticists, whom he pigeonholes as practitioners of the *genus tenue*. He does not reject Atticism, but rather accords it a place at smaller venues demanding less oratorical vigor: "if it's the mark of the *Attici* to speak in a restrained and meager manner, let them by all rights be *Attici*; but let them come to the *comitium* and speak before a standing judge: the court benches require a greater and fuller voice" (*si anguste et exiliter dicere est Atticorum, sint sane Attici; sed in comitium veniant, ad stantem iudicem dicant: subsellia grandiorem et pleniorem vocem desiderant*, 289).

This provisional acceptance of Atticism is possible only because Cicero exploits ambiguities in his own redefinitions of *Atticus*. He first criticizes it as a wrongly assumed label ("Roman Atticism"), when in fact it should designate the great range of Athenian models ("Real Atticism"). Since the

---

[64] Calvus' learning comes through clearly: *litteris eruditior, scienter, doctis* (283).

Atticists insist on their style of speech, however, Cicero finally concedes that it can designate a minimum level of competence, the faultless employment of the *genus tenue*. The status of Atticism as a kind of minimum level of adequacy is essentially a negative definition, the prospect that "the mark of the Atticists is to have nothing bothersome or inept" (*nihil habere molestiarum nec ineptiarum Atticorum est*, 315). By aligning Atticism with the *genus tenue* he can then claim that any true *orator* must, by definition, have mastered that stylistic register.

With greater precision he later distinguishes the Attic from the grand style:

> If, however, they accept a style that is sharp and sensible while at the same time direct, firm, and dry, and if they don't rely on heavier oratorical embellishment and they understand this to be properly Attic, they praise it rightly. There's a place, you see, in an art form so capacious and varied, for even this small-scale precision. The result is that not all who speak in the Attic style speak well, but that all who speak well speak also in the Attic style.

> sin autem acutum, prudens et idem sincerum et solidum et exsiccatum genus orationis probant nec illo graviore ornatu oratorio utuntur et hoc proprium esse Atticorum volunt, recte laudant. est enim in arte tanta tamque varia etiam huic minutae subtilitati locus. ita fiet, ut non omnes qui Attice idem bene, sed ut omnes qui bene idem etiam Attice dicant. (291)

Cicero has redefined Roman Atticism not to reject it out of hand but in such a way that allows him to acknowledge its value as one weapon in the full rhetorical arsenal. His minimalist definition of Atticism and maximalist definition of the orator allow him to coopt Atticism, placing it safely under the all-encompassing umbrella of Ciceronian force, fullness, and variety. Cicero's style here reinforces the conceptual point (as we saw with *brevitas* at the beginning of this chapter). This conclusion to the diatribe against Atticism uses a distinctly Attic flourish: a smooth *sententia* with simple terse language and an unobtrusively chiastic word arrangement.[65]

Cicero disagrees with the Roman Atticists not to defend himself against charges of being "Asian" but to stake a claim as to what "Attic" properly means and what type of orator best represents an ideal that draws on Athenian models. Cicero's response is essentially "I have no problem with Atticism, as long as we understand what it actually means. As a result, I'm

---

[65] *Attice idem bene ~ bene idem Attice*. See *Orat.* 79 for the *sententia* as a crucial feature of the *genus tenue*.

at least as Attic as anyone else, but more importantly, I'm not *just* Attic."
For all the arguments against Atticism, the movement is not in itself his
main opponent in the *Brutus*, and his aim is hardly to accurately document
a doctrinal disagreement with fidelity.[66] Atticism is as much a foil as it is
a target.

It is certainly true that the multifaceted criticisms made in the *Brutus*
anticipate the strict equation of the Attic style with the *genus tenue* and its
duty to instruct (*docere*) in the *Orator*.[67] Yet the *Brutus* integrates the
Atticism debate into the narratives of artistic evolution, stylistic appropriation and Roman identity, contemporary politics, and Cicero's aesthetic
commitments. The *Orator* criticizes Atticism in different terms and to
different ends, once again pigeonholing the Atticists as practitioners of the
plain style, but in order to provide a rhetorical and intellectual justification
of prose rhythm. Considerable overlap exists between the *Brutus* and the
Orator, but the local requirements in each text are what ultimately shape
the local forms of Atticism.[68] The importance of history in the *Brutus*
means that opposing Cicero's values ultimately means being on the wrong
side of Roman history, failing to understand that Roman oratory depends
on the diversity found in the Greek and Roman traditions. Aesthetic
history in the *Brutus* is inextricable from civic history, which places
Cicero's detractors in a bind: to deny his stylistic argument is to deny
the greatness of Rome's past and thus to render oratory meaningless in the
present.

---

[66] Lebek (1970) 94: "Cicero schreibt nicht, um die Nachwelt über den Attizismus seiner Zeit zu
informieren." Lebek (1970) 89 is, however, unwilling to draw the likely conclusion that Cicero
distorts the terms of the disagreement.
[67] Cf. Guérin (2014).
[68] Cicero's later proposal of Thrasymachus as the originator of prose rhythm (*Orator*) rather than
Isocrates (32; cf. *de Orat.* 3.173) may not result from revised opinion or access to new knowledge.
Each choice is thoroughly plausible in its own context and each best serves the historical narrative of
the text in which it appears. See Gotoff (1979) 37–66 on the polemical discussion of style and
rhythm in the *Orator*.

CHAPTER 8

Minerva, Venus, and Cicero's Judgments on Caesar's Style

But the Athenians also benefited more from having strong roofs over their houses than the most beautiful ivory statue of Minerva; yet I'd still rather be Phidias.

sed Atheniensium quoque plus interfuit firma tecta in domiciliis habere quam Minervae signum ex ebore pulcherrimum; tamen ego me Phidiam esse mallem.
– *Brutus* 257 (on Cicero's accomplishments)

You see, they're nude, upright, charming, with all adornment of speech, like a garment, removed.

nudi enim sunt, recti et venusti, omni ornatu orationis tamquam veste detracta.
– *Brutus* 262 (on Caesar's *commentarii*)

Probably the most famous single judgment of literary criticism in Greco-Roman antiquity is Cicero's assessment in the *Brutus* of Julius Caesar's historical writings (*commentarii*) on the Gallic War. The passage's fame stems from its documentation of two political greats of the late republic who were also eloquent masters of the Latin language, so much so that they would become canonical models for what was long termed "the best prose," imitated in degrees ranging from obsequious to creative ever since their first publication, and defining even today the standard of "classical" prose for composition courses. This passage also yields up a rare gem in the history of literary criticism, one contemporary assessing the creative output of another, and that as a response (Cicero's) to an earlier evaluation (Caesar's) of stylistic and political merits. Caesar, in his treatise on language usage, *de Analogia*, had said that Cicero was virtually the first inventor of fullness (*copia*) and had served well the fame and esteem of the Roman people.[1]

---

[1] At 252, repeated at 253. On *commentarius* see Riggsby (2006) 133–55, Nousek (2018), Raaflaub (2018) 17. Cicero probably means *de Bello Gallico*; most scholars think *de Bello Civili* was published posthumously; see Raaflaub (2009) 180–82, Grillo (2012) 178–80.

Cicero's assessment identifies several qualities of Caesar's writings, traditionally understood as "unadorned" (*nudi*), "direct" (*recti*), and "pleasing" (*venusti*). The subsequent characterization seems to explain Caesar's unembellished narratives as much as his use of simple, choice language. Succinctness is praised: "you see, nothing is more pleasing in history than pure and plain brevity" (*nihil est enim in historia pura et inlustri brevitate dulcius*, 262). This last sentence reiterates the initial description with modified attributes: *pura* ≈ *nudi*; *inlustris/brevitas* ≈ *recti*; *dulcius* ≈ *venusti*. In addition to narrative simplicity, the language of the initial judgment, *ornatus orationis* ("embellishment of style," "rhetorical artifice"), also indicates a lack of adornment. Cicero describes Caesar's slick narrative style and his famed linguistic simplicity (*elegantia*, cf. 252, 261).

The description undoubtedly reflects most readers' experience of Caesar's writings. Yet its language and the accompanying simile, suggesting or describing a physical body and its clothing, are remarkable for several reasons.[2] Cicero inherited the analogies to the human physique or clothing from Isocrates and subsequent Hellenistic theorists, yet he also differs from that tradition.[3] As descriptors of style, the first two adjectives (*nudi, recti*) are somewhat unusual and are not necessarily complimentary. *Nudus* occurs infrequently to mean wanting adornment, sometimes as a consequence of *brevitas*.[4] *Rectus* meaning "direct" or "straightforward" first appears here in Latin (and so may have been quite striking), but never really catches on in the critical lexicon. Subsequent usage does not greatly increase our understanding of Cicero's exact meaning.[5] Admittedly, the lexicon of Roman criticism is notoriously vague, but it also tends toward

---

[2] Kraus (2005) discusses technical aspects of the terms and the language's suggestiveness.

[3] Van Hook (1905) 18–23 on metaphors of dress and the body. Fantham (2006) 251 emphasizes the unorthodox descriptions of Cicero's body in the Ciceropaideia.

[4] Cf. *OLD* s.v. *nudus* 8b (Van Hook 1905 has no entry for γυμνός); Lausberg (1998) 283 (citing Isidore, where it indicates unfigured language, not so unlike the uses of *rectus* cited in the note below) and 343 with Quint. *Inst.* 8.6.41 (negatively describing language that lacks epithets); it is connected to *brevitas* and lack of embellishment: "praise speeches … have bare and unadorned brevity" (*laudationes … brevitatem habent nudam atque inornatam*, *de Orat.* 2.341); cf. *ieiuna atque nuda*, *de Orat.* 1.218; *nuda atque inornata*, *Rhet. Her.* 4.69. The commonality is that the term is markedly negative, not just "unadorned" but "wanting adornment." It is also typically a doublet, with a more common explanatory synonym.

[5] For *rectus*/ὀρθός Van Hook (1905) 17 (without examples). Lausberg (1998) 754–55 gives examples indicating "propriety" in an ethical, grammatical, or terminological sense, or to denote correct usage. It also denotes proper pronunciation and natural gesture. After the *Brutus* the small number of examples like Cicero's (e.g. Seneca the Elder, Quintilian, and Fronto) indicate non-figured language, "straightforward" speech that does not rely on a *schema* ("figure") used to avoid giving offense. In these technical instances *rectus* modifies a word denoting speech (*oratio, sermo*, etc.). *TLL* XI.2.818.53–70 [Pieroni, 2020].

uniformity and repetition.[6] The third term (*venusti*) is more common and applies to a broad range of attractive or charming phenomena: (erotic) attractiveness, graceful gesture, deft humor, or well-ordered narrative. It is used to describe the effects of several types of rhetorical figures of speech in the *Rhetoric to Herennius* (see below). Our passage may be a calque on Greek χάρις, indicating graceful succinct narration, but the judgment, as Brian Krostenko remarks, "has been enlivened here by alluding to another of the lexeme's senses, 'gracefully shaped,' said of the human body."[7] Lastly, it remains unclear how the simile of clothing removed clarifies the terms of the judgment. It offers and then embellishes a visual image more than it elucidates the preceding adjectives.[8] Cicero's point about lack of adornment (*ornatus*) could be made without it, and the insistence on the removal of all adornment (*omnis ornatus*) is harder to square with Caesar's writing.[9]

However seemingly artless or plain his prose, Caesar still employed various embellishments, although with restraint and alongside his famed lexical selectivity (*elegantia*).[10] Rhetorical treatises demand adornment in all stylistic registers. The *Rhetoric to Herennius* tells us that "rhetorical figures lend each style distinction" (*omne genus orationis ... dignitate adficiunt exornationes, Rhet. Her. 4.16*).[11] The *Orator* associates *elegantia* above all with the low style (*genus tenue*), which requires a variety of rhetorical effects (*Orat. 78–90*). Caesar is no exception, as Christopher

---

[6] The description of Caesar's oratory is traditional, if restricted to language and delivery. For bibliography on Caesar's oratory see van der Blom (2016) 147 n.3. Cicero praised Caesar in a (lost) letter to Nepos (Suet. *Jul.* 55.2).

[7] Krostenko (2001) 109. This paragraph is heavily indebted to Krostenko (2001) 40–51, 99–111 on *venust(us)*.

[8] Cicero's embellishment to describe unembellished language seems hardly innocent: he uses assonance (*om-, or-, or-*), a simile, and hyperbaton of *detracta*, which enables its attraction to the gender of *vestis*; in addition, *venustus*, on Krostenko's reading (above), suggests two senses simultaneously (as does *ornatus*; see note 9 below) and may be Cicero's calque on a Greek word. I hope to discuss the passage in another venue along with Cicero's response to *de Analogia* and the relevant historiographical background of Cic. *Att.* 2.1.2 (SB 21).

[9] Lausberg (1998) 163–90 notes that *brevitas* still requires some *ornatus*; see esp. 174–76. *Ornatus* can indicate "attire" or "outfitting" and perfectly fits its sartorial simile; cf. Fantham (1972) 166–68, Innes (2003) 7–8. On the tension between style and content in *ornatus*, May and Wisse (2001) 326–27 note that "the two are in fact inseparable."

[10] Caesar's style is more complex and varied than Cicero's description indicates: Schlicher (1936), Deichgräber (1950), Eden (1962), Leeman (1963) 156–59, Rambaud (1979), Gotoff (1984), Williams (1985), von Albrecht (1989) 54–67, Damon (1994), Gotoff (1993) xxvi–xxvii, Riggsby (2006) 28–32, Kraus (2005) and (2009), Krebs (2018). Grillo (2012) 2–5 succinctly outlines modern misconceptions of Caesar's "simple style" (focusing on *de Bello Civili*). Krostenko (2001) 34–39, 114–23 on *elegantia*.

[11] Krostenko (2001) 103–6 on *venust(us)* and rhetorical figures from the *Rhetoric to Herennius*.

Krebs remarks: "Almost any passage of the *Commentarii* will reveal an assortment of the most common rhetorical devices."[12] In short, Cicero's judgment, while accurate on the surface, merits circumspection. It describes the *commentarii* fairly reasonably, yet scholars have increasingly called attention to the corporeal imagery of the judgment and have proposed different interpretations of its suggestiveness. Several features in the description and several contexts in and beyond the *Brutus* give good reason to think that this is more than just a straightforward assessment of Caesar's *commentarii*.[13]

The following discussion offers the most speculative argument of this book, proposing that Cicero has a specific physical image in mind. The corporeal and sartorial imagery evokes a distinct and symbolically laden object: a statue of Venus, and specifically, a nude (*nudi*) upright (*recti*) Venus (*venusti*), with her clothing removed, such as Praxiteles' renowned Aphrodite of Knidos. Reference to Venus, given her importance to Caesarian self-presentation, and Cicero's prominent mention of Minerva in the digression on Caesar (quoted above) establish a meaningful antithesis between the two godesses. Cicero draws on symbolic and historical differences in the representations of Minerva and Venus, prompting us to consider the political and aesthetic divide that separates Cicero from Caesar. Far from being just a famous literary judgment, the assessment of Caesar's *commentarii* is also an intervention in the civic crisis, an attempt to communicate a set of ideals that are in competition with Caesar's ideals.[14]

Though cautious in its criticisms, the *Brutus* is a masterfully orchestrated response to Caesarian ideology and aesthetics. As Chapter 3 discussed, Cicero does not criticize Caesar directly, but rather argues that military achievement for self-promotion ultimately endangers the Roman community. Cicero's countervailing model of civic action, and his own historiography, the *Brutus* itself, offer an alternative political vision built on the legacies of Rome's oratorical and textual pasts.

---

[12] Krebs (2018) 119.

[13] E.g. Douglas (1966a), A. Powell (1998), Dugan (2005), Kraus (2005), discussed further below.

[14] C. Steel (2005) 146: "He and Caesar, in radically different ways, demonstrated to other politicians how to transcend the limitations of memoir and produce texts which enact contemporaneous engagement with public life." Cf. Walter (2010). I recognize that some readers might resist the possibility that Cicero alludes to the Aphrodite of Knidos. In that case, I hope that Cicero's discussion of Minerva and use of *venustus* make plausible the arguments (which do not depend on identifying the statue) about the symbolic and ideological resonances of the two goddesses and their celebrants: Minerva (Cicero) and Venus (Caesar).

Four distinct yet interrelated topics contextualize Cicero's references to Minerva and Venus and they will be discussed in turn: (1) Cicero's long-standing appeal to Minerva as an ideological ally, which begins at least as early as the 50s and is especially prominent in his dispute over Clodius' statue of Libertas on the Palatine; (2) statuary analogies in Greco-Roman literary criticism and in the *Brutus*; (3) the larger conversational exchange concerning Caesar (251–62); and (4) statues of Athena/Minerva and Aphrodite/Venus and their aesthetic and political implications for Cicero's judgment of Caesar.

Minerva in the 50s

A decade before the *Brutus*, in September 57 BCE, Cicero returned from exile, he repeatedly reminds us, to great acclamation. Physically restored to the city after eighteen months, he still had to undertake the protracted, painstaking journey toward political restoration.[15] That journey ultimately proved endless: he stumbled against the renewed alliance of Caesar, Pompey, and Crassus, saw Clodius defeated only after Milo murdered him on the Appian Way near Bovillae on 18 January 52, failed to secure Milo's acquittal with one of the best Latin speeches ever produced, and soon witnessed Rome succumb first to Caesar and then to the triumvirate and the proscriptions that cost him his life.

Upon returning he sought the restoration of his Palatine house, which Clodius had plundered in March 58 in order to build a far more lavish home with an ostentatious portico and shrine dedicated to the goddess Libertas. On 29 September 57, Cicero pled his case before the pontiffs, seeking annulment of Clodius' consecration of Cicero's property. They ruled in his favor, and reconstruction began the following year. The full details of the speech *de Domo sua* are less relevant for our purposes than the crucial rhetorical subplot concerning two statues and the ideological dispute at whose center they stood. This similar dispute over the symbolic differences between two statues provides crucial background for the *Brutus'* references to statuary and tutelary goddesses.

Cicero challenged the erection of Clodius' statue of the goddess Libertas in various ways, claiming or suggesting repeatedly that Clodius had treated the Roman people like slaves (who by definition cannot enjoy *libertas*): "were you placing an image of Liberty in the very house that itself had been a sign of your most cruel lordship and of the most wretched servitude

---

[15] Kaster (2006) 1–14, Kenty (2018) 253–57 discuss Cicero's post-consular self-presentation.

of the Roman people?" (*Libertatis simulacrum in ea domo conlocabas, quae domus erat ipsa indicium crudelissimi tui dominatus et miserrimae populi Romani servitutis?, Dom.* 110).[16] He also recasts *libertas* into the neighboring yet negative value associated with it, *licentia* ("license," "wantonness"): "you set up an image not of public liberty but license" (*simulacrum non libertatis publicae, sed licentiae conlocasti, Dom.* 113).[17] Connected to this moral reframing is the assertion that the statue actually depicted a foreign prostitute: "It's said to have been some courtesan from Tanagra" (*Tanagraea quaedam meretrix fuisse dicitur, Dom.* 111).[18]

Against Clodius' immorality stands Cicero's allegiance to Minerva:

> Witty fellow, you introduce urbane and charming rumors that I often call myself Jupiter and even claim that Minerva is my sister. I'm not so arrogant in calling myself Jupiter as ignorant in thinking Minerva his sister. I do claim that my sister is a virgin, which you won't let your sister be. Yet perhaps you often call yourself Jupiter on the grounds that you can rightly call the same woman both sister and wife.

> homo facetus inducis etiam sermonem urbanum ac venustum, me dicere solere esse me Iovem, eundemque dictitare Minervam esse sororem meam. Non tam insolens sum, quod Iovem esse me dico, quam ineruditus, quod Minervam sororem Iovis esse existimo; sed tamen ego mihi sororem virginem adscisco, tu sororem tuam virginem esse non sisti. Sed vide ne tu te soleas Iovem dicere, quod tu iure eandem sororem et uxorem appellare possis. (*Dom.* 92)

We do not have Clodius' speech, to which Cicero colorfully responds with rhetoric perfectly calculated to culminate in a favorite punchline: Clodius' affair with his sister Clodia.[19] Cicero's initial attachment to Minerva – an icon of chastity set against Clodius' sexual wantonness – takes a serious turn later on: "and you, Minerva, do I pray to and beseech, guardian of Rome, who has always stood fast to aid my plans and witness my deeds" (*te, custos urbis, Minerva, quae semper adiutrix consiliorum meorum, testis laborum exstitisti, precor atque quaeso, Dom.* 144). Plutarch has this language in mind when he writes that Cicero, just before leaving Rome for

---

[16] Cicero had just claimed that Clodius took liberty from the whole city (*Libertas . . . quam ex urbe tota sustulisti,* 110).

[17] Clodius' actions are impudent mockery (*ludibrium impudentiae, Dom.* 131); cf. his tribunician wantonness (*libidini tribuniciae, Dom.* 106).

[18] Cf. *signum de busto meretricis* (*Dom.* 112). Tanagra, in Boeotia, was highly regarded for its terracotta figurines, sometimes also deposited in graves, which might explain the statue's alleged provenance from a tomb (*imaginem meretricis, ornamentum sepulcri, Dom.* 112). Clodius' brother, Appius Claudius Pulcher, brought the statue back to Rome.

[19] Corbeill (2018b) reconstructs what Clodius may have said in *de Haruspicum Responso.*

exile, "took the statue of Athena, which he had long since set up at his home and honored exceedingly, to the Capitol and dedicated it with the inscription 'To Athena, Protectress of Rome'" (τὸ μὲν ἄγαλμα τῆς Ἀθηνᾶς, ὃ πολὺν χρόνον ἔχων ἐπὶ τῆς οἰκίας ἱδρυμένον ἐτίμα διαφερόντως, εἰς Καπιτώλιον κομίσας ἀνέθηκεν ἐπιγράψας "Ἀθηνᾷ Ῥώμης φύλακι," Plut. *Cic.* 31.6).

Cicero pinned his political hopes on Minerva for the last two decades of his life. He boasted of being savior of Rome for having quashed the Catilinarian conspiracy.[20] His self-depiction as *custos urbis* likens his own role to that of Minerva (*custodem urbis*, Dom. 40; *custodem patriae*, Dom. 102).[21] In *de Legibus*, composed in the mid-50s but never completed, Cicero revisits his care for this statuette of Minerva when he abandoned his house and departed Rome in exile: "I brought her from my house into the father's and was esteemed savior of the fatherland by the judgment of the senate, Italy, and all peoples" (*eamque ex nostra domo in ipsius patris domum detulimus, iudicia senatus, Italiae, gentium denique omnium conservatae patriae consecuti sumus, Leg.* 2.42). He trades on an equivalence that is suggested throughout his career and that governed his actions during and after the Catilinarian conspiracy: his welfare is inextricable from that of the Roman state. As John Bodel says, "The gesture, both personal and public, effectively suggested that the fate of the *res publica* was tied to Cicero's own well-being, even as (more conventionally) his personal salvation depended upon the integrity of the *res publica*."[22]

It's worth reprising several features of the dispute with Clodius, because they resurface in 46 BCE. At the broadest level statuary, its varied symbolism and potential associations, becomes a vehicle through which to craft and convey ideological and rhetorical disputes. Minerva is central to Cicero's self-depiction as savior of the Roman state, manifested in physical representations of her in Rome. In matching Minerva against Clodius and Libertas he differently interprets his opponent's favored goddess: connecting her to individual rather than communal well-being, alluding to provocative or sexualized characteristics of the physical statue (versus

[20] Cf. *urbis servatorem* (*Dom.* 101), *patriae conservatorem* (*Har.* 58).
[21] Pina Polo (2003) tantalizingly suggests that Cicero's rhetoric drew on a (now largely lost) tradition of representing Minerva as the *custos urbis*. He considers two inscriptions (*CIL* 6.529 and *CIL* 5.6489) and material from a tower on the city walls of Tarraco (modern Tarragona, in northeast Spain), the first Roman city founded outside of Italy. See also Hesberg (1998), Dyck (2003) 366–67. Cf. Athena's guardianship of citadels at Catul. 64.8: *diva quibus retinens in summis urbibus arces*.
[22] Bodel (2008) 252.

Minerva's chastity), and portraying Minerva as the community's true champion.

Statuary Analogies

Moving from the historical to the literary-historical, statuary in the *Brutus* surfaces in the long passage on Cato (61–69), the first orator of note after the first orator of record, Marcus Cornelius Cethegus (57–60).

> Who in fact of those who now consider the lesser things doesn't understand that Canachus' sculptures are too stiff to imitate reality? Calamis' are certainly hard, but still softer than Canachus'; Myron's are not yet sufficiently realistic, but you still wouldn't hesitate to call them beautiful. Polyclitus' are more beautiful and already distinctly perfect, as they typically seem, to me at least. A similar relationship holds for painting, in which we praise Zeuxis, Polygnotus, and Timanthes, and the forms and outlines of those who didn't use more than four colors. Yet in Aetion, Nicomachus, Protogenes, and Apelles already everything is perfect.

> Quis enim eorum qui haec minora animadvertunt non intellegit Canachi signa rigidiora esse quam ut imitentur veritatem? Calamidis dura illa quidem, sed tamen molliora quam Canachi; nondum Myronis satis ad veritatem adducta, iam tamen quae non dubites pulchra dicere; pulchriora Polycliti et iam plane perfecta, ut mihi quidem videri solent. similis in pictura ratio est: in qua Zeuxim et Polygnotum et Timanthem et eorum, qui non sunt usi plus quam quattuor coloribus, formas et liniamenta laudamus; at in Aetione Nicomacho Protogene Apelle iam perfecta sunt omnia. (70)

The passage explains inclusion of Cato in the catalogue of orators by noting his place in the early stages of stylistic evolution. The sculptural analogy includes an important formulation of stylistic change as a series of progressions across time, with each artist representing a different stage in the evolution from the stiff crudeness of Canachus to the polished realism of Polyclitus.[23] Set against the subsequent analogy to painting, which includes only two stages, an earlier and later group divided by the richness of their palette, the statuary analogy importantly sets up gradual evolution as a crucial principle for the *Brutus*. Cicero avoids the traditional and schematic division into "old" and "new" and establishes a framework that accounts for gradual change over time.[24] The innovations in his

---

[23] Goldberg (1995) 3–12 illuminates Cicero's evolutionary scheme. Jucker (1950) 118–46 on such analogies in Varro and Cicero. Dahlmann (1962) 591 n.1 claims Varro (without evidence) as Cicero's source for the analogies.

[24] D. A. Russell (1981) 159 on "old" versus "new."

conceptual system are made clear by contrast with the simpler bipartite division among painters. The second analogy does not provide further, simpler clarification of the same point but instead indicates, by way of contrast, the *Brutus'* crucial emphasis on sequential evolution.

Yet while Cicero here indicates a methodological premise of his history, revisited and refined in the course of the dialogue, the analogy has provocatively left out Phidias. As long ago as 1978, Doreen C. Innes valuably observed that Cicero ostentatiously excludes him.[25] Readers familiar with the topos would expect a reference to the premier sculptor of the classical period.[26] Greek thinkers, as Jerome Pollitt notes, thought that "the art of Phidias represents the supreme achievement of Greek sculpture and that the most perfect rhetoric of the past should be compared to Phidias in its grandeur and perfection."[27] Because Phidias would be the next stage in the catalogue, Innes argued, his absence criticizes the less-developed Atticists, while Phidias implicitly represents the perfection of Cicero's hero, Demosthenes.

The abbreviated catalogue is undoubtedly striking, considering both the history of Greek sculpture and the deployment of the topos elsewhere. Within the context of the *Brutus*, however, including two explicit mentions of Phidias later, the omission is more complex than a limited intervention in the Atticism/Asianism debate. In the course of the dialogue Cicero extends not only the temporal range of sculptors mentioned, both backward and forward, but also the explanatory power of such comparisons. Right away in the next passage and the next literary judgment, of Rome's first poet, Livius Andronicus, we hear that "the Latin Odyssey is like some piece from Daedalus and also his plays do not merit a second read" (*et Odyssia Latina est sic [in] tamquam opus aliquod Daedali et Livianae fabulae non satis dignae quae iterum legantur*, 71). The beginning of Latin literature is likened to the beginning of Greek sculpture, and the alignments are further contrived by making the first

[25] Innes (1978); however, she does not address two later citations of Phidias and two additional references to other sculptors, already discussed by Jucker (1950) 128. Douglas (1973) 108–15 argues that the catalogue of sculptors (70) emphasizes realism (*veritas*) in bronze statuary and therefore culminates in the technical maturity of Polyclitus. This does not diminish the expectation that Phidias appear in comparisons of sculpture to rhetoric. Douglas notes references to Phidias, but fails to connect the different analogies. Innes (1978) 470 n.1 objects to Douglas' claim that Cicero restricts his catalogue to bronze-casting (Cicero does not mention the medium).

[26] For other examples of the topos, see Isoc. *Antid.* 2, Cic. *de Orat.* 3.26, *Orat.* 8–9, Quint. *Inst.* 12.10.7–9, Dem. *Eloc.* 14, Dion. Hal. *Isai.* 4 and *Isoc.* 3; cf. Plin. *Nat.* 36.20–21, Sen. *Con.* 10.5.8, [Longinus], *Subl.* 36.3–4; building marvelously on this tradition, Dio Chrysostom ventriloquizes Phidias to defend the spoken word over the plastic arts in his Olympic Oration (Dio *Or.* 12).

[27] Pollitt (1974) 61.

Latin poet correspond to the first Greek poet by mention of Livius' Latin *Odyssia*, resulting in the neatly schematic trio of firsts: Homer–Daedalus–Livius.[28] Mention of Livius' status as un-rereadable also expands the analogy beyond mere stylistic assessment, because the contemporary artistic utility of older texts emerges as a central problem.[29] Yet in addition to providing a schematic structure for the different stages of development, such analogies also make substantive claims about the pedagogical (and ultimately political) relevance of an author.[30]

Phidias' centrality to any catalogue of sculptors will soon emerge: "the talent of Quintus Hortensius while he was a very young man was approved of as soon as it was seen, like a statue of Phidias" (*Q. Hortensi admodum adulescentis ingenium ut Phidiae signum simul aspectum et probatum est*, 228). Phidias is the quintessence of sculpture: his creative accomplishments and renown are as immediately recognizable as the pieces he produces.[31] It also can hardly be coincidence that Cicero names Phidias, so central a figure to Greek art and rhetorical analogies, along with Hortensius. He was a crucial colleague and rival, his death inspired the *Brutus*, and Cicero wrested from him the mantle of Rome's premier orator.

Another example adds artistic imitation to the terms of the analogy: "just as Lysippus used to say about the Doryphorus of Polyclitus, so you are now saying that the speech on the Servilian law was your master" (*ut Polycliti doryphorum sibi Lysippus aiebat, sic tu suasionem legis Serviliae tibi magistram fuisse*, 296). The claim comes from Atticus, who, despite his real-world penchant for antiquarian researches strikes an aggressively presentist pose in the dialogue's fiction. We find him challenging the canonization of allegedly outdated orators such as Cato and Crassus. Atticus responds to Cicero's former adoption as a role model of Crassus' speech promoting the *lex Servilia* of 106 BCE (161). Mention of Polyclitus in this context touches on the initial catalogue of four sculptors, where he

---

[28] The circle of firstness is closed by the fact that Daedalus appears in the literary record in Homer (in connection with the shield of Achilles, wrought by Hephaestus, *Il.* 18.591–92), and his name is already synonymous in Homer with good craftsmanship. Cicero had just cited Homer as the first poet of record (despite possible forerunners). That Livius' first play in 240 precedes his Latinized *Odyssey* suggests that Cicero sought out the alignment. He could have reversed the terms of assessment (plays Daedalian, *Odyssia* readable once) while asserting Livius' crude antiquity.

[29] I assume that judgment of the *fabulae* applies to the *Odyssia*, that is, Livius is universally antiquated. The point is that Livius will not repay in-depth study.

[30] The reference to Naevius' *bellum Poenicum* as "like a work of Myron" (*quasi Myronis opus*, 75) creates a tripartite lineage for epic poetry: Livius–Naevius–Ennius, with Ennius figured as Polyclitus: *perfecta* (70) – *perfectior* (76).

[31] The statue is the summit of artistry (*Minerva illa Phidiae*, *Parad.* 5), outranking the lowly workmanship of the *Paradoxa Stoicorum*.

was the developmental endpoint. With the addition of Lysippus the entire catalogue now contains seven sculptors.[32] This last analogy also introduces the imitation of artistic works, which was implicit in the earlier assessment of Livius Andronicus (71, quoted above), since the pragmatic value of reading and rereading, in addition to the recreational purpose of enjoyment, is to find material suitable for imitation. Cicero expands the traditional analogy to statuary in order to include the likening of the specific works produced by an author to the specific works produced by a sculptor.[33] The comparison might seem inevitable, but other works do not so extensively elaborate the topos. Among other theorists, statuary analogies tend to elucidate the relative development of an author (Demetrius, Dionysius of Halicarnassus) or a specific quality or characteristic of style (Quintilian).[34] Cicero has instead interwoven both sides of this analogy to give it greater explanatory power, as authors no less than sculptors engage with a tradition of past works as part of their own artistic development. Just as Lysippus studied and imitated Polyclitus' renowned statue of a nude warrior, so Cicero relied on a prominent deliberative speech by his role model, Crassus, to improve his eloquence. Statuary and eloquence are more complexly intertwined in the *Brutus* than anywhere else.

Chronology should be borne in mind as well, since Lysippus takes us into the later classical period, well after Polyclitus and Phidias, and suggests one guiding principle of the *Brutus*: change continues beyond a notional classical acme. Lysippus (*fl.* 330) was a somewhat younger contemporary of Praxiteles (*fl.* 360) and along with him is seen as a great innovator who helped to establish the bridge from the late classical period into the Hellenistic.[35] If the initial catalogue of four sculptors was surprising for having suppressed mention of Phidias, especially given its listing of figures from the sixth and fifth centuries and the notion of artistic perfection, the absence of Praxiteles is notorious, since the larger range of analogies offered in the *Brutus* brings us well into the fourth century.

It is noteworthy that only in the digression on Caesar does Cicero directly identify himself with a sculptor producing a work of art, claiming

---

[32] The number of sculptors cited across the *Brutus* thus equals the total number of painters cited. Cf. *de Orat.* 3.26–27, in which Cicero creates a neat symmetry in groups of three for sculptors (Myro, Polyclitus, Lysippus), painters (Zeuxis, Aglaophon, Apelles), Roman tragedians (Ennius, Pacuvius, Accius), and Greek tragedians (Aeschylus, Sophocles, Euripides).

[33] Precision replaces the vagueness used for Livius: *opus aliquod Daedali*.

[34] See Jucker (1950) 118–46, Fantham (1972) 141–43 on Cicero's analogies with visual arts, and Squire (2015); generally, Pollitt (1974).

[35] For the (not always reliable) *floruit* dating I rely on Stewart (1990).

that he would prefer to be Phidias crafting a Minerva than a useful workman (*ego me Phidiam esse mallem*, 257, discussed below). Other examples compare statuary to style in general or individual speakers and speeches, while Cicero essentially collapses the analogy, identifying himself with Phidias' cultural and political relevance. He asks not merely *What object does Phidias produce?*, but *How is artistic production meaningful in the broadest sense?* By inserting himself into the digression on Caesar's style and emphasizing the importance of his own actions over those of other military commanders, Cicero sets himself up to be compared to Caesar. To then liken himself to a Phidias producing a Minerva prompts the inevitable question: what sculptor and sculpture might we associate with Caesar in comparison? From there it is no great interpretive leap for Cicero to suggest that Caesar in producing his *commentarii* is essentially a Praxiteles producing a Venus. Yet even with the conceptual framework in place, and even in light of the *Brutus'* repeated tendency to have readers posit comparisons and meaningfully fill in conceptual gaps, the identification still requires further evidence connecting Caesar to the statuary analogies.[36]

The Conversational Exchange (251–62)

The evaluation of Caesar comes as part of an extended, complex, and animated exchange on a range of topics. It is the most intricate digression in the *Brutus* and among the liveliest scenes from any of Cicero's dialogues, dramatically reminiscent perhaps of the mid-conversation exchange that opens *de Legibus* or the occasional Socratic back-and-forth between Laelius and Scipio in *de Republica*. The digression on Caesar challenges the value of military triumphs while promoting Cicero's civic and oratorical achievements. All three interlocutors participate, a rarity in the dialogue, and the trio together evaluates no other orator. Coupled with the evaluation of Marcus Claudius Marcellus (248–50), the topic also seems to violate the injunction to discuss only the dead, further marking its importance.[37]

---

[36] On filling in the gaps in the *Brutus*, see Chapter 1 on the Ciceropaideia and Chapter 4 on the syncrisis of Coriolanus and Themistocles. Longinus offers a similarly tantalizing "riddle" in comparing an unidentified "Colossus" with the Doryphorus of Polyclitus (*Subl.* 36.3). De Jonge (2013) argues for an identification with Phidias' Zeus at Olympia.

[37] Age should not have prevented Brutus from hearing Caesar's oratory (248; cf. Chapter 1). Badian (1967) 229 says Cicero means forensic oratory, but that overlooks the importance of deliberative. Van der Blom (2016) remarks that Caesar's "entire career is characterized by vigorous political and oratorical activity when in Rome." Cic. *Lig.* 30 says that Cicero frequently pled alongside Caesar.

Cicero begins by seeking Atticus' opinion of Caesar (251), while Brutus vainly recalls the intention to evaluate only the dead, before Atticus gives a brief account (252–53) and hands over to Brutus (254–55); he quickly yields to Cicero (255–58) and his inbuilt digression on the true utility of eloquence over military achievement, in which Cicero fields the imagined objections of a fictive interlocutor; Atticus picks up the relay (258–59), followed by Brutus' query of Atticus' mentioning Sisenna and C. Rusius (260), prompting Atticus to relay the notorious *sputatilica* story (260), to discuss the analogical method, and to note Caesar's oratorical *elegantia* (261); Brutus then moves from the *orationes* to the *commentarii* (262), which Cicero takes up in the well-known judgment (262) before urging a return from the digression to the main account (*revertamur*, 262).

The topics broached are central to the dialogue and indeed encapsulate the most essential themes in it: the use of language (analogy and anomaly), the utility of public achievement (military and civic), state well-being (*salus civitatis*), communal memory (*historia*), literary exchange, aesthetic evaluation, and Greek culture as a model for explaining Roman artistic practices (Phidias' Athena/Minerva). Formally and topically the long digression is a masterpiece of rhetoric.[38] The key to understanding the judgment of Caesar lies in Cicero's mention of Phidias' famed statue:

> The great orator far excels petty commanders ... It was also of greater utility to the Athenians to have sturdy roofs over their houses than to have that most beautiful ivory statue of Minerva. I'd still rather be Phidias than the best setter of roof beams. That's why we must weigh carefully not a man's utility but his true value, especially since only a few can paint or sculpt remarkably, but you can't have a lack of workmen and heavy lifters.
>
> multo magnus orator praestat minutis imperatoribus ... Atheniensium quoque plus interfuit firma tecta in domiciliis habere quam Minervae signum ex ebore pulcherrimum; tamen ego me Phidiam esse mallem quam vel optumum fabrum tignuarium. quare non quantum quisque prosit, sed quanti quisque sit ponderandum est; praesertim cum pauci pingere egregie possint aut fingere, operarii autem aut baiuli deesse non possint. (256–57)

Mention of Minerva is almost an afterthought, a fortuitous example to support his dismissal of the average commander and his triumphs and to promote his own civic achievements as an orator and politician. Cicero does not challenge the triumph outright but revises the values attached to

[38] See Chapter 3 for fuller quotation and discussion.

it and offers countervailing sources of civic value, a strategy already prominent in his dialogues of the 50s and in many respects the distinguishing feature of his self-fashioning.[39]

Cicero's association of himself with Minerva, while it feeds into the larger network of statuary analogies, is different from them in character. It underscores a key theme in Cicero's history of oratory: the interrelationship of the Roman state and stylistic practice. He transposes the statuary comparison to the political plane, underscoring how Phidias and Athena are central to Athenian civic identity in the classical period. Phidias, of course, was inherently tied to Pericles, the orator-statesman who plays a surprisingly outsize role in the *Brutus*.[40] The association of Cicero with Phidias and Minerva, inserted into the digression on Caesar, provides an interpretive framework for Atticus' subsequent analysis of Caesar's style. Even if Atticus does not explicitly cite Praxiteles and his vastly influential Venus, Cicero has primed us to expect an artistic analogy in the discussion of Caesar.

The Aesthetic and Political Judgment of Caesar

Statuary's importance to the *Brutus* is signaled early, if indirectly, in the dialogue's dramatic setting: after the long preface the speakers sit in a small meadow near a statue of Plato (*in pratulo propter Platonis statuam consedimus*, 24). Reference to spatial settings and their physical objects within dialogue-frames typically allude to a Platonic forerunner and foreshadow a significant theme in the Ciceronian version.[41] In no other dialogue does Cicero insert a statue of Plato into the dramatic transition from preface to discussion, and the detail, along with mention of the meadow, points us to the setting of Plato's *Phaedrus*, with its *locus amoenus*, statuettes, and shrine. Statuary there crucially elucidates the work's analysis of writing, rhetoric, and philosophy, and refers to specific individuals in the Athenian social and political milieu.[42]

---

[39] Dugan (2005) and van der Blom (2010) on Cicero' self-presentation and his use of role models.

[40] For a comparable affiliation of Pericles with Phidias and his creation of statues, see Dio Chrys. *Or.* 12 (the *Olympic Oration*) and Plut. *Per.* 31.4–5.

[41] See Zetzel (2003) on the *pulvinus* and Plato's pillows, as well as the plane tree (*platanus*), in Cicero's *de Oratore*. On the *pratulus*, compare Cic. *Rep.* 18.4: *in aprico maxime pratuli loco*; *Att.* 12.6.2 (SB 306), and Chapter 2.

[42] See Morgan (1994) on indirect references in the *Phaedrus* to golden statues set up in honor of Gorgias and the meaning of these references for the dialogue.

Direct reference to statues of Plato and Minerva in the *Brutus* are likely of special significance for the conversation in which they are engaged, a significance underscored by the fact that Cicero has otherwise modeled the *Brutus* less on the dialogues of Plato (or his follower, Heraclides of Pontus) in the way that he did for *de Oratore* and *de Republica*, and more on those of Aristotle, in which the author takes the leading role in exposition of the material rather than use intermediaries such as Socrates (Plato's works), Scipio (*de Republica*), or Crassus (*de Oratore*). Given the formal design of the dialogue, the reference to Plato in the dramatic setting, including reference to Plato's *Phaedrus*, is striking and indicates the thematic relevance not just of oratory but also of statuary as a crucial theme in the *Brutus*.

Evidence for Cicero's admiration of statuary and its representative potential in his own life abounds. Despite occasionally feigned dilettantism and criticism of statuary's extravagance in the *Verrines*, Cicero knew Greek art well and was alert to the intellectual and symbolic value of objects and images.[43] He eagerly sought a Hermathena, a double-faced composite bust with Hermes and Athena, for the gymnasium in his Tusculan villa nicknamed the Academy, probably a peristyle garden. "That decoration is appropriate to my Academy," he tells Atticus, "because Hermes is common to all (such) places and Minerva is the special symbol of that gymnasium" (*est ornamentum Academiae proprium meae, quod et Hermes commune omnium et Minerva singulare est insigne eius gymnasi*, Att. 1.4.3 [SB 9]).[44]

Both the language and the structure of the digression on Caesar's style are closely connected to the analogies with the visual arts. After mentioning Phidias, Cicero notes that sculptors are valuable, "especially since few men can paint or sculpt with excellence" (*praesertim cum pauci pingere egregie possint aut fingere*, 257). Given that Cicero has only just offered an analogy to statuary, the additional mention of painting, which otherwise serves no purpose, points beyond the immediate context. First, it directs us back to the double analogy of style to painting and statuary earlier in the work (70), connecting the contents of the later digression with the earlier statements about the development of style. The claim *pauci . . . possint* also reinforces at a general level the close connection between the visual arts and the production of oratory, since this "*paucitas* motif" is one of the crucial premises of the *Brutus* (and of Cicero's rhetorical dialogues in

---

[43] Vasaly (1993) discusses his references to physical space in Rome's urban landscape.

[44] Cf. *Att.* 1.1.5 (SB 10). Cicero frequently discusses art and its collection in the first book of letters to Atticus: 1.1.5 (SB 10), 1.3.1 (SB 8), 1.4.3 (SB 9), 1.5.7 (SB 1), 1.6.2 (SB 2), 1.8.2 (SB 4), 1.9.2 (SB 5), 1.10.3–4 (SB 6), 1.11.3 (SB 7). He elsewhere criticizes the inept choices of M. Fadius Gallus in selecting for him (*Fam.* 7.23 [SB 209]).

general): only few men achieve greatness in oratory because oratory is so difficult and therefore valuable.[45] Employment of this motif here further aligns the creative uniqueness of visual artists to the rare skills of the true orator.

Second, the two verbs *pingere* and *fingere* also direct us forward to the description of Julius Caesar himself, in which Caesar is likened to an artist producing works of art, first as a painter and then as a sculptor.

> Atticus said, "Caesar, however, systematically fixes faulty and corrupt usage with pure and uncorrupted usage. And so when he adds to this elegance of Latin diction – which is still necessary, even if you're not an orator and just a well-bred Roman citizen – those oratorical decorations of speech, it then seems as if he places well-painted pictures in good light. This distinction is uniquely his, yet I don't see to whom he should give pride of place in shared virtues. He has a marvelous and hardly routine manner of speech, with voice, movement, and physical appearance even grand and well-bred in a certain way."
>
> Then Brutus said, "I certainly admire his speeches greatly. I've read a great many and even his *commentarii*, which he wrote about his affairs."
>
> I said, "They really are remarkable; you see, they're nude, upright, and charming, with all adornment of speech, like a garment, removed. But while he intended to ready materials for others wanting to write history, he perhaps did a favor for the fools who'll intend to burn them with curling irons: sensible men at any rate he scared off from writing. You see, in history nothing is more pleasing than pure and lucid brevity. But, if you're willing, let's get back to those who are no longer living."

> Caesar autem rationem adhibens consuetudinem vitiosam et corruptam pura et incorrupta consuetudine emendat. itaque <u>cum ad hanc elegantiam verborum Latinorum – quae, etiam si orator non sis et sis ingenuus civis Romanus, tamen necessaria est – adiungit illa oratoria ornamenta dicendi, tum videtur tamquam tabulas bene pictas conlocare in bono lumine.</u> hanc cum habeat praecipuam laudem, in communibus[46] non video cui debeat cedere. splendidam quandam minimeque veteratoriam rationem dicendi tenet, voce motu forma etiam magnificam et generosam quodam modo.
>
> Tum Brutus: orationes quidem eius mihi vehementer probantur. com-pluris autem legi; atque etiam commentarios quosdam scripsit rerum suarum.
>
> Valde quidem, inquam, probandos; <u>nudi enim sunt, recti et venusti, omni ornatu orationis tamquam veste detracta.</u> sed dum voluit alios habere

---

[45] The *paucitas* motif: 182, 244, 270, 299, 333, *de Orat.* 1.8, *Orat.* 20; difficulty of the *ars*: *rem unam esse omnium difficillimam* (25); cf. e.g. 137, 199.
[46] The comma is moved forward before *in communibus* (Kaster, following Douglas).

parata, unde sumerent qui vellent scribere historiam, ineptis gratum fortasse
fecit, qui volent illa calamistris inurere: sanos quidem homines a scribendo
deterruit; nihil est enim in historia pura et inlustri brevitate dulcius. sed ad
eos, si placet, qui vita excesserunt, revertamur. (261–62)

Caesar's speeches abound in oratorical adornment. *Ornamenta* is a
related if more specific version of the abstract *ornatus* that his *commentarii*
allegedly lack, and the cognate terms align the qualities of his speeches with
the (absent) qualities of his histories.[47] The metaphor, signaled by *tamquam*, presents Caesar as a painter: his use of ornament allows him to paint
pictures well and place them in good lighting.[48]

In describing Caesar as a painter (261) Cicero paves the way for us to
discern his role as sculptor (262): Caesar's speeches are like painting, his
commentarii like statuary. The later language *nudi, recti, venusti*, etc. thus
continues the idea of Caesar as a producer of artworks but shifts from
painting to statuary. Given Cicero's earlier mention of Phidias' Minerva it
also suggests that in his *commentarii* Caesar creates a specific sculpture.
The questions remain, which one and why?

Praxiteles' Aphrodite of Knidos

When read with attention to its visual elements, Cicero's judgment of the
commentarii most closely suggests a nude upright statue of Venus:
Praxiteles' Aphrodite of Knidos. Nudity is evident (*nudi*). *Recti* in the
sense of "upright" identifies the Knidian original while differentiating that
version from variations – all the major variations present Aphrodite as less
upright than the Knidia.[49] The term *venusti* plays on the name of the
goddess, who was, of course, so central to Caesarian ideology: Venus.[50] As
Christina S. Kraus observes, "any application of *venustus* to Caesar must
conjure up the image of the most famous Julian ancestor, the goddess of
love herself."[51] Lastly, the detail concerning the clothing removed also
perfectly matches the typology of the Knidian Venus, who alluringly holds
in her left hand the garment removed for bathing. Simply put, Cicero's

---

[47] Mankin (2011) 213 on *ornamenta* versus *ornatus*.
[48] Note too *tamquam* in 262, *tamquam veste detracta*, another parallel between the two passages on the
visual arts.
[49] *OLD* s.v. *rectus* 7b and below for the variations.
[50] See Weinstock (1971) 15–18 and *passim* on Venus in Caesarian ideology. Krostenko (2001) 42–43
discusses puns on the name of Venus; Cic. *Verr.* 2.5.142 puns on Venus and Cupid. A. Powell
(1998) 114 suggests a connection to Caesar's sexual peccadillos. Cic. *N.D.* 2.69 implausibly
connects Venus to *venire*.
[51] Kraus (2005) 112.

description of Caesar's *commentarii* corresponds to Praxiteles' Aphrodite of Knidos, the paradigmatic upright statue of a nude Venus.

Praxiteles' innovative and controversial Knidia is thought to be the first rendering of a full-size female nude in the plastic arts. She inspired several formal variations that became immensely popular beginning (probably) at the end of the second century BCE and would even establish themselves in the iconography of self-presentation for respectable Roman matrons in the imperial period.[52] There was the crouching Venus tying her sandals or putting up her hair, or Venus rising from the sea, reclined, as we see in a fresco from Pompeii – rather than upright as Botticelli portrayed Venus' emergence into the world.

Other explanations of the language have argued that it indicates the shape of a human form in general, Caesar's body itself, or Caesar portrayed in the Greek tradition of the heroic nude.[53] Several objections to these identifications can be made. There is no evidence that by 46 BCE the heroic male nude had claimed a spot at Rome in the repertoire of artistic self-presentation among the political class. There exists, certainly, a history of the Roman heroic nude from roughly the second century BCE onward, although a controversial history in many respects. Cicero excoriates Verres' son for one such statue in Greek-speaking Sicily in the 70s.[54] In the *pro Rabirio Postumo* (54/53 BCE) Cicero defends Rabirius' choice to don Greek attire at the court of King Ptolemy XIII Auletes of Alexandria by noting that Scipio Asiagenus was honored with a statue on the Capitol depicting him wearing a *chlamys* and *crepides* for his victory over Antiochus III of Syria in 189 BCE.[55] As Christopher Hallett notes, that this was the only example Cicero cites (or perhaps could cite) "must make it extremely

---

[52] Understandably, the more diffident "Capitoline" type became the norm. On the statue and its various transformations and receptions in the Greco-Roman world, see *LIMC* II s.v. "Aphrodite" nos. 391–422, Havelock (1995), D'Ambra (1996), Stewart (1997) 96–106, Hallett (2005) 199, 201, 219–22, 260, 331–32, Kousser (2010), Stewart (2010). On republican Rome and Venus' cooption by Sulla, Pompey, and Caesar, see Schilling (1982) 272–345, Kousser (2010) 289–91.

[53] Douglas (1966a) 191: "the human form as represented in sculpture"; Dugan (2005) 185: heroic nude; Kraus (2005) is the most extensive discussion of the passage in comparison to Caesar's historiography; she interprets this as an eroticized representation of Caesar in statuary terms ("The physical image ... is unabashedly masculine," 112). Cf. also Pelling (2006). I differ from Dugan and Kraus in arguing for a statue of Venus, although that identification would still support some of their arguments, even if (or in part because) the intermediary layer of irony is removed.

[54] Cicero's criticism in the *Verrines* merits circumspection: its persuasive effect, regardless of attitudes toward heroic nudity, depends on rhetorical wordplay, to link *nudus* with the spoliation of Sicily (*statua ... nuda fili - nudata provincia, Ver.* 2.4.143).

[55] The statue was commissioned not by Scipio, however, but by local Greeks.

unlikely that the heroic portrait was a generally accepted part of Roman self-representation at this date."[56]

The first clear examples we have of individuals portraying themselves in this way do not appear until Sextus Pompey's and Octavian Caesar's issuance of coinage after the death of Caesar, and they appear to be an innovative attempt to portray their martial virtue and filial piety during the propaganda wars of the triumviral period: Octavian as son of *divus Iulius*, Sextus as son of Neptune/Pompey. Such portrayals were fostered in large measure by the association of the Greek nude with the idealized physique of young men. For Caesar and Pompey, however, we have no clear evidence of their self-presentation using the heroic nude.[57] Perhaps like the triumviral successors years later, Cicero in the *Brutus* might have been appealing to a possibility latent but not yet realized in the repertoire of celebratory iconography at Rome.[58] His audience surely will have been able to make this and other conceptual leaps along with him. Yet arguing against such a reference is the unquestionably honorific nature of such a portrayal, even if we allow for hints of ironic criticism in the polysemy of the description: reference to the heroic nude would associate Caesar with the majesty of a Hellenistic ruler or the great heroes of mythology. "The costume," in the words of Michael Koortbojian, "declared that they were to be thought of as having achieved a level of *honor et gloria* far beyond the norms toward which all good Romans might ordinarily strive."[59] Such panegyric hardly accords with Cicero's desire to downplay Caesar's achievements and to express displeasure at the contemporary distress of the Roman state.

Furthermore, despite the potential erotic connotations of nudity, *venustus* is hardly an attribute of the heroic male nude, which emphasized grandeur, reverence, and military virtue above all else. It justified nudity

---

[56] Hallett (2005) 153. On statues of Caesar at Rome, See Cadaro (2006), Zanker (2009), Koortbojian (2013), esp. 191–226 on the nude costume. Koortbojian (2013) 194 remarks: "Several much-contested examples of nude or seminude statues survive that may well date from the late second century (although none of them can be dated with certainty)." Such honors from others were more acceptable, and Cicero could have honored Caesar in this way. Yet he has every reason to avoid the celebratory heroic nude in a text that challenges martial accomplishments.

[57] This is not to say that Sextus and Octavian could not have been imitating their fathers or appealing to already acceptable norms, but there is no clear evidence of widespread acceptance at an earlier time. It seems far more likely that they were pursuing their own innovative ends while tying them back to claims of legitimacy through familial inheritance.

[58] Silver denarii issued by Caesar in 47/46 do represent Venus on the obverse and on the reverse a heroic nude Aeneas carrying Anchises and the Palladium with the legend "CAESAR," but no coins show Caesar himself in the heroic nude. See *RRC* 458/1.

[59] Koortbojian (2013) 194.

through the associations with physical training, competitive fighting, exploits in battle, and the heroes and gods of mythology. In addition, the nudity of the heroic nude is paradoxically not really "nude." Such statues do not have the garment, typically the Greek battle cloak, the *chlamys*, fully removed, but rather at a minimum draped over the left shoulder and accompanied by weaponry, such as a sword, spear, or *balteus* (swordbelt). Nudity is a feature of the statues insofar as they show the genitalia, but the heroic nude is a type of costumed portrait with accoutrements. While *nudus* is a flexible term, typically meaning not "nude" but "mostly nude" or "unadorned," Cicero's specific description – *omni ornatu orationis tamquam veste detracta* – better fits the versions of a fully disrobed Venus, in which the nudity itself, including the presence of the garment fully removed for bathing, is a crucial element of the statuary typology and an integral part of its erotic appeal, all tied back to Praxiteles' innovations. Quite differently, the nudity of the portrait in heroic costume was, paradoxically, a representation in which the nudity itself was important but was not the sole emphasis; rather, nudity in conjunction with the military apparatus formed a crucial mode of dress that symbolized an entire Hellenic world of martial and mythological heroism. It was not nudity alone that was on display for visual consumption but rather the heroic majesty and virtue of which nudity was an index and iconographic convention.[60]

The questions are essentially twofold: which of two standard topoi does Cicero refer to, and how does each of those topoi determine the analogy he uses? The first commonplace is *talis oratio, qualis vita*, which aligns in largely moral terms the qualities of an author's style with his own life. The scholarship thus far has largely emphasized this topos. The operative analogy in this case is that Caesar's writings are a reflection of Caesar as a person (and thus are meant to describe him).[61] The second possibility is the commonplace that likens writings to monuments, structures, or objects.[62] On this second explanation, the analogy compares Caesar's writings to another object, specifically a statue.

---

[60] Koortbojian (2013) 195 does underscore the symbolic effectiveness of "the sheer material radiance of such nude images."

[61] Möller (2004) capaciously studies the topos.

[62] Cicero's *de Orat.* 3.180 offers an analogy to a temple; cf. Tac. *Dial.* 20.7, 22.4. Architectural analogies are more commonly a poetic topos and go back at least to Pindar (*Ol.* 6.1–7); the most famous Latin example is Vergil's promise of a *templum* to Augustus in the *Georgics* (3.4–12; presumably the *Aeneid*).

It is true that Cicero's indirectness, his innovations with statuary analogies in the *Brutus*, and the subsequent history of the topos might suggest a comparison of Caesar's works to his physical body, thus creating the possibility of moral judgment of that body. Elements in the surrounding discussion, such as the mention of the *calamistri* ("curling irons") applied by imitators (262), are used by authors such as Seneca and Tacitus to describe a figure such as Maecenas; they rework the passage precisely in line with the topic *talis oratio, qualis vita*. However, the subsequent reception may mislead us about the original text's purpose. While the two topoi are closely related, they have fundamentally different aims; the second topos – the comparison of written texts to objects – has a crucially different focus: not on the craftsman but the craft he produces.

Cicero's judgment does describe a human or human-like form, but the target of the analogy is not Julius Caesar but rather the object that Caesar by analogy produces in his writings: the *commentarii* are like the Aphrodite of Knidos. Praxiteles' Aphrodite and Phidias' Athena, probably the two most celebrated female statues of Greco-Roman antiquity, are crucial to the work's political and aesthetic commitments. Cicero's reference to Venus offers a potent and contextually relevant criticism of Caesar, bringing into focus the symbolism that separates Minerva from Venus.

Cicero's Minerva: The Symbolic and the Real

The symbolic contrast between Minerva and Venus is the greatest strength of the implicit comparison. Cicero portrays himself as the defender of state and civic order in his actions and writings and reprises the association with Minerva he first made in battling Clodius. Phidias' Athena and Praxiteles' Aphrodite embody fundamentally different attitudes and contexts for producing statuary, and Cicero aligns himself with the former in order to promote a specific vision of Rome modeled on Athenian learning, Periclean Athens, and its martial and civic accomplishments. Phidias represents classical Athens at its highpoint, after the defeat of the Persians, which was accompanied by a sense of Athenian supremacy in the military and artistic spheres. Praxiteles, by contrast, whatever his artistic fame, represents a subsequent phase of Athenian history, the decline of Athens that would culminate in capitulation to Macedonian rule. Minerva marvelously encapsulates Cicero's promotion of his theoretical and historical ideology as a countervailing force against military accomplishment. As the quintessential goddess of Athens and learning, Athena/Minerva suits Cicero's attempts in the 50s and 40s to align Roman civic identity with broad-based theoretical learning derived from Greek sources.[63] Thus Minerva's championing of the learned arts crucially supports Cicero's rejection of military triumph as Rome's main source of greatness.

This is not to deny a martial connection. Athena/Minerva is a goddess of war, but symbolizes war combined with wisdom, guided policy to benefit the polity, and battle conducted with strategic deliberation.[64] She differs from her typically bloodthirsty, glory-seeking counterpart, Ares/ Mars, who in the worst versions represents the brutal aspects of warfare and destructive slaughter.[65] Most notably, Athena symbolizes the salvation of Athens from the great Persian enemy, and her monumental function as the protectress of Greece underpins Cicero's self-description as the savior of Rome. Built in the 450s and 440s, the Parthenon celebrated Athenian victory over the invading Persian forces and offered tribute to the gods for their assistance. The temple was rebuilt over the older temple to Athena, which the occupying Persians had destroyed in 480. It contained Phidias' massive chryselephantine statue of Athena, dressed in a peplos, with a shield lowered to the ground and supported upright by her left hand while she held a statue of Nike in her right.[66] The temple complex, with its central position in the city, massive size, elaborate friezes, and dazzling statue of its patron goddess celebrated Athenian victory, thus suggesting for Cicero's audience an alternative vision of triumphal success, one based not solely on military conquest, but on defending the welfare of the state and promoting civic harmony.

This emphasis emerges in Brutus' remark that Cicero's *supplicatio* (of 63 BCE, rather than 51 BCE) outranks Caesar's praise for Cicero's oratorical accomplishments, which in turn outranks the triumphs of many men (*hanc autem, inquit, gloriam testimoniumque Caesaris tuae quidem supplicationi non, sed triumphis multorum antepono*, 255). The hierarchy is a crucial

---

[63] Quint. *Inst.* 11.1.24 (probably citing *de Consulatu suo* 1) notes that Minerva trained Cicero in the arts (*Minervam quae artes eum edocuit*). That Minerva represents Athens, while Praxiteles' Venus is associated with Knidos in Asia Minor, conveniently aligns Cicero with Athens (versus Asia), yet again challenging the Atticists by reversing the terms of debate.

[64] Cic. *N.D.* 3.53 cites her reputation as the founder of warfare (*quam principem et inventricem belli ferunt*).

[65] Further details are beyond the scope of the present study, but the Roman Mars is generally portrayed in a better light than his Greek counterpart Ares. In mythology Ares/Mars is closely connected to Aphrodite/Venus.

[66] Cicero's description of the ivory features identifies the Athena Parthenon as opposed to Phidias' bronze Athena Promachos, which stood between the Parthenon and the Propylaea. Cf. the reference to the shield of Athena Parthenon at *Orator* 234; *LIMC* II.212–33, 574–631 s.v. "Athena."

reminder that great oratory must serve great political ends. It also cautiously locates Caesar in that hierarchy even as it demotes military honor. Caesar had unabashedly promoted Venus as the patron of his military success. He vowed a temple to Venus Genetrix at the battle of Pharsalus in 48 and dedicated it on 24 September 46, the last day of his magnificent quadruple triumph. It is important, of course, to keep in mind that at the writing of the *Brutus* Caesar had received *supplicationes* but had yet to triumph, and thus Cicero's prioritization of his own *supplicatio* likens their achievements while giving pride of place to Cicero. He offers a deliberate countermodel to Caesar's self-representation as a descendant of Venus and to his impending celebration of victory.

Phidias' Athena was also a prime example of civic benefaction and especially of Pericles' centrality to classical Athens. Cicero's emphasis on the statue dovetails remarkably with Pericles' political and oratorical prominence, emphasized in the *Brutus* far more than in any other dialogue.[67] Pericles is the first Greek orator of merit (28) and anticipates the first Roman orator, Marcus Cornelius Cethegus (cos. 204). Cicero excludes orators prior to Pericles/Cethegus by claiming not to know or not to value earlier texts.[68] Pericles also assumes a notably Ciceronian profile as the first to introduce learning (*doctrina*) to his oratory, allegedly through his philosophical association with Anaxagoras. Pericles, seeming to follow Ciceronian prescriptions, turned abstruse philosophical knowledge into material for public speeches, and in addition to stylistic fullness (*ubertas, copia*) he also mastered powerful, almost violent, persuasion: "they [the Athenians] feared the terrifying force of his speech" (*vim dicendi terroremque timuerunt*, 44). His applied *doctrina*, *ubertas*, and *copia*, as well as a command of *vis* ("forcefulness") makes him resemble Crassus, Antonius, or Cicero much more than a politician active well before the classical canon of Greek speakers.

Pericles also crops up, somewhat unexpectedly, at the "beginning" of Roman oratory, since Cicero claims, probably wrongly, that Ennius' description of Cethegus as the "marrow of persuasion" (*Suadai medulla*) was crafted in imitation of Eupolis' description of *Peitho* sitting on the lips of Pericles (59). He plays a crucial role not only in the history of Greek oratory, but also in the history of literary history at Greece and Rome. Pericles becomes a forerunner for Cicero's stylistic and political values.

---

[67] See Noël (2014) on Pericles in the *Brutus*, Chapter 5 on Pericles/Cethegus.

[68] Pericles' role as the beginning is brought further into relief by his contrast with the alleged endpoint of Greek oratory, Demetrius of Phalerum (38), who lacks Pericles' forceful stings (*aculei*).

By likening himself to Phidias Cicero associates himself with Periclean Athens and underscores his political and artistic superiority.[69]

The juxtaposition of Minerva and Venus also trades on the opposition of virginal purity to licentiousness that was central to criticizing Clodius' statue of Libertas in the previous decade.[70] Minerva's chaste adult maidenhood is wholly unlike Venus' associations of sexual frivolity and sensual pleasure.[71] The absence of Venus' *vestis* also pointedly contrasts with Athena's most prominent garment, the *peplos* presented to Athena (Polias) at the Panathenaia each summer.[72] Cicero thus represents the Greek civic and artistic worlds so that they match up with his own political and aesthetic designs. He draws on the symbolism of Minerva as a foil to Caesar's Venus-driven ideology and to promote a coherent and powerfully persuasive civic and artistic alternative for Rome and its past.

The Real Goddess Minerva

When Cicero claims that he would rather be a Phidias sculpting a Minerva, he indulges not in fantasy but fact. In one very real sense he was a creator of Minerva, having crafted a Roman equivalent to Athena at the center of Roman public worship by transferring a Minerva from his domestic *sacrarium* to the Capitoline (discussed above). The statue still

---

[69] Dio Chrysostom (*Orat.* 12.6) associates Pericles and Phidias and makes a further connection between artisan and politician in the crafting of Minerva: Phidias depicted both men on the shield of Athena Promachos (cf. Plut. *Per.* 31.4–5).

[70] And against Clodius he reprises criticism first crafted against Verres: "he relocated the treasures of the maiden Minerva into the house of a courtesan" (*hic ornamenta Minervae virginis in meretriciam domum transtulit*, *Ver.* 2.4.123). There may be a (tenuous) connection between Minerva and the allegory of *eloquentia* as a *virgo* needing protection (330). Stroup (2003) on the *adulta virgo*.

[71] Other Roman representations of Venus, including Caesar's Venus Genetrix, traditionally associate her with war (and Mars) rather than with the sensual eroticism of Aphrodite (and accordingly emphasize her nudity less); cf. Kousser (2010). Cicero, however, in alluding to the Aphrodite of Knidos, need not accurately portray the martial versions of Venus. If anything, such distortion is crucial to his rhetoric, reframing what Caesar's Venus means by presenting a different version of her. My interpretation requires only that the association Aphrodite/Venus *could* be made. The syncretism of Aphrodite/Venus is underway by the late second century; see Schilling (1982) 378–79.

[72] Barber (1992) on the *peplos* in the festival. Would a reference to the Knidia evoke Caesar's rumored affair with Nicomedes IV Philopator, which led Bibulus to dub him "the Queen of Bithynia" (*Bithynicam reginam*, Suet. *Jul.* 49.2)? Nicomedes IV may have acquired the statue from Knidos in return for the cancellation of debts; cf. Pollitt (1990) 84, Stewart (1990) 279, and Havelock (1995) 63, with Plin. *Nat.* 36.20. Cicero may well have known about the bid for the statue in 70 BCE: *Ver.* 2.4.135: *quid Cnidios ut Venerem marmoream?* If it was this Nicomedes, then Cicero marvelously challenges Caesar's association with Venus by putting it into the least favorable context. Cicero once quipped that the son of Venus was deflowered in Bithynia (Suet. *Jul.* 49.3).

occupied its place, presumably in Minerva's precinct as part of the Capitoline Triad, in 46 BCE and stayed beyond Caesar's (and probably Cicero's) death.[73] In a letter of 43 to Cornificius she again makes an appearance: "on that very day [19 March, Quinquatrus, the festival of Minerva] the senate decreed that our Minerva, guardian of Rome, whom a gale overturned, be set up again" (*eo ipso die senatus decrevit, ut Minerva nostra, custos urbis, quam turbo deiecerat, restitueretur, Fam.* 12.25.1 [SB 373]). The real-life placement of Minerva on the Capitoline and her textual notice in the *Brutus* connect the location of Cicero's Minerva on the heights of the Capitol to its monumental equivalent in Athens, the Parthenon, perched above the city Athena protected.[74] Cicero's dedication of Minerva as he departed Rome may even have been calculated to recall the dedication of Athens to Athena as citizens abandoned the city to the invading enemy during the Persian War.[75] The gesture is inseparable from the subsequent triumph of Athens over the Persians and claims to superiority over other Greeks. Once again Cicero's ingenuity found a way to indulge the *Brutus'* obsessive creation of meaningful parallels between Athens and Rome. This masterful manipulation of spatial and geographical resonances throws into relief Caesar's Venus, still in search of a place in Rome's urban topology. Cicero knew this well, since, in conjunction with Caesar's financial creature-in-Rome, Oppius, he already in 54 was busy helping to secure land for Caesar's forum with its temple of Venus Genetrix.[76]

Cicero may also be responding to Caesarian provocation. Caesar too had sought to lay claim to Minerva and to connect her to Julian propaganda. Almost contemporaneous with the *Brutus* is Caesar's issuance in 47/46 BCE of silver denarii with Venus on the obverse and Aeneas fleeing Troy with Anchises on his left shoulder and, crucially, the Palladium in his right hand. This wooden image of Pallas Athena may have been stolen by Diomedes and/or Odysseus; the mythological differences are part of the complex story of post-Homeric reception. Somehow, it arrived at Rome and was housed in the temple of Vesta. Caesar's numismatic vision is clear: Aeneas brought her to Rome and therefore it is Caesar who protects Rome during the civil war. It will also have reinforced Caesar's already prominent

[73] The cella to the right of Jupiter was dedicated to Minerva. *LTUR* III.146, with Liv. 7.3.5.
[74] Mont Allen reminds me that the considerable overlap in the iconography of Minerva and Roma reinforces the overlap in their function as tutelary deities.
[75] Isoc. *Antid.* 233, *Paneg.* 96, Lys. 2.33–43, Plut. *Them.* 10.2–3.
[76] Cic. *Att.* 4.16 (SB 89), *LTUR* II.306–7. It surely formed part of his rivalry with Pompey: *LTUR* v.35–38 on Pompey's theater complex with a temple of Venus Victrix.

connection to Troy via Venus, since the Palladium was given by Zeus to Ilus, Troy's mythical founder. And as *pontifex maximus* Caesar had a close connection to the Palladium, since the Vestal Virgins were its sacred keepers in the temple of Vesta and were in turn under control of the pontifical college. Caesar appears to have crafted an East–West lineage of devotion to the Roman state, and Cicero through Minerva similarly matches Caesar's efforts at crafting an eastern precedent as part of civic ideology.[77]

Caesar's citation of the Palladium on coinage is also a claim on her powers of intellectual and artistic production. Caesar ranked, after all, among the chief intellectuals of his day and was no less eager than Cicero to emerge victorious from the ideological battles that depended on rhetorical skill and the manicured presentation of public image. His *commentarii* and *de Analogia* are both products of that scholarly persona, but no less so are his administrative reforms, such as the solar Julian calendar, established from new knowledge derived from Greco-Egyptian scholars.[78] Caesar's calendrical reforms were in full effect by the end of 46 BCE, the monstrous year bloated beyond all measure to allow the new calendar to begin in 45. Cicero, for his part, acutely felt the imperious weight of knowledge turned into power: once told that Lyra, the constellation, would soon rise, he quipped, "Well of course, it's been ordered to" (Plut. *Caes.* 59.6).[79]

From this larger network of complex representation, of claims and counterclaims about knowledge, authority, and civic duty, emerges Cicero's citation of Phidias' famed statue of Athena on the Acropolis. Certainly it is much more than part of the local argument against the limited value of military triumphs. Allusion to Venus in Cicero's judgment of the *commentarii* strikes directly at the heart of Caesarian self-promotion through his familial claim of descent from Venus, a point perhaps given special piquancy in light of Atticus' composition of family histories, including of the Julii.[80] It is as if Cicero says defiantly, "You may have

---

[77] Assenmaker (2007) and (2010) on the Palladium in late republican and Augustan contexts, respectively. R. M. A. Marshall (2017) 70–71. Cic. *Scaur.* 48 relates how the *pontifex maximus*, L. Metellus, once snatched the Palladium from the burning temple of Vesta; it guarantees the safety of the Roman state (*pignus nostrae salutis atque imperi*).

[78] Feeney (2007) 197 on the reforms as "part of a larger revolution of systematizing and personal control in many departments of Roman life, by which Caesar's name and presence were made indispensably central." I also discuss this in the Introduction.

[79] Volk (2021), chap. 6 suggests that Cicero may have been ridiculing an error in the timing of Lyra's rise.

[80] Cf. Nepos *Att.* 18.3. Varro also traced the ancestry of the Julii to Troy, although his work's date is unknown; see *FRHist* I: 421; on Varro's historical writings: *FRHist* I: 412–23, II: 836–43, III: 513–17.

Venus, Caesar, for yourself and your family, but that is all. Minerva is mine, just as she and I belong to Rome."

Much as Cicero manipulated the antithesis between Minerva and Libertas (or Licentia, as he calls her) to attack Clodius, so in the *Brutus* does he repeat the rhetorical ploy. Yet in place of Libertas and her statue emerges Venus, so crucially associated with Caesar and the *gens Iulia*, allegedly descended from Aeneas, son of the Trojan Anchises and the goddess Venus. The shift in statuary reflects Cicero's shifting struggles against Rome's turbulent self-destruction in the 50s and then the emerging problem of autocratic rule in the 40s. It also reflects, in his literary career, the shift from the (begun-and-then-abandoned?) *de Legibus*, with its emphasis on Clodius, to the *Brutus*, with Caesar occupying his energies and Clodius barely an afterthought.

The *Brutus* crucially contextualizes Caesar's attempts to define his public image and his divine descent, a reminder of the extent to which the elevation of Venus and the promotion of Julian ancestry from her were a long and contested process that may only have seemed complete with the rise of Augustus and the writing of Vergil's *Aeneid*. Yet if we fast-forward nearly half a century, then perhaps Vergil too produces a distant and sympathetic echo of Cicero's claims on Minerva. Aeneas is depicted fleeing Troy with Anchises and the Penates, but Vergil makes no mention of the Palladium, and this despite the famous Caesarian denarius showing Aeneas fleeing, Palladium in hand.[81] There are of course any number of explanations, yet it's tempting to ask if Vergil, out of sympathy for the lost cause and with full knowledge of Cicero's Minervan attachments, conceded this small yet meaningful ideological battle in a war that Cicero and his like-minded contemporaries would never win.

Cicero, for his part, well imagined that powerful weapons against Caesar, or perhaps just refuge, could be found in Minerva, who, in a single potent symbol, commanded the arts of learning, and of resistance. She had long buoyed him in the ideological maelstrom of the late republic and would continue to do so even after the dictator's death. In the crisis of 46, the crucial moment of the *Brutus*, Minerva became the last hope-filled image of salvation before the political iconoclasm that Caesar and his lovely Venus would bring soon enough.

---

[81] See Serv. ad *Aen.* 2.166 with Assenmaker (2007) 392 and (2010) 41–2.

Conclusion

A dreary overstuffed catalogue of bygone orators or a magnificent intellectual achievement? A swan song for public speech or an apology for the art of eloquence? A timid retreat into academic leisure or a brazen challenge to civil war and Caesar? Despite the divergent viewpoints of these questions, it is hard to come away from Cicero's *Brutus* without seeing merit in each of them. There is some of almost everything in Cicero's stunning dialogue, and for that reason its seeming hodgepodge of intellectual curiosity, political statement, and documentary diligence has spurred modern observers to widely differing interpretations.

Cicero's *Brutus* is a rhetorical masterpiece steeped in the intellectual vibrancy of the late republic and its Greco-Roman traditions. "Rhetorical" remains the operative word, since its literary history is not history in the modern sense, but rather a careful mélange of plain fact, suggestive coincidence, and egregious mischaracterization. Many of its aims, and the techniques by which it persuades us, are hidden or only dimly hinted at. Indirection is its lifeblood. The scholarly veneer of scrupulously chronicling notable speakers masks just how ingeniously deceptive Cicero can be. He partially and tendentiously illuminates the history of Roman oratory, something paradoxically akin to hanging a veil of light over the past.

This book has examined the *Brutus* from political, aesthetic, and intellectual perspectives, with each contributing to a larger picture of the dialogue's message and aims. Certainly there were forerunners for parts of Cicero's undertaking, but it deserves greater recognition than A. E. Douglas' tentative appreciation: "without any certainly known precedent" and "perhaps completely novel."[1] Douglas' emphasis on historical actors made him focus on the integration of historical biographies and the dialogue form, which had some precedent in Peripatetic (Aristotle)

---

[1] Douglas (1966a) xxii–xxiii. Cf. Rawson (1972) 34; Gowing (2000) 39: "an unusual work written to fulfill an unusual purpose." Again, for a discussion of several intellectual forerunners, see Chapter 2.

and Academic (Heraclides of Pontus) writers and in Hellenistic scholarship.[2]

There were also Roman precedents in the field of biography and memoir: we learn of the writings of Scaurus and Catulus (both over-shadowed by Xenophon's *Cyropaideia*). Rutilius' memoirs are not cited but some content may be smuggled in as the "conversation" Cicero claims to have had with him. Sulla's massive twenty-two-book autobiography, like any reference to the dictator's oratory, is passed over in one of the dialogue's blaring silences.[3] Cicero had happily written about his own life, in both Greek and Latin, seeking to slot himself into this tradition of political memoirists.[4] Among Greco-Roman scholars Varro seems to have most closely paralleled Cicero's endeavors, although we again have no evidence or reason to think that, despite their shared interest in the literary past, the two intellectual rivals developed the same theoretical framework.[5]

The greatest contribution of the *Brutus* must be stated outright: Cicero invented literary history, or at least literary history as we have come to understand its main features in the tradition of European letters. His major accomplishment was to compose (in the original sense of *componere*, "put together") a framework for documenting the history of an artistic practice, and he did so by selecting from the diverse and sometimes contradictory literary and scholarly talk of the late republic. There is no need to claim that, in a stroke of genius and in isolation, he created literary historiography without precedents. No creative mind advances in this way. His accomplishment is in having interwoven diverse strands of thought on how to conceptualize and represent cultural production across time.[6]

Crafting such a "modern" literary history meant not only incorporating several competing discourses but also countenancing their inevitable con-flicts and limitations. Cicero chose teleology as his model for literary development, documenting the various contributions and stages of improvement within an artistic tradition. His choices were not the only

---

[2] Nünlist (2015) 713–14 gives a succinct overview and bibliography.
[3] Scholz, Walter, and Winkle (2013) on republican memoirs.
[4] Isocrates' *Antidosis* presented a partial bio-rhetorical template for the Ciceropaideia.
[5] I am aware, in light of how much of Varro is lost, that we cannot know with certainty how different their conceptions of literary history were.
[6] Vasari's magnum opus, *Le vite de' più eccellenti pittori, scultori e architettori* (1550, rev. 1568), shows that Cicero's framework was relevant not just to literature. See Gombrich (1960) and (1966). Several expected features of modern literary history listed in Most (2008) 198–200 are present in the *Brutus*, as well as at least some attempt to craft what he calls "a genuinely *literary* literary history," that is, "a distortion of the past of literature into an open future" (206). Cf. Hunter (2009), Farrell (2010), Grethlein (2017).

possibilities and ushered in several abiding problems, such as the conflict between antiquarianism and presentism in canon formation. Directly related to this problem is the conflict between absolute and relative standards: should one apply the standards of today or the past in judging a work of literature? As so often, Cicero looked to historical context for a workaround: the effectiveness of stylistic change in its contemporary setting secures it a place in literary history.

Investigating the literary past also means peering into the murky regions of meaningful change and causes: which innovations merit documentation and how do we know what caused them? Cicero partly advocates for contextualism, acknowledging the role history plays in shaping literature, but unlike many modern critical cults, he does not idolize historical context alone as the guiding genius of literary evolution. The syncrisis of Cato with Lysias, and indeed the entire question of how to appropriate past models, Greek or Roman, exemplifies the crucial gulf between the history of an art and the circumstances that effect artistic change. Authors do not respond solely to immediate contexts, but also fashion their craft on past models or alien traditions that are historically or contextually out of sync with the immediate lived experience of an author. This is one of the reasons why literary history cannot be accounted for by the same causal narratives that explain the histories of events (which are also imperfectly accounted for, but for different reasons). For all that we may acknowledge historicism's power, when speaking of literary causes we cannot reduce them to historical determinism any more than pure formalism.[7]

Cicero's historically informed view of literary models is the conceptual underpinning of his stylistic agenda in the *Brutus*. Diversity and forcefulness are derived from the history of oratorical styles documented throughout the dialogue. He thereby avoids relying on purely aesthetic justifications for style, citing the exemplary contributions of the past to promote his contemporary stylistic program. Greek and Roman luminaries have all contributed to the panoply of stylistic possibilities. We typically speak of this model as evolutionary or teleological, which is true, but it is also accretive, as each speaker or generation supplements past innovations and refinements. The exposition of Rome's oratorical past thereby becomes the greatest argument in support of Ciceronian style. While *de Oratore* presents his values dogmatically through the authority of Crassus, Antonius, and their fellow

---

[7] Perkins (1992) 128: "Historical contextualism tends to suppress critical intelligence." See also the seminal discussion by Wellek and Warren (1956) 263–82, with Wellek (1963) 37–53. Hinds (2010) teases out the rival claims of historicism and formalism for textual interpretation in classics.

travelers,[8] the *Brutus* presents a compelling diachronic basis for those values: oratorical diversity, culminating in *vis* and *copia*, must be the inevitable result of oratory's long trajectory at Rome.

This historical view of style also required a significant shift in the doctrine on diversity, which coincided with renewed appreciation of Demosthenes.[9] Demosthenes was exemplary because he remained publicly relevant and his style possessed the greatest range of effects: "you'd easily say that Demosthenes doesn't lack anything at all" (*cui nihil admodum desit Demosthenem facile dixeris*, 35).[10] He is not the sole model, however, because we may emulate his effectiveness but cannot imitate his style. Hence the transition in Cicero's thinking, as Elaine Fantham has remarked, from *imitatio* directed at a single forerunner to *imitatio* that champions a wealth of styles – this second model would win out among later authors who found it so alluring in Cicero's *Brutus*.[11]

Quintilian, for example, adamantly champions Cicero as *the* canonical figure, but equally champions diversity, and however simplistic, even pedantic, Book 10's pairing of authors with stylistic traits might seem, his *Institutio* underlines the need for the budding orator to master the greatest number of styles, which are to be found in the breadth offered by Rome's literary past. Seneca the Elder's declamatory encyclopedia displays a wealth of examples, and is billed as such for the edification of his sons. Pliny's *Epistles* elevate *varietas* to the chief compositional virtue of the epistolary corpus.[12]

But it was Pliny's contemporary and literary confidant, Tacitus, who endowed the Ciceronian lesson with a historical sensibility and ensured the powerful afterlife of Cicero's doctrine of diversity. Marcus Aper

---

[8] E.g. "Another [requirement for pleading], in which that divinely forceful excellence of the orator is perceived, is to state what needs to be said with embellishment, fullness, and variety" (*alterum est, in quo oratoris vis illa divina virtusque cernitur, ea, quae dicenda sunt, ornate, copiose varieque dicere, de Orat.* 2.221).

[9] This appreciation also dovetails nicely with the political appeal to Demosthenes in the *Philippics*. Set against the development in Greece and the ultimate futility of Demetrius' pleasing style, Cicero's criticism of the Atticists underscores their civic irrelevance. See Wooten (1983), Bishop (2019) 173–218. It was in some sense a revival of his post-consular exuberance and the "Demosthenic" corpus of consular speeches; cf. *Att.* 2.1.3 (SB 21), which emphasizes deliberative oratory and the combination of word and deed (perhaps as a better alternative to the uninspiring Greek commentary on his consulship, discussed at 2.1.2). Cape (2002) discusses the consular speeches.

[10] The passage is followed by a careful listing of his fullness, emphasized through pleonasm of *nihil* (×10) in Section 35. Cf. the definition of the *genus grande* in the *Orator*, connected to Demosthenes: "full, rich, serious, adorned, in which there is surely the greatest power" (*amplus copiosus, gravis ornatus, in quo profecto vis maxima est, Orat.* 97). Wooten (1997) is a salutary reminder of Cicero's skewed take on Demosthenes in the *Orator*.

[11] Fantham (1978a) and (1978b).   [12] Fitzgerald (2016), esp. 84–100 on Pliny.

reformulates the wealth of styles into a principle of change: "eloquence doesn't have one look alone, but even among those whom you dub ancients many sorts are found; what's different isn't automatically worse" (*non esse unum eloquentiae vultum, sed in illis quoque quos vocatis antiquos pluris species deprehendi, nec statim deterius esse quod diversum est, Dial.* 18.3). Cassius Severus, the watershed dividing ancient from modern oratory, let history and context prompt his innovations (Aper, again): "you know, he saw, as I was just saying, that the form and appearance of oratory must adapt in sync with the circumstances of a period and changes in taste" (*vidit namque, ut paulo ante dicebam, cum condicione temporum et diversitate aurium formam quoque ac speciem orationis esse mutandam, Dial.* 19.2). The observation explains why Cicero cannot be the sole model of style, as Tacitus adapts Ciceronian lessons in the spirit in which Cicero first appropriated Greeks and Romans.

The choice to make Demosthenes an ideal, the doctrine of diversity, and the desire to preserve past contributions also bear directly on conceptions and constructions of literary canons. The *Brutus* contains a powerful utilitarian justification for the diversity of the canon, which merits repeating amidst the sallies and retreats of the still-ongoing culture wars. Great models are meaningless without others to contextualize them, to instruct us, and to offer new perspectives. In the case of English literature, for example, it is not despite but because of Shakespeare's greatness that we should also read, say, Toni Morrison.[13] The canon anxiety of the 1990s was largely based on a misunderstanding of the reality that closed canons, in the secular tradition at least, have been the exception rather than the norm.[14] Indeed, the most productive interventions – those that would themselves become part of the canon – have always been, in one form or another, challenges to it.

Cicero's provocative staging of a canon debate shows that no one version can be correct. We possess, after all, every reason to challenge his excommunication of Appius Claudius Caecus from oratory's hallowed

---

[13] If we have absorbed the lessons of the *Brutus*, then one Ciceronian dictate is clear: any reasonable person will insist that reading Toni Morrison is valuable and required. No appeal to the School of Resentment (to use Harold Bloom's phrase) can deny the aesthetic value of her novels for expressing the experience of America.

[14] Well put by the philosopher John Searle in "The Storm Over the University," a review article in the *New York Review of Books* (6 Dec. 1990): "In my experience there never was, in fact, a fixed 'canon'; there was rather a certain set of tentative judgments about what had importance and quality. Such judgments are always subject to revision, and in fact they were constantly being revised." See further T. Gelzer (1975), Gorak (1997), Vardi (2003), Citroni (2006), Döpp (2008), and essays in Flashar (1979).

lists, the very man who deserves to inaugurate oratorical history at Rome. The delicious irony of Atticus' needling presentism – Cicero brilliantly makes this antiquarian play the ultra-modernist – only underscores the contingency of Cicero's oratorical catalogue. Instead it emerges from the *Brutus* that tussling with the canon, and coming to understand the political and intellectual stakes of canonization, are part and parcel of what literary histories not only can but in fact *must* do. Such debates never end, nor should they, and Cicero's inventive solution – to have Brutus say that he wishes to read authors who might otherwise elude a presentist canon – places pedagogical principles above the dictates of modern fashion.[15]

This debate is related to the uncertain status of oratory as a literary genre. Oratory and its texts are portrayed as subject to several cultural codes that also govern poetry. This hardly means that the two genres are the same, but it is a powerful reminder that literary history must accommodate its canons not only to new authors but to new and different types of cultural production. Generic expansion occurs not by assigning texts categorically to the abstract notion of literature (as it is, that modern term was foreign to Romans); instead, it requires identifying cross-generic similarities in the creation, circulation, evaluation, and employment of texts as literary artifacts. It is these social functions that eventually determine the canonical place of emerging types of literature.[16]

Another key emphasis of Cicero's literary history is the relationship of literature to the communal world, both the community of today and of the past. He offers an open-ended teleology by refusing to make himself the sole endpoint of all oratorical development. For all the self-serving gestures, he crafts a normative framework that can encompass Rome's oratorical future no less than its past. This teleology without a telos ultimately becomes a bridge from the aesthetic world of criticism to the political world of contemporary Rome: we write not only for ourselves now, but for a community in the future.

Cicero always sought to align individual and communal interests: "so we must all have the same aim in mind, that utility be the same for each individual and for all together" (*unum debet esse omnibus propositum, ut eadem sit utilitas uniuscuiusque et universorum, Off.* 3.26). Sean Gurd has argued that the community of revision in the *Brutus* is essentially political,

---

[15] As Richard Rorty (1998) 135 puts it: "canons are temporary, and touchstones replaceable." Morrison (1989) cogently defends canonical texts while showing how canons must necessarily evolve under the pressure of new contexts.
[16] See Farrell (2003), with bibliography, on classical genres.

that Caesarian perfection in his *commentarii* and his rule-bound analogical system preclude communal intervention in linguistic production and literary tradition.[17] Cicero insists on the principle of change, on the need for the revision of communal standards, and on the orator's accommodation to the audience. Stylistic developments are inevitable in any art and are inherently political in oratory: they form the basis for communal contributions to the state through public speech, unlike Caesar's perfect, yet isolated, *commentarii*.

Cicero embeds in his normative historiographical framework a means by which the Roman community will, indeed must, remain attached to the past, not by accepting it wholesale, which is the dirty business of classicism, but by valuing the past and the need for change at the same time. This is the privilege and burden of each generation of critics, scholars, and readers. Only a future community that can both revere and criticize past luminaries can sustain the communal connections that Cicero envisions as part of the *res publica*. Put pointedly: to espouse a closed canon is to be severed from the community, to be bereft of any communal value toward others or oneself.

The close interconnection of oratory with the community and civil order brings us back to Cicero's own view of oratory's purpose and its future under Caesarian rule. The *Brutus* shows that oratory thrives even in conditions of external war and civil unrest. Jarrett Welsh has argued that the choice to follow Varro and to place the beginnings of Latin poetry, and therefore literature, in 240 BCE also followed Varro's desire to place the beginning of Latin poetry in a time of peace rather than war. Leaving aside his compelling arguments and the valuable recovery of the Accian and Porcian mindsets, it is worth considering Cicero's stated claims about oratory's rise.[18]

Cicero had earlier remarked that oratory flourishes in the absence of internal and external conflict:

> You see, the passion for speaking doesn't usually arise among those who are establishing a government or warring or who are impeded and chained up by the domination of kings. Eloquence is the companion of peace, the associate of leisure, and the nursling as it were of a well-ordered state.

---

[17] Gurd (2012) 57–58.

[18] Welsh (2011) shows that Cicero has tendentiously suppressed Accius' dating of Livius' *Hymn to Juno Regina* in 207, in which Accius probably followed the Porcian chronology. Varro's *de Poetis* made 240 the beginning of poetry. Cicero's adoption of Varro's chronology need not entail adoption of his ideology *en bloc*. Cicero could just as easily have used Varro's redating of the beginning of Latin poetry as a convenient screen for different views on the history of oratory and its relationship to literature.

nec enim in constituentibus rem publicam nec in bella gerentibus nec in impeditis ac regum dominatione devinctis nasci cupiditas dicendi solet. pacis est comes otique socia et iam bene constitutae civitatis quasi alumna quaedam eloquentia. (45)

He may have had in mind Aristotle, who placed the development of Greek artistic practices in the period of leisure after the Persian Wars:[19]

Through wealth they found greater leisure and greater passion for virtue, emboldened by their deeds before and after the Persian Wars, searching after and acquiring all manner of knowledge indiscriminately.

σχολαστικώτεροι γὰρ γιγνόμενοι διὰ τὰς εὐπορίας καὶ μεγαλοψυχότεροι πρὸς τὴν ἀρετήν, ἔτι τε πρότερον καὶ μετὰ τὰ Μηδικὰ φρονηματισθέντες ἐκ τῶν ἔργων, πάσης ἥπτοντο μαθήσεως, οὐδὲν διακρίνοντες ἀλλ᾽ ἐπιζητοῦντες. (Arist. *Pol.* 1341a 28–32)

Yet in considering the possible beginnings of oratory and the general turmoil of the late republic, it is difficult to accept Cicero's connection of oratory to peace. Cethegus, best known as an ally of Scipio Africanus, inaugurates oratory while his career falls in the flush of the Second Punic War, and in fact Cicero's Ennius portrays his eloquence as integral to that war. The alternative beginning Cicero considered, Caecus' speech against Pyrrhus, shares this martial shortcoming. Cicero's larger claims about oratory and peace are undermined by the very examples he cites (or overlooks) for the beginnings of Roman oratory. The placement of Livius at the beginning of literature may well have been a concession to the idea that peace rather than war should accompany the beginning of literature. But Cicero's own options for oratory, be it his explicit choice, Cethegus, or the overlooked option, Caecus, place oratory's beginnings amidst war.

Furthermore, the last century of the republic was similarly marked by frequent, often violent, political strife, much of which fostered (and was fostered by) the use of oratory. If anything, the rise of oratory and its documentation in Cicero's own writings repeatedly align state disorder with the practice of oratory. Oratory may ensure peace by quelling or even instituting its own ordering violence, but aligning its development with peace is far less plausible. Perhaps no greater example exists than Cicero's monumental *de Oratore*, which stands as a testament to the oratorical

---

[19] Horace probably alludes to this passage to explain the rise of the arts: *Epist.* 2.1.93–102. See Brink (1963) 115, 196–98, (1982) 133–34, Citroni (2013) 202. Brink believes that 45 draws on Aristotle's Συναγωγὴ Τεχνῶν, but Cicero's citation seems (to me) to begin at 46. On the topos cf. also *de Orat.* 1.14, 1.30, 2.33.

greats whose fates were intertwined with the political upheaval of the 90s and 80s and the causes and fallout of the Social and Civil Wars. Cicero in fact built his reputation on public speech in times of public upheaval; witness the Catilinarian conspiracy – sedition quelled by oratory, and capital violence. Cicero even likened his deeds to Rome's salvation from the Germans by Marius and from Hannibal by Scipio.[20] Soon after the *Brutus* he wrote in the Demosthenic tradition passionate and monumental speeches against Antony, urging that Antony be declared a public enemy.

Tacitus draws the right conclusions:

> I'm not speaking of some inactive and calm thing and one that enjoys approval and restraint, but that great and notorious eloquence is the nursling of license, which fools call freedom. It's the companion of seditious actions, the goad of an unbridled people, lacking compliance, lacking sternness, contumacious, reckless, arrogant, and does not occur in well-ordered states.

> non de otiosa et quieta re loquimur et quae probitate et modestia gaudeat, sed est magna illa et notabilis eloquentia alumna licentiae, quam stulti libertatem vocant, comes seditionum, effrenati populi incitamentum, sine obsequio, sine severitate, contumax temeraria arrogans, quae in bene constitutis civitatibus non oritur. (Tac. *Dial.* 40.2)

The passage reverses the alignment of oratory with peaceful circumstances, offering not only several allusions to Cicero but a correction of his apparent claim.[21] At a distance of a century and a half, Tacitus understood the insurmountable discrepancy between Cicero's argument and the tumultuous reality of civic life in the late republic. Yet there may be underlying optimism in Cicero too: if war and upheaval in fact do not inhibit oratory, then the work's allusions to the civil war might also hold out the promise of a future for oratory and reinforce the importance of continuing to cultivate it in the present. Under Caesar oratory was on hiatus, not dead.[22]

Traditional readings of the *Brutus* have done much to obscure the uniqueness of Cicero's inquiry, in large part because they have not accounted for the complexity of the *Brutus* as a work of literature itself. They take the teleology to be the central point of the work and relegate the digressions to a position of adornment and distraction or, occasionally and

---

[20] Cic. *Cat.* 4.21.
[21] Tacitus also draws in part on Cic. *de Orat.* 2.35 (Antonius: *et languentis populi incitatio et effrenati moderatio*) and *Rep.* 1.68 (Scipio: *ex hac nimia licentia, quam illi solam libertatem putant*).
[22] Cf. Gowing (2000), C. Steel (2002), Charrier (2003).

less grudgingly, of doctrinal assertion. Yet the digressions contain the methodological reflections on literary history, while the teleology of orators in successive stages is a pretext that creates a place for the digressions. Of course neither the digressions nor the teleology could exist without one another in the *Brutus*. The digressions alone could only amount to what we call literary theory, while the teleological catalogue alone would be nothing but failed literary history.[23]

The much larger issue is how we choose to read a text such as the *Brutus* and whether we are willing to acknowledge it for what it is. My reading is intended to be more broadly applicable to other literary texts in the critical tradition. A work such as the *Brutus* must be read first on its own terms, which means carefully considering the literary elements before us: meaningful repetitions and omissions, parallels and images, the rhetorical manipulation of the material under discussion, and a host of other characteristics. In most cases, only after first getting a view of the work's larger construction is it then possible to determine how its constituent elements fit into that construction and how they are meaningful.

Chapter 8's discussion of Julius Caesar's *commentarii* offers an important caveat for appreciating Roman criticism and suggests that different interpretive assumptions can lead to very different readings of a literary-critical text such as the *Brutus*. The work's so-called digressions, including the most digressive parts of those digressions, are integral to its aesthetic and political claims. Scholars have not shied away from locating secondary allusions to Caesar's life in the judgment, and this book's claim that Cicero likens Caesar's *commentarii* to a nude statue of Venus (Praxiteles' Aphrodite of Knidos) is not intended to deny other possibilities. Cicero's description may well have been crafted with the understanding that different audiences might have different interpretations. Some may also prefer the traditional reading: Cicero depicts with reasonable accuracy the main stylistic features of Caesar's histories. However, a modern scholar who takes this immediate judgment as accurate contemporary evidence for Caesar's style may also face a disconcerting question: in a different context and for different purposes, how differently might Cicero have described Caesar's style?

The passage is a powerful reminder of the danger faced in extracting isolated statements from texts of ancient literary criticism. The oft-assumed status of such works as technical or theoretical treatises has made

---

[23] As de Man (1970) 401 provocatively put it: "a positivistic history of literature, treating it as if it were a collection of empirical data, can only be a history of what literature is not."

them liable to the curse of excerption, the tendency to read an isolated statement as the immediately transparent view of the author. Such statements then become mobile and redeployable, borrowed, traded, or pilfered like artifacts for museums of thought.

His judgment of Caesar serves as a reminder that Cicero's arguments are often as rhetorical as they are logical and that, however pathbreaking his conceptualization of literary history, not all claims merit the same recognition. Cicero's specious diatribe against the Atticists has largely gone unchallenged by modern scholars, while, for example, the arguments of Marcus Aper in Tacitus' *Dialogus* on the definition of *antiquus* have been dismissed as reductive sophistry that disqualifies his defense of imperial oratory (Tac. *Dial.* 17). Unlike Cicero, Aper has both literary precedent (Horace and Cicero) and a sounder analytical framework (the relationship between qualitative categories and chronology) to back his claims. The different receptions demonstrate well how scholarly preconceptions produce wildly varying treatments of similar material. Prejudices about political aims (anti- and pro-autocracy) have largely determined scholarly acceptance: the choice to believe Cicero and disbelieve Aper rests more on assumptions about their politics than on the strength of their arguments.

The dialogue's apparent flaws, including Cicero's remarkable penchant to select, suppress, or manipulate evidence, have limited our recognition of his literary-critical innovations. So have misunderstandings of the work's multifaceted purpose, as well as prejudices against ancient, and especially Roman, literary criticism. The orthodoxy has long held that ancient criticism is intrinsically flawed, a nascent stage of the art, whose complexity could only be revealed by modern theorists and critics millennia later. Such shortcomings are doubly felt for Roman critics because of supposed inferiority to their Greek confrères; as Michael Winterbottom notes, "Cicero, Horace and Quintilian, authoritative and influential though they were, not only rank inferior to the best Greek critics: they are not competing in the same field."[24] The rules of the game – to respond in kind to this scholar's metaphor – have yet to be adequately laid out, which accounts for our neglect of such texts and misunderstanding of the enduring value of Roman criticism.

The brilliance of Cicero's intellect would radiate for centuries across the field of oratory – or better put, rhetorical education and so all education – and across the field of philosophy too, oratory and philosophy being the

---

[24] Winterbottom (1982) 33.

main divisions in his twin afterlives.[25] The fate of his criticism, unless it fell under one of these two areas, was less fortunate. Roman criticism, much like Roman philosophy, has suffered greatly from not looking more like its Greek counterparts, whose aggressive forms of inquiry and abstract categorization, readily suspected by Cicero for being tedious hair-splitting without public relevance, have a shape more familiar and therefore more palatable to modern scholars. His great English biographer, Elizabeth Rawson, notes that he had "a sensitive and receptive, but not a deeply original, mind."[26] Even so great an advocate of Roman intellectual history would not balk at calling him unsympathetically derivative, an opinion, or prejudice, unquestioningly repackaged and retailed by some of even the most devoted students of Greco-Roman criticism.

Yet the contributions to literary historiography and to Greco-Roman criticism, if the readings of this book are valid, undoubtedly belong to a capacious and innovative mind. Cicero did not think it sufficient to offer a catalogue of oratory and to connect oratory to the governing of the *res publica*, although that alone would have been a great achievement. Instead he also crafted a critical framework and a critical idiom with which to write a compelling and pleasing account of an artistic past. He drew not only from the vibrant intellectual discourses of the late republic, but also from the urgent realization that the republic he had known might cease to exist.

In the *Brutus* Cicero has contributed more than any other thinker in the Western tradition to the foundation on which accounts of the literary past continue to be built. It is a kind of revolution in literary criticism and history, not the astronomical revolution of Copernicus noted in this book's Introduction, but the kind of fundamental reconceptualization that Kant's first *Kritik* would signal for modern philosophy at the end of the eighteenth century. In crafting a new and enduring framework for literary historiography, Cicero was outdone not by any of the Greeks before him and from whom he first learned both literature and how to judge it, not by any of his contemporaries, who avidly pursued new possibilities for literary expression and documenting the past, and, despite unquestionable advances and occasional relapses in the intervening millennia, not by any thinker since.

---

[25] For documentation of Cicero's imperial afterlife, see Gowing (2013), MacCormack (2013), Bishop (2015), Keeline (2018), and La Bua (2019).

[26] Rawson (1983) 3. The preface to the second edition, written as she was completing the exemplary *Intellectual Life in the Late Roman Republic* (1985), does acknowledge that Cicero possessed "greater intellectual maturity than most of his contemporaries" (Rawson 1983 vi).

References

Adamietz, J. (ed.) (1966) *Quintiliani Institutionis oratoriae liber iii*. Munich: Fink.
Allen, W. (1954) "Cicero's Conceit," *TAPhA* 85: 121–44.
Altman, W. H. F. (2016) *The Revival of Platonism in Cicero's Late Philosophy: Platonis aemulus and the Invention of Cicero*. Lanham, MD: Lexington.
André, J. M. (1966) *L'otium dans la vie morale et intellectuelle romaine: des origines à l'époque augustéenne*. Paris: Presses Universitaires de France.
Assenmaker, P. (2007) "'Pignus salutis atque imperii': l'enjeu du Palladium dans les luttes politiques de la fin de la République," *LEC* 75: 381–412.
  (2010) "La place du Palladium dans l'idéologie augustéenne: entre mythologie, religion et politique," in I. Baglioni (ed.), *Storia delle religioni e archeologia: discipline a confronto*. Rome: Alpes Italia. 35–64.
Assfahl, G. (1932) *Vergleich und Metapher bei Quintilian*. Stuttgart: Kohlhammer.
Atkins, J. W. (2013) *Cicero on Politics and the Limits of Reason: The Republic and Laws*. Cambridge University Press.
  (2018) *Roman Political Thought*. Cambridge University Press.
Atkins, J. W. H. (1934) *Literary Criticism in Antiquity: A Sketch of Its Development*. Cambridge University Press.
Aubert, S. (2010) "La polémique cicéronienne contre Atticistes et Stoiciens autour de la santé du style," in P. Chiron and C. Lévy (eds.), *Les noms du style dans l'antiquité gréco-latine*. Louvain; Walpole, MA: Peeters. 87–111.
Aubert-Baillot, S. (2014) "La rhétorique du Stoïcien Rutilius Rufus dans le Brutus," in Aubert-Baillot and Guérin (eds.), 123–40.
Aubert-Baillot, S. and Guérin, C. (eds.) (2014) *Le Brutus de Cicéron: rhétorique, politique et histoire culturelle*. Leiden and Boston, MA: Brill.
Badian, E. (1964) *Studies in Greek and Roman History*. Oxford: Blackwell.
  (1967) Review of E. Malcovati: Cicero, *Brutus*; and A. E. Douglas: Cicero, *Brutus*, *JRS* 57: 223–30.
  (1969) "Quaestiones Variae," *Historia* 18: 447–91.
  (1972) "Ennius and His Friends," in O. Skutsch (ed.), *Ennius*. Geneva: Fondation Hardt. 149–208.
Bakhtin, M. M. (1981) *The Dialogic Imagination: Four Essays*, ed. M. Holquist, tr. C. Emerson and M. Holquist. Austin: University of Texas Press.
Balbo, A. (2013) "Marcus Junius Brutus the Orator: Between Philosophy and Rhetoric," in C. Steel and H. van der Blom (eds.), *Community and*

Communication: Oratory and Politics in Republican Rome. Oxford University Press. 315–28.

Baraz, Y. (2012) *A Written Republic: Cicero's Philosophical Politics.* Princeton University Press.

Barber, E. J. W. (1992) "The Peplos of Athena," in J. Neils (ed.), *Goddess and Polis: The Panathenaic Festival in Ancient Athens.* Princeton University Press. 103–17.

Barchiesi, M. (1962) *Nevio epico.* Padua: Cedam.

Barwick, K. (1963) *Das rednerische Bildungsideal Ciceros.* Berlin: Akademie.

Beard, M. (2007) *The Roman Triumph.* Cambridge University Press.

   (2013) *"Quousque tandem . . . ?"* (review of Everitt 2001), in *Confronting the Classics: Traditions, Adventures, and Innovations.* New York: Liveright. 79–87.

Beck, H. (2005) *Karriere und Hierarchie: die römische Aristokratie und die Anfänge des Cursus Honorum in der mittleren Republik.* Berlin: Akademie.

Bell, A. J. E. (1997) "Cicero and the Spectacle of Power," *JRS* 87: 1–22.

Bennett, C. (2003) "The Early Augustan Calendars in Rome and Egypt," *ZPE* 142: 221–40.

Bernstein, F. (1998) *Ludi Publici: Untersuchungen zur Entstehung und Entwicklung der öffentlichen Spiele im republikanischen Rom.* Stuttgart: Franz Steiner.

Berthold, H. (1965) "Die Gestalt des Themistokles bei M. Tullius Cicero," *Klio* 43: 38–48.

Bishop, C. (2015) "Roman Plato or Roman Demosthenes? The Bifurcation of Cicero in Ancient Scholarship," in W. H. F Altman (ed.), *Brill's Companion to the Reception of Cicero.* Leiden: Brill. 283–306.

   (2019) *Cicero, Greek Learning, and the Making of a Roman Classic.* Oxford University Press.

Blösel, W. (2011) "Die Demilitarisierung der römischen Nobilität von Sulla bis Caesar," in W. Blösel and K.-J. Hölkeskamp (eds.), *Von der militia equestris zur militia urbana: Prominenzrollen und Karrierefelder im antiken Rom.* Stuttgart: Steiner. 55–80.

Bodel, J. P. (2008) "Cicero's Minerva, Penates, and the Mother of the Lares: An Outline of Roman Domestic Religion," in J. P. Bodel and S. M. Olyan (eds.), *Household and Family Religion in Antiquity.* Malden, MA, and Oxford: Blackwell. 248–75.

Bolonyai, G. (1993) "Iudicium docti indoctique," *AAntHung* 34: 103–37.

Bonner, S. (1977) *Education in Ancient Rome: From the Elder Cato to the Younger Pliny.* Berkeley: University of California Press.

Bowersock, G. W. (1979) "Historical Problems in Late Republican and Augustan Classicism," in Flashar (ed.), 57–78.

Boyancé, P. (1940) "Sur Cicéron et l'histoire (*Brutus,* 41–43)," *REA* 42: 388–92.

   (1941) *"Cum dignitate otium,"* *REA* 43: 172–91.

Bréguet, E. (1967) "A propos de quelques exemples historiques dans le *De re publica* de Cicéron, I, 3, 5–6," *Latomus* 26: 597–608.

Brennan, T. C. (2000) *The Praetorship in the Roman Republic.* 2 vols. Oxford University Press.

(2014) "Power and Process under the Republican 'Constitution,'" in H. Flower (ed.), *The Cambridge Companion to the Roman Republic*. Cambridge University Press. 19–53.

Bringmann, K. (1971) *Untersuchungen zum späten Cicero*. Göttingen: Vandenhoeck & Ruprecht.

Brink, C. O. (1963) *Horace on Poetry: Prolegomena to the Literary Epistles*. Cambridge University Press.

(1982) *Horace on Poetry: Epistles, Book II*. Cambridge University Press.

(1989) "Quintilian's *De Causis Corruptae Eloquentiae* and Tacitus' *Dialogus de Oratoribus*," *CQ* 39: 472–503.

Brittain, C. (2001) *Philo of Larissa: The Last of the Academic Sceptics*. Oxford: Clarendon Press.

Brunt, P. A. (1988) *The Fall of the Roman Republic and Related Essays*. Oxford: Clarendon Press.

Burke, K. (1973) *The Philosophy of Literary Form: Studies in Symbolic Action*, 3rd ed. Berkeley: University of California Press.

Cadario, M. (2006) "Le statue di Cesare a Roma tra il 46 e il 44 a.C.: la celebrazione della vittoria e il confronto con Alessandro e Romolo," *Acme* 59: 25–70.

Cape, R. W. (2002) "Cicero's Consular Speeches," in May (ed.), 113–58.

Castorina, E. (1952) *L'atticismo nell'evoluzione del pensiero di Cicerone*. Catania: Giannotta.

Cavarzere, A. (1998) "La funzione di Ortensio nel prologo del *Brutus*," *Lexis* 16: 149–62.

(2012) "Coscienza del progresso e consapevolezza del presente: Cicerone, *Brutus* 22–23," in M. Citroni (ed.), *Letteratura e civitas: transizioni dalla Repubblica all'Impero: in ricordo di Emanuele Narducci*. Pisa: ETS. 99–115.

(2018) "Gaius Titius, Orator and Poeta. (Cic. Brut. 167 and Macrob. Sat. 3.16.4–16)," in Gray et al. (eds.), 153–70.

Charrier, S. (2003) "Les années 90–80 dans le *Brutus* de Cicéron (§§ 304–312): la formation d'un orateur au temps des guerres civiles," *REL* 81: 79–96.

Chassignet, M. (2003) "La naissance de l'autobiographie à Rome: *laus sui* ou *apologia de vita sua*?" *REL* 81: 65–78.

Chiron, P. (2014) "Démétrios de Phalère dans le *Brutus*," in Aubert-Baillot and Guérin (eds.) 105–20.

Cichorius, C. (1922) *Römische Studien*. Leipzig: Teubner.

Citroni, M. (2001) "Affermazioni di priorità e coscienza di progresso artistico nei poeti latini," in E. A. Schmidt (ed.), *L'histoire littéraire immanente dans la poésie latine*. Geneva: Fondation Hardt. 267–314.

(2005) "Orazio, Cicerone, e il tempo della letteratura," in J. P. Schwindt (ed.), *La représentation du temps dans la poésie augustéenne / Zur Poetik der Zeit in augusteischer Dichtung*. Heidelberg: Winter. 123–39.

(2006) "The Concept of the Classical and the Canons of Model Authors in Roman Literature," in J. I. Porter (ed.), *Classical Pasts: The Classical Traditions of Greece and Rome*. Princeton University Press. 204–34.

(2013) "Horace's *Epistle* 2.1, Cicero, Varro, and the Ancient Debate about the Origins and the Development of Latin Poetry," in J. A. Farrell and D. P. Nelis (eds.), *Augustan Poetry and the Roman Republic*. Oxford University Press. 180–204.

Corbeill, A. P. (2001) "Education in the Roman Republic: Creating Traditions," in Y. L. Too (ed.), *Education in Greek and Roman Antiquity*. Leiden: Brill. 261–87.

(2018a) "Anticato," in Grillo and Krebs (eds.), 215–22.

(2018b) "Clodius' Contio de haruspicum responsis," in Gray et al. (eds.), 171–90.

Courtney, E. (2003) *The Fragmentary Latin Poets*. Oxford University Press.

Craig, C. P. (1993) *Form as Argument in Cicero's Speeches: A Study of Dilemma*. Atlanta, GA: Scholars Press.

Crane, R. S. (1971) *Critical and Historical Principles of Literary History*. University of Chicago Press.

Crawford, J. W. (1984) *M. Tullius Cicero: The Lost and Unpublished Orations*. Göttingen: Vandenhoeck & Ruprecht.

(ed.) (1994) *M. Tullius Cicero: The Fragmentary Speeches: An Edition with Commentary*, 2nd ed. Atlanta, GA: Scholars Press.

Crook, J. A. (1995) *Legal Advocacy in the Roman World*. Ithaca, NY: Cornell University Press.

Culham, P. (1989) "Archives and Alternatives in Republican Rome," *CPh* 134: 100–15.

Dahlmann, H. (1953) *Varros Schrift De poematis und die hellenistisch-römische Poetik*. Wiesbaden: Steiner.

(1962) *Studien zu Varro De poetis*. Wiesbaden: Steiner.

(1963) "Zu Varros Literaturforschung, besonders in 'De poetis,'" in H. Dahlmann et al. (eds.), *Varron*. Geneva: Fondation Hardt. 1–31.

Dahlmann, H. and Heisterhagen, R. (1957) *Varronische Studien I: zu den Logistorici*. Mainz: Steiner.

D'Alton, J. F. (1931) *Roman Literary Theory and Criticism: A Study in Tendencies*. New York: Russell & Russell.

D'Ambra, E. (1996) "The Calculus of Venus: Nude Portraits of Roman Matrons," in N. B. Kampen (ed.), *Sexuality in Ancient Art: Near East, Egypt, Greece, and Italy*. Cambridge University Press. 219–32.

Damon, C. (1994) "Caesar's Practical Prose," *CJ* 89: 183–95.

Dangel, J. (ed. and tr.) (1995) *Accius: Oeuvres (Fragments)*. Paris: Les Belles Lettres.

D'Anna, G. (1984) "Il problema delle origini della poesia latina nel *Brutus* di Cicerone," *Ciceroniana* 5: 81–90.

(1996) "La cronologia dei poeti latini arcaici in Cicerone," in *Per Enrica Malcovati: atti del convegno di studi nel centenario della nascita*. Como: New Press. 91–104.

David, J.-M. (1992) *Le patronat judiciaire au dernier siècle de la République romaine*. Rome: École française de Rome.

(2014) "La function des modèles dans l'articulation chronologique du *Brutus*," in Aubert-Baillot and Guérin (eds.), 19–38.

Degl'Innocenti Pierini, R. (1980) *Studi su Accio*. Florence: CLUSF.

Deichgräber, K. (1950) "Elegantia Caesaris: zu Caesars Reden und 'Commentarii.'" *Gymnasium* 57: 112–23.

de Jonge, C. C. (2013) "Longinus 36.3: The Faulty Colossus and Plato's *Phaedrus*," *Trends in Classics* 5: 318–40.

(2014) "The Attic Muse and the Asian Harlot: Classicizing Allegories in Dionysius and Longinus," in C. Pieper and J. Ker (eds.), *Valuing the Past in the Greco-Roman World*. Leiden: Brill. 388–409.

Delarue, F. (1982) "L'asianisme à Rome," *REL* 60: 166–85.

de Man, P. (1970) "Literary History and Literary Modernity," *Daedalus* 99: 384–404.

(1986) *The Resistance to Theory*. Minneapolis: University of Minnesota Press.

Dench, E. (2009) "The Roman Historians and Twentieth-century Approaches to Roman History," in Feldherr (ed.), 394–406.

Desmouliez, A. (1952) "Sur la polémique de Cicéron et des atticistes," *REL* 30: 168–85.

(1982) "A propos du jugement de Cicéron sur Caton l'ancien (Brutus XVI–XVIII 63–69 et LXXXV–LXXXVII 292–300)," *Philologus* 126: 70–89.

Dettenhofer, M. H. (1992) *Perdita iuventus: zwischen den Generationen von Caesar und Augustus*. Munich: Beck.

Dihle, A. (1957) "Analogie und Attizismus," *Hermes* 85: 170–205.

(1977) "Der Beginn des Attizismus," *A&A* 23: 162–77.

Döpp, S. (2008) "Klassik in lateinischer Literatur: antike Ansätze zur Konstituierung der Epoche," *Gymnasium* 115: 47–67.

Douglas, A. E. (1955a) "M. Calidius and the Atticists," *CQ* 5: 241–47.

(1955b) "The Aristotelian Συναγωγὴ Τεχνῶν after Cicero, *Brutus*, 46–48," *Latomus* 14: 536–39.

(1966a) *M. Tulli Ciceronis Brutus*. Oxford: Clarendon Press.

(1966b) "*Oratorum Aetates*," *AJPh* 87: 290–306.

(1973) "The Intellectual Background of Cicero's Rhetorica: A Study in Method," *ANRW* 1/3: 95–138.

Driediger-Murphy, L. G. (2019) *Roman Republican Augury: Freedom and Control*. Oxford University Press.

Due, B. (1989) *The Cyropaedia: Xenophon's Aims and Methods*. Aarhus University Press.

Dugan, J. (2005) *Making a New Man: Ciceronian Self-Fashioning in the Rhetorical Works*. Oxford University Press.

(2012) "*Scriptum* and *voluntas* in Cicero's *Brutus*," in M. Citroni (ed.), *Letteratura e civitas: transizioni dalla Repubblica all'Impero: in ricordo di Emanuele Narducci*. Pisa: ETS. 117–28.

(2018) "Netting the Wolf-Fish: Gaius Titius in Macrobius and Cicero," in Gray et al. (eds.), 135–48.

Dupraz, E. (2007) "Appius Claudius Caecus comme fondateur de la littérature latine," in B. Bureau and C. Nicolas (eds.), *Commencer et finir: débuts et fins dans les littératures grecque, latine et néolatine*. Lyon: Éditions CERGR. 21–42.

Dyck, A. R. (1996) *A Commentary on Cicero, De officiis*. Ann Arbor: University of Michigan Press.

(2003) *A Commentary on Cicero, De legibus*. Ann Arbor: University of Michigan Press.

(2008) "Rivals into Partners: Hortensius and Cicero," *Historia* 57: 142–73.

(2012) *Marcus Tullius Cicero: Speeches on Behalf of Marcus Fonteius and Marcus Aemilius Scaurus*. Oxford University Press.

Earl, D. C. (1967) *The Moral and Political Tradition of Rome*. London: Thames & Hudson.

Eckert, A. (2018) "Roman Orators between Greece and Rome: The Case of Cato the Elder, L. Crassus, and M. Antonius," in Gray et al. (eds.), 19–32.

Edelstein, L. (1967) *The Idea of Progress in Classical Antiquity*. Baltimore, MD: Johns Hopkins University Press.

Eden, P. T. (1962) "Caesar's Style: Inheritance versus Intelligence," *Glotta* 40: 74–117.

Elliott, J. (2013) *Ennius and the Architecture of the Annales*. Cambridge University Press.

Erasmus, D. (1528 [1986]) *Dialogus Ciceronianus*, tr. B. I. Knott, in A. H. T. Levi (ed.), *Collected Works of Erasmus*, vol. XXVIII. University of Toronto Press.

Everitt, A. (2001) *Cicero: The Life and Times of Rome's Greatest Politician*. London: John Murray.

Fairweather, J. (1981) *Seneca the Elder*. Cambridge University Press.

Fantham, E. (1972) *Comparative Studies in Republican Latin Imagery*. University of Toronto Press.

(1977) "Cicero, Varro, and M. Claudius Marcellus," *Phoenix* 31: 208–13.

(1978a) "Imitation and Evolution: The Discussion of Rhetorical Imitation in Cicero *De Oratore* 2. 87–97 and Some Related Problems of Ciceronian Theory," *CPh* 73: 1–16.

(1978b) "Imitation and Decline: Rhetorical Theory and Practice in the First Century after Christ," *CPh* 73: 102–16.

(1979) "On the Use of *Genus*-Terminology in Cicero's Rhetorical Works," *Hermes* 107: 441–59.

(1981) "The Synchronistic Chapter of Gellius (*NA* 17.21) and Some Aspects of Roman Chronology and Cultural History between 60 and 50 B.C.," *LCM* 6: 7–17.

(1988) "*Varietas* and *satietas*: *De oratore* 3.96–103 and the Limits of *ornatus*," *Rhetorica* 6: 275–90.

(2004) *The Roman World of Cicero's De oratore*. Oxford University Press.

(2006) Review of J. Dugan, *Making a New Man: Ciceronian Self-fashioning in the Rhetorical Works*. *Hermathena* 181: 249–52.

Farrell, J. A. (2003) "Classical Genre in Theory and Practice," *New Literary History* 34: 383–408.

(2010) "Literary Criticism," in A. Barchiesi and W. Scheidel (eds.), *The Oxford Handbook of Roman Studies*. Oxford University Press. 176–87.

Feeney, D. C. (2002) "*Una cum scriptore meo*: Poetry, Principate and the Traditions of Literary History in the Epistle to Augustus," in T. Woodman and D. C. Feeney (eds.), *Traditions and Contexts in the Poetry of Horace*. Cambridge University Press. 172–86.

   (2005) "The Beginnings of a Literature in Latin: Review Article," *JRS* 95: 226–40.

   (2007) *Caesar's Calendar: Ancient Time and the Beginnings of History*. Berkeley: University of California Press.

   (2010) "Time and Calendar," in A. Barchiesi and W. Scheidel (eds.), *The Oxford Handbook of Roman Studies*. Oxford University Press. 882–94.

   (2016) *Beyond Greek: The Beginnings of Latin Literature*. Cambridge, MA: Harvard University Press.

Feldherr, A. (ed.) (2009) *The Cambridge Companion to the Roman Historians*. Cambridge University Press.

Filbey, E. J. (1911) "Concerning the Oratory of Brutus," *CPh* 6: 325–33.

Fitzgerald, W. (2016) *Variety: The Life of a Roman Concept*. University of Chicago Press.

Flaig, E. (2003) *Ritualisierte Politik: Zeichen, Gesten und Herrschaft im Alten Rom*. Göttingen: Vandenhoeck & Ruprecht.

Flashar, H. (ed.) (1979) *Le classicisme à Rome aux I^{ers} siècles avant et après J.-C.* Geneva: Fondation Hardt.

Flower, H. I. (1996) *Ancestor Masks and Aristocratic Power in Roman Culture*. Oxford University Press.

   (2010) *Roman Republics*. Princeton University Press.

   (2014) "Memory and Memoirs in Republican Rome," in G. K. Galinsky (ed.), *Memoria Romana: Memory in Rome and Rome in Memory*. Ann Arbor: University of Michigan Press. 27–40.

Fogel, J. (2007) "The Descent of Style in Cicero's *Brutus*," *Scholia* 16: 42–68.

Föllinger, S. and Müller, G. M. (eds.) (2013) *Der Dialog in der Antike: Formen und Funktionen einer literarischen Gattung zwischen Philosophie, Wissensvermittlung und dramatischer Inszenierung*. Berlin: de Gruyter.

Ford, A. (2002) *The Origins of Criticism: Literary Culture and Poetic Theory in Classical Greece*. Princeton University Press.

Fortenbaugh, W. W. (1988) "*Benevolentiam conciliare* and *animos permovere*: Some Remarks on Cicero's *De Oratore* 2.178–216," *Rhetorica* 6: 259–73.

Fox, M. (2007) *Cicero's Philosophy of History*. Oxford University Press.

   (2009) "Heraclides of Pontus and the Philosophical Dialogue," in W. W. Fortenbaugh and E. Pender (eds.), *Heraclides of Pontus: Discussion*. New Brunswick, NJ: Transaction. 41–68.

Frampton, S. (2019) *Empire of Letters: Writing in Roman Literature and Thought from Lucretius to Ovid*. New York: Oxford University Press.

Frazel, T. D. (2009) *The Rhetoric of Cicero's In Verrem*. Göttingen: Vandenhoeck & Ruprecht.

Frisch, P. (1985) "Cicero, *Brutus* 218–219 – eine Episode mit Widerhaken," *ZPE* 58: 297–99.

Gadamer, H.-G. (1989) *Truth and Method*, 2nd ed., tr. rev. J. Weinsheimer and D. G. Marshall. London: Continuum.

Gagarin, M. (2002) *Antiphon the Athenian: Oratory, Law, and Justice in the Age of the Sophists*. Austin: University of Texas Press.

Gaines, R. N. (1995) "Cicero's Response to the Philosophers in *De oratore*, Book 1," in W. B. Horner and M. Leff (eds.), *Rhetoric and Pedagogy: Its History, Philosophy, and Practice: Essays in Honor of James J. Murphy*. Mahwah, NJ: Erlbaum. 43–56.

Gallagher, C. and Greenblatt, S. (2000) *Practicing New Historicism*. University of Chicago Press.

Garcea, A. (2012) *Caesar's De analogia*. Oxford University Press.

Geffcken, K. A. (1973) *Comedy in the Pro Caelio, with an Appendix on the In Clodium et Curionem*. Leiden: Brill.

Gelzer, M. (1938) "Ciceros *Brutus* als politische Kundgebung," *Philologus* 93: 128–31.
(2014) *Cicero: ein biographischer Versuch*, 3rd ed., ed. W. Riess. Stuttgart: Steiner.

Gelzer, T. (1975) "Klassik und Klassizismus," *Gymnasium* 82: 147–73.
(1979) "Klassizismus, Attizismus und Asianismus," in Flashar (ed.), 1–41.

Gera, D. L. (1993) *Xenophon's Cyropaedia: Style, Genre, and Literary Technique*. Oxford: Clarendon Press.

Gibson, R. and Steel, C. (2010) "The Indistinct Literary Careers of Cicero and Pliny the Younger," in P. Hardie and H. Moore (eds.), *Classical Literary Careers and Their Reception*. Oxford University Press. 118–37.

Gildenhard, I. (2003) "The 'Annalist' before the Annalists: Ennius and His *Annales*," in U. Eigler, U. Gotter, N. Luraghi, and U. Walter (eds.), *Formen römischer Geschichtsschreibung von den Anfängen bis Livius: Gattungen, Autoren, Kontexte*. Darmstadt: Wissenschaftliche Buchgesellschaft. 93–114.
(2007) *Paideia Romana: Cicero's Tusculan Disputations*. Cambridge Philological Society.
(2011) *Creative Eloquence: The Construction of Reality in Cicero's Speeches*. Oxford University Press.
(2013a) "Of Cicero's Plato: Fictions, Forms, Foundations," in Schofield (ed.), 225–75.
(2013b) "Cicero's Dialogues: Historiography Manqué and the Evidence of Fiction," in Föllinger and Müller (eds.), 225–74.
(2018) "A Republic in Letters: Epistolary Communities in Cicero's Correspondence, 49–44 BCE," in P. Ceccarelli, L. Doering, T. Fögen, and I. Gildenhard (eds.), *Letters and Communities: Studies in the Socio-political Dimensions of Ancient Epistolography*. Oxford University Press. 205–38.

Gildenhard, I. and Zissos, A. (2004) "Ovid's 'Hecale': Deconstructing Athens in the *Metamorphoses*," *JRS* 94: 47–72.

Goh, I. (2018) "An Asianist Sensation: Horace on Lucilius as Hortensius," *AJPh* 139: 641–74.

Goldberg, S. M. (1995) *Epic in Republican Rome.* Oxford University Press.

(2005) *Constructing Literature in the Roman Republic: Poetry and Its Reception.* Cambridge University Press.

(2006) "Ennius after the Banquet," *Arethusa* 39: 427–47.

Goltz, A. (2000) "*Maiestas sine viribus*: die Bedeutung der Lictoren für die Konfliktbewältigungsstrategien römischer Magistrate," in B. Linke and M. Stemmler (eds.), *Mos maiorum: Untersuchungen zu den Formen der Identitätsstiftung und Stabilisierung in der römischen Republik.* Stuttgart: Steiner. 237–67.

Gombrich, E. H. (1960) "Vasari's *Lives* and Cicero's *Brutus*," *JWI* 23: 309–11.

(1966) "The Debate on Primitivism in Ancient Rhetoric," *JWI* 29: 24–38.

Gorak, J. (1997) "Canons and Canon Formation," in H. B. Nisbet and C. Rawson (eds.), *The Cambridge History of Literary Criticism*, vol. IV: *The Eighteenth Century.* Cambridge University Press. 560–84.

Görler, W. (1974) *Untersuchungen zu Ciceros Philosophie.* Heidelberg: Winter.

(1988) "From Athens to Tusculum: Gleaning the Background of Cicero's *De oratore*," *Rhetorica* 6: 215–35.

Gotoff, H. C. (1979) *Cicero's Elegant Style: An Analysis of the Pro Archia.* Urbana: University of Illinois Press.

(1984) "Towards a Practical Criticism of Caesar's Prose Style," *ICS* 9: 1–18.

(1993) *Cicero's Caesarian Speeches: A Stylistic Commentary.* Chapel Hill: University of North Carolina Press.

(2002) "Cicero's Caesarian Orations," in May (ed.), 219–71.

Gowing, A. M. (2000) "Memory and Silence in Cicero's *Brutus*," *Eranos* 98: 39–64.

(2013) "Tully's Boat: Responses to Cicero in the Imperial Period," in C. Steel (ed.), 233–50.

Granatelli, R. (1990) "L'*in utramque partem disserendi exercitatio* nell'evoluzione del pensiero retorico e filosofico dell'antichità," *Vichiana*, 3rd ser., 1–2: 165–81.

Graver, M. (2002) *Cicero on the Emotions: Tusculan Disputations 3 and 4.* University of Chicago Press.

Gray, C., Balbo, A., Marshall, R. M. A., and Steel, C. (eds.) (2018) *Reading Republican Oratory: Reconstructions, Contexts, Receptions.* Oxford University Press.

Greenidge, A. H. J. (1901) *The Legal Procedure of Cicero's Time.* Oxford: Clarendon Press.

Grethlein, J. (2017) "Literary History! The Case of Ancient Greek Literature," in Grethlein and Rengakos (eds.), 11–29.

Grethlein, J. and Rengakos, A. (eds.) (2017) *Griechische Literaturgeschichtsschreibung: Traditionen, Probleme und Konzepte.* Berlin: de Gruyter.

Griffin, M. T. (ed.) (2009) *A Companion to Julius Caesar.* Malden, MA: Wiley-Blackwell.

Grillo, L. (2012) *The Art of Caesar's Bellum Civile: Literature, Ideology, and Community.* Cambridge University Press.

Grillo, L. and Krebs, C. B. (eds.) (2018) *The Cambridge Companion to the Writings of Julius Caesar.* Cambridge University Press.

Gruen, E. S. (1966) "Political Prosecutions in the 90's B.C.," *Historia* 15: 32–64.

(1967) "Cicero and Licinius Calvus," *HSPh* 71: 215–33.

(1968) *Roman Politics and the Criminal Courts, 149–78 B.C.* Cambridge, MA: Harvard University Press.

(1974) *The Last Generation of the Roman Republic.* Berkeley: University of California Press.

(1990) *Studies in Greek Culture and Roman Policy.* Leiden: Brill.

(1991) "The Exercise of Power in the Roman Republic," in A. Molho, K. A. Raaflaub and J. Emle (eds.), *City States in Classical Antiquity and Medieval Italy: Athens and Rome, Florence and Venice.* Stuttgart: Steiner. 251–67.

(1992) *Culture and National Identity in Republican Rome.* Ithaca, NY: Cornell University Press.

Guérin, C. (2011) *Persona: l'élaboration d'une notion rhétorique au Ier siècle av. J.-C.,* vol. II: *Théorisation cicéronienne de la persona oratoire.* Paris: Vrin.

(2014) "*Oratorum bonorum duo genera sunt:* la définition de l'excellence stylistique et ses conséquences théoriques dans le *Brutus*," in Aubert-Baillot and Guérin (eds.), 161–89.

(2015) *La voix de la vérité: témoin et témoignage dans les tribunaux romains du Ier siècle avant J.-C.* Paris: Les Belles Lettres.

Gunderson, E. (2000) *Staging Masculinity: The Rhetoric of Performance in the Roman World.* Ann Arbor: University of Michigan Press.

Gurd, S. A. (2012) *Work in Progress: Literary Revision as Social Performance in Ancient Rome.* Oxford University Press.

Gutzwiller, K. (2014) "Contests of Style and Uses of the Middle in Canon Making," in M. Cojannot-Le Blanc, C. Pouzadoux, and É. Prioux (eds.), *L'héroïque et le champêtre 2: appropriation et déconstruction des théories stylistiques dans la pratique des artistes et dans les modalités d'exposition des œuvres.* Nanterre: Press Universitaires de Paris Ouest. 15–31.

Habinek, T. N. (1998) *The Politics of Latin Literature: Writing, Identity, and Empire in Ancient Rome.* Princeton University Press.

(2005) *The World of Roman Song: From Ritualized Speech to Social Order.* Baltimore, MD: Johns Hopkins University Press.

Haenni, P. R. (1905) *Die litterarische Kritik in Ciceros "Brutus."* Diss. University of Fribourg.

Hall, J. (2009) "Serving the Times: Cicero and Caesar the Dictator," in W. J. Dominik, J. Garthwaite, and P. A. Roche (eds.), *Writing Politics in Imperial Rome.* Leiden: Brill. 89–110.

(2014) "Cicero's *Brutus* and the Criticism of Oratorical Performance," *CJ* 110: 43–59.

Hall, U. (1990) "Greeks and Romans and the Secret Ballot," in E. M. Craik (ed.), *Owls to Athens: Essays on Classical Subjects Presented to Sir Kenneth Dover.* Oxford: Clarendon Press. 191–99.

(1998) *"Species libertatis*: Voting Procedure in the Late Roman Republic," in M. M. Austin, J. Harries, and C. J. Smith (eds.), *Modus operandi: Essays in Honour of Geoffrey Rickman*. Institute of Classical Studies, University of London. 15–30.

Hallett, C. H. (2005) *The Roman Nude: Heroic Portrait Statuary, 200 BC–AD 300*. Oxford University Press.

Halliwell, S. (1986) *Aristotle's Poetics*. Chapel Hill: University of North Carolina Press.

Hanchey, D. (2013) *"Otium* as Civic and Personal Stability in Cicero's Dialogues," *CW* 106: 171–97.

Hantos, T. (1988) *Res publica constituta: die Verfassung des Dictators Sulla*. Stuttgart: Steiner.

Hardie, P. R. (1993) *The Epic Successors of Virgil: A Study in the Dynamics of a Tradition*. Cambridge University Press.

Harris, W. V. (1979) *War and Imperialism in Republican Rome, 327–70 B.C.* Oxford University Press.

Havelock, C. M. (1995) *The Aphrodite of Knidos and Her Successors*. Ann Arbor: University of Michigan Press.

Heldmann, K. (1982) *Antike Theorien über Entwicklung und Verfall der Redekunst*. Munich: Beck.

Hellegouarc'h, J. (1972) *Le vocabulaire latin des relations et des partis politiques sous la République*, 2nd ed. Paris: Les Belles Lettres.

Hendrickson, G. L. (1904) "The Peripatetic Mean of Style and the Three Stylistic Characters," *AJPh* 25: 125–46.

(1906) "Literary Sources in Cicero's *Brutus* and the Technique of Citation in Dialogue," *AJPh* 27: 184–99.

(1926) "Cicero's Correspondence with Brutus and Calvus on Oratorical Style," *AJPh* 47: 234–58.

(1962) *Brutus*, in *Cicero: Brutus; Orator*, rev. ed. Cambridge, MA: Harvard University Press. 2–293.

Hesberg, H. von (1998) "Minerva Custos Urbis: zum Bildschmuck der Porta Romana in Ostia," in P. Kneissl and V. Losemann (eds.), *Imperium Romanum: Studien zur Geschichte und Rezeption: Festschrift für Karl Christ zum 75. Geburtstag*. Stuttgart: Steiner. 370–78.

Hiebel, D. (2009) *Rôles institutionnel et politique de la contio sous la république romaine (287–49 av. J.-C.)*. Paris: De Boccard.

Hinds, S. (1998) *Allusion and Intertext: Dynamics of Appropriation in Roman Poetry*. Cambridge University Press.

(2010) "Between Historicism and Formalism," in A. Barchiesi and W. Scheidel (eds.), *The Oxford Handbook of Roman Studies*. Oxford University Press. 369–85.

Hirzel, R. (1895) *Der Dialog: ein literarhistorischer Versuch*. 2 vols. Leipzig: S. Hirzel.

Hodgson, L. (2017) "'A Faded Reflection of the Gracchi': Ethics, Eloquence and the Problem of Sulpicius in Cicero's *De Oratore*," *CQ* 67: 163–81.

Hölkeskamp, K.-J. (1995) "*Oratoris maxima scaena*: Reden vor dem Volk in der politischen Kultur der Republik," in M. Jehne (ed.), *Demokratie in Rom? Die Rolle des Volkes in der Politik der römischen Republik.* Stuttgart: Steiner. 11–49.

(2010) *Reconstructing the Roman Republic: An Ancient Political Culture and Modern Research.* Princeton University Press.

(2011a) "Self-Serving Sermons: Oratory and the Self-Construction of the Republican Aristocrat," in C. Smith and R. Covino (eds.), *Praise and Blame in Roman Republican Rhetoric.* Swansea: Classical Press of Wales. 17–34.

(2011b) "The Roman Republic as Theatre of Power: The Consuls as Leading Actors," in H. Beck, A. Duplá, M. Jehne, and F. Pina Polo (eds.), *Consuls and Res Publica: Holding High Office in the Roman Republic.* Cambridge University Press. 161–81.

(ed.) (2017) *Libera Res Publica: die politische Kultur des antiken Rom: Positionen und Perspektiven.* Stuttgart: Steiner.

Horsfall, N. (1976) "The Collegium Poetarum," *BICS* 23: 79–95.

(1989) *Cornelius Nepos: A Selection, Including the Lives of Cato and Atticus.* Oxford: Clarendon Press.

Hose, M. (1999) "Die zweite Begegnung Roms mit den Griechen; oder: zu politischen Ursachen des Attizismus," in G. Vogt-Spira, B. Rommel, and I. Musäus (eds.), *Rezeption und Identität: die kulturelle Auseinandersetzung Roms mit Griechenland als europäisches Paradigma.* Stuttgart: Steiner. 274–88.

Hösle, V. (2006) *Der philosophische Dialog: eine Poetik und Hermeneutik.* Munich: Beck.

(2008) "Cicero's Plato," *WS* 121: 145–70.

Humm, M. (2004) "Numa et Pythagore: vie et mort d'un mythe," in P.-A. Deproost and A. Meurant (eds.), *Images d'origines, origines d'une image: hommages à Jacques Poucet.* Louvain-la-Neuve: Academia Bruylant. 125–37.

(2005) *Appius Claudius Caecus: la République accomplie.* Rome: École française de Rome.

(2009) "Rome et l'Italie dans le discours d'Appius Claudius Caecus contre Pyrrhus," *Pallas* 79: 203–20.

Hunter, R. L. (2009) *Critical Moments in Classical Literature: Studies in the Ancient View of Literature and Its Uses.* Cambridge University Press.

Hutchinson, G. O. (2013) *Greek to Latin: Frameworks and Contexts for Intertextuality.* Oxford University Press.

Innes, D. C. (1978) "Phidias and Cicero, *Brutus* 70," *CQ* 28: 470–71.

(2003) "Metaphor, Simile, and Allegory as Ornaments of Style," in G. R. Boys-Stones (ed.), *Metaphor, Allegory, and the Classical Tradition: Ancient Thought and Modern Revisions.* Oxford University Press. 7–27.

Jacotot, M. (2014) "*De republica esset silentium*: pensée politique et histoire de l'éloquence dans le *Brutus*," in Aubert-Baillot and Guérin (eds.), 193–214.

Jahn, O., Kroll, W., and Kytzler, B. (1964) *Brutus*, 7th ed. Berlin: Weidmann.

Janson, T. (1964) *Latin Prose Prefaces: Studies in Literary Conventions*. Stockholm: Almqvist & Wiksell.

Jastrow, J. (1900) *Fact and Fable in Psychology*. Boston, MA: Houghton Mifflin.

Jauss, H. (1982) *Toward an Aesthetic of Reception*. Minneapolis: University of Minnesota Press.

Jazdzewska, K. (2014) "From 'Dialogos' to Dialogue: The Use of the Term from Plato to the Second Century CE," *GRBS* 54: 17–36.

   (forthcoming) *Greek Dialogue in Antiquity: Post-Platonic Transformations*. Oxford University Press.

Jehne, M. (1993) "Geheime Abstimmung und Bindungswesen in der römischen Republik," *HZ* 257: 593–613.

Jocelyn, H. D. (1969) "The Poet Cn. Naevius, P. Cornelius Scipio, and R. Caecilius Metellus," *Antichthon* 3: 32–47.

Johnson, W. A. (2009) "The Ancient Book," in R. S. Bagnall (ed.), *The Oxford Handbook of Papyrology*. Oxford University Press. 256–81.

   (2012) *Readers and Reading Culture in the High Roman Empire: A Study of Elite Communities*. Oxford University Press.

Jones, C. P. (1970) "Cicero's *Cato*," *RhM* 113: 188–96.

Jones, R. E. (1939) "Cicero's Accuracy of Characterization in His Dialogues," *AJPh* 60: 307–25.

Jucker, H. (1950) *Vom Verhältnis der Römer zur bildenden Kunst der Griechen*. Frankfurt: Klostermann.

Kaster, R. (1995) *C. Suetonius Tranquillus: De Grammaticis et Rhetoribus*. Oxford University Press.

   (1998) "Becoming 'CICERO,'" in P. E. Knox and C. Foss (eds.), *Style and Tradition: Studies in Honor of Wendell Clausen*. Stuttgart: Teubner. 248–63.

   (2005) *Emotion, Restraint, and Community in Ancient Rome*. Oxford University Press.

   (2006) *Cicero: Speech on Behalf of Publius Sestius*. Oxford University Press.

   (2020) *Cicero: Brutus and Orator*. Oxford University Press.

Keeline, T. J. (2018) *The Reception of Cicero in the Early Roman Empire: The Rhetorical Schoolroom and the Creation of a Cultural Legend*. Cambridge University Press.

Keith, A. M. (1999) "Slender Verse: Roman Elegy and Ancient Rhetorical Theory," *Mnemosyne* 52: 41–62.

Kennedy, G. A. (1972) *The Art of Rhetoric in the Roman World, 300 B.C.–A.D. 300*. Princeton University Press.

Kenty, J. (2018) "The Political Context of Cicero's Oration *De domo sua*," *Ciceroniana*, n.s. 2/2: 245–64.

   (2020) *Cicero's Political Personae*. Cambridge University Press.

Kierdorf, W. (1980) *Laudatio funebris: Interpretationen und Untersuchungen zur Entwicklung der römischen Leichenrede*. Meisenheim am Glan: A. Hain.

Kim, L. (2010) "The Literary Heritage as Language: Atticism and the Second Sophistic," in E. J. Bakker (ed.), *A Companion to the Ancient Greek Language*. Oxford: Wiley-Blackwell. 468–82.

(2017) "Atticism and Asianism," in D. S. Richter and W. A. Johnson (eds.), *The Oxford Handbook of the Second Sophistic*. Oxford University Press. 41–66.

Kinsey, T. E. (ed.) (1971) *Pro P. Quinctio oratio, Edited with Text, Introduction, and Commentary*. Sidney University Press.

Koortbojian, M. (2013) *The Divinization of Caesar and Augustus: Precedents, Consequences, Implications*. Cambridge University Press.

Kousser, R. (2010) "Augustan Aphrodites: The Allure of Greek Art in Roman Visual Culture," in A. C. Smith and S. Pickup (eds.), *Brill's Companion to Aphrodite*. Leiden: Brill. 285–306.

Kraus, C. S. (ed.) (1999) *The Limits of Historiography: Genre and Narrative in Ancient Historical Texts*. Leiden and Boston, MA: Brill.

(2005) "Hair, Hegemony, and Historiography: Caesar's Style and Its Earliest Critics," in T. Reinhardt, M. Lapidge, and J. H. Adams (eds.), *Aspects of the Language of Latin Prose*. Oxford: British Academy. 97–115.

(2009) *"Bellum Gallicum,"* in Griffin (ed.), 157–74.

Krebs, C. B. (2018) "A Style of Choice," in Grillo and Krebs (eds.), 110–30.

Kronenberg, L. (2009) *Allegories of Farming from Greece and Rome: Philosophical Satire in Xenophon, Varro and Virgil*. Cambridge University Press.

Krostenko, B. A. (2001) *Cicero, Catullus, and the Language of Social Performance*. University of Chicago Press.

(2005) "Style and Ideology in the *Pro Marcello*," in K. E. Welch, T. W. Hillard, and J. Bellemore (eds.), *Roman Crossings: Theory and Practice in the Roman Republic*. Swansea: Classical Press of Wales. 279–312.

Kunkel, W. (1962) *Untersuchungen zur Entwicklung des römischen Kriminalverfahrens in vorsullanischer Zeit*. Munich: Beck.

Kurczyk, S. (2006) *Cicero und die Inszenierung der eigenen Vergangenheit: auto-biographisches Schreiben in der späten Römischen Republik*. Cologne: Böhlau.

Kytzler, B. (1970) *Cicero: Brutus*. Munich: Heimeran.

La Bua, G. (2019) *Cicero and Roman Education: The Reception of the Speeches and Ancient Scholarship*. Cambridge University Press.

Laird, A. (ed.) (2006) *Oxford Readings in Ancient Literary Criticism*. Oxford University Press.

Langlands, R. (2018) *Exemplary Ethics in Ancient Rome*. Cambridge University Press.

Laurence, R. and Smith, C. J. (1995) "Ritual, Time and Power in Ancient Rome," *Accordia Research Papers* 6: 133–51.

Lausberg, H. (1998) *Handbook of Literary Rhetoric: A Foundation for Literary Study*. Leiden: Brill.

Lebek, W. D. (1970) *Verba prisca: die Anfänge des Archaisierens in der lateinischen Beredsamkeit und Geschichtsschreibung*. Göttingen: Vandenhoeck & Ruprecht.

Leeman, A. D. (1963) *Orationis ratio: The Stylistic Theories and Practice of the Roman Orators, Historians and Philosophers*. Amsterdam: Hakkert.

Lehmann, A. (2002) *Varron critique littéraire: regard sur les poètes latins archaïques*. Brussels: Latomus.

(2004) "Les débuts de la critique littéraire à Rome," in L. De Poli and Y. Lehmann (eds.), *Naissance de la science dans l'Italie antique et moderne.* Berne: Lang. 139–62.

Lehoux, D. (2012) *What Did the Romans Know? An Inquiry into Science and Worldmaking.* University of Chicago Press.

Lendon, J. E. (2009) "Historians without History: Against Roman Historiography," in Feldherr (ed.), 41–61.

Leo, F. (1901) *Die griechisch-römische Biographie nach ihrer literarischen Form.* Leipzig: Teubner.

(1912) *Plautinische Forschungen: zur Kritik und Geschichte der Komödie,* 2nd ed. Berlin: Weidmann.

(1913) *Geschichte der römischen Literatur. Erster Band.* Berlin: Weidmann.

(1960) *Ausgewählte kleine Schriften,* vol. II. Rome: Edizione di Storia e Letteratura.

Levene, D. S. (2004) "Tacitus' *Dialogus* as Literary History," *TAPhA* 134: 157–200.

Lévêque, P. (1957) *Pyrrhos.* Paris: De Boccard.

Linderski, J. (1986) "The Augural Law," *ANRW* II 16/3: 2146–312.

Lintott, A. W. (1974) "Cicero and Milo," *JRS* 64: 62–78.

(1992) *Judicial Reform and Land Reform in the Roman Republic: A New Edition, with Translation and Commentary, of the Laws from Urbino.* Cambridge University Press.

(1999) *The Constitution of the Roman Republic.* Oxford: Clarendon Press.

(2004) "Legal Procedure in Cicero's Time," in J. G. F. Powell and J. Paterson (eds.), *Cicero the Advocate.* Oxford University Press. 61–78.

(2008) *Cicero as Evidence: A Historian's Companion.* Oxford University Press.

Long, A. A. (1995) "Cicero's Plato and Aristotle," in J. G. F. Powell (ed.), *Cicero the Philosopher: Twelve Papers.* Oxford University Press. 37–61.

Lowrie, M. (2008) "Cicero on Caesar or Exemplum and Inability in the *Brutus,*" in A. H. Arweiler and M. Möller (eds.), *Vom Selbst-Verständnis in Antike und Neuzeit / Notions of the Self in Antiquity and Beyond.* Berlin: de Gruyter. 131–54.

Luce, T. J. (1989) "Ancient Views on the Causes of Bias in Historical Writing," *CPh* 84: 16–31.

MacCormack, S. (2013) "Cicero in Late Antiquity," in C. Steel (ed.), 251–305.

MacKendrick, P. (1989) *The Philosophical Books of Cicero.* New York: St. Martin's.

MacRae, D. (2016) *Legible Religion: Books, Gods, and Rituals in Roman Culture.* Cambridge, MA: Harvard University Press.

(2018) "*Diligentissumus investigator antiquitatis*? 'Antiquarianism' and Historical Evidence between Republican Rome and the Early Modern Republic of Letters," in K. Sandberg and C. Smith (eds.), *Omnium Annalium Monumenta: Historical Writing and Historical Evidence in Republican Rome.* Leiden: Brill. 137–56.

Maltby, R. (1991) *A Lexicon of Ancient Latin Etymologies.* Leeds: Francis Cairns.

Mankin, D. (2011) *Cicero: De Oratore Book III.* Cambridge University Press.

Manuwald, G. (2011) *Roman Republican Theatre.* Cambridge University Press.

Marinone, N. (2004) *Cronologia Ciceroniana, Secunda Edizione aggiornata e corretta con nuova versione interattiva in CD-rom,* ed. E. Malaspina. Bologna: Centro di Studi Ciceroniani Pàtron.

Marmorale, E. V. (1967) *Naevius Poeta: introduzione biobibliografica, testo dei frammenti e commento,* 2nd ed. Florence: La nuova Italia.

Marr, J. (1995) "The Death of Themistocles," *G&R* 42: 159–67.

Marrou, H.-I. (1971) *Histoire de l'éducation dans l'antiquité,* 6th ed. Paris: Éditions du Seuil.

Marshall, A. J. (1984) "Symbols and Showmanship in Roman Public Life: The Fasces," *Phoenix* 38: 120–41.

Marshall, A. M. (1993) "Atticus and the Genealogies," *Latomus* 52: 307–17.

Marshall, R. M. A. (2017) "Varro, Atticus, and *Annales,*" *BICS* 60/2: 61–75.

Martha, J. (1960) *Cicéron: Brutus.* Paris: Les Belles Lettres.

Martin, P. M. (2014) "Entre prosopographie et politique: la figure et l'ascendance de Brutus dans le *Brutus,*" in Aubert-Baillot and Guérin (eds.), 215–35.

May, J. M. (1988) *Trials of Character: The Eloquence of Ciceronian Ethos.* Chapel Hill: University of North Carolina Press.

  (1990) "The Monologistic Dialogue as a Method of Literary Criticism: Cicero, *Brutus* 285–289 and Horace, *Epistle* 2.1.34–39," *Athenaeum* 68: 177–80.

  (ed.) (2002) *Brill's Companion to Cicero: Oratory and Rhetoric.* Leiden and Boston, MA: Brill.

May, J. M. and Wisse, J. (2001) *Cicero: On the Ideal Orator.* Oxford University Press.

Mazzarino, S. (1966) *Il pensiero storico classico,* vol. II, part 2. Bari: Laterza.

McDermott, W. C. (1972) "Curio Pater and Cicero," *AJPh* 93: 381–411.

McGill, S. (2012) *Plagiarism in Latin Literature.* Cambridge University Press.

Millar, F. (1998) *The Crowd in Rome in the Late Republic.* Ann Arbor: University of Michigan Press.

Mitchell, T. N. (1979) *Cicero: The Ascending Years.* New Haven, CT: Yale University Press.

  (1991) *Cicero: The Senior Statesman.* New Haven, CT: Yale University Press.

Moatti, C. (1997) *La raison de Rome: naissance de l'esprit critique à la fin de la République.* Paris: Seuil.

  (2003) "Experts, mémoire et pouvoir à Rome, à la fin de la République," *RH* 626: 303–25.

Möller, M. (2004) *Talis oratio – qualis vita: zu Theorie und Praxis mimetischer Verfahren in der griechisch-römischen Literaturkritik.* Heidelberg: Winter.

Momigliano, A. D. (1950) "Ancient History and the Antiquarian." *JWI* 13: 285–315.

  (1990) *The Classical Foundations of Modern Historiography.* Berkeley: University of California Press.

Montana, F. (2015) "Hellenistic Scholarship," in F. Montanari, S. Matthaios, and A. Rengakos (eds.), *Brill's Companion to Ancient Greek Scholarship.* Leiden: Brill. 60–183.

Monteleone, C. (2003) *La "Terza Filippica" di Cicerone: retorica e regolamento del Senato, legalità e rapporti di forza*. Fasano: Schena.

Moreau, P. (1982) *Clodiana religio: un procès politique en 61 av. J.-C.* Paris: Les Belles Lettres.

Moretti, G. (1995) *Acutum dicendi genus: brevità, oscurità, sottigliezze e paradossi nelle tradizioni retoriche degli Stoici*. Bologna: Pàtron.

Morgan, K. A. (1994) "Socrates and Gorgias at Delphi and Olympia: *Phaedrus* 235d6–236b4," *CQ* 44: 375–86.

Morrell, K. (2017) *Pompey, Cato, and the Governance of the Roman Empire*. Oxford University Press.

  (2018) "Cato, Pompey's Third Consulship and the Politics of Milo's Trial," in H. van der Blom, C. Gray, and C. Steel (eds.), *Institutions and Ideology in Republican Rome: Speech, Audience and Decision*. Cambridge University Press. 165–80.

Morrison, T. (1989) "Unspeakable Things Unspoken: The Afro-American Presence in American Literature," *Michigan Quarterly Review* 28: 1–34.

Morstein-Marx, R. (2004) *Mass Oratory and Political Power in the Late Roman Republic*. Cambridge University Press.

Most, G. W. (2008) "What Was Literary History?" in J. Berthold and B. Previšić (eds.), *Texttreue: komparatistische Studien zu einem masslosen Massstab*. Bern: Lang. 195–207.

Mouritsen, H. (2001) *Plebs and Politics in the Late Roman Republic*. Cambridge University Press.

  (2013) "From Meeting to Text: The *Contio* in the Late Republic," in C. Steel and H. van der Blom (eds.), *Community and Communication: Oratory and Politics in Republican Rome*. Oxford University Press. 63–82.

Münzer, F. (1905) "Atticus als Geschichtschreiber," *Hermes* 40: 50–100.

Narducci, E. (1997) *Cicerone e l'eloquenza romana: retorica e progetto culturale*. Rome: Laterza.

  (2002) "*Brutus*: The History of Roman Eloquence," in May (ed.), 401–25.

Nicolet, C. (1972) "Les lois judiciaires et les tribunaux de concussion," *ANRW* 1/2: 197–214.

Noël, M.-P. (2003) "La Συναγωγή τεχνῶν d'Aristote et la polémique sur les débuts de la rhétorique chez Cicéron," in C. Lévy, B. Besnier, and A. Gigandet (eds.), *Ars et ratio: sciences, art et métiers dans la philosophie hellénistique et romaine: actes du colloque international organisé à Créteil, Fontenay et Paris du 16 au 18 octobre 1997*. Paris: Latomus. 113–25.

  (2014) "Périclès et les débuts de la rhétorique grecque dans le *Brutus*," in Aubert-Baillot and Guérin (eds.), 88–104.

Norden, E. (1898) *Die antike Kunstprosa vom VI. Jahrhundert v. Chr. bis in die Zeit der Renaissance*. Leipzig: Teubner.

North, J. (1990) "Democratic Politics in Republican Rome," *P&P* 126: 3–21.

Nousek, D. L. (2018) "Genres and Generic Contaminations: The *Commentarii*," in Grillo and Krebs (eds.), 97–109.

Novara, A. (1982) *Les idées romaines sur le progrès d'après les écrivains de la République*. Paris: Les Belles Lettres.

Nünlist, R. (2015) "Poetics and Literary Criticism in the Framework of Ancient Greek Scholarship," in F. Montanari, S. Matthaios, and A. Rengakos (eds.), *Brill's Companion to Ancient Greek Scholarship*. Leiden: Brill. 706–55.

Osgood, J. W. (2005) "Cicero's *Pro Caelio* 33–34 and Appius Claudius' *Oratio de Pyrrho*," *CPh* 100: 355–58.

O'Sullivan, N. (1997) "Caecilius, the 'Canons' of Writers, and the Origins of Atticism," in W. J. Dominik (ed.), *Roman Eloquence: Rhetoric in Society and Literature*. London: Routledge. 32–49.

  (2015) "'Rhetorical' vs 'Linguistic' Atticism: A False Dichotomy?" *Rhetorica* 33: 134–46.

Otto, A. (1890) *Die Sprichwörter und sprichwörtlichen Redensarten der Römer*. Leipzig: Teubner.

Paul, H. (2011) *Hayden White: The Historical Imagination*. Cambridge: Polity.

Peirano, I. (2013) "*Non subripiendi causa sed palam mutuandi*: Intertextuality and Literary Deviancy between Law, Rhetoric, and Literature in Roman Imperial Culture," *AJPh* 134: 83–100.

Pelling, C. (2006) "Judging Julius Caesar," in M. Wyke (ed.), *Julius Caesar in Western Culture*. Oxford: Wiley. 1–26.

Perkins, D. (1991) "Introduction," in D. Perkins (ed.), *Theoretical Issues in Literary History*. Cambridge, MA: Harvard University Press. 1–8.

  (1992) *Is Literary History Possible?* Baltimore, MD: Johns Hopkins University Press.

Perlwitz, O. (1992) *Titus Pomponius Atticus*. Stuttgart: Steiner.

Pezzini, G. (2018) "Caesar the Linguist: The Debate about the Latin Language," in Grillo and Krebs (eds.), 173–92.

Pfeiffer, R. (1968) *History of Classical Scholarship: From the Beginnings to the End of the Hellenistic Age*. Oxford University Press.

Pina Polo, F. (1996) *Contra arma uerbis: der Redner vor dem Volk in der späten römischen Republik*. Stuttgart: Steiner.

  (2003) "Minerva: *Custos Urbis* de Roma y de Tarraco," *AEA* 76: 111–19.

  (2011) *The Consul at Rome: The Civil Functions of the Consuls in the Roman Republic*. Cambridge University Press.

  (2012) "*Contio, Auctoritas* and Freedom of Speech in Republican Rome," in S. Benoist (ed.), *Rome, a City and Its Empire in Perspective: The Impact of the Roman World through Fergus Millar's Research*. Leiden: Brill. 45–58.

Piras, G. (2012) "Tradizione indiretta e testi frammentari: Ennio, *Ann.* 303–308 V.² (304–308 Sk.), Cicerone e Gellio," in L. Gamberale, M. De Nonno, C. Di Giovine, and M. Passalacqua (eds.), *Le strade della filologia: per Scevola Mariotti*. Rome: Edizione di Storia e Letteratura. 41–69.

  (2017) "La prosopopea di Appio Claudio Cieco (Cic. *Cael.* 33–34): tradizione letteraria, memoria familiare e polemica politica," in P. De Paolis (ed.), *Cicerone oratore: atti dell'VIII Simposio Ciceroniano, Arpino 6 maggio 2016*. Cassino: Università degli Studi di Cassino e del Lazio Meridionale. 63–100.

Pollitt, J. J. (1974) *The Ancient View of Greek Art: Criticism, History, and Terminology.* New Haven, CT: Yale University Press.

(1990) *The Art of Ancient Greece: Sources and Documents.* Cambridge University Press.

Powell, A. (1998) "Julius Caesar and the Presentation of Massacre," in K. E. Welch and A. Powell (eds.), *Julius Caesar as Artful Reporter: The War Commentaries as Political Instruments.* London: Duckworth. 111–37.

Powell, J. G. F. (1988) *Cicero: Cato Maior de senectute.* Cambridge University Press.

(2010a) "Court Procedure and Rhetorical Strategy in Cicero," in D. H. Berry and A. Erskine (eds.), *Form and Function in Roman Oratory.* Cambridge University Press. 21–36.

(2010b) "Hyperbaton and Register in Cicero," in E. Dickey and A. Chahoud (eds.), *Colloquial and Literary Latin.* Cambridge University Press. 163–85.

Raaflaub, K. (2009) "*Bellum Gallicum*," in Griffin (ed.), 175–91.

(2018) "Caesar, Literature, and Politics at the End of the Republic," in Grillo and Krebs (eds.), 13–28.

Rambaud, M. (1979) "César et la rhétorique: a propos de Cicéron (*Brutus*, 261–262)," in *La rhétorique à Rome: colloque des 10–11 décembre 1977, Paris.* Paris: Les Belles Lettres. 19–39.

Ramsey, J. T. (2016) "How and Why Was Pompey Made Sole Consul in 52 BC?" *Historia* 65: 298–324.

Rathofer, C. (1986) *Ciceros Brutus als literarisches Paradigma eines Auctoritas-Verhältnisses.* Frankfurt am Main: A. Hain.

Rawson, E. (1972) "Cicero the Historian and Cicero the Antiquarian," *JRS* 62: 33–45.

(1979) "L. Cornelius Sisenna and the Early First Century B.C.," *CQ* 29: 327–46.

(1982) "*Crassorum Funera*," *Latomus* 41: 540–49.

(1983) *Cicero: A Portrait*, 2nd ed. Bristol Classical Press.

(1985) *Intellectual Life in the Late Roman Republic.* London: Duckworth.

(1986) "Cassius and Brutus: The Memory of the Liberators," in I. S. Moxon, J. D. Smart, and A. J. Woodman (eds.), *Past Perspectives: Studies in Greek and Roman Historical Writing.* Cambridge University Press. 101–19.

Richards, E. G. (1998) *Mapping Time: The Calendar and Its History.* Oxford University Press.

Richlin, A. (2011) "Old Boys: Teacher-Student Bonding in Roman Oratory," *CW* 105: 91–107.

Riggsby, A. M. (2006) *Caesar in Gaul and Rome: War in Words.* Austin: University of Texas Press.

(2010) *Roman Law and the Legal World of the Romans.* Cambridge University Press.

Robinson, E. A. (1951) "The Date of Cicero's *Brutus*," *HSPh* 60: 137–46.

Roller, M. B. (2018) *Models from the Past in Roman Culture: A World of Exempla.* Cambridge University Press.

Rollinger, C. (2017) "Ciceros *supplicatio* und aristokratische Konkurrenz im Senat der späten Republik," *Klio* 99: 192–225.

Rorty, R. (1998) *Achieving Our Country: Leftist Thought in Twentieth-Century America.* Cambridge, MA: Harvard University Press.

Rösch-Binde, C. (1998) *Vom "δεινὸς ἀνερ" zum "diligentissimus investigator anti-quitatis": zur komplexen Beziehung zwischen M. Tullius Cicero und M. Terentius Varro.* Munich: Utz.

Rosenstein, N. (2007) "Military Command, Political Power, and the Republican Elite," in P. Erdkamp (ed.), *A Companion to the Roman Army.* Malden, MA: Blackwell. 132–47.

Rosillo-López, C. (ed.) (2017) *Political Communication in the Roman World.* Leiden: Brill.

Rüpke, J. (2011) *The Roman Calendar from Numa to Constantine: Time, History, and the Fasti.* Malden, MA: Wiley-Blackwell.

(2012) *Religion in Republican Rome: Rationalization and Ritual Change.* Philadelphia: University of Pennsylvania Press.

Russell, D. A. (1979) "*De Imitatione*," in D. West and A. J. Woodman (eds.), *Creative Imitation and Latin Literature.* Cambridge University Press. 1–16.

(1981) *Criticism in Antiquity.* Berkeley: University of California Press.

Russell, J. B. (1991) *Inventing the Flat Earth: Columbus and Modern Historians.* New York: Praeger.

Ryan, F. X. (1998) *Rank and Participation in the Republican Senate.* Stuttgart: Steiner.

Saintsbury, G. (1900) *A History of Criticism and Literary Taste in Europe: From the Earliest Texts to the Present Day,* vol. 1. Edinburgh: Blackwood.

Salerno, F. (1999) *Tacita libertas: l'introduzione del voto segreto nella Roma repub-blicana.* Naples: Edizioni Scientifiche Italiane.

Schaaf, L. (1979) "Die Todesjahre des Naevius und des Plautus in der antiken Überlieferung," *RhM* 122: 24–33.

Schenkeveld, D. M. (1988) "*Iudicia vulgi*: Cicero, *De oratore* 3.195ff. and *Brutus* 183ff.," *Rhetorica* 6: 291–305.

Schilling, R. (1982) *La religion romaine de Vénus depuis les origines jusqu'au temps d'Auguste,* 2nd ed. Paris: De Boccard.

Schironi, F. (2007) "Ἀναλογία, *Analogia, Proportio, Ratio*: Loanwords, Calques and Reinterpretations of a Greek Technical Word," in L. Basset, F. Biville, B. Colombat, P. Swiggers, and A. Wouters (eds.), *Bilinguisme et terminologie grammaticale gréco-latine.* Leuven; Paris; Dudley, MA: Peeters. 321–38.

Schlicher, J. J. (1936) "The Development of Caesar's Narrative Style," *CPh* 31: 212–24.

Schofield, M. (2008) "Ciceronian Dialogue," in S. Goldhill (ed.), *The End of Dialogue in Antiquity.* Cambridge University Press. 63–84.

(ed.) (2013) *Aristotle, Plato and Pythagoreanism in the First Century BC: New Directions for Philosophy.* Cambridge University Press.

Scholz, P., Walter, U., and Winkle, C. (2013) *Fragmente römischer Memoiren.* Heidelberg: Antike.

Schöpsdau, K. (1969) *Antike Vorstellungen von der Geschichte der griechischen Rhetorik.* Diss. Saarland University.

(1994) "Das Nachleben der Technon synagoge bei Cicero, Quintilian und in den griechischen Prolegomena zur Rhetorik," in W. W. Fortenbaugh and D. C. Mirhady (eds.), *Peripatetic Rhetoric after Aristotle.* New Brunswick, NJ: Transaction. 192–216.

Schütrumpf, E. (1988) "Platonic Elements in the Structure of Cicero *De oratore* Book I," *Rhetorica* 6: 237–58.

Schwindt, J. (2000) *Prolegomena zu einer "Phänomenologie" der römischen Literaturgeschichtsschreibung: von den Anfängen bis Quintilian.* Göttingen: Vandenhoeck & Ruprecht.

Sciarrino, E. (2015) "Schools, Teachers, and Patrons in Mid-Republican Rome," in W. M. Bloomer (ed.), *A Companion to Ancient Education.* Malden, MA: Wiley-Blackwell. 226–39.

Scourfield, J. H. D. (2013) "Towards a Genre of Consolation," in H. Baltussen (ed.), *Greek and Roman Consolations: Eight Studies of a Tradition and Its Afterlife.* Swansea: Classical Press of Wales. 1–36.

Sedley, D. (1997) "The Ethics of Brutus and Cassius," *JRS* 87: 41–53.

(ed.) (2012) *The Philosophy of Antiochus.* Cambridge University Press.

Sehlmeyer, M. (2003) "Die Anfänge der antiquarischen Literatur in Rom: Motivation und Bezug zur Historiographie bis in die Zeit von Tuditanus und Gracchanus," in U. Eigler, U. Gotter, N. Luraghi, and U. Walter (eds.), *Formen römischer Geschichtsschreibung von den Anfängen bis Livius: Gattungen, Autoren, Kontexte.* Darmstadt: Wissenschaftliche Buchgesellschaft. 157–71.

Shackleton Bailey, D. R. (1971) *Cicero.* New York: Scribner.

Shorey, P. (1909) "Φύσις, Μελέτη, Ἐπιστήμη," *TAPhA* 40: 185–201.

Shorn, S. (2004) *Satyros aus Kallatis: Sammlung der Fragmente mit Kommentar.* Basel: Schwabe.

Skutsch, O. (1985) *The Annals of Q. Ennius.* Oxford University Press.

Smith, C. J. (2009) "Sulla's Memoirs," in C. J Smith and A. Powell (eds.), *The Lost Memoirs of Augustus and the Development of Roman Autobiography.* Swansea: Classical Press of Wales. 65–86.

(2018) "Varro and the Contours of Roman Antiquarianism," *Latomus* 77: 1090–1118.

Squire, M. (2015) "Aesthetics and Latin Literary Reception," in E. A. Friedland, M. G. Sobocinski, and E. K. Gazda (eds.), *The Oxford Handbook of Roman Sculpture.* Oxford University Press. 589–605.

Steel, C. (2002) "Cicero's *Brutus*: The End of Oratory and the Beginning of History?" *BICS* 46: 195–211.

(2005) *Reading Cicero.* London: Duckworth.

(2012) "Cicero's Autobiography: Narratives of Success in the Pre-Consular Orations," *CCG* 23: 251–66.

(2013a) "Structure, Meaning and Authority in Cicero's Dialogues," in Föllinger and Müller (eds.), 221–34.

(ed.) (2013b) *The Cambridge Companion to Cicero*. Cambridge University Press.

(2016) "Early-career Prosecutors: Forensic Activity and Senatorial Careers in the Late Republic," in P. Du Plessis (ed.), *Cicero's Law: Rethinking Roman Law of the Late Republic*. Edinburgh University Press. 205–27.

Steel, D. (2000) *Marking Time: The Epic Quest to Invent the Perfect Calendar*. Malden, MA: Wiley-Blackwell.

Stem, S. R. (2005) "The First Eloquent Stoic: Cicero on Cato the Younger," *CJ* 101: 37–49.

Stern, S. (2012) *Calendars in Antiquity: Empires, States, and Societies*. Oxford University Press.

(2017) "Calendars, Politics, and Power Relations in the Roman Empire," in J. Ben-Dov and L. Doering (eds.), *The Construction of Time in Antiquity: Ritual, Art, and Identity*. Cambridge University Press. 31–49.

Stewart, A. F. (1990) *Greek Sculpture: An Exploration*. New Haven, CT: Yale University Press.

(1997) *Art, Desire and the Body in Ancient Greece*. Cambridge University Press.

(2010) "A Tale of Seven Nudes: The Capitoline and Medici Aphrodites, Four Nymphs at Elean Kerakleia, and an Aphrodite at Megalopolis," *Antichthon* 44: 12–32.

Stockton, D. L. (1971) *Cicero: A Political Biography*. Oxford University Press.

Strasburger, H. (1990) *Ciceros philosophisches Spätwerk als Aufruf gegen die Herrschaft Caesars*, ed. G. Strasburger. Hildesheim: Olms.

Stroup, S. C. (2003) *"Adulta Virgo*: The Personification of Textual Eloquence in Cicero's *Brutus*," *MD* 50: 115–40.

(2010) *Catullus, Cicero, and a Society of Patrons: The Generation of the Text*. Cambridge University Press.

Stull, W. (2011) *"Deus ille noster*: Platonic Precedent and the Construction of the Interlocutors in Cicero's *De oratore*," *TAPhA* 141: 247–63.

Suerbaum, W. (1995) "Rhetorik gegen Pyrrhos: zum Widerstand gegen den Feind aus dem Osten in der Rede des Appius Claudius Caecus 280/279 v. Chr. nach Ennius, Oratorum Romanorum fragmenta und B. G. Niebuhr," in C. Schubert and K. Brodersen (eds.), *Rom und der griechische Osten*. Stuttgart: Steiner. 251–65.

(1996/1997) "Vorliterarische römische Redner (bis zum Beginn des 2. Jhs. v. Chr.) in Ciceros *Brutus* und in der historischen Überlieferung," *WJA* 21: 169–98.

(1997) "Fehlende Redner in Ciceros *Brutus*? Nebst Hinweisen auf fehlende Entwicklung, fehlende Belege und fehlende Ernsthaftigkeit in einer Geschichte der römischen Beredsamkeit," in B. Czapla, T. Lehmann, and S. Liell (eds.), *Vir bonus dicendi peritus: Festschrift für Alfons Weisch*. Wiesbaden: Reichert. 407–19.

(ed.) (2002) *Die archaische Literatur: von den Anfängen bis Sullas Tod: die vorliterarische Periode und die Zeit von 240 bis 78 v. Chr.* Munich: Beck.

Sumner, G. V. (1973) *The Orators in Cicero's Brutus: Prosopography and Chronology.* University of Toronto Press.

Syme, R. (1939) *The Roman Revolution.* Oxford University Press.

(1980) "The Sons of Crassus," *Latomus* 39: 403–8.

Tan, J. (2008) "*Contiones* in the Age of Cicero," *CA* 27: 163–201.

Tatum, J. (1989) *Xenophon's Imperial Fiction: On the Education of Cyrus.* Princeton University Press.

Tatum, W. J. (1991) "Cicero, the Elder Curio and the Titinia Case," *Mnemosyne* 44: 364–71.

(2011) "The Late Republic: Autobiographies and Memoirs in the Age of the Civil Wars," in G. Marasco (ed.), *Political Autobiographies and Memoirs in Antiquity.* Leiden: Brill. 161–87.

Taylor, L. R. (1949) *Party Politics in the Age of Caesar.* Berkeley: University of California Press.

(1966) *Roman Voting Assemblies from the Hannibalic War to the Dictatorship of Caesar.* Ann Arbor: University of Michigan Press.

Tempest, K. (2011) *Cicero: Politics and Persuasion in Ancient Rome.* London: Continuum.

(2013) "An *Ethos* of Sincerity: Echoes of the *De Republica* in Cicero's *Pro Marcello*," *G&R* 60: 262–80.

(2017) *Brutus: The Noble Conspirator.* New Haven, CT: Yale University Press.

Todd, S. C. (tr.) (2000) *Lysias.* Austin: University of Texas Press.

Treggiari, S. (2015) "The Education of the Ciceros," in W. M. Bloomer (ed.), *A Companion to Ancient Education.* Malden, MA: Wiley-Blackwell. 240–51.

van den Berg, C. S. (2008) "The *Pulvinar* in Roman Culture," *TAPhA* 138: 239–73.

(2014) *The World of Tacitus' Dialogus de Oratoribus: Aesthetics and Empire in Ancient Rome.* Cambridge University Press.

(2019) "The Invention of Literary History in Cicero's Brutus," *CPh* 114: 573–603.

(2021) "Phaedrus in the Forum: Plautus' *Pseudolus* and Plato's *Phaedrus*," in C. W. Marshall (ed.), *Festschrift for Susanna Morton Braund.* London; New York: Routledge. 91–106.

van der Blom, H. (2010) *Cicero's Role Models: The Political Strategy of a Newcomer.* Oxford University Press.

(2016) *Oratory and Political Career in the Late Roman Republic.* Cambridge University Press.

Van Hook, L. (1905) *The Metaphorical Terminology of Greek Rhetoric and Literary Criticism.* Diss. University of Chicago.

Vardi, A. (2003) "Canons of Literary Texts at Rome," in M. Finkelberg and G. G. Stroumsa (eds.), *Homer, the Bible, and Beyond: Literary and Religious Canons in the Ancient World.* Leiden: Brill. 131–52.

Vasaly, A. (1987) "Personality and Power: Livy's Depiction of the Appii Claudii in the First Pentad," *TAPhA* 117: 203–26.

(1993) *Representations: Images of the World in Ciceronian Oratory.* Berkeley: University of California Press.

Volk, K. (2020) "Varro and the Disorder of Things," *HSPh* 110: 184–212.
  (2021) *The Roman Republic of Letters: Scholarship, Philosophy, and Politics in the Age of Cicero and Caesar.* Princeton University Press.
Volk, K. and Zetzel, J. E. G. (2015) "Laurel, Tongue and Glory (Cicero, *De Consulatu Suo* Fr. 6 Soubiran)," *CQ* 65: 204–23.
von Albrecht, M. (1989) *Masters of Roman Prose from Cato to Apuleius,* tr. N. Adkin. Leeds: Cairns.
Wallace-Hadrill, A. (1997) "*Mutatio morum*: The Idea of a Cultural Revolution," in T. Habinek and A. Schiesaro (eds.), *The Roman Cultural Revolution.* Cambridge University Press. 3–22.
Walter, U. (2010) "'Caesar macht Geschichte': Memorialpolitik und Historiographie zwischen Konvention und Innovation," in G. Urso (ed.), *Cesare: precursore o visionario? Atti del convegno internazionale, Cividale del Friuli, 17–19 settembre 2009.* Pisa: ETS. 59–73.
Walters, B. (2020) *The Deaths of the Republic: Imagery of the Body Politic in Ciceronian Rome.* Oxford University Press.
Wardle, D. (2014) *Suetonius: Life of Augustus.* Oxford University Press.
Wassmann, H. (1996) *Ciceros Widerstand gegen Caesars Tyrannis: Untersuchungen zur politischen Bedeutung der philosophischen Spätschriften.* Bonn: Habelt.
Weinstock, S. (1971) *Divus Julius.* Oxford: Clarendon Press.
Welch, K. E. (1996) "T. Pomponius Atticus: A Banker in Politics?" *Historia* 45: 450–71.
Wellek, R. (1963) *Concepts of Criticism.* New Haven, CT: Yale University Press.
Wellek, R. and Warren, A. (1956) *Theory of Literature,* 3rd ed. New York: Harcourt, Brace & World.
Welsh, J. T. (2011) "Accius, Porcius Licinus, and the Beginning of Latin Literature," *JRS* 101: 31–50.
White, H. (1987) *The Content of the Form: Narrative Discourse and Historical Representation.* Baltimore, MD: Johns Hopkins University Press.
Whitton, C. L. (2013) *Pliny the Younger: Epistles, Book II.* Cambridge University Press.
Wilamowitz, U. von (1900) "Asianismus und Atticismus," *Hermes* 35: 1–52.
Wilcox, D. J. (1987) *The Measure of Times Past: Pre-Newtonian Chronologies and the Rhetoric of Relative Time.* University of Chicago Press.
Williams, M. F. (1985) "Caesar's Bibracte Narrative and the Aims of Caesarian Style," *ICS* 10: 215–26.
Winsbury, R. (2009) *The Roman Book: Books, Publishing and Performance in Classical Rome.* London: Duckworth.
Winterbottom, M. (1982) "Literary Criticism," in E. J. Kenney (ed.), *The Cambridge History of Classical Literature II: Latin Literature.* Cambridge University Press. 33–50.
Wirszubski, C. (1954) "Cicero's *cum dignitate otium*: A Reconsideration." *JRS* 44: 1–13.
Wiseman, T. P. (1971) *New Men in the Roman Senate, 139 B.C.–A.D. 14.* Oxford University Press.

(1974) "Legendary Genealogies in Late-Republican Rome," *G&R* 21: 153–64.
(1979) *Clio's Cosmetics: Three Studies in Greco-Roman Literature.* Leicester University Press.
(2009) *Remembering the Roman People: Essays on Late-Republican Politics and Literature.* Oxford University Press.
Wisse, J. (1989) *Ethos and Pathos from Aristotle to Cicero.* Amsterdam: Hakkert.
   (1995) "Greeks, Romans, and the Rise of Atticism," in J. G. J. Abbenes, S. R. Slings, and I. Sluiter (eds.), *Greek Literary Theory after Aristotle.* Amsterdam: VU University Press. 65–82.
Wistrand, M. (1979) *Cicero Imperator: Studies in Cicero's Correspondence, 51–47 B.C.* Göteborg: Acta Universitatis Gothoburgensis.
Woodman, A. J. (1988) *Rhetoric in Classical Historiography: Four Studies.* London: Croom Helm.
Woolf, R. (2015) *Cicero: The Philosophy of a Roman Sceptic.* London; New York: Routledge.
Wooten, C. W. (1983) *Cicero's Philippics and Their Demosthenic Model: The Rhetoric of Crisis.* Chapel Hill: University of North Carolina Press.
   (1997) "Cicero and Quintilian on the Style of Demosthenes," *Rhetorica* 15: 177–92.
Yakobson, A. (1992) "*Petitio et Largitio*: Popular Participation in the Centuriate Assembly of the Late Republic," *JRS* 82: 32–52.
   (1995) "Secret Ballot and Its Effects in the Late Roman Republic," *Hermes* 123: 426–42.
   (1999) *Elections and Electioneering in Rome: A Study in the Political System of the Late Republic.* Stuttgart: Steiner.
Zanker, P. (2009) "The Irritating Statues and Contradictory Portraits of Julius Caesar," in Griffin (ed.), 288–314.
Zerubavel, E. (2003) *Time Maps: Collective Memory and the Social Shape of the Past.* University of Chicago Press.
Zetzel, J. E. G. (1972) "Cicero and the Scipionic Circle," *HSPh* 76: 173–79.
   (1981) *Latin Textual Criticism in Antiquity.* New York: Arno.
   (1995) *De re publica: Selections.* Cambridge University Press.
   (2003) "Plato with Pillows: Cicero on the Uses of Greek Culture," in D. Braund and C. Gill (eds.), *Myth, History and Culture in Republican Rome: Studies in Honour of T. P. Wiseman.* University of Exeter Press. 119–38.
   (2007) "The Influence of Cicero on Ennius," in W. Fitzgerald and E. Gowers (eds.), *"Ennius perennis": The "Annals" and Beyond.* Cambridge Philological Society. 1–16.
   (2009) *Cicero: Ten Speeches.* Indianapolis: Hackett.
   (2013) "Political Philosophy," in Steel (ed.), 181–95.
   (2017) *Cicero: On the Commonwealth and On the Laws.* 2nd ed. Cambridge University Press.
   (2018) *Critics, Compilers, and Commentators: An Introduction to Roman Philology, 200 BCE–800 CE.* Oxford University Press.
Zoll, G. (1962) *Cicero Platonis aemulus: Untersuchung über die Form von Ciceros Dialogen, besonders von De oratore.* Zurich: Juris-Verlag.

General Index

absolutism 166, 169–72, 174–76, 180
Academy (Cicero's villa) 231
Accius, Lucius 11, 15, 70, 113–16, 132, 164
 Didascalica 113–14
achievements (military/civic) 3, 83, 229
 Caecus 138–39, 141, 148
 Caesar 91–92, 220
 Cicero 22, 72, 86–88, 229–30, 238–39
adornment see *ornatus*
Aelius Stilo, Lucius 164
Aemilius Lepidus, Marcus *see* Lepidus
Aeschines 210
allegory, of eloquence (*eloquentia*) 34–35, 153,
 158–59, 240n68
Analogy/Anomaly debate 65
Anaxagoras 152, 155–57
Anicius, Lucius 174
Annaeus Lucanus, Marcus *see* Lucan
Anomaly *see* Analogy/Anomaly debate
Antiochus of Ascalon 32
anti-philhellenism 180–84
Antiphon 156
antiquarianism 166, 174, 188–89, 192, 205–6,
 249, 254
 see also outdated authors
Antonius, Marcus 109
 comparisons 108–9
 martial metaphors in speeches 83
Antonius, Marcus (Mark Antony) 113, 252
Aper, Marcus 172, 197–98
 on *antiquus* 254
 diversity of style 247–48
Aphrodite of Knidos (statue) (Praxiteles) 220, 233–37
 see also Venus
Apollonius Molon 28, 31–33, 36–38
Aquilius Gallus, C. 109
Aristotle 153
 on the development of arts 251
 influence on the *Brutus* 60, 231
 Poetics, biology of a genre 72
 Συναγωγὴ Τεχνῶν 60, 158

Asianism 9, 24, 28–35, 192–94, 203
assassination, Julius Caesar 75–77, 83
Athena/Minerva statue (Phidias) 87–89, 159,
 220, 228–31
Atticism 9, 24, 28–35, 64, 118, 174, 176–80,
 191–96, 254
Atticus
 diatribe against 199–210
 history of 199
 Lysias and Cato 198–99
 and the *Orator* 64–67
 style of oratory 64, 193–96
 term 193, 196, 200–2
 redefinition 210–15
 see also Analogy/Anomaly debate
Atticus (Titus Pomponius Atticus) 4, 45–46,
 153–54
 as inspiration for *Brutus* 52–59
 Liber Annalis ("Yearly Book") 4, 7, 53–56, 59,
 79–80, 155
 inspired by *de Republica* 68
 in *Orat.* 66
 and the term *Atticus* 196–213
augurs, college of 47–48
Augustus (Octavian Caesar) 5, 113, 235
Aurelius Cotta, C. *see* Cotta
Aurelius Cotta, Lucius 174
autobiography 22–43, 181–82

biography/memoir 245
 Cicero 20–22, 245
 Ciceropaideia 22–43, 192
 development of 151n51
 and philhellenism 181–82
birth dates, and chronology 126–27
Bodel, John 223
brevity (*brevitas*) 191–92, 219n8
Brutus (Marcus Junius Brutus) 61
 age 30–31n32, 45–46
 Appius Claudius Pulcher defense 40
 and Caesar 77

281

Index Locorum

For EU product safety concerns, contact us at Calle de José Abascal, 56–1°, 28003 Madrid, Spain or eugpsr@cambridge.org.

www.ingramcontent.com/pod-product-compliance
Ingram Content Group UK Ltd.
Pitfield, Milton Keynes, MK11 3LW, UK
UKHW020358140625
459647UK00020B/2534